ANGELS

ARTWORK BY PHILIP HOWE

SPIRITUAL OIL PAINTINGS

DREAM IMAGERY ~ STUDIES ~ DRAWINGS

INCLUDES OVER 40 PAGES OF DEMONSTRATIONS

Philip Howe's paintings are best described as a return to classic realism. Each image is created to convey a sense of mood and emotion, yet designed to invite each viewer to think, to explore. His fluid technique is honed from doing thousands of illustration jobs for international clients, but the work within this book is removed from any commercial application. This is the work of an artist painting for himself and for those who appreciate masterful technique and spiritual subjects with an illustrative approach.

"For over three decades Philip Howe has been creating finely crafted art for himself and the pleasure of his many varied clients and collectors. He has treated his craft with the tenacity of a lifetime student. He is always stretching his skills while never truly finding the perfect painting, all while continuing to develop his abilities and establish himself as one of the finest narrative painters in the country. The body of work contained in this book is a testament to Philip's ability and passion. How he feels about his art is beautifully expressed in each heartfelt narrative."

Chris Hopkins, nationally recognized painter and illustrator

"Spiritual and Dream imagery have been a source of inspiration for artists since the beginning of painting. The work contained within this book represents many of the oil paintings I did in the last decade, as well as some earlier work and my studies. These are personal paintings, unfettered by any commercial constraints and rendered for the pure pleasure of conveying spiritual and meditative messages as I wanted to express them. I hope people will appreciate their content as much as the technique. I always work hard to achieve accurate figure work and I think the realism is necessary to convey an almost mystical mood that I like to achieve in my work.

Traditional realism, especially today, is primarily very conservative and nature based. Most of my fine art falls outside of contemporary realism. It's just how I think. I like creative avenues that are inventive and cerebral, not fantasy, with sophisticated design and content where the final image has something to say, like a good novel, often with hidden meaning for each viewer to interpret in their own way.

I can usually see the image pretty clearly in my head, and then it's just a matter of getting it onto the canvas. The extensive demo section in this book details my process and is added for artists and others interested in my technical approach.

These pieces are a reflection of my own ideas, dreams, and spiritual imagination. Inventive work, like Angel and dream imagery, is always exciting to do and inspires me to come up with unique interpretations that hopefully convey a thought provoking mood, beauty, something positive and uplifting, and concepts that enlighten and stimulate each viewer who sees them."

Philip Howe

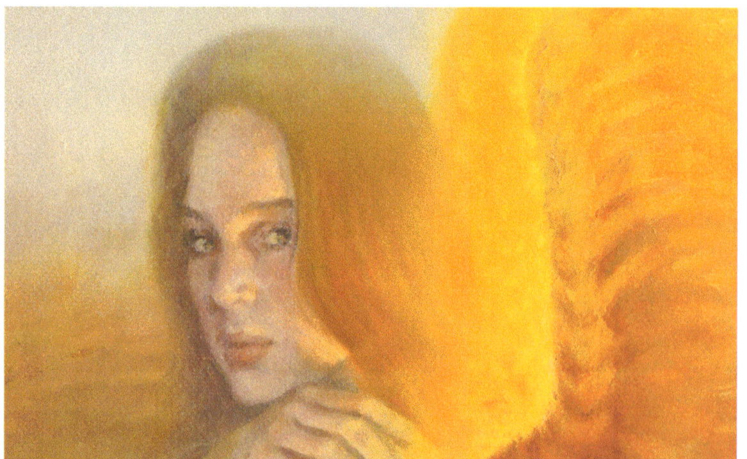

For more information on these and other paintings, prints, demos, and the artist's technical notes- please visit www.philiphowe.com or- www.illustratedimages.com

We hope these paintings will inspire and move you.

Thank you for purchasing an Illustrated Images Book.

Angels ~ Spiritual and Dream Imagery
Artwork by Philip Howe

Published by Illustrated Images Books 2009

ISBN 978-0-9843198-2-4

Artwork, poetry, and book design by Philip Howe © 2009

Calligraphy flourishes by Glenn Yoshiyama

First Edition

Printed in the United States of America

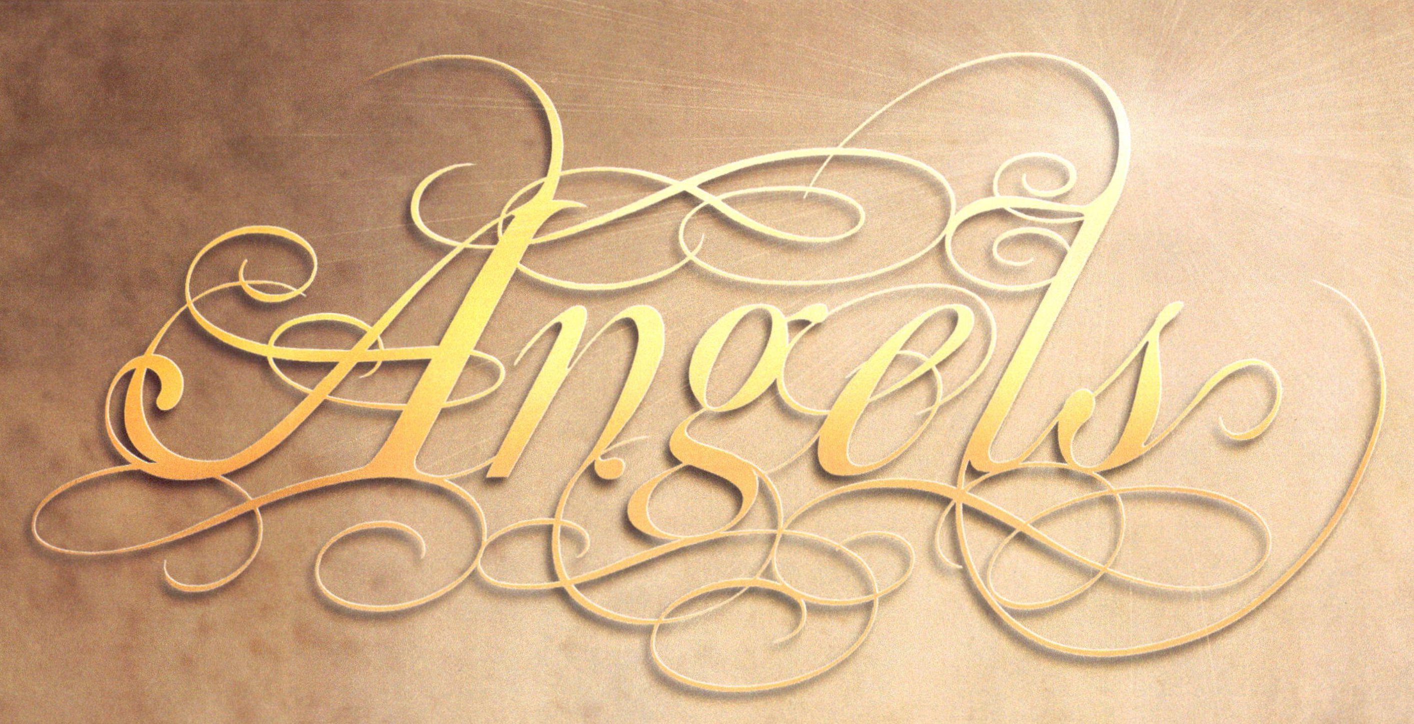

Spiritual and Dream Imagery

The Artwork of Philip Howe

Contents

Angels and Dream Paintings 4-63

Oil Studies 64-83

Earlier Work 84-87

Figure Drawings 88-89

Demonstrations 90-133

Far Below

Waiting for the moment

to drift into the world

outside of spirit,

where time exists for mortal beings

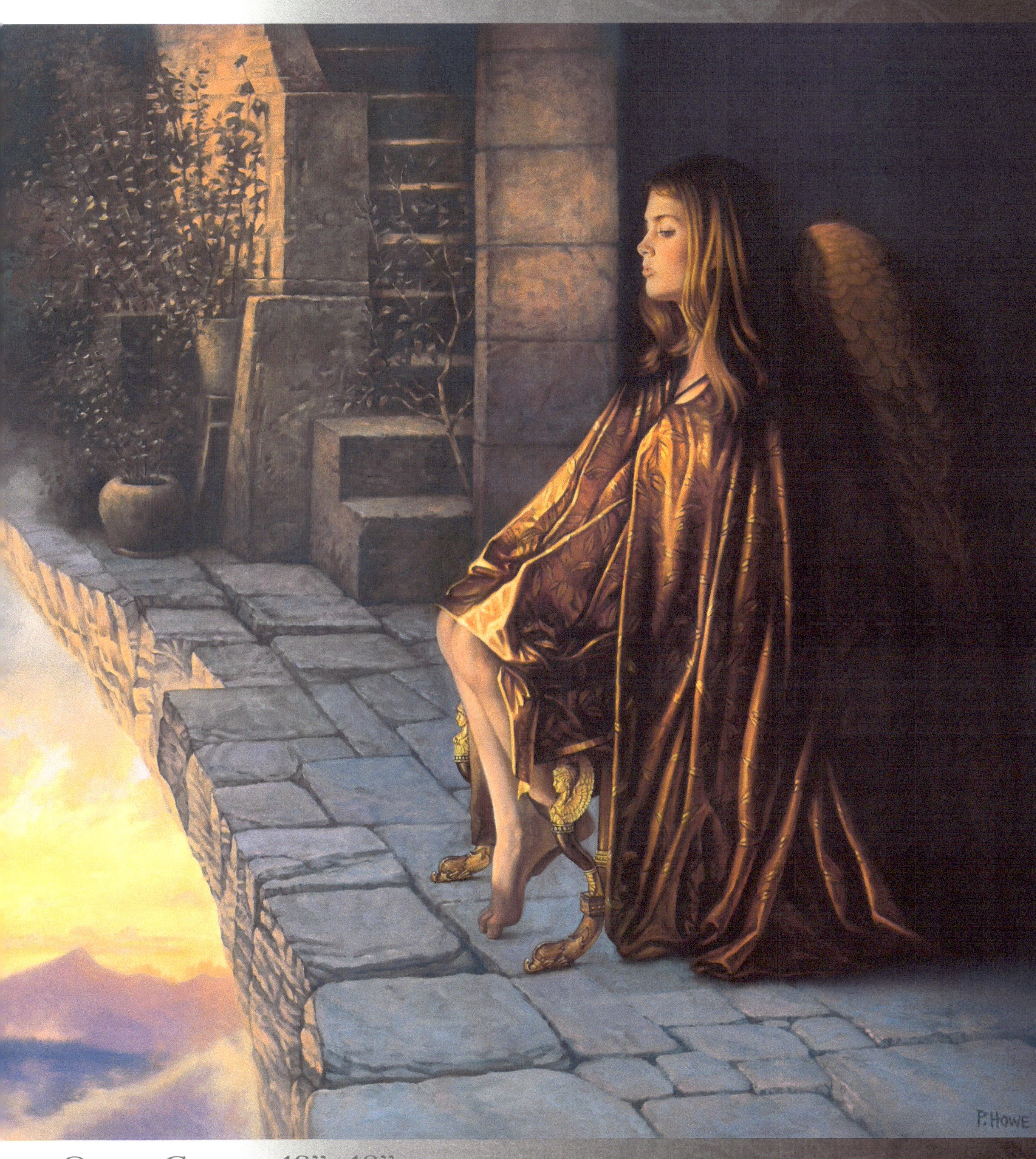

Oil on Canvas 48"x48"

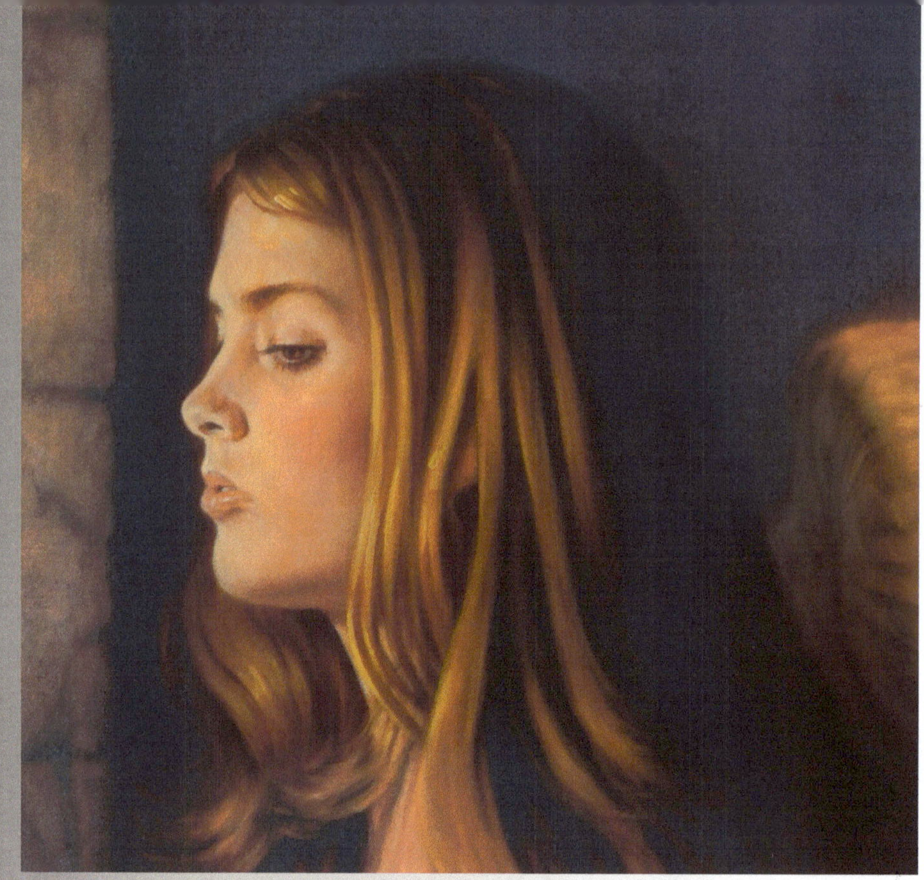

Far Below- Details

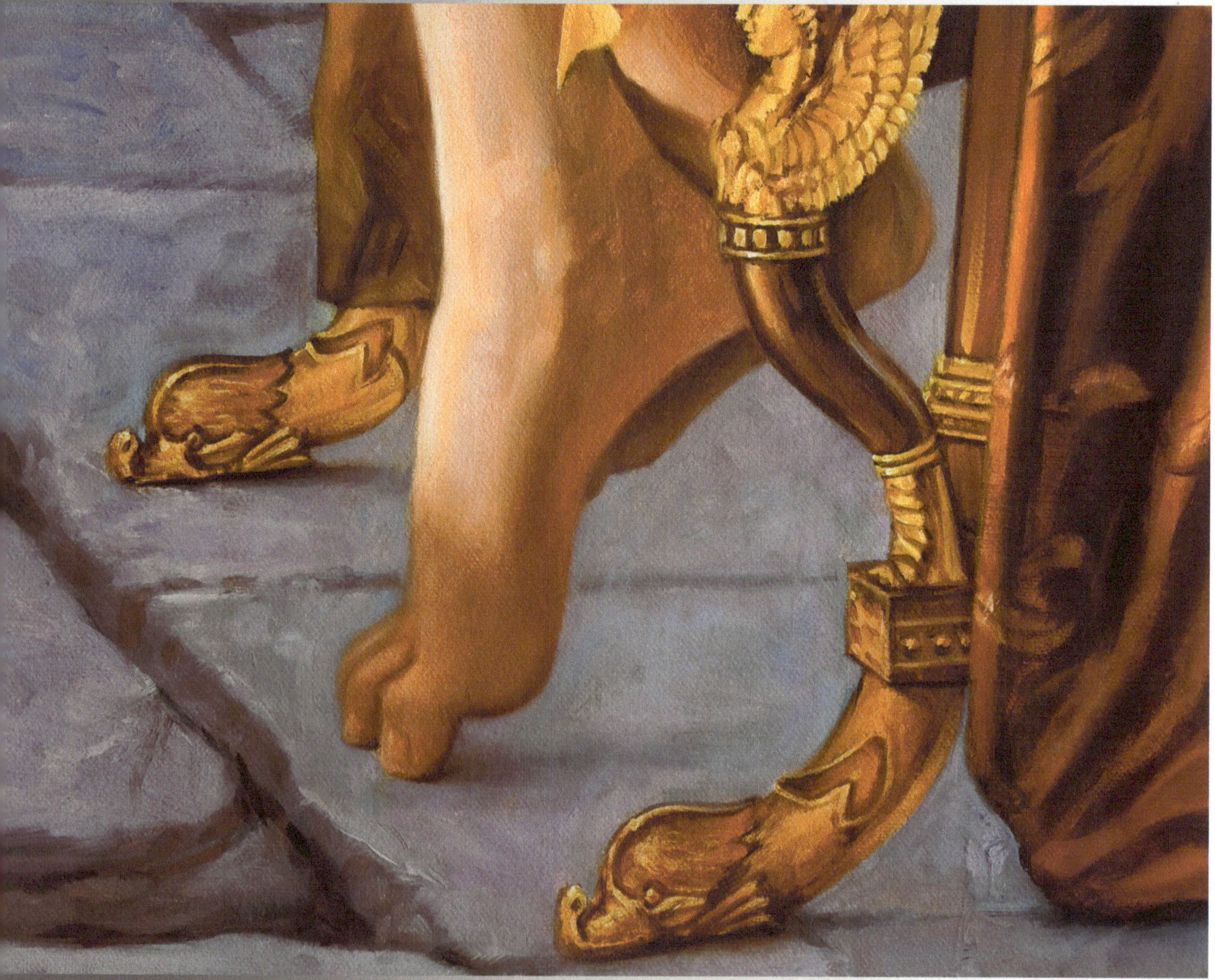

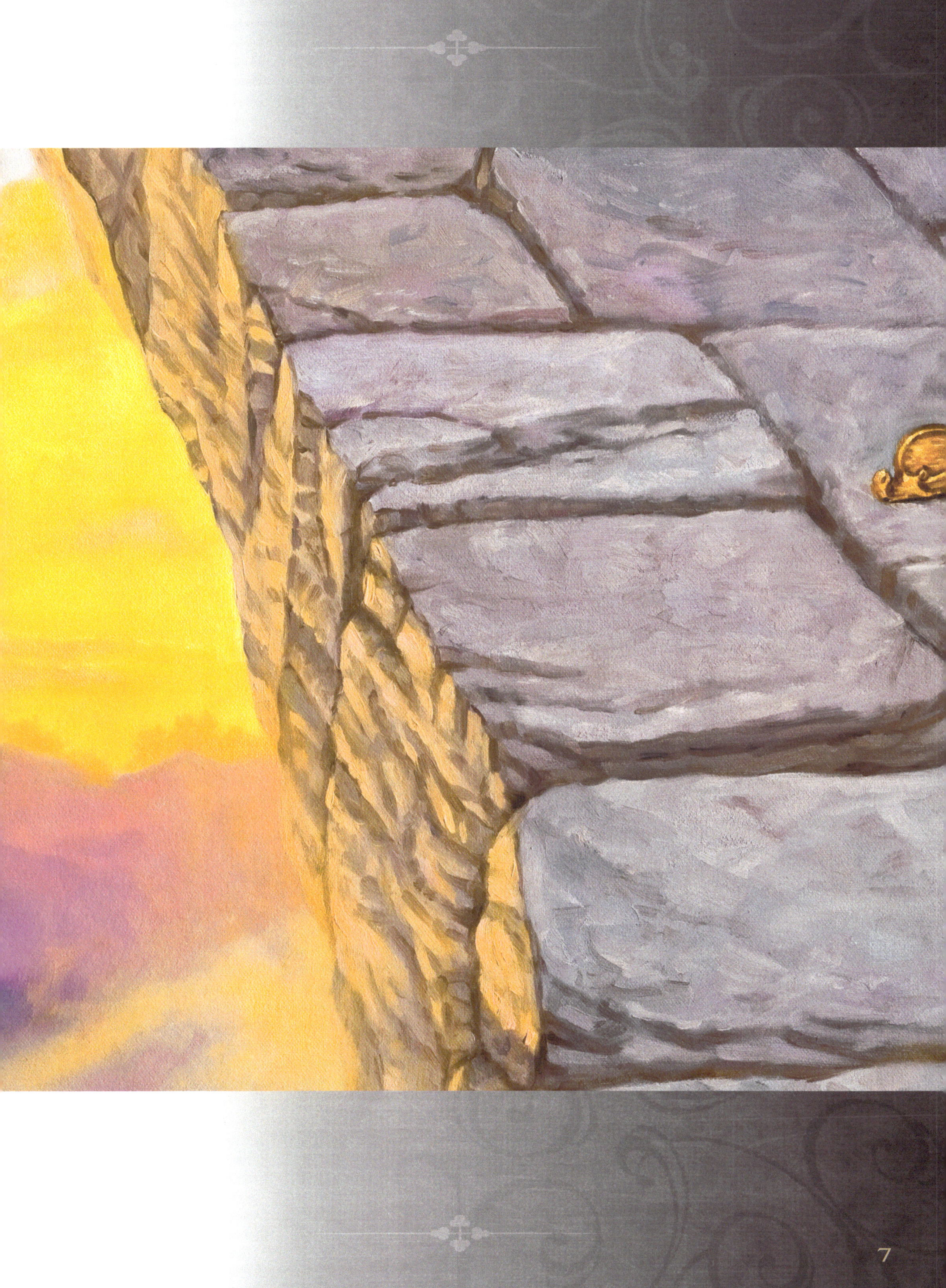

The Heart of a Tree

In all living things known to man or spirit

a soul begins and grows and ages.

Yet the deepest part

is still the heart

within the soul

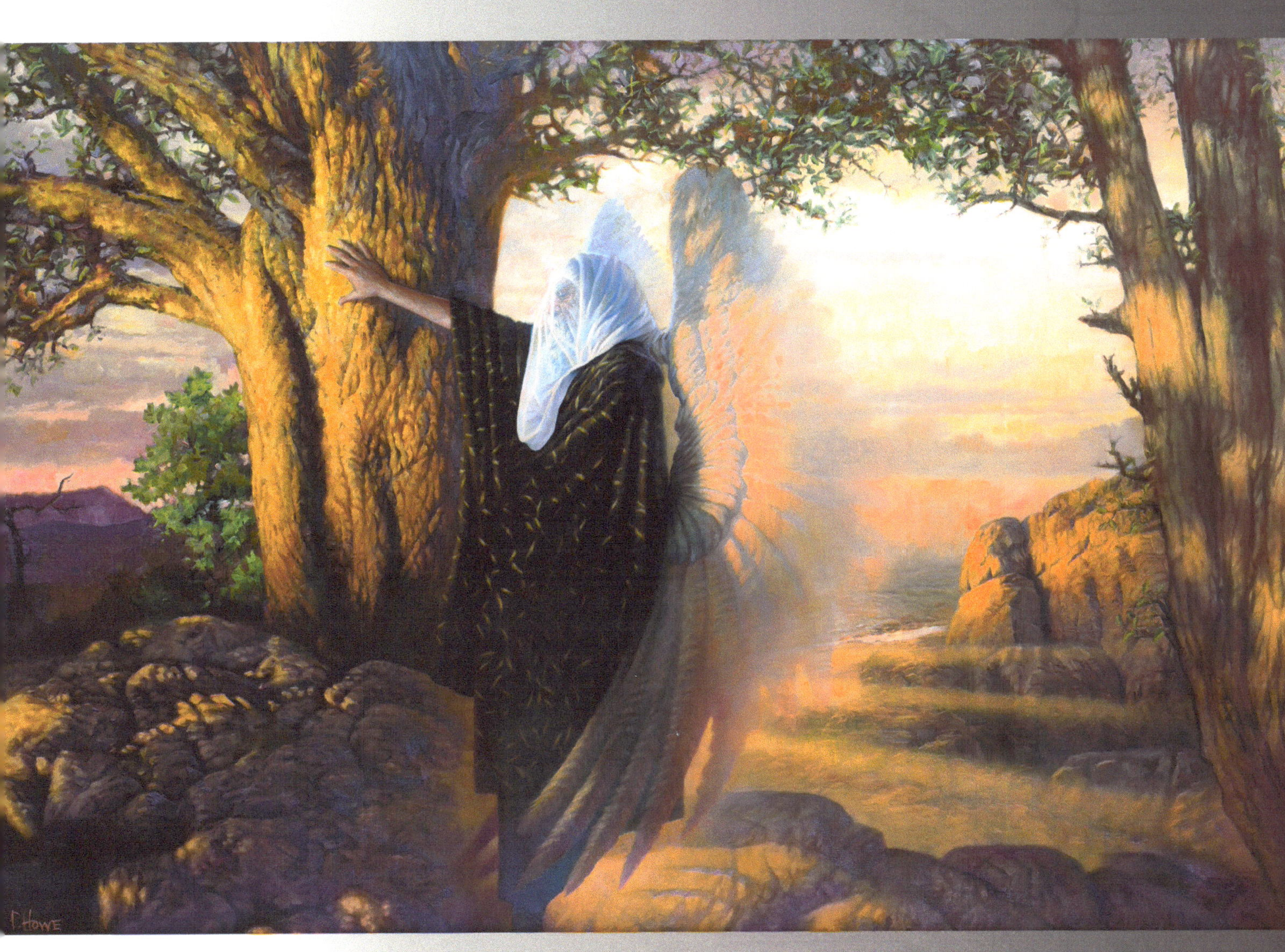

Oil on Canvas 34"x 52"

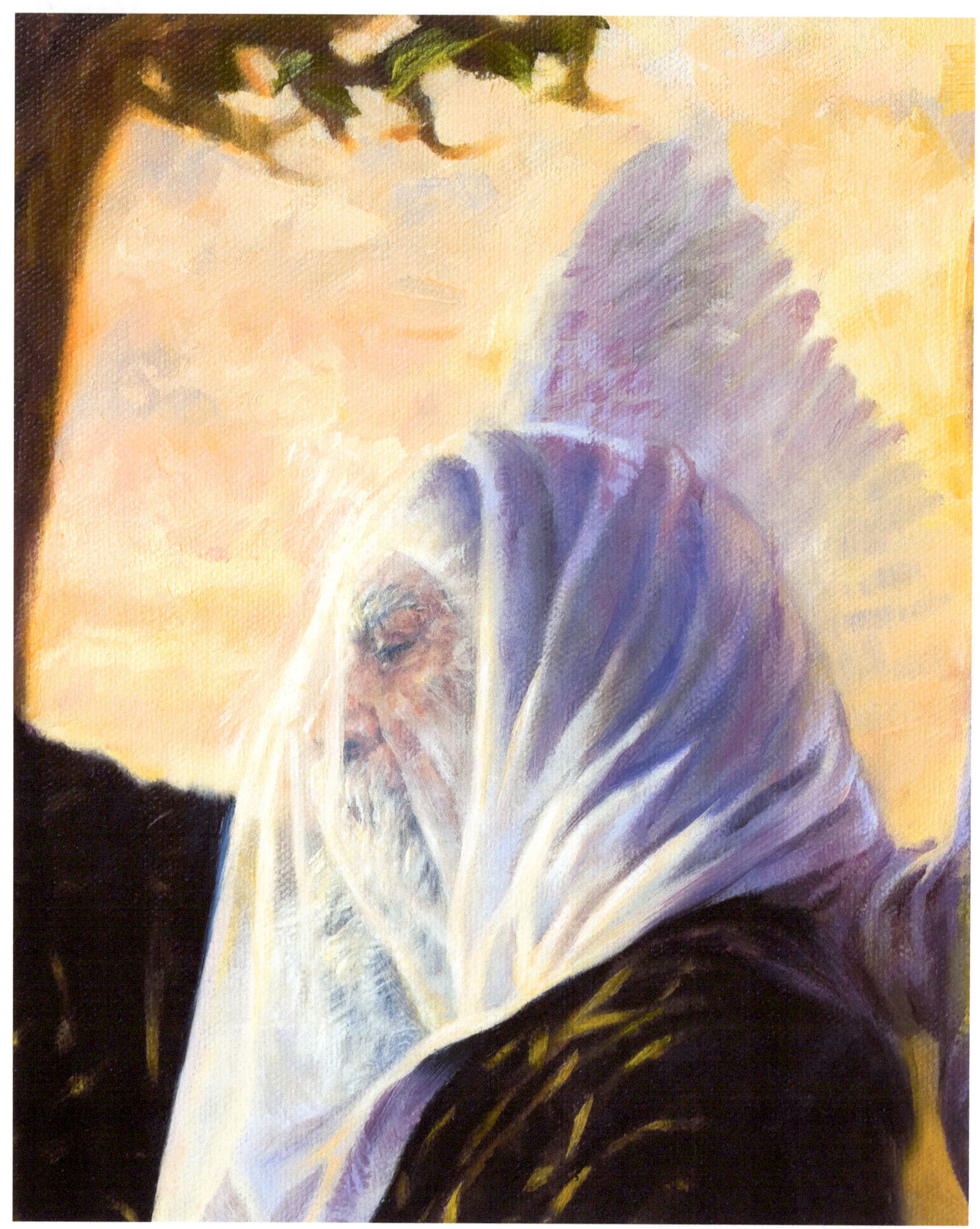

The Heart of a Tree- Details

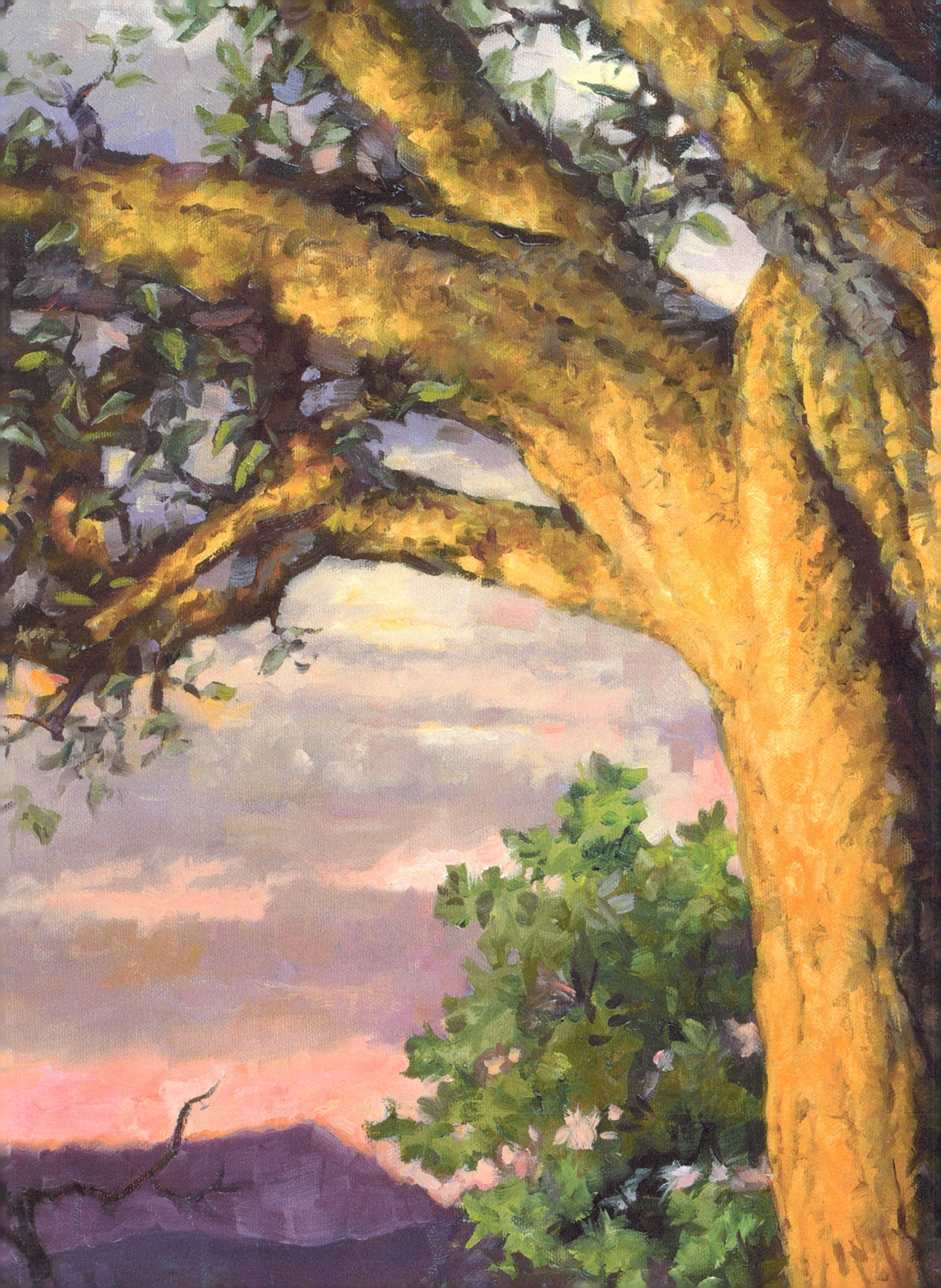

The Sentinel

Oil on Canvas 32" x 44"

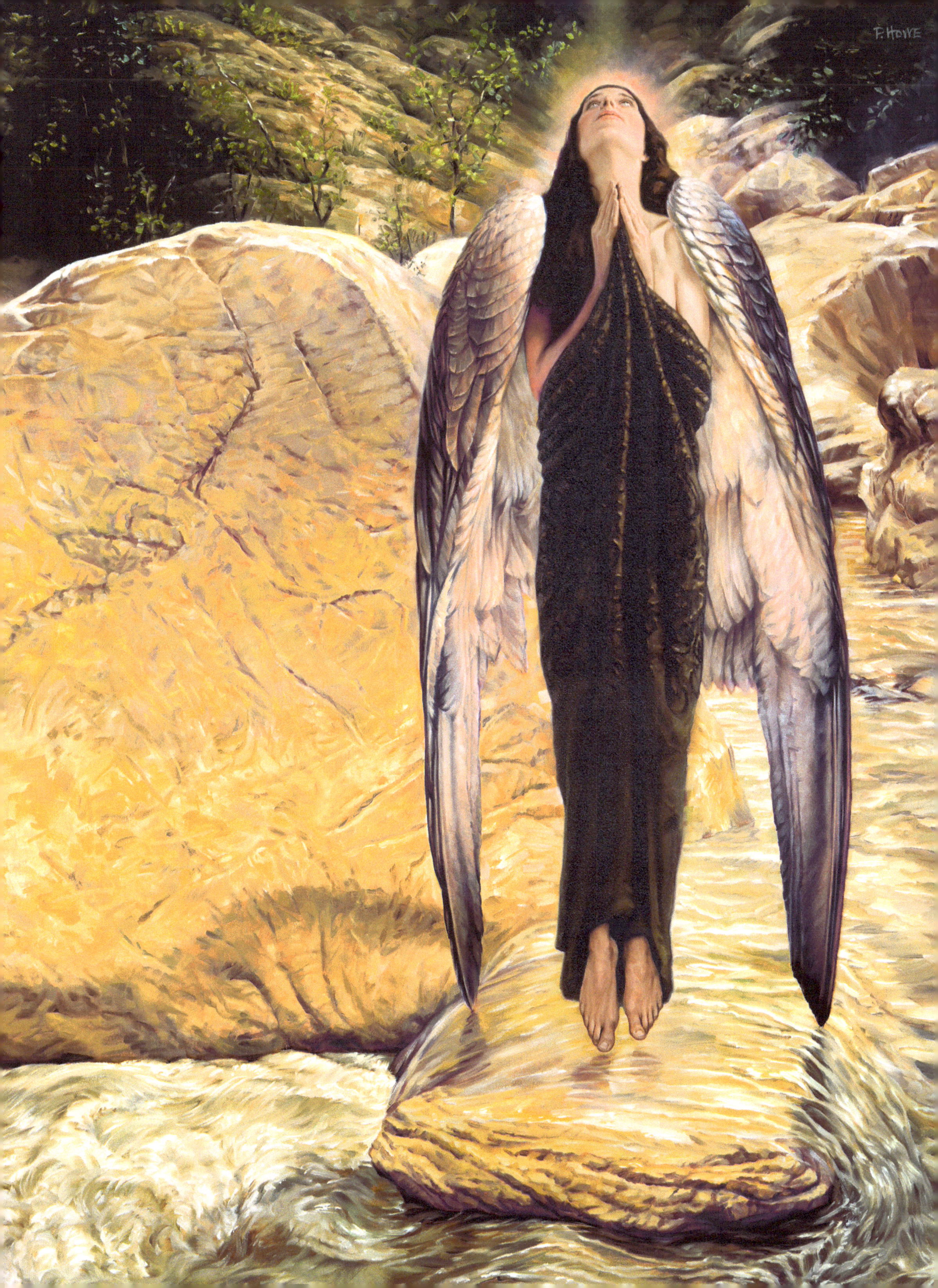
P. HOWE

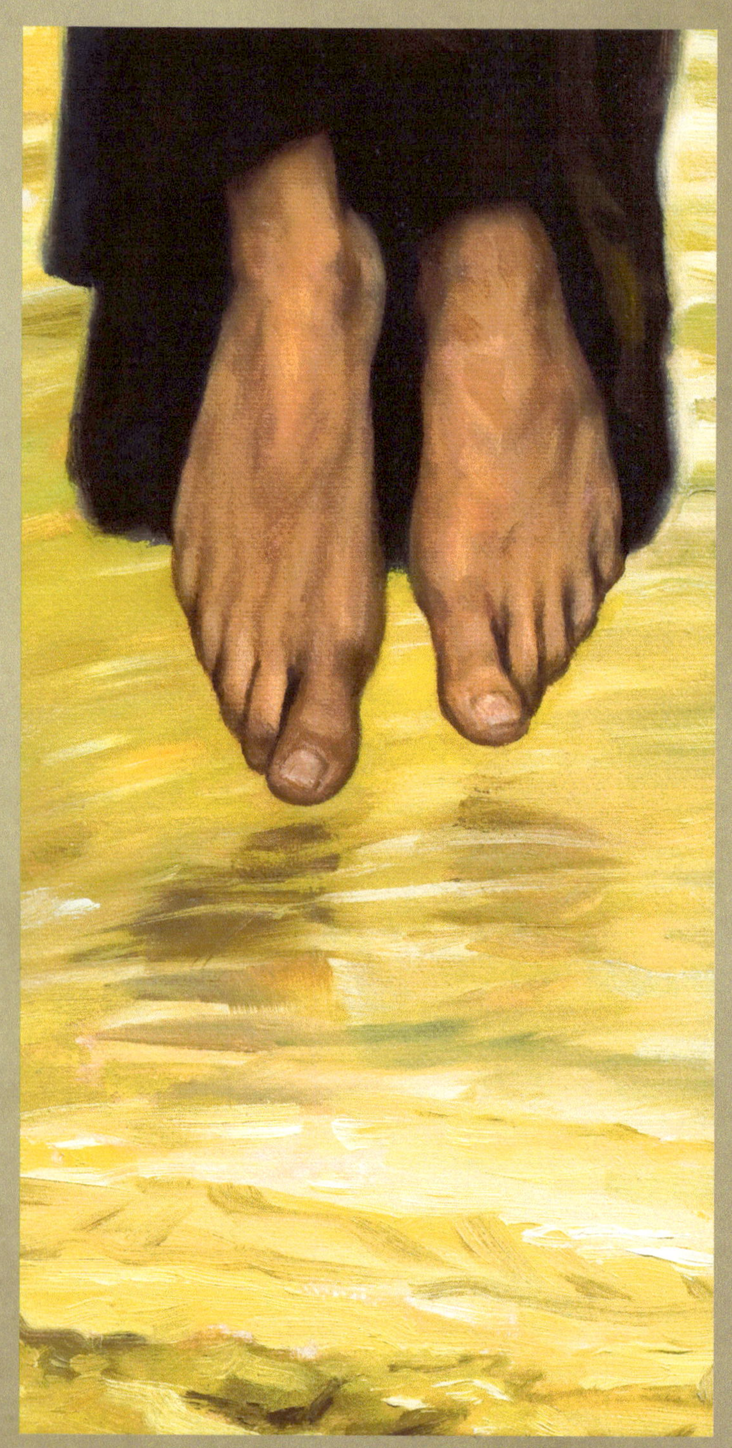

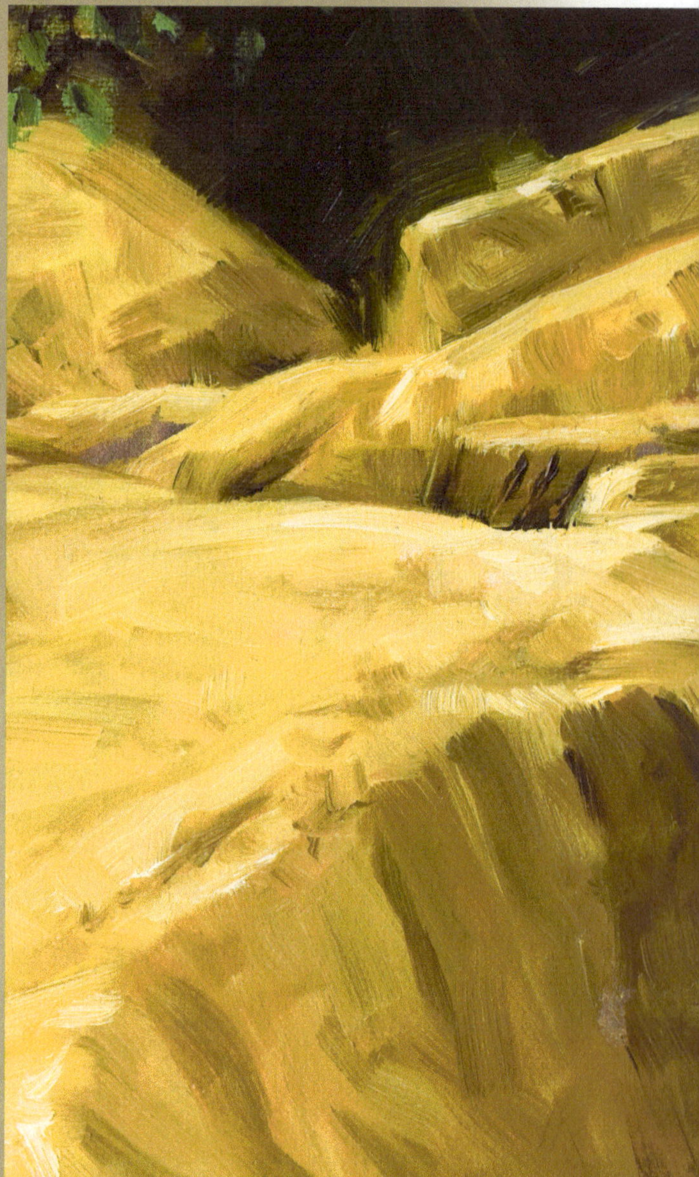

Sentinel - Details

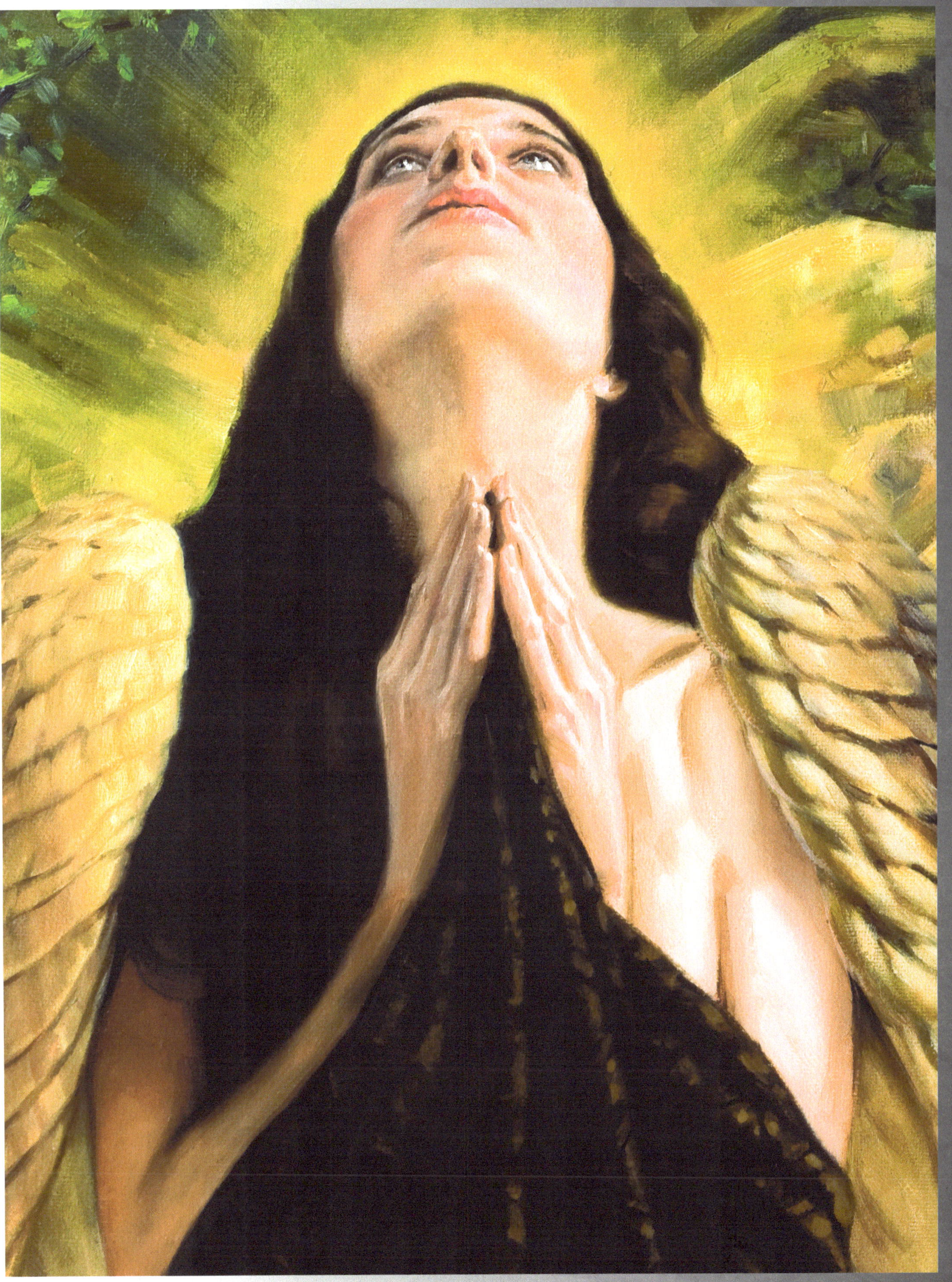

Mary's House

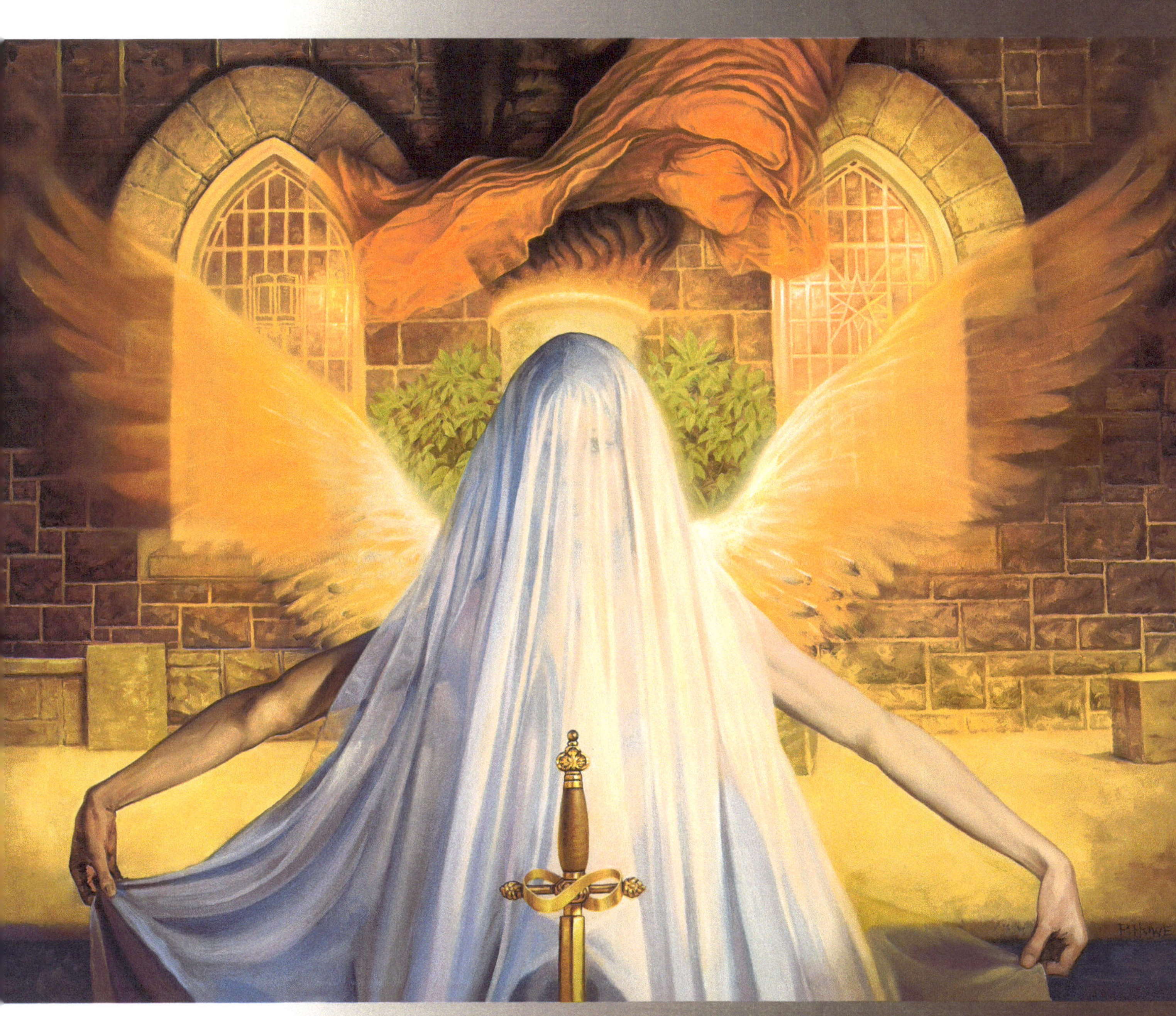

Oil on Canvas 42" x 56"

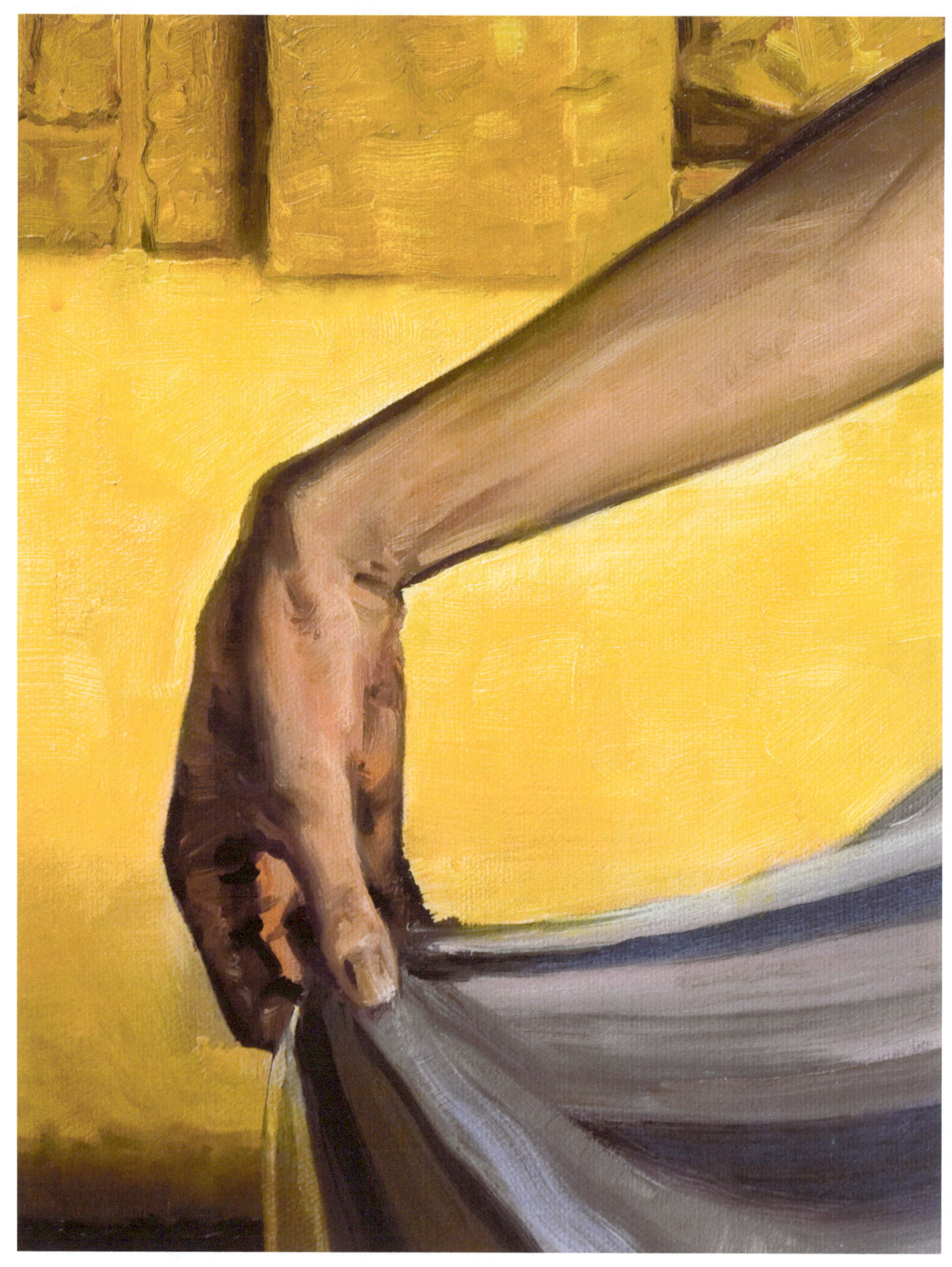

Mary's House - Details

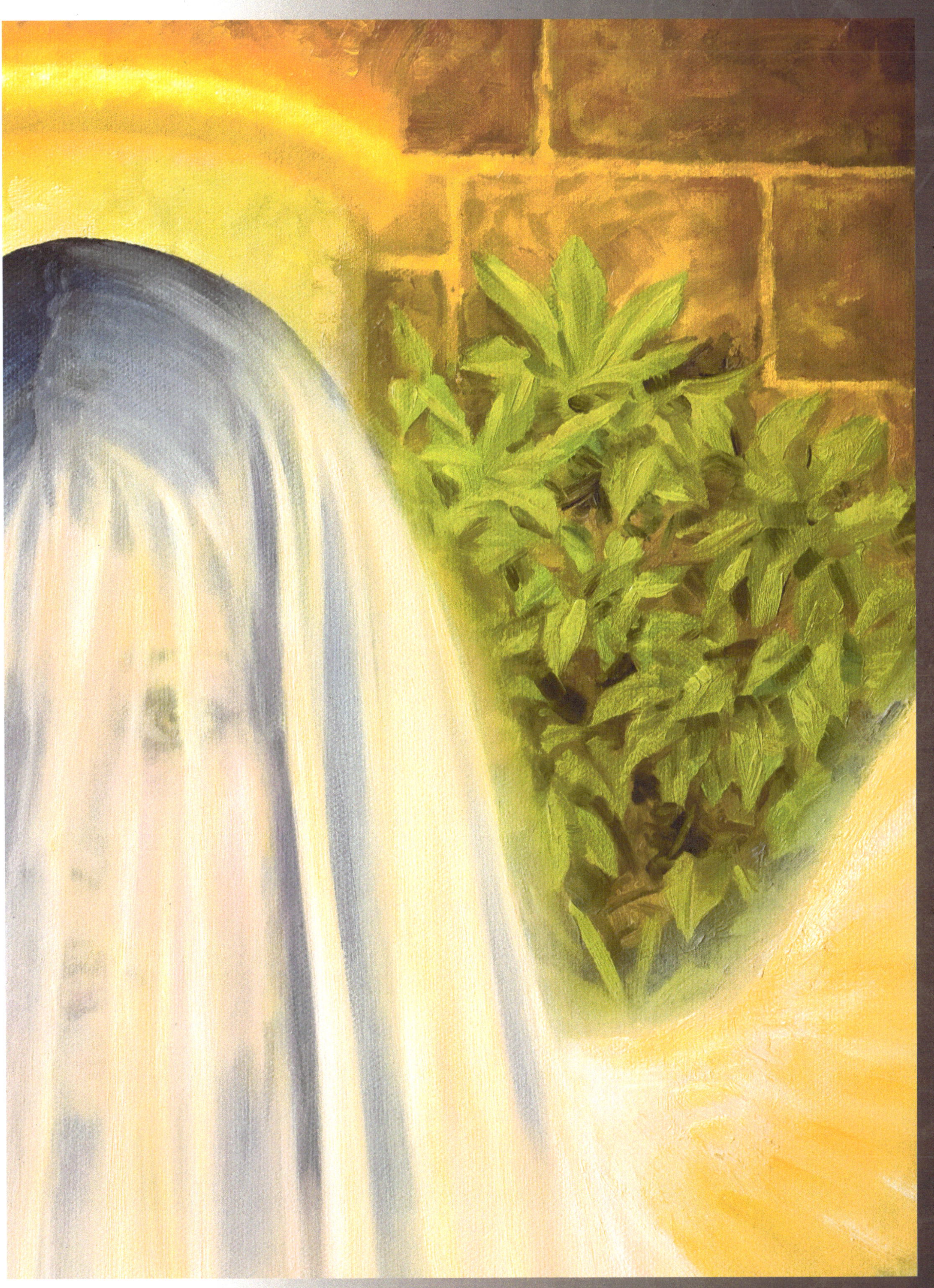

Caverna Magica

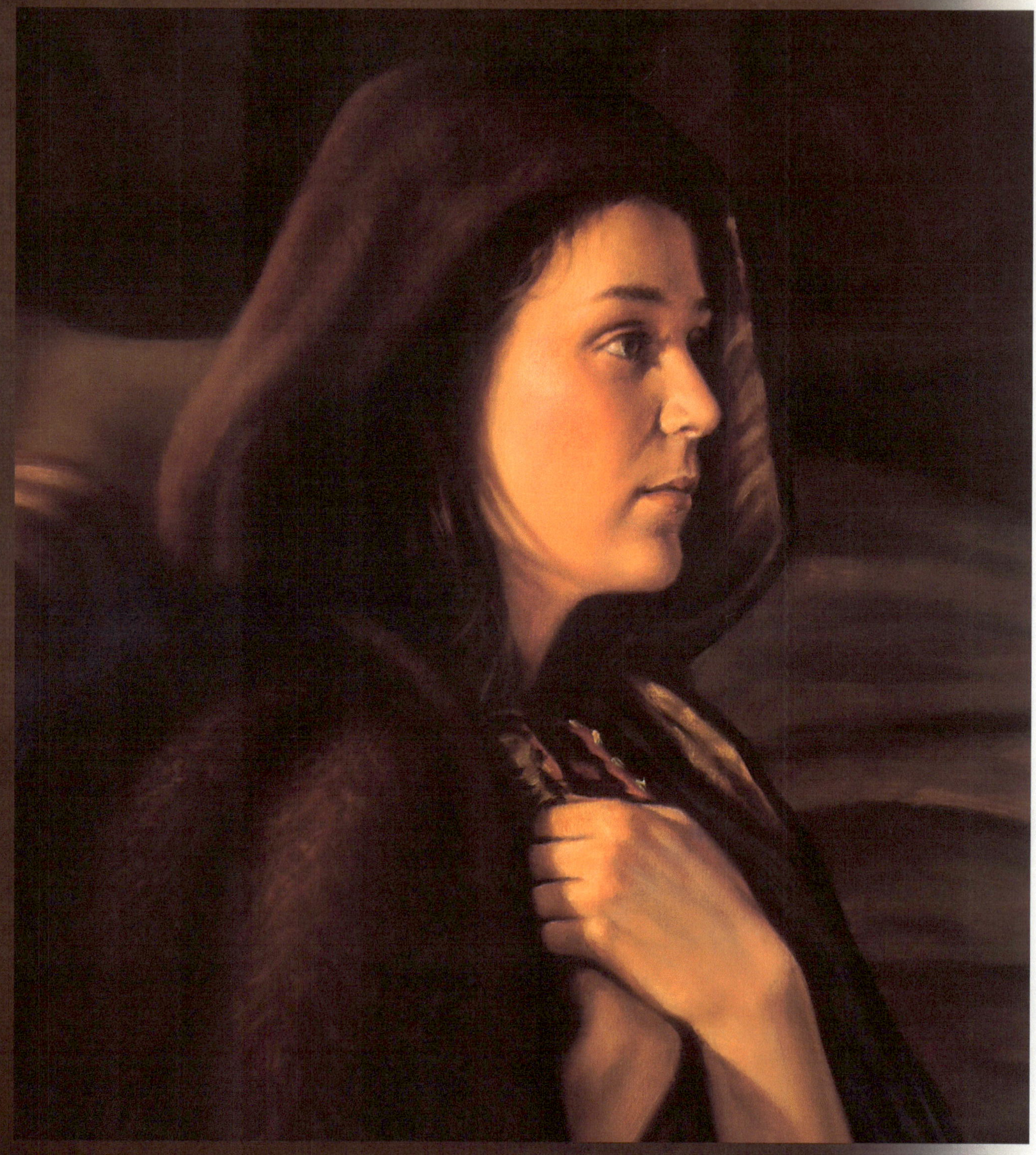

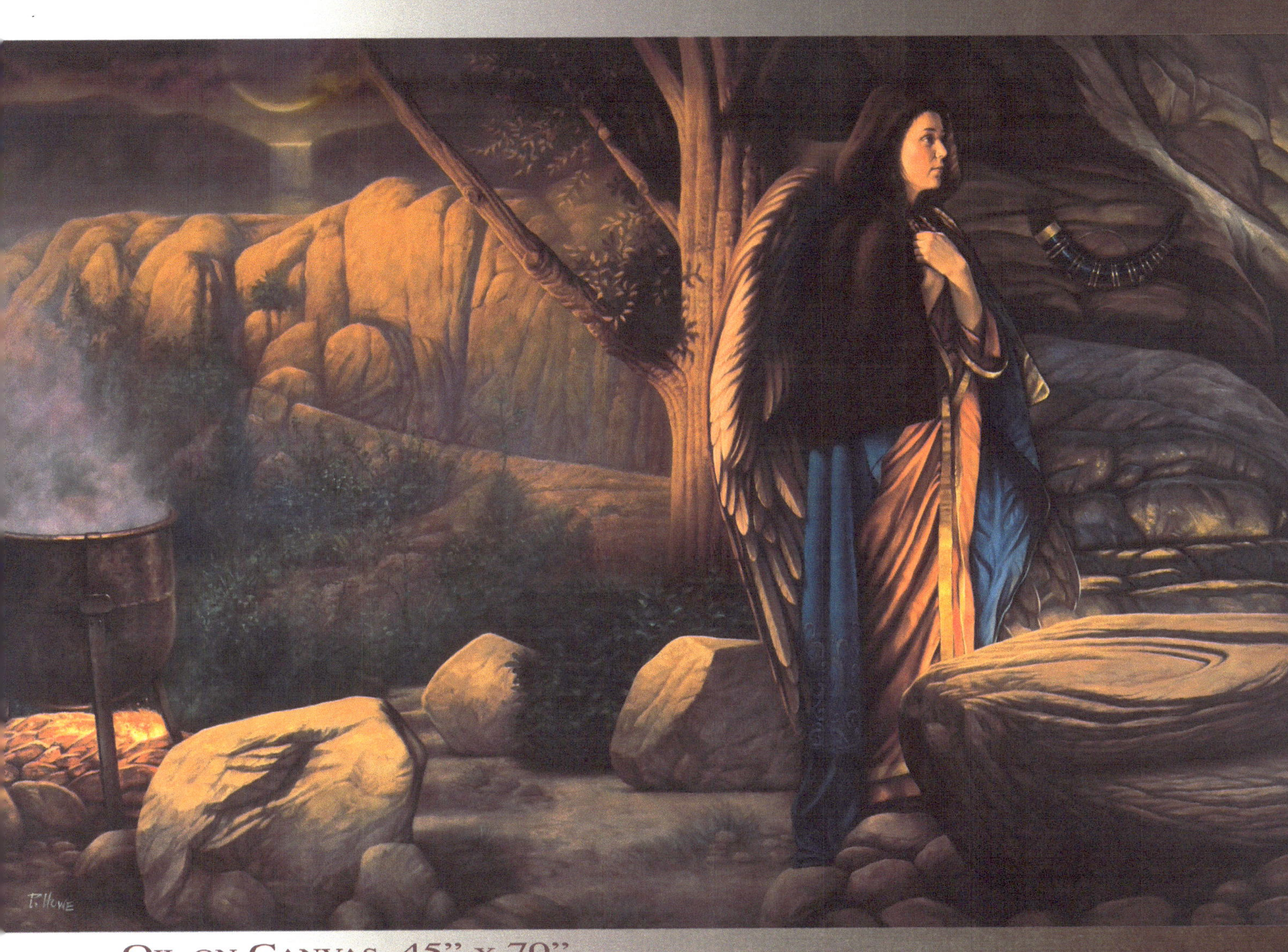

Oil on Canvas 45" x 70"

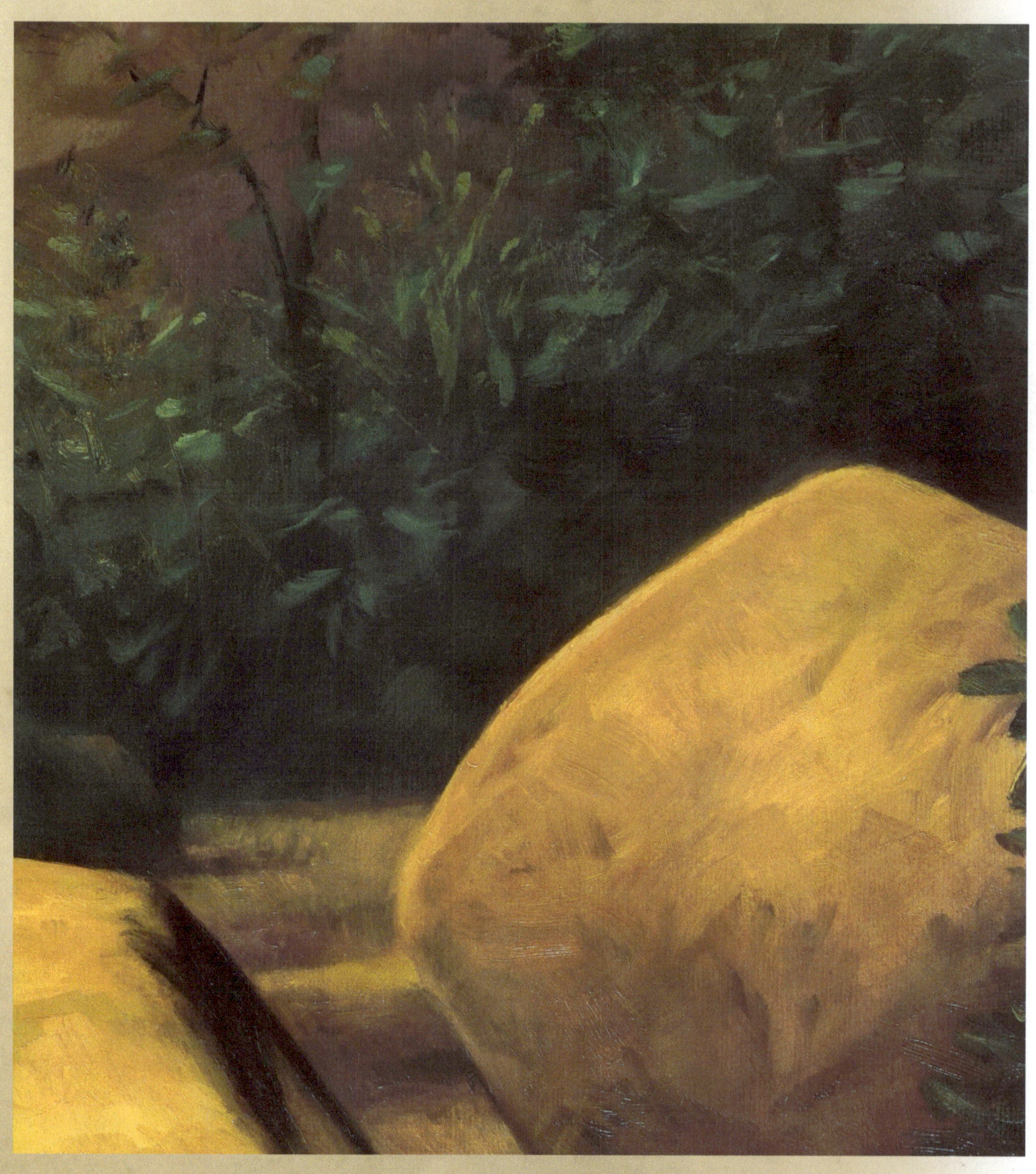

Caverna Magica - Details

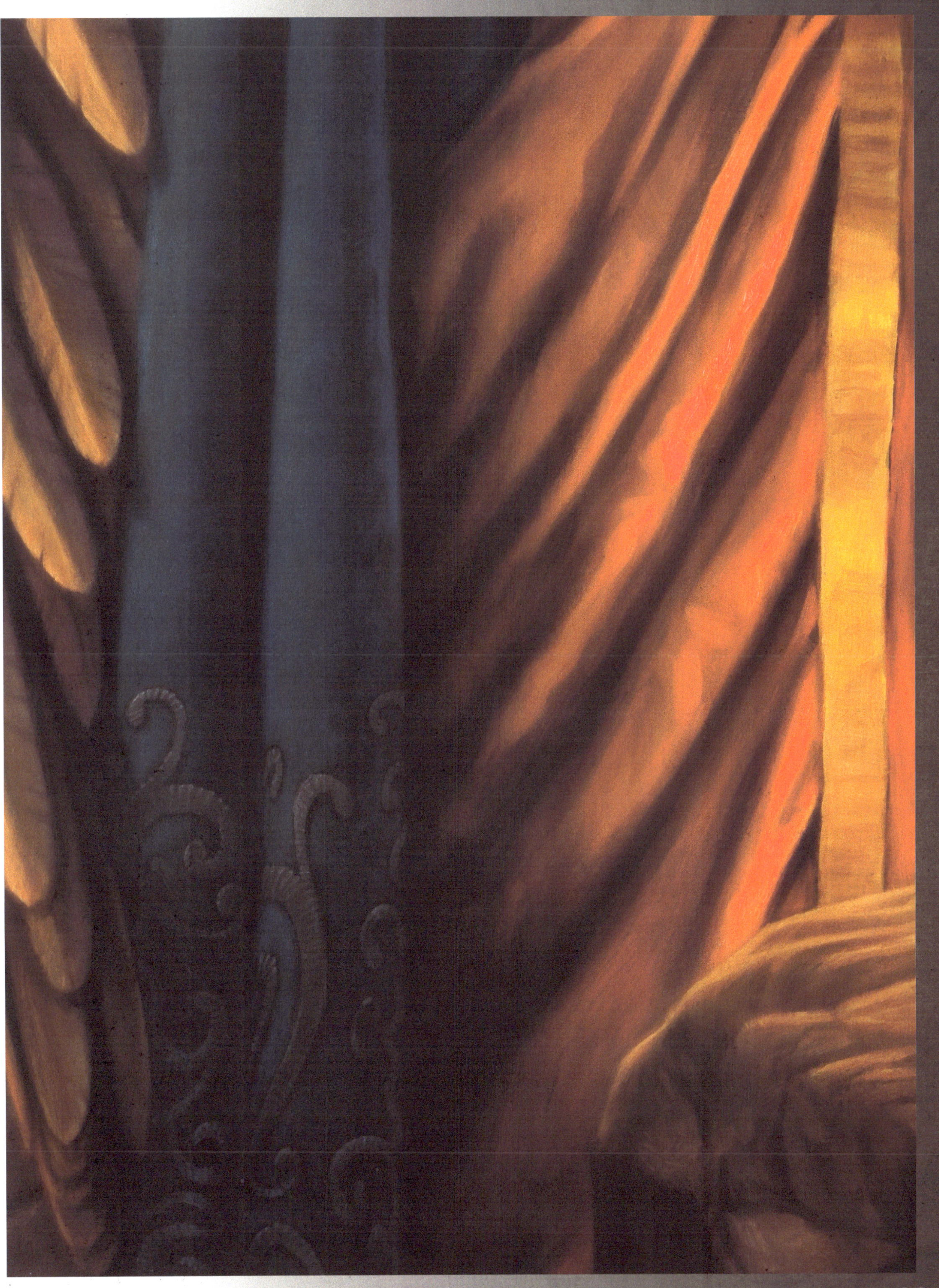

New Beginnings

Oil on Canvas 45" x 70"

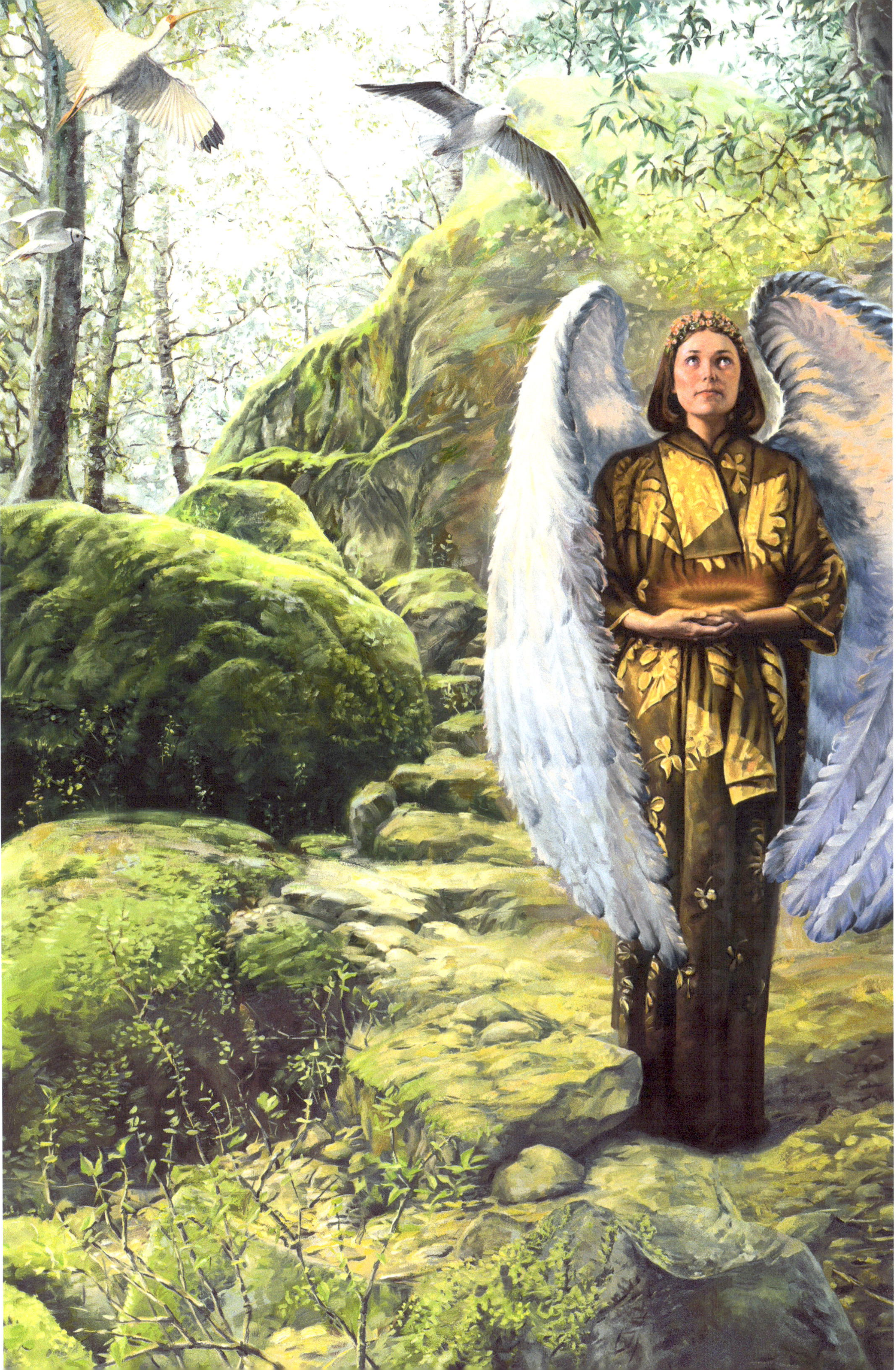

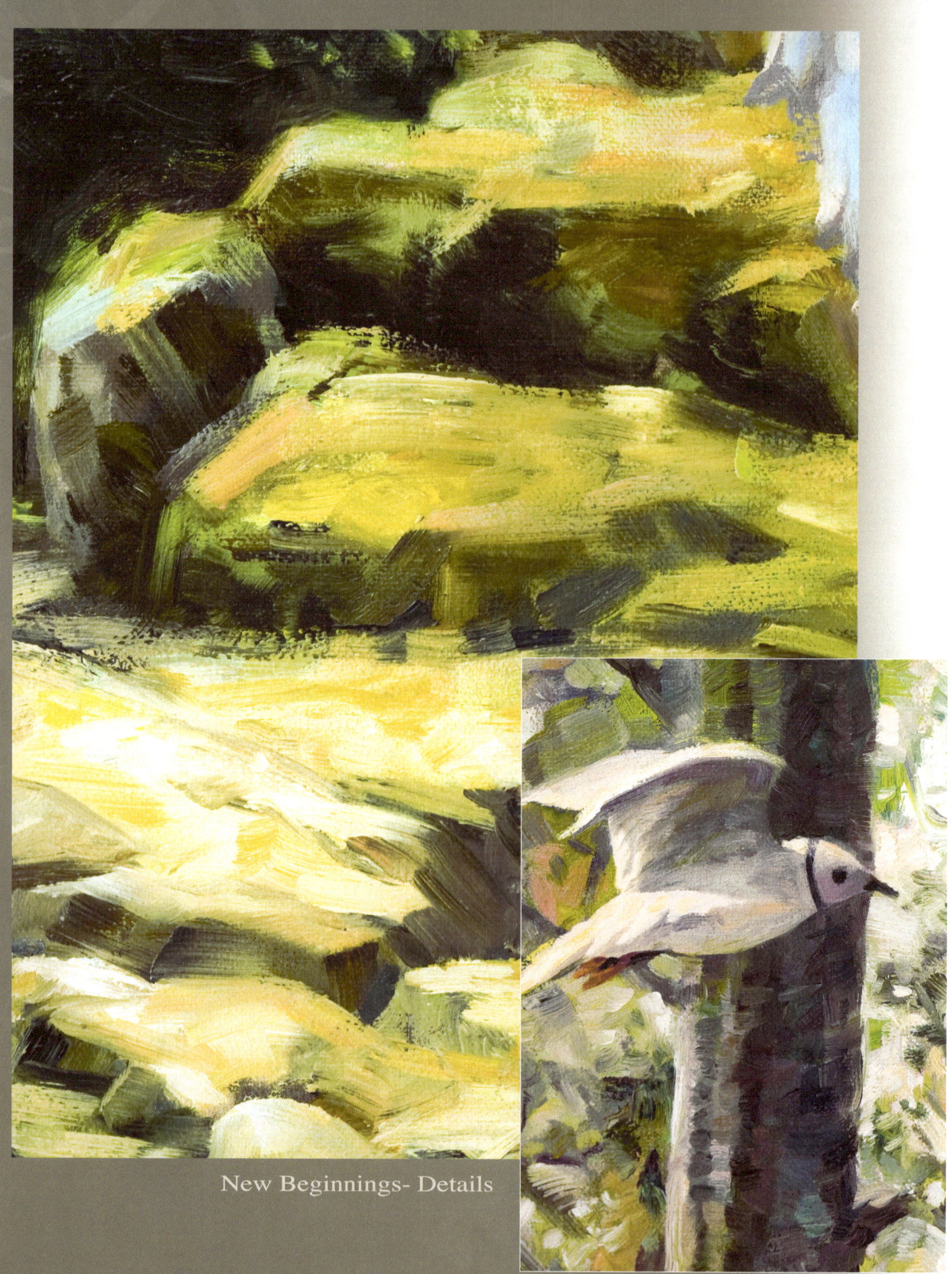

New Beginnings- Details

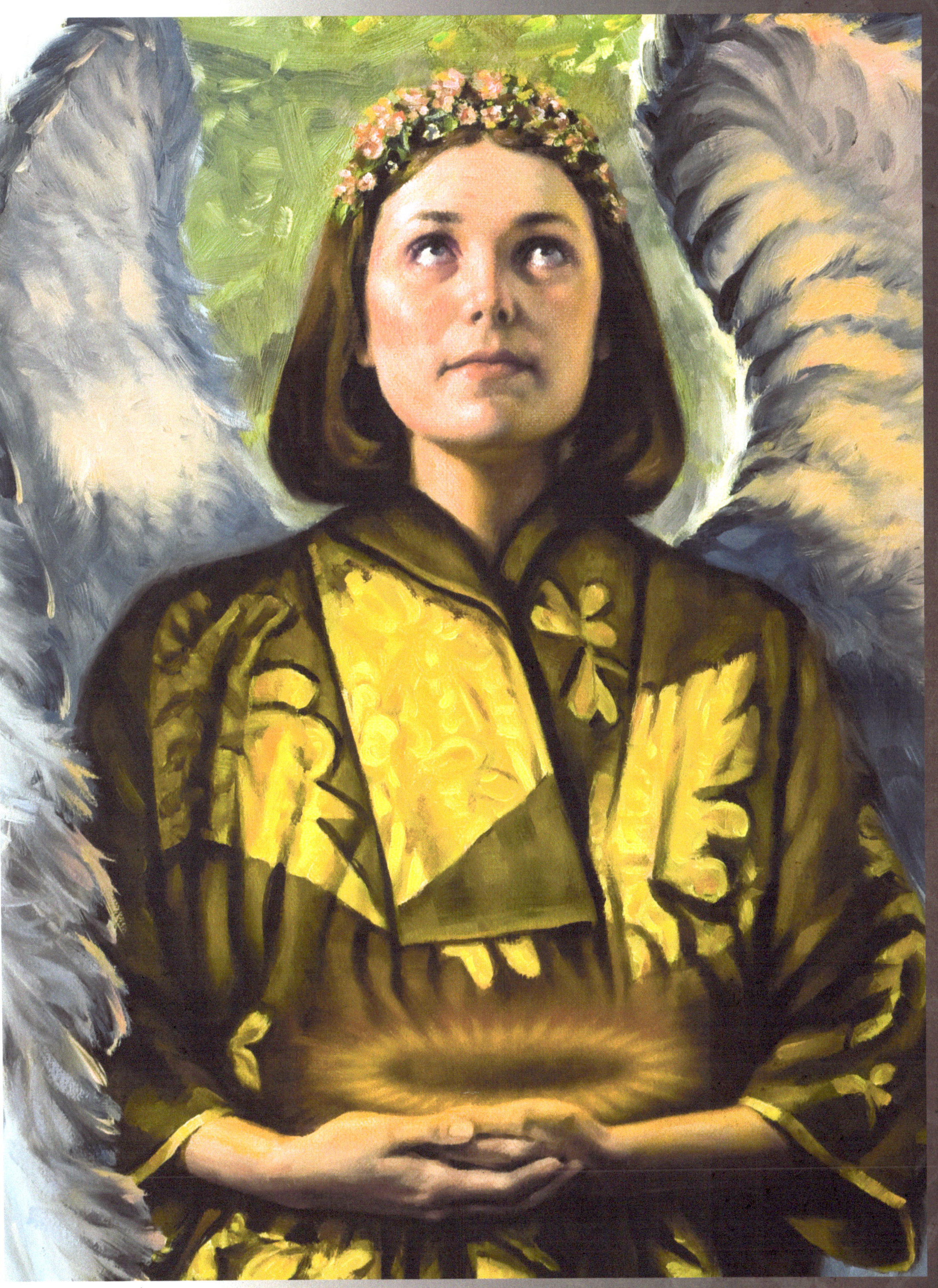

Passing On

Oil on Canvas 42" x 56"

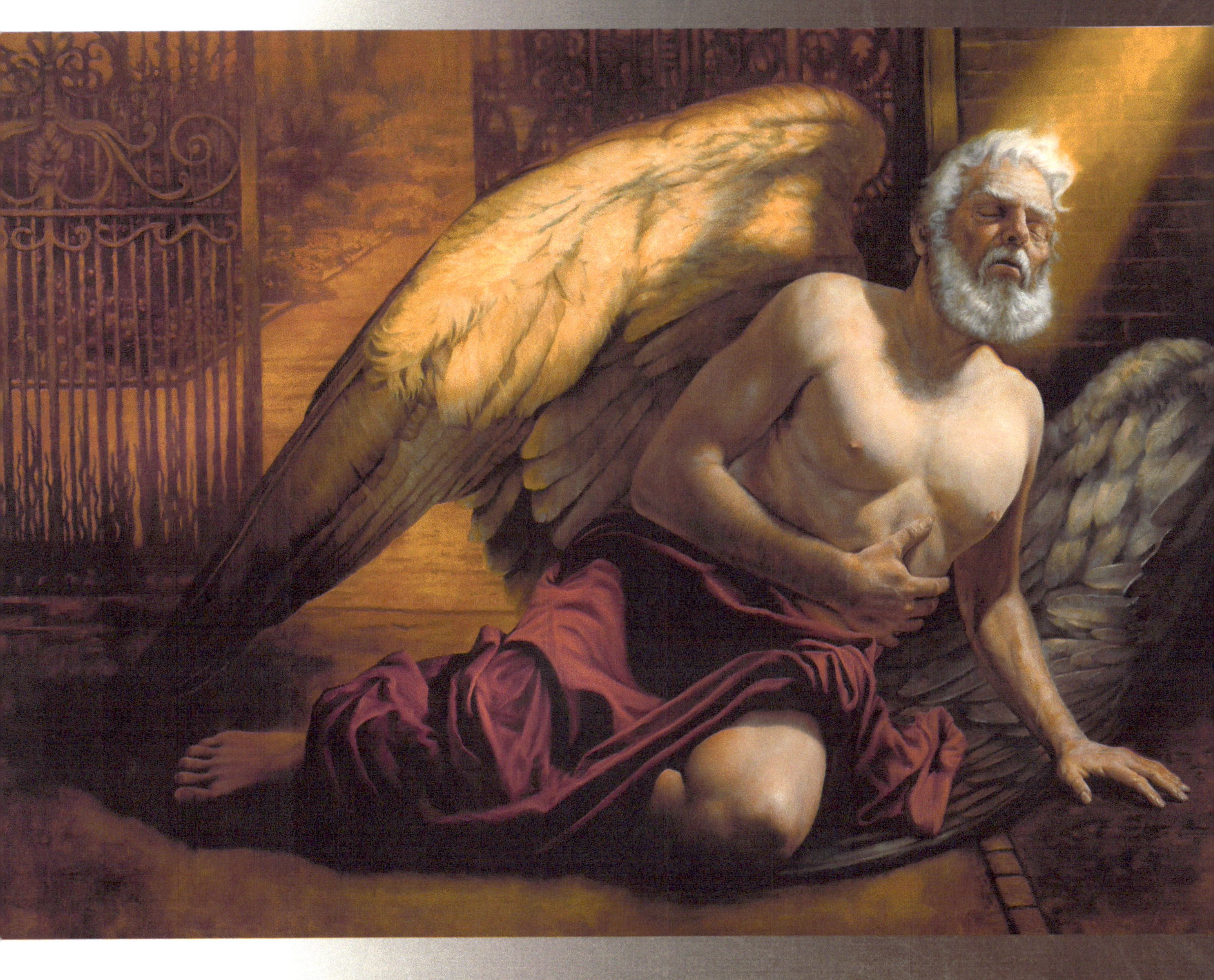

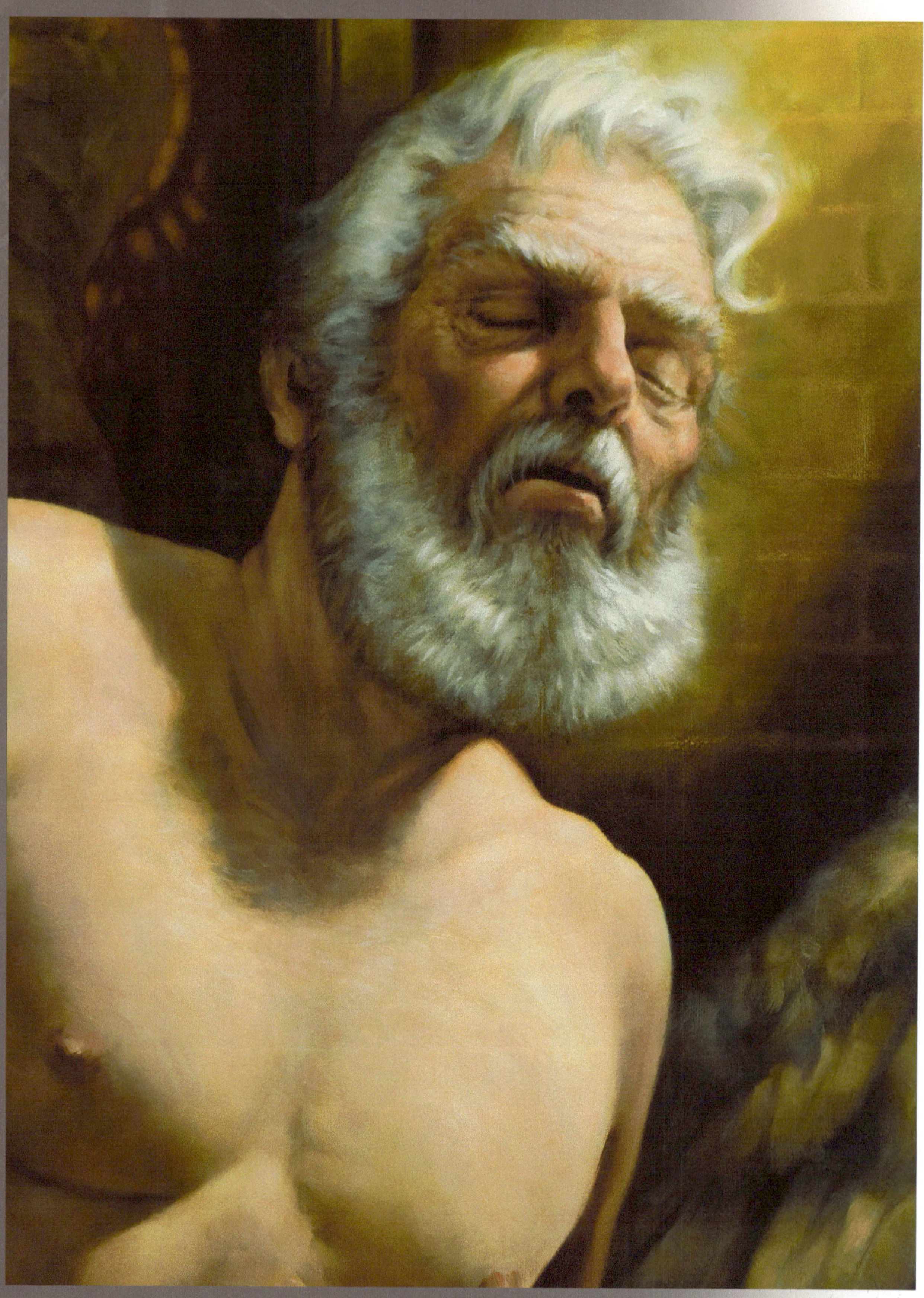

New Beginnings- Details

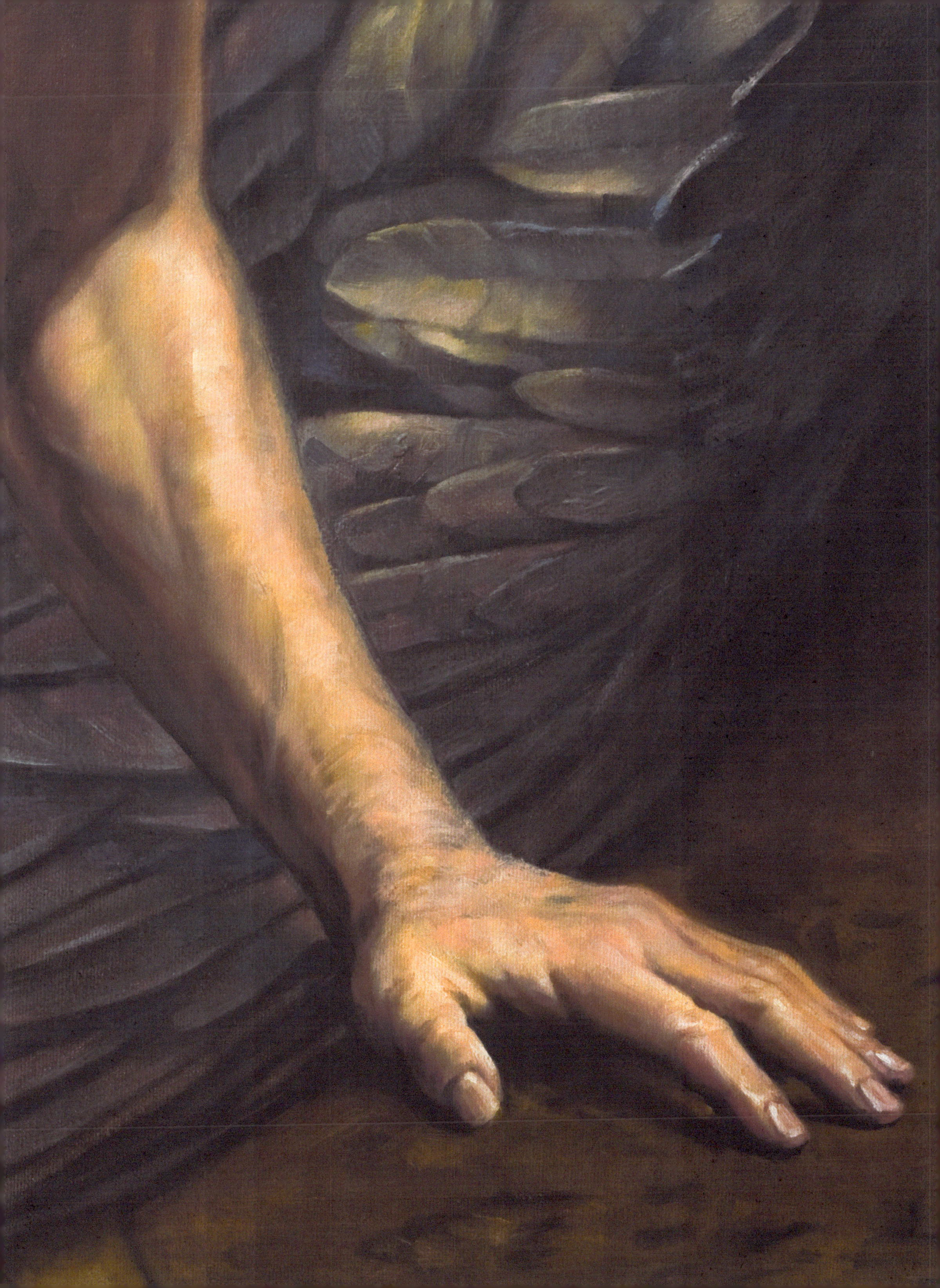

To Be Mortal

Embers of lost faith

stir among the Angels

who seek to know

the pleasures of mortality

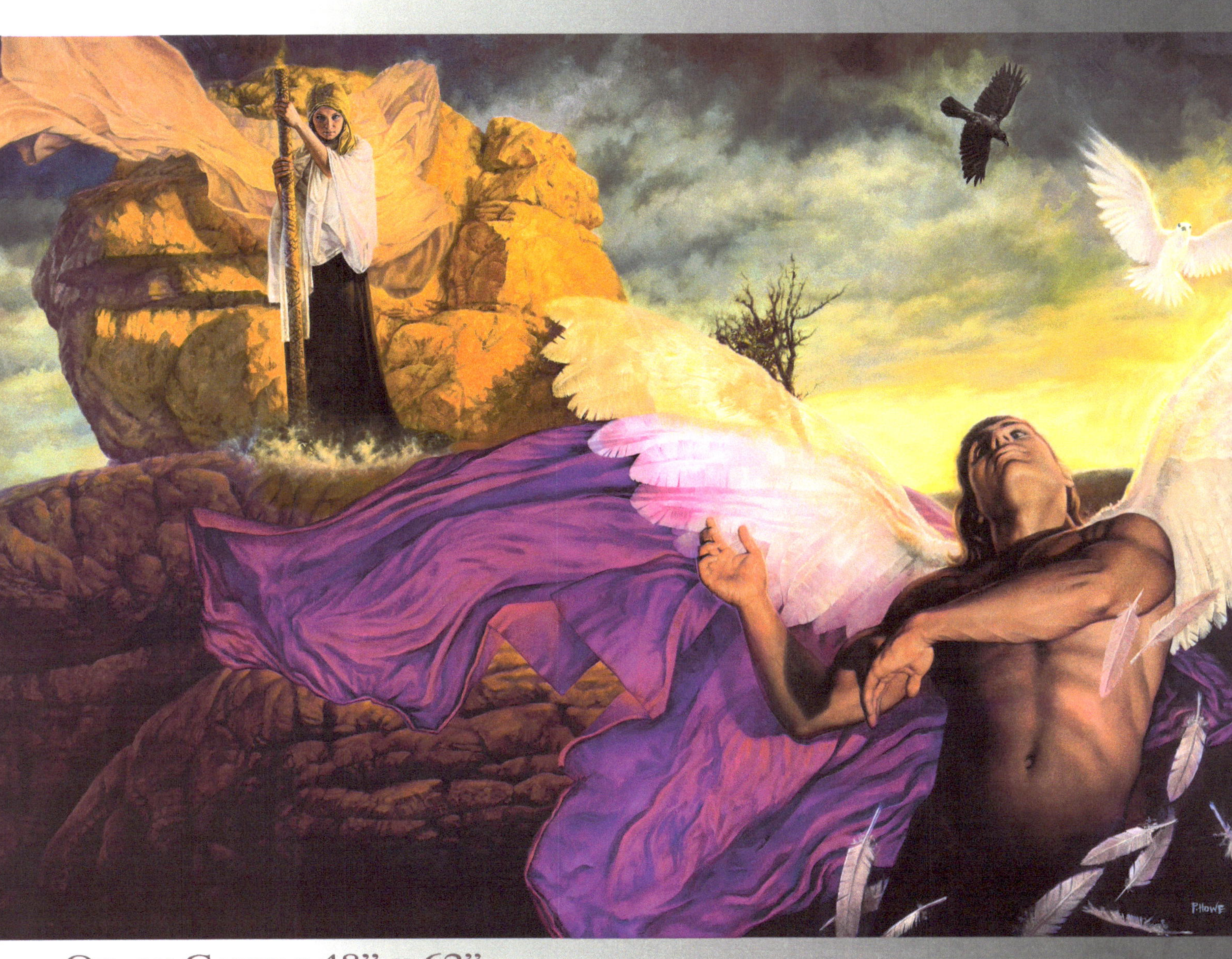

Oil on Canvas 48" x 62"

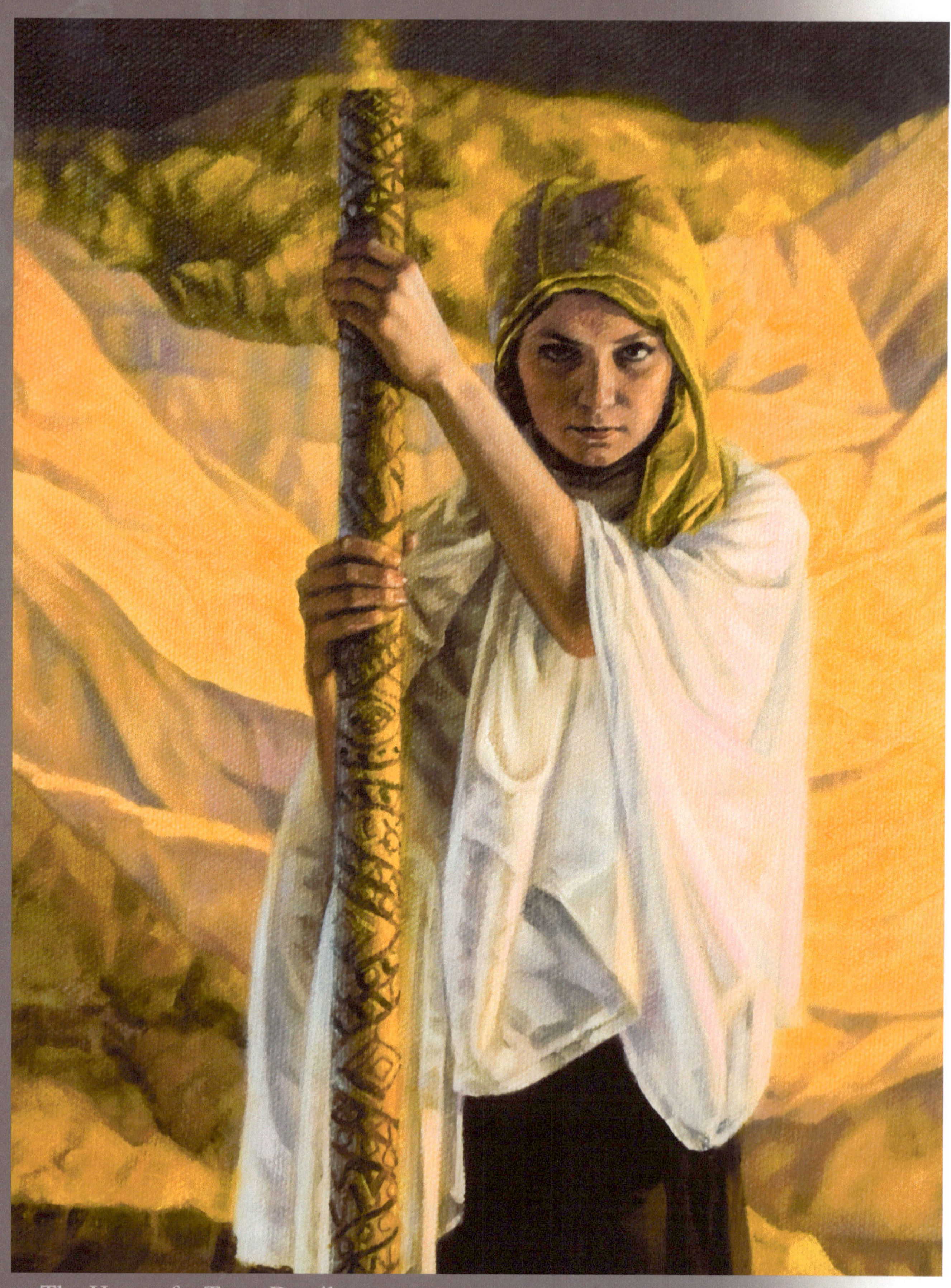

The Heart of a Tree- Details

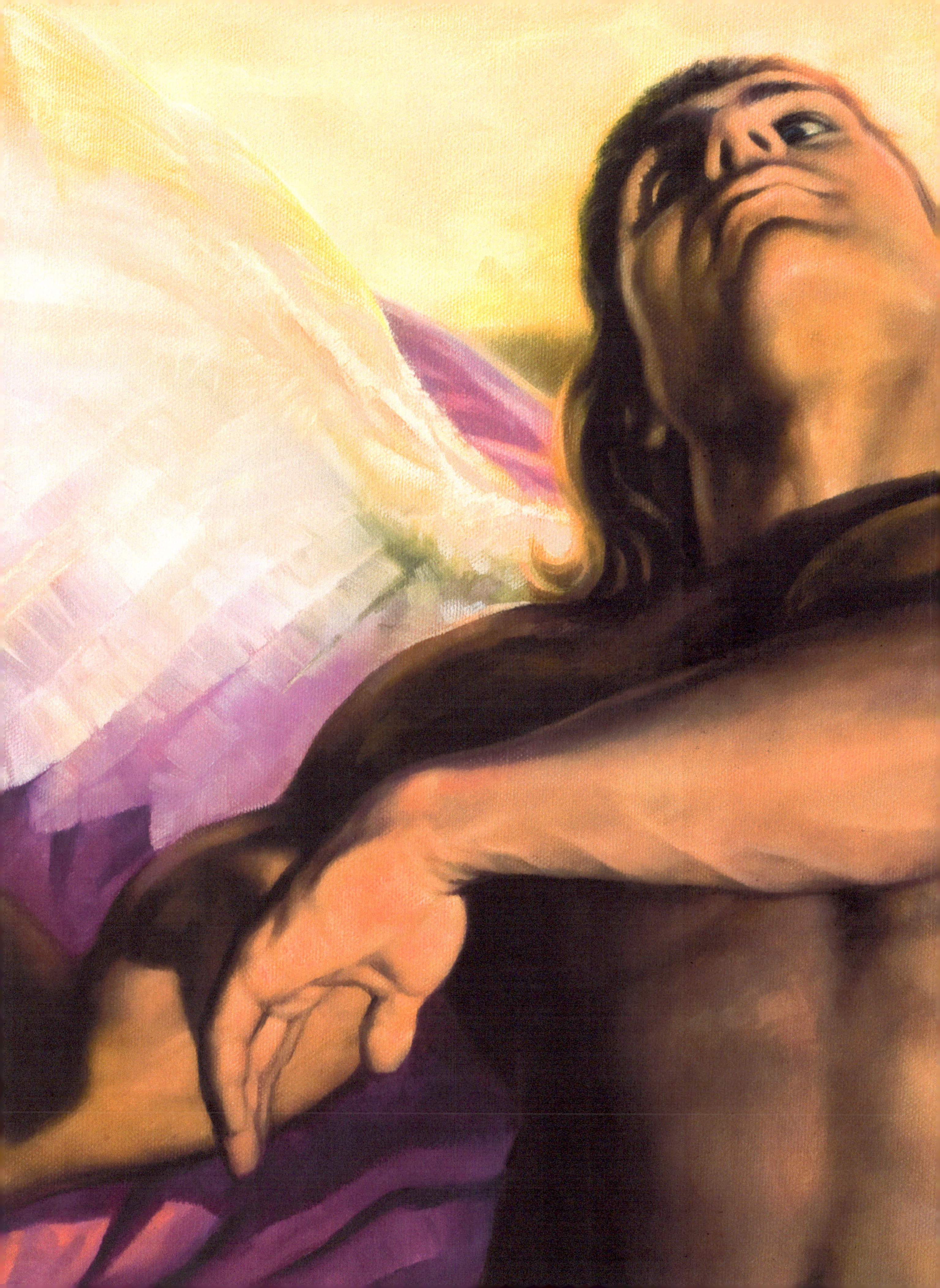

By the Sword

Oil on Canvas 32" x 50"

No higher spirit is bound by such tools,

when faith challenges the courage

of human existence

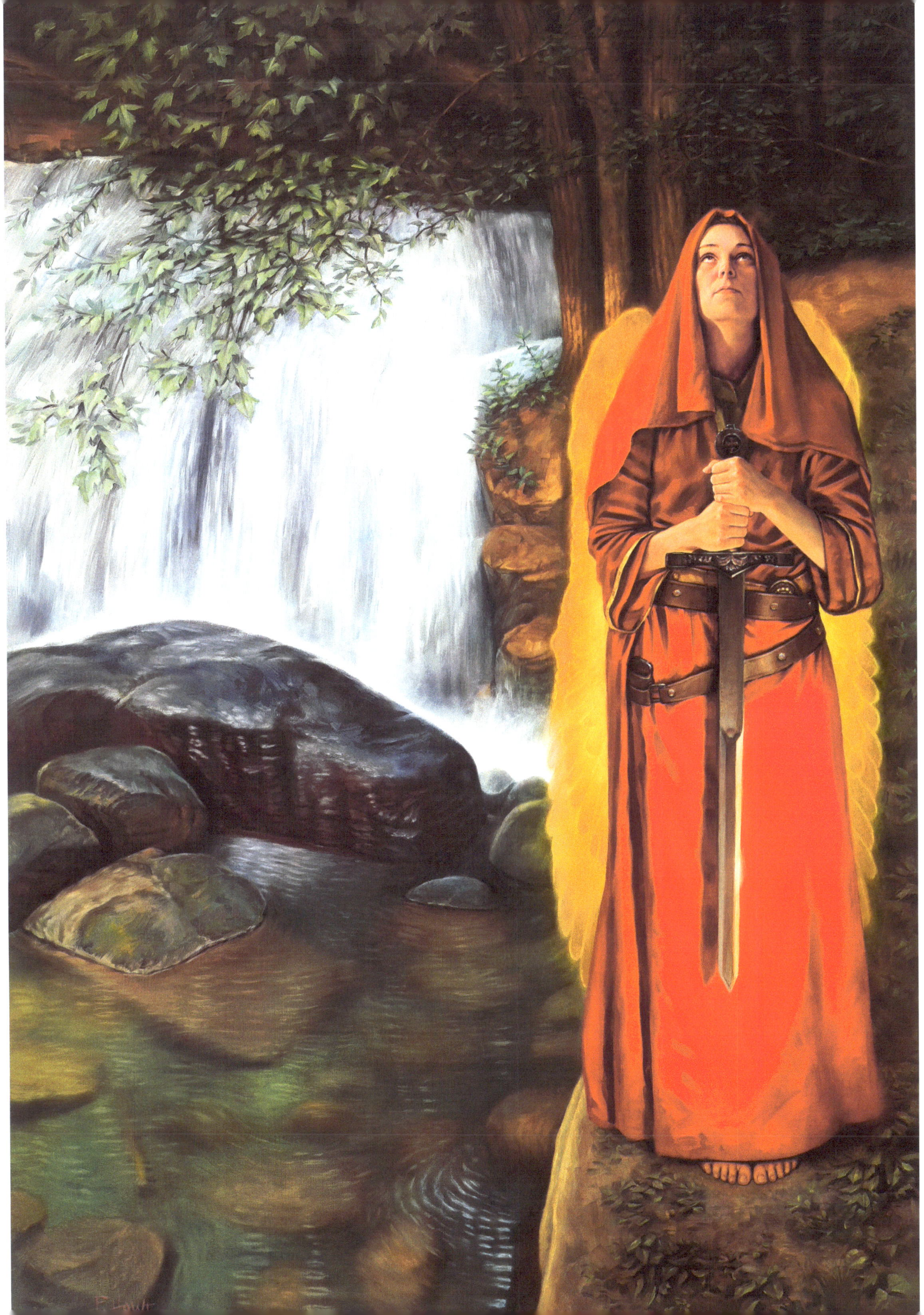

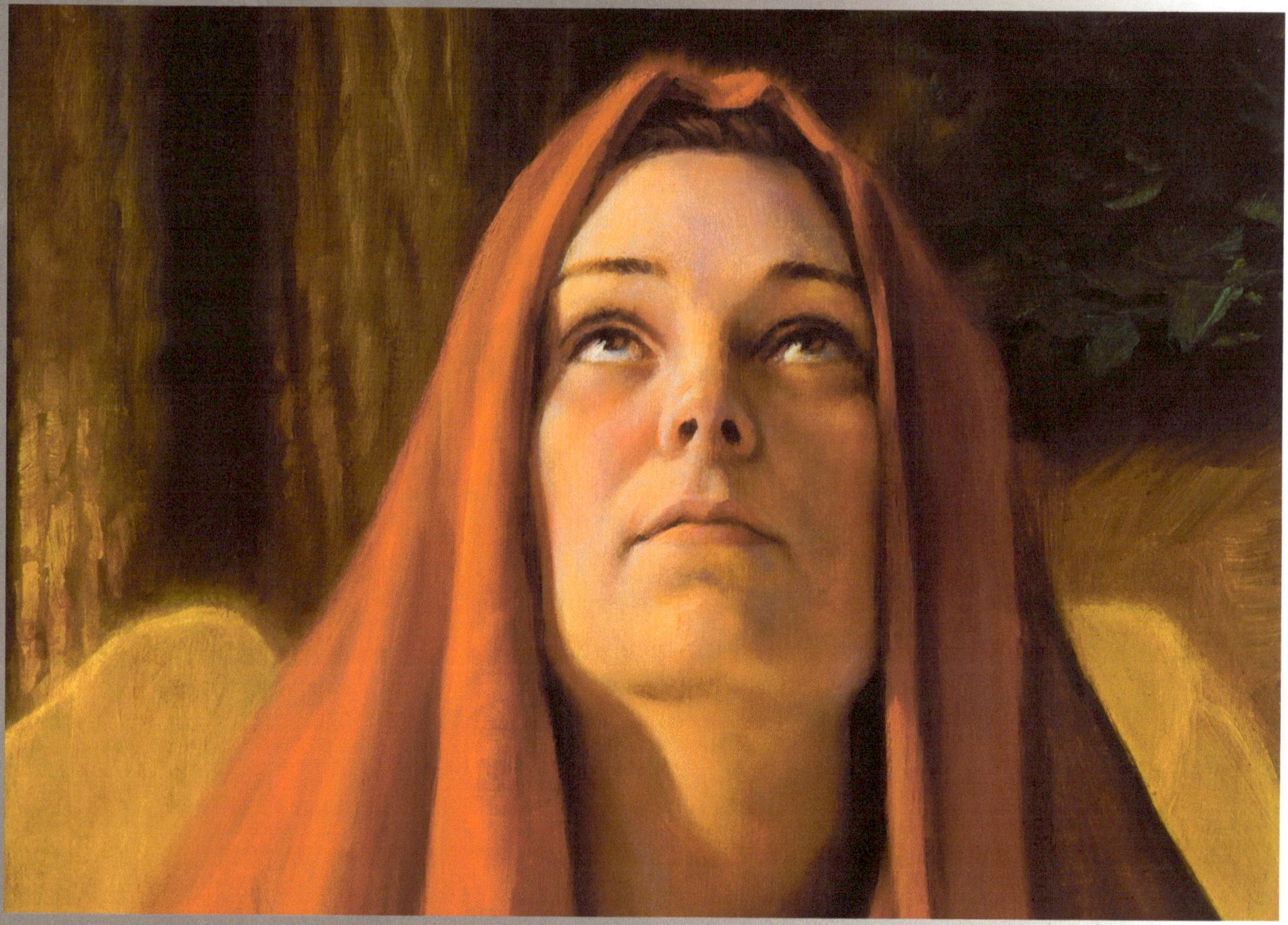

The Heart of a Tree- Details

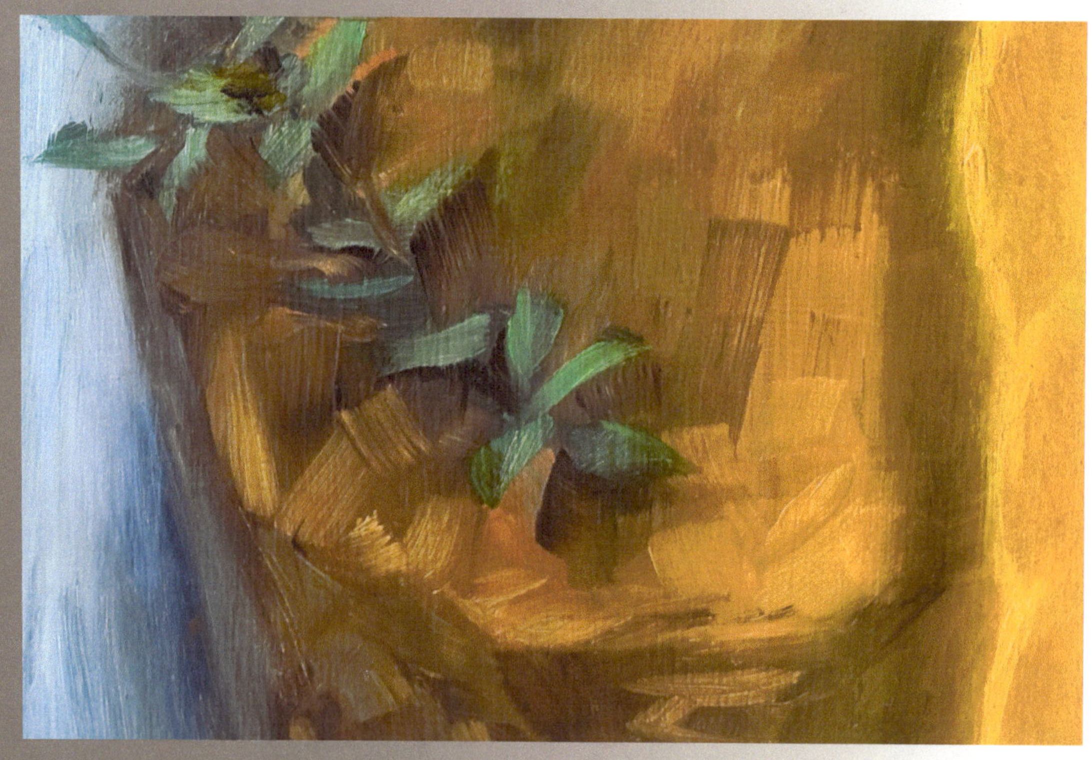

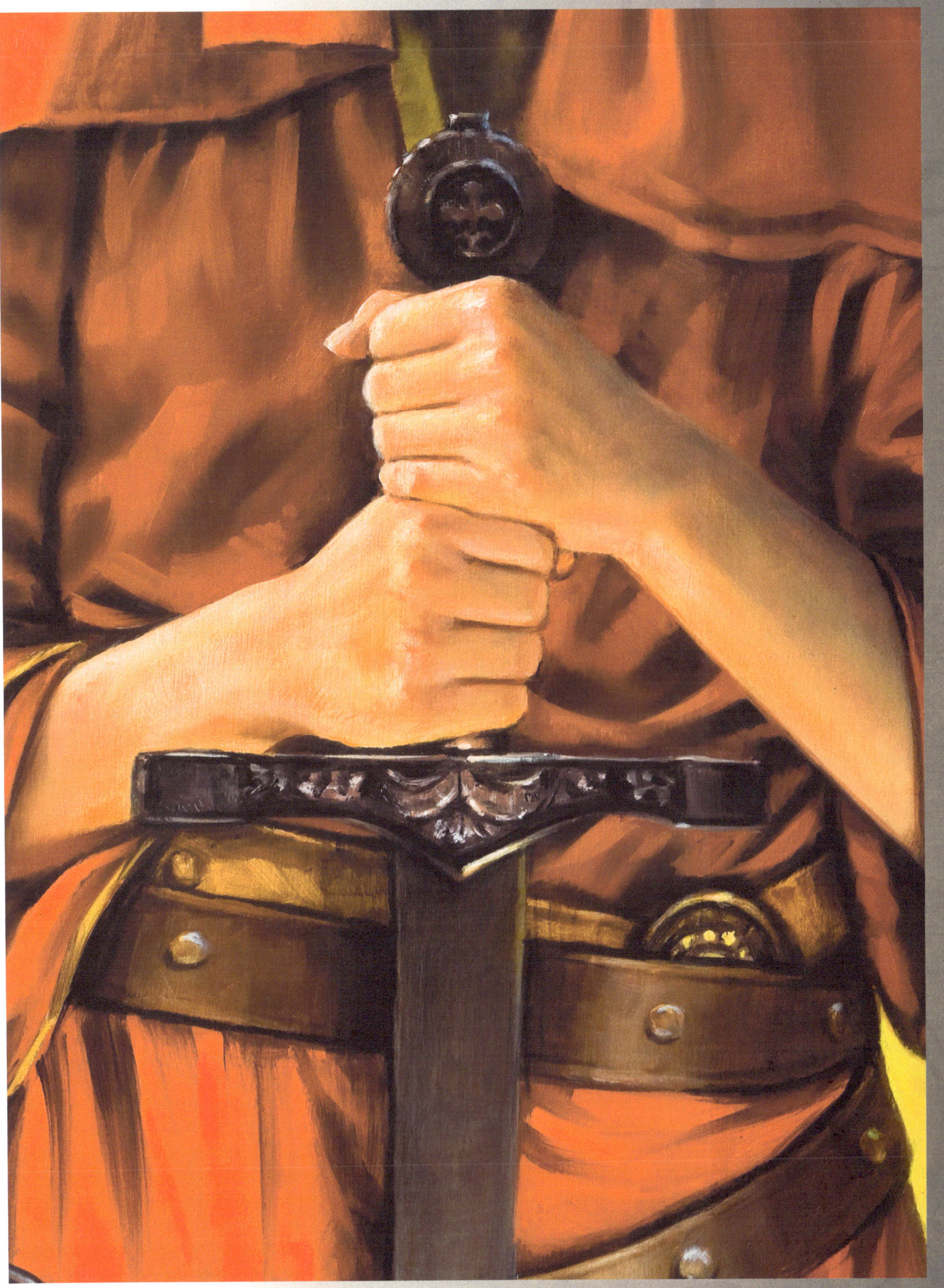

At the Gate

Oil on Canvas 48" x 70"

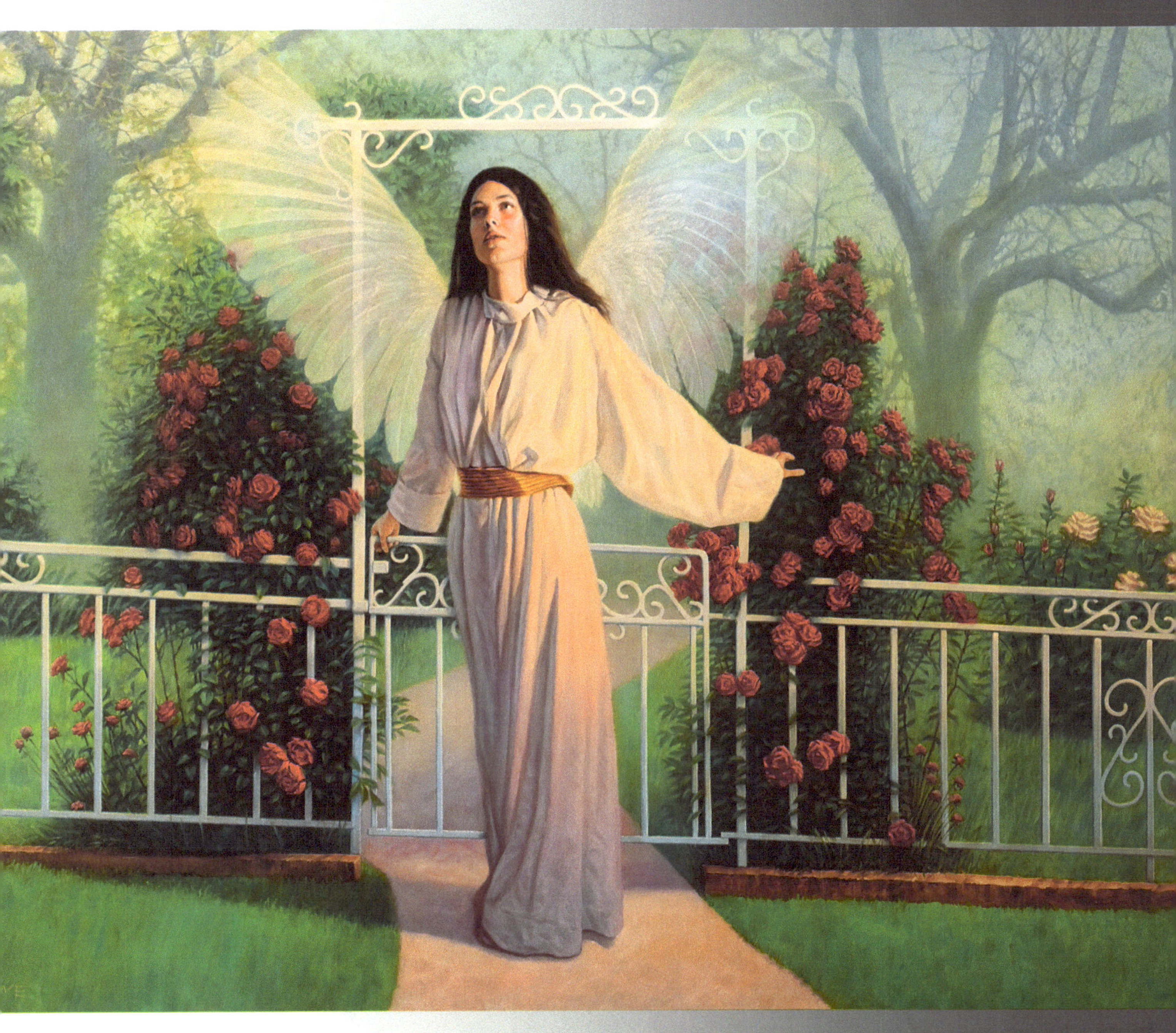

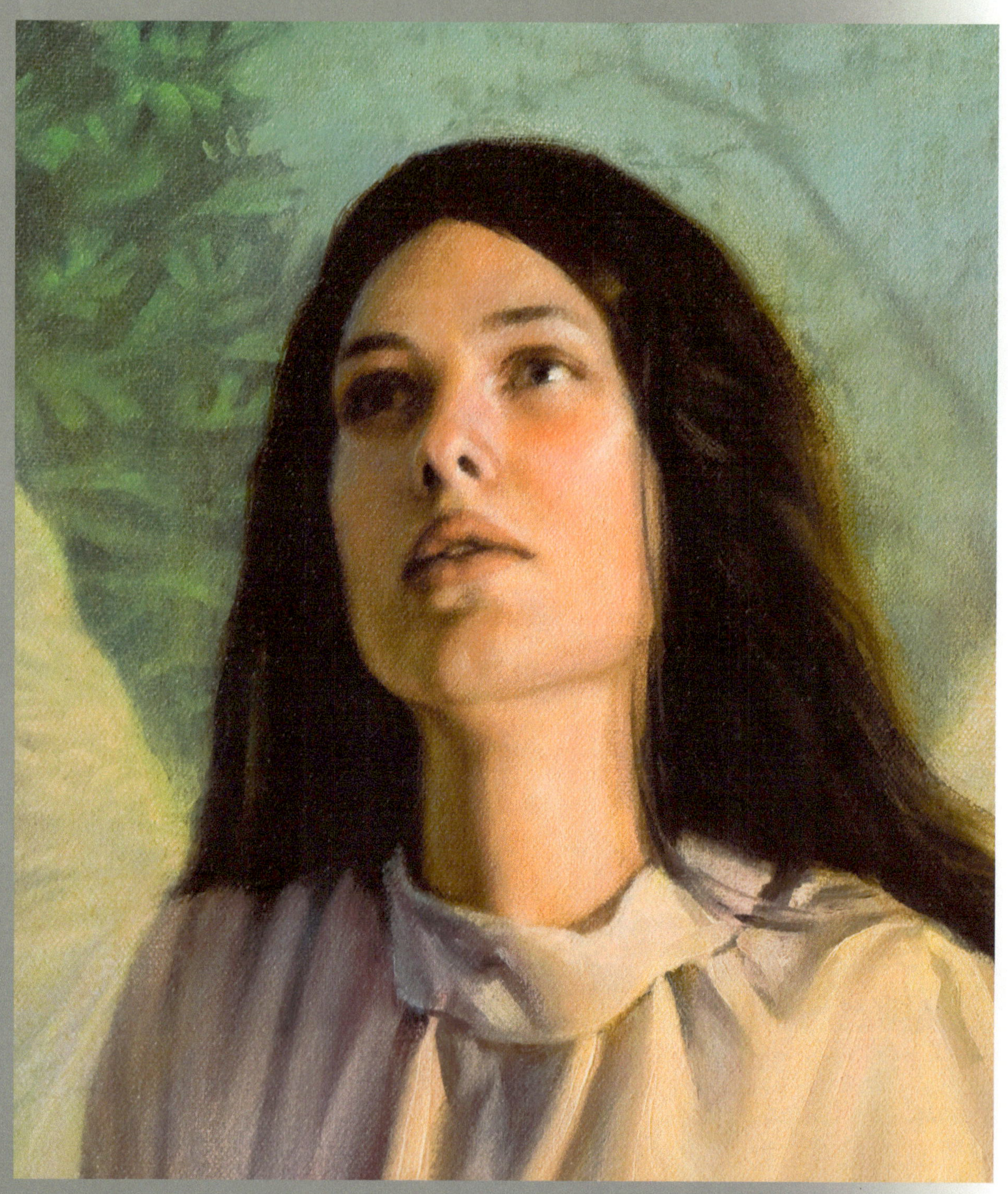

At the Gate - Details

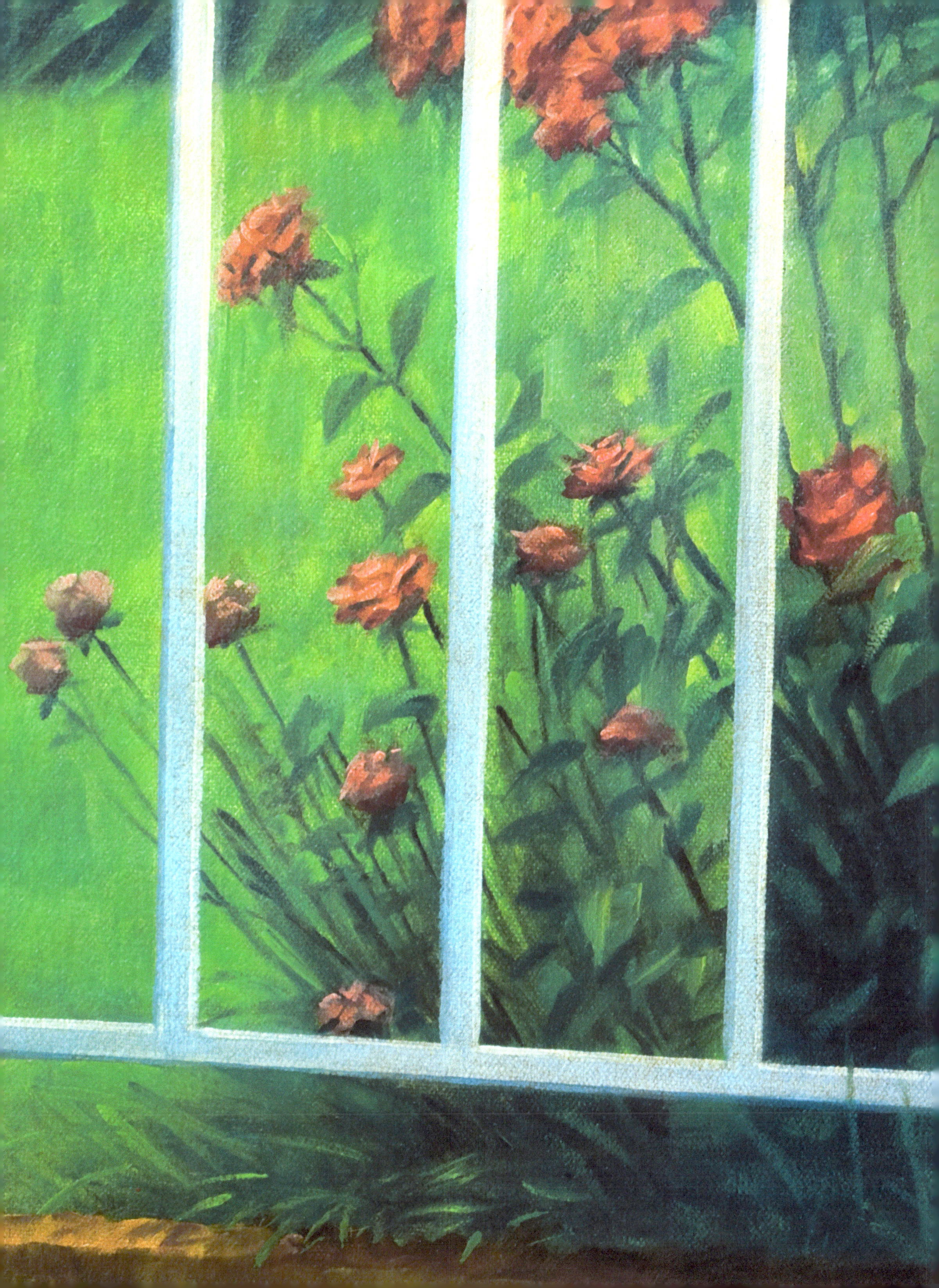

The Tranquil Sea

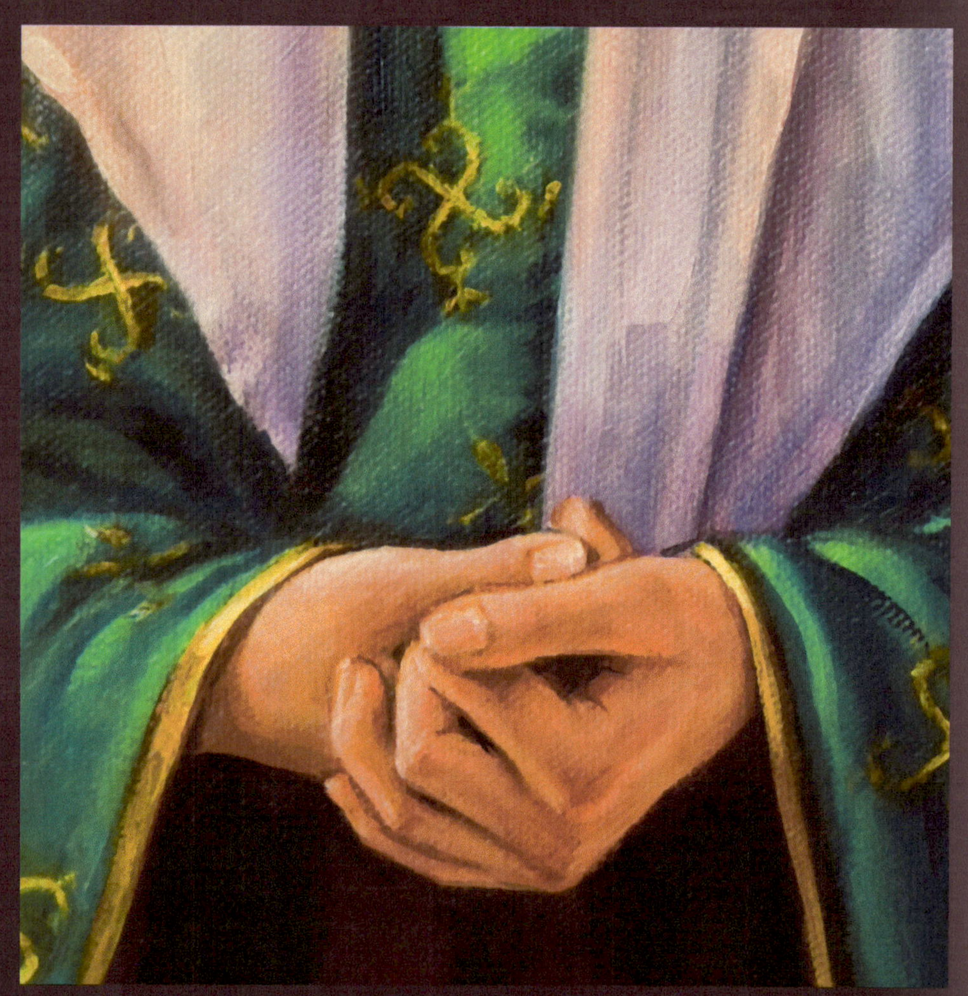

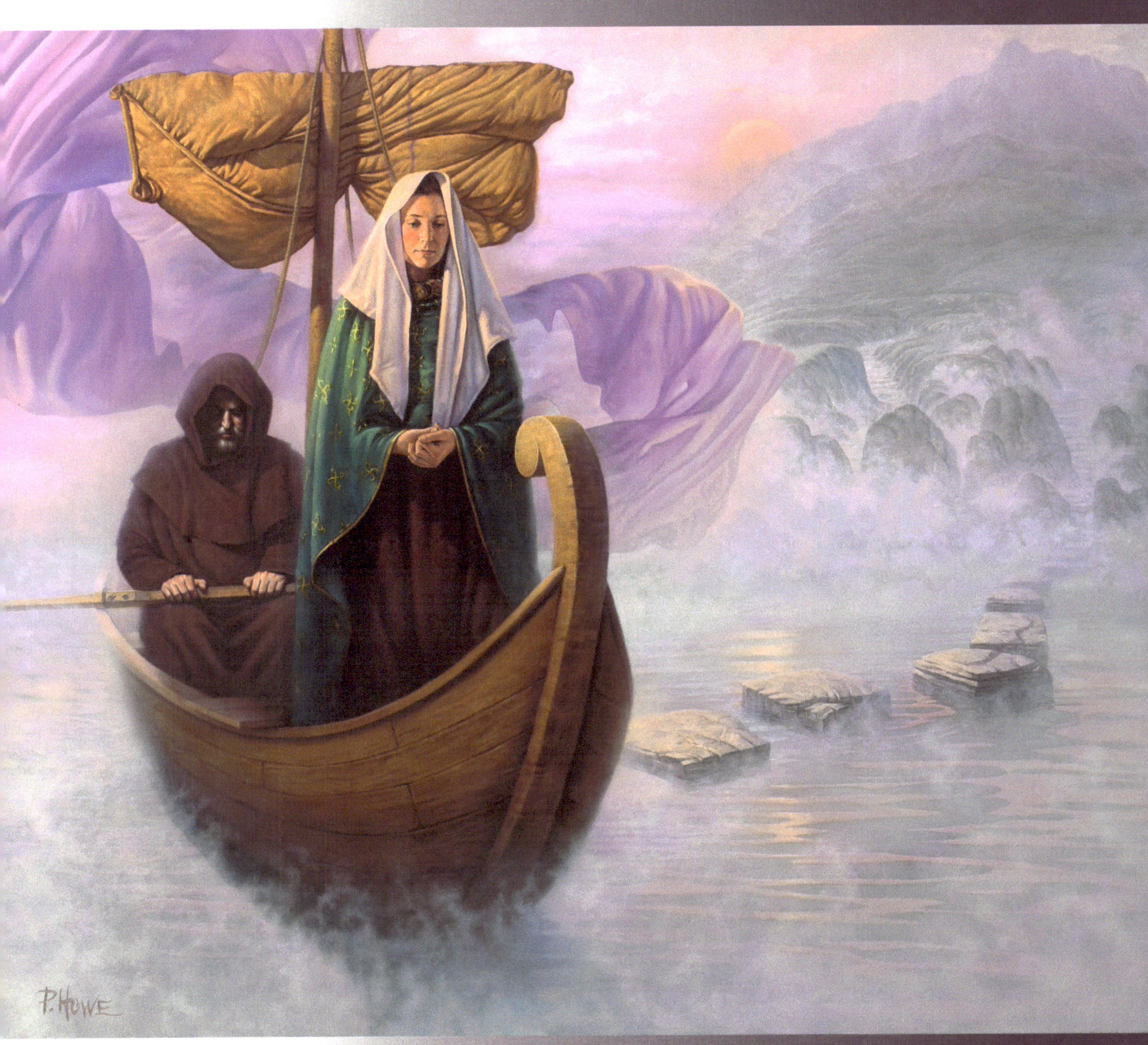

Oil on Canvas 48" x 58"

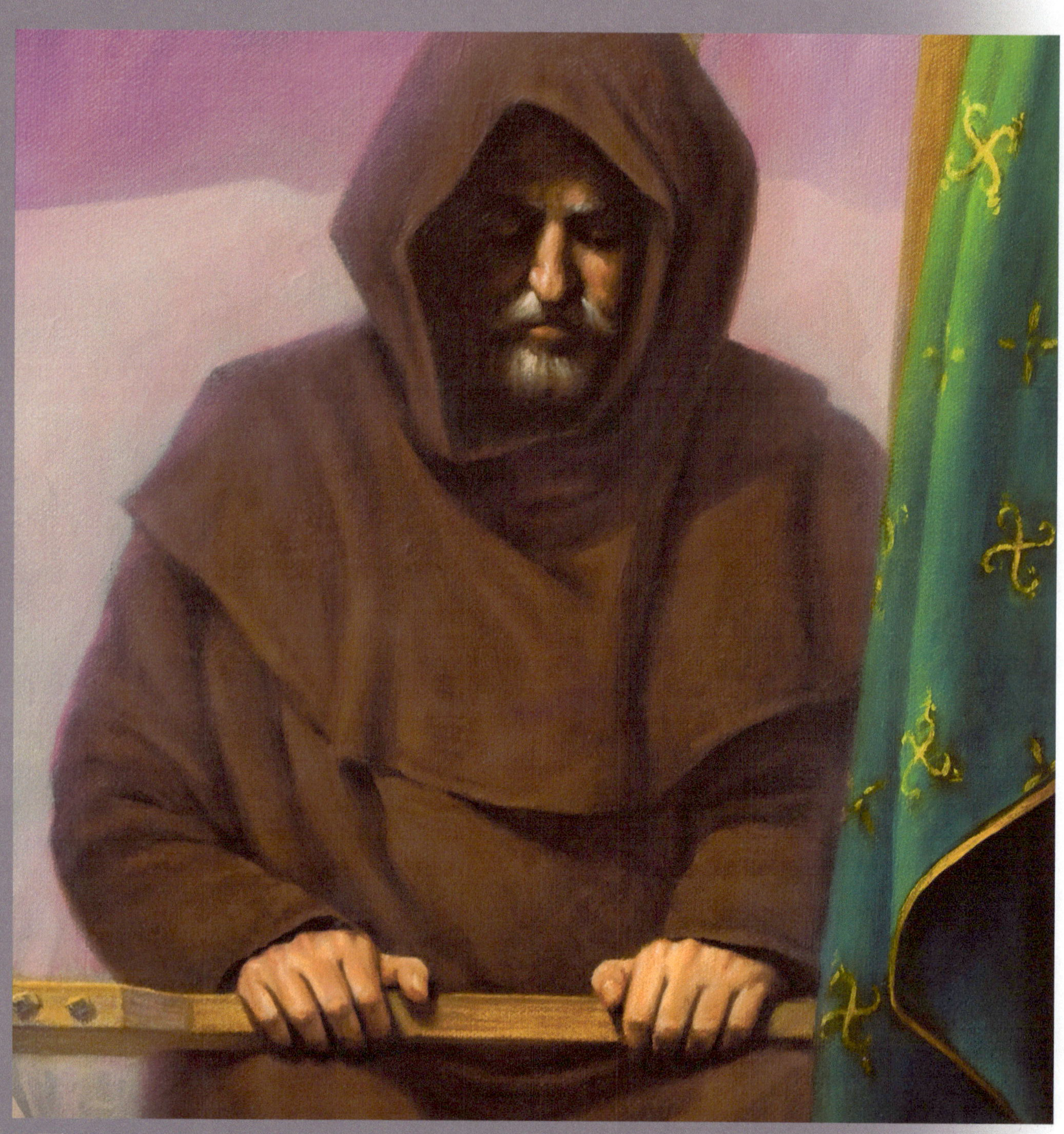
The Tranquil Sea - Details

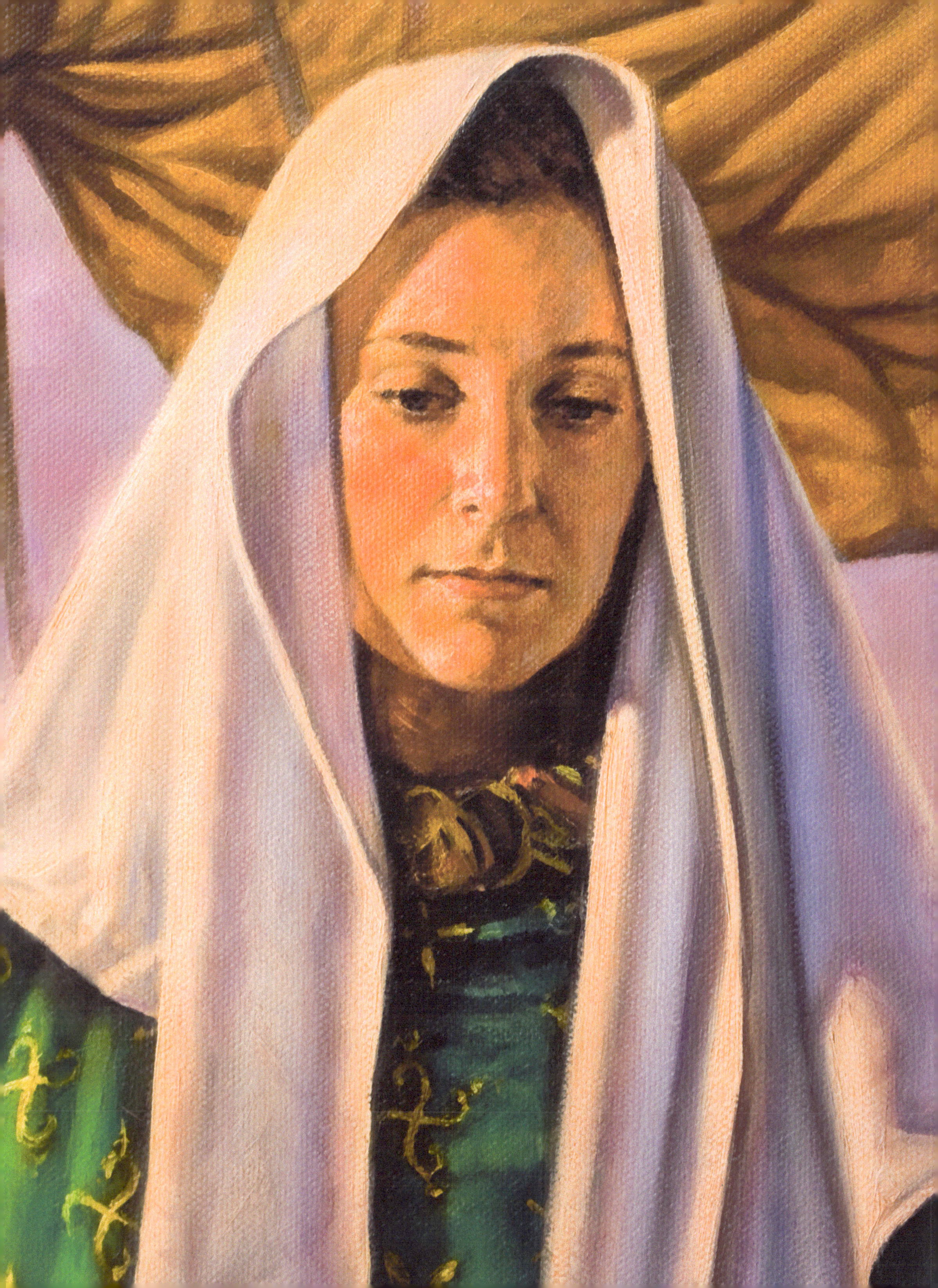

Sail Away

Oil on Canvas 48" x 60"

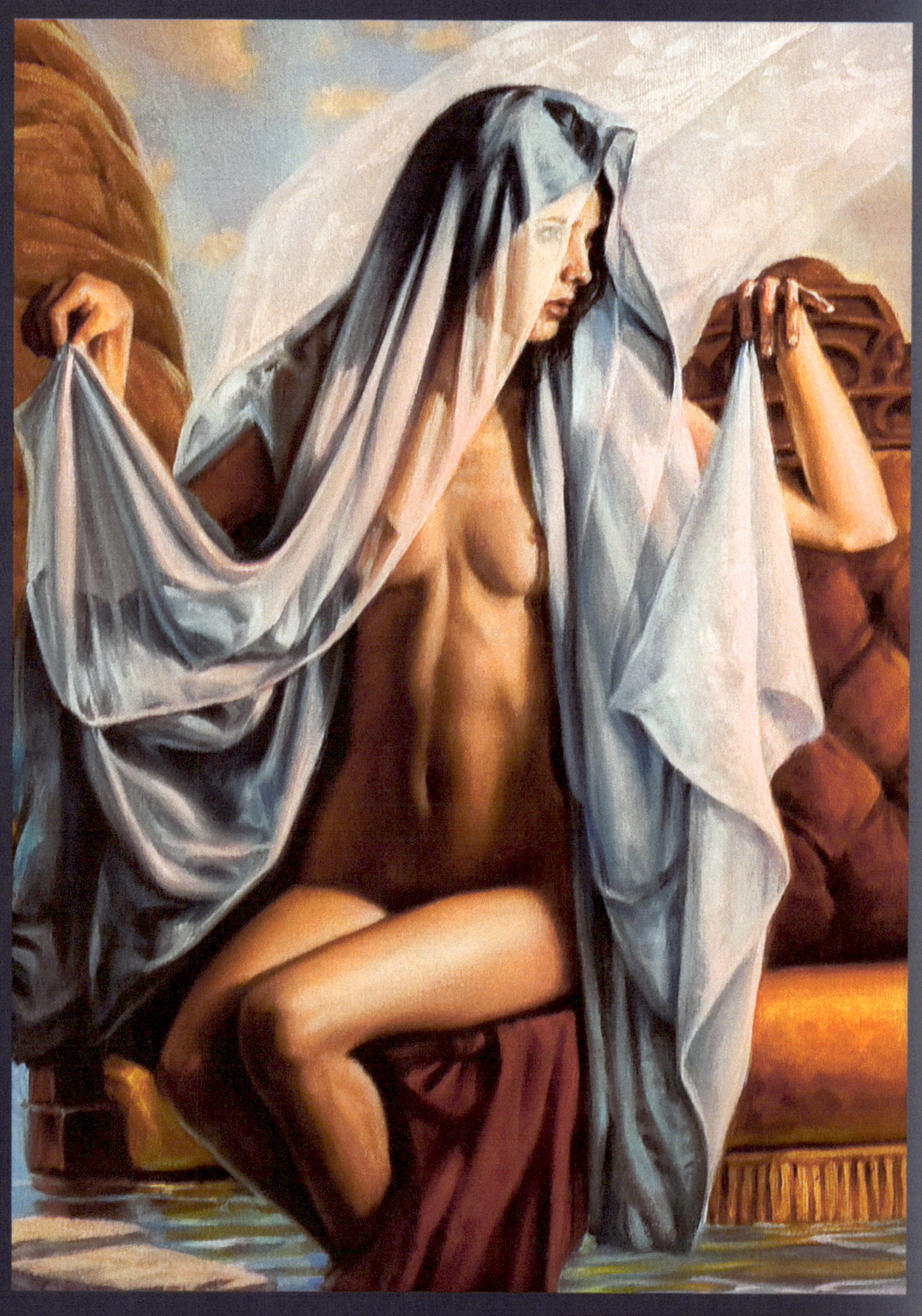

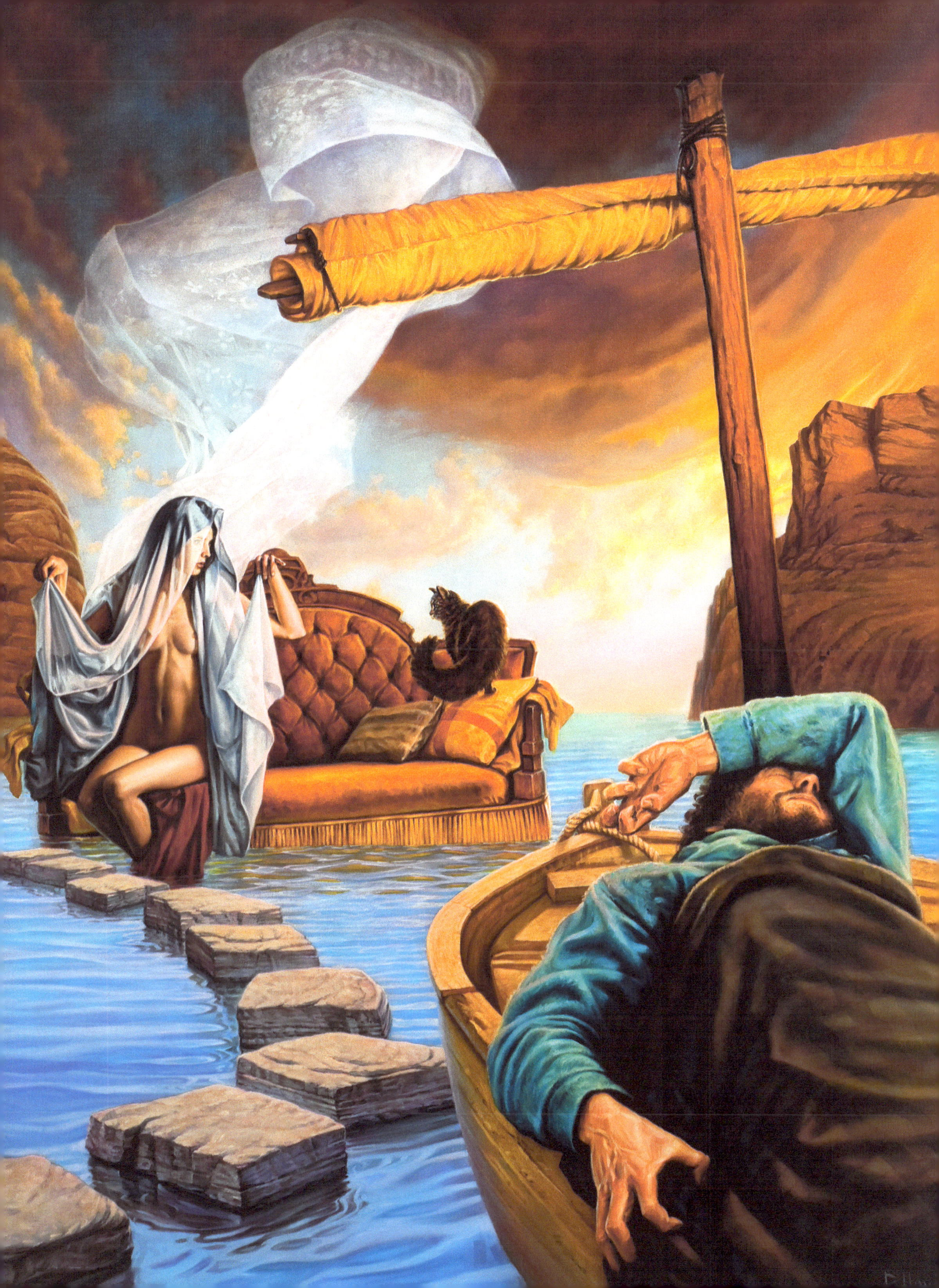

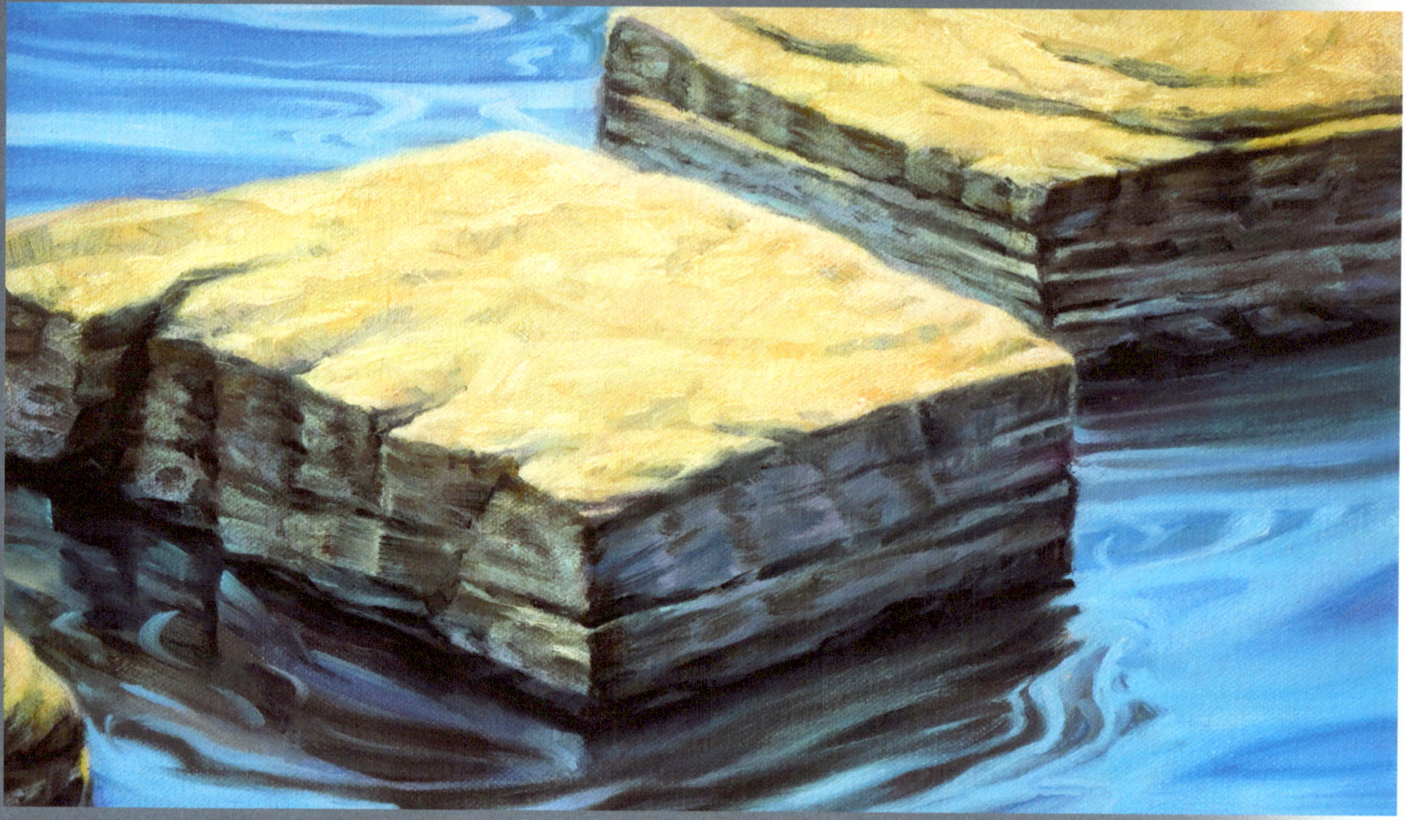

Sail Away- Details

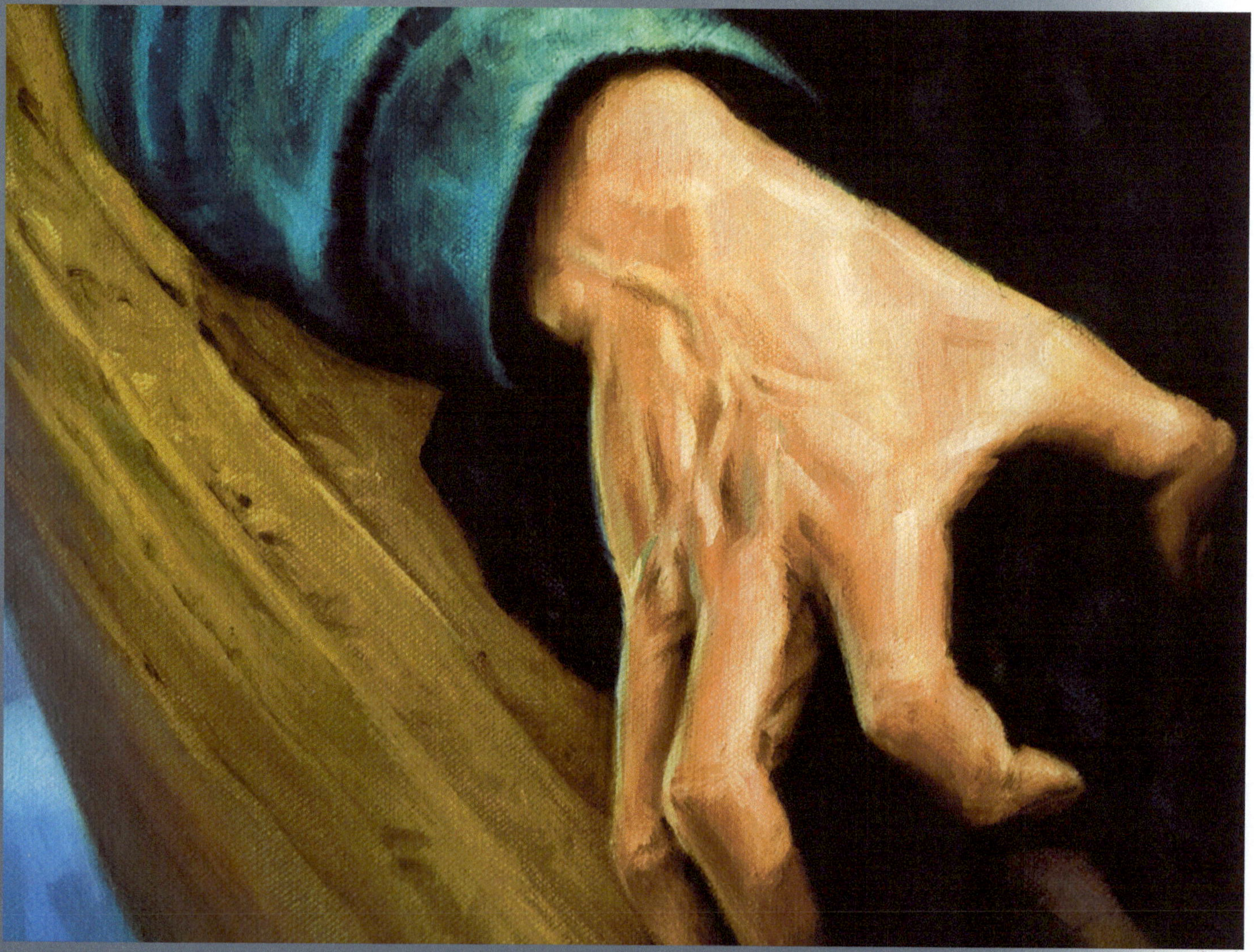

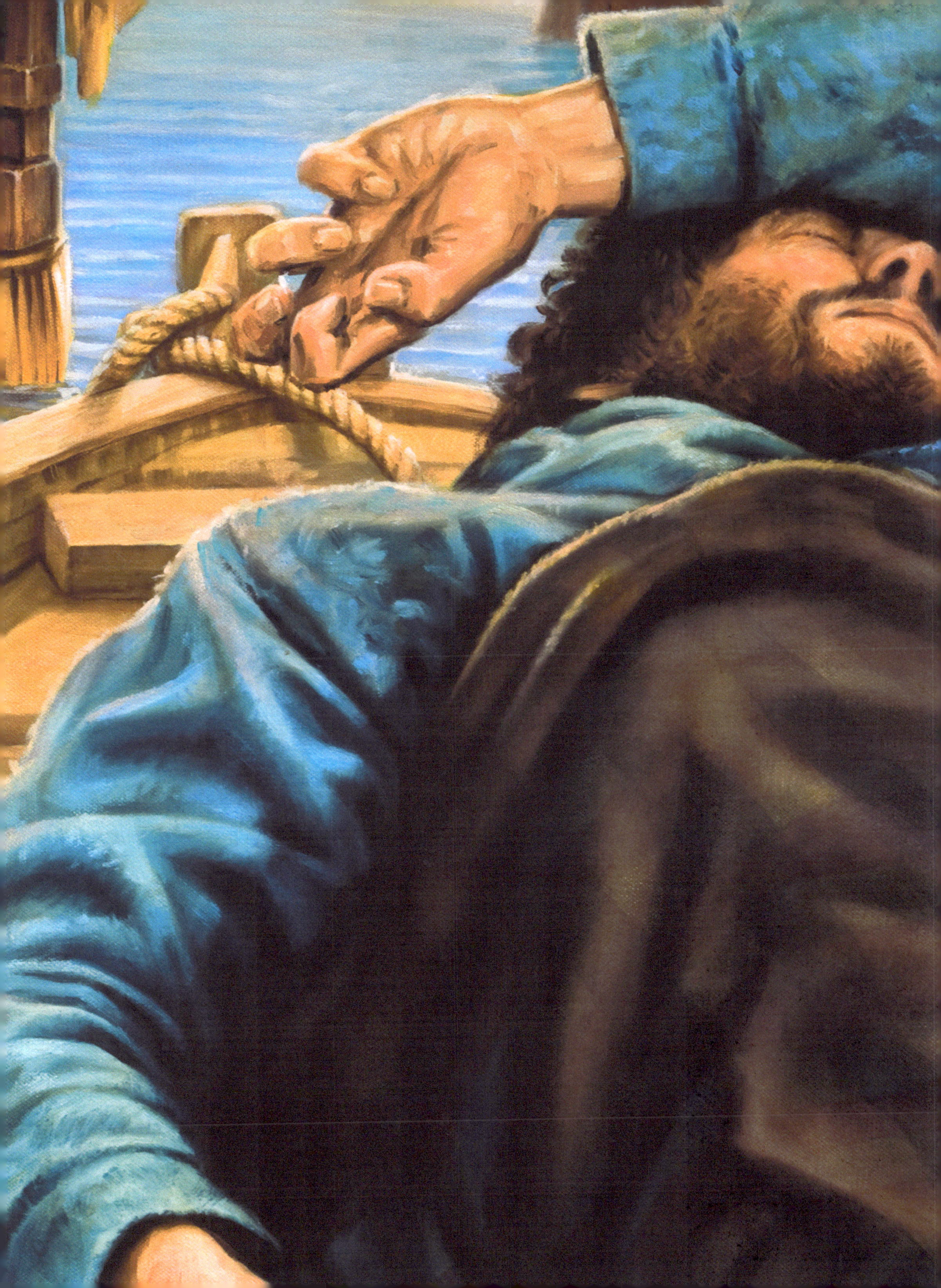

Morning

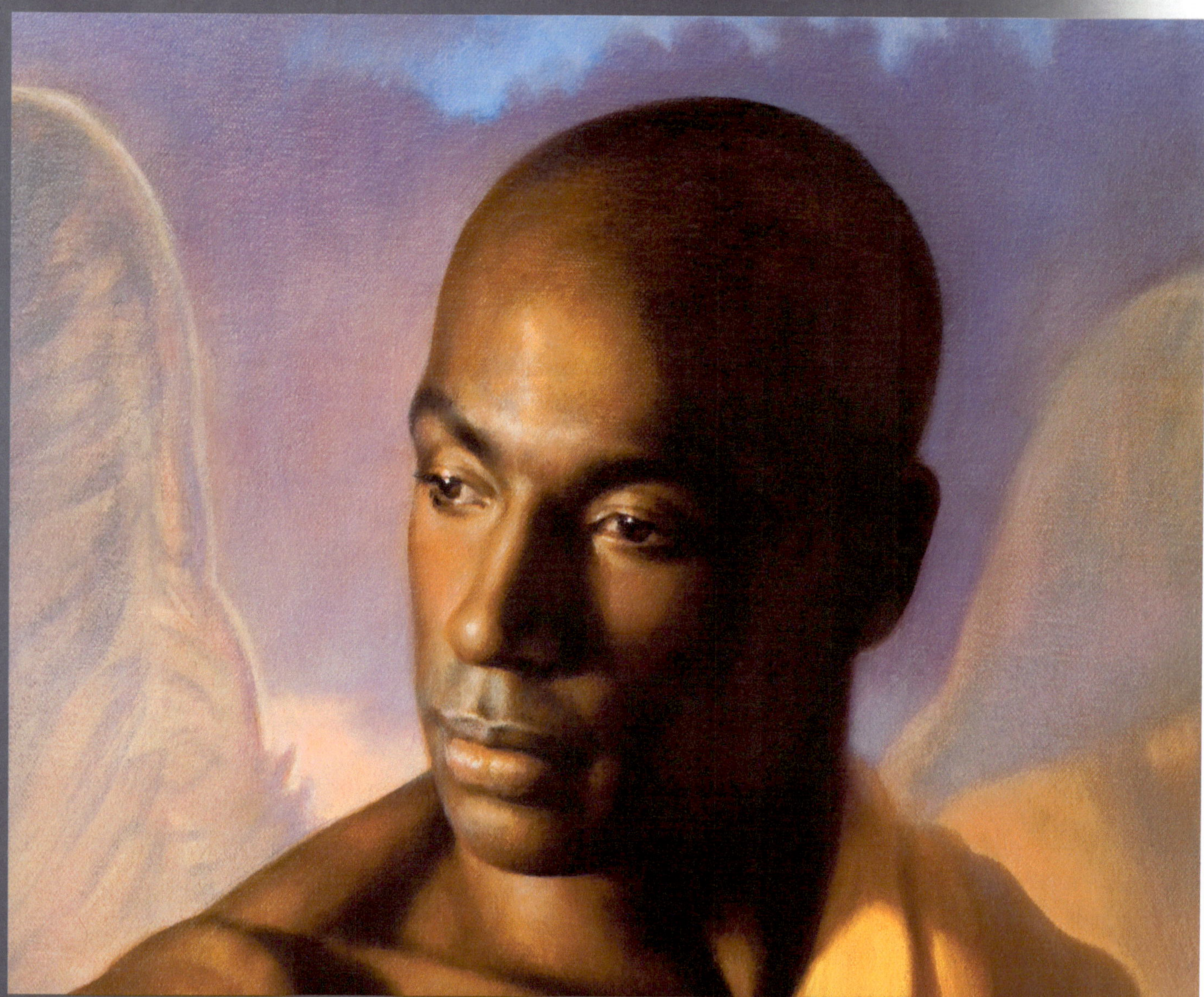

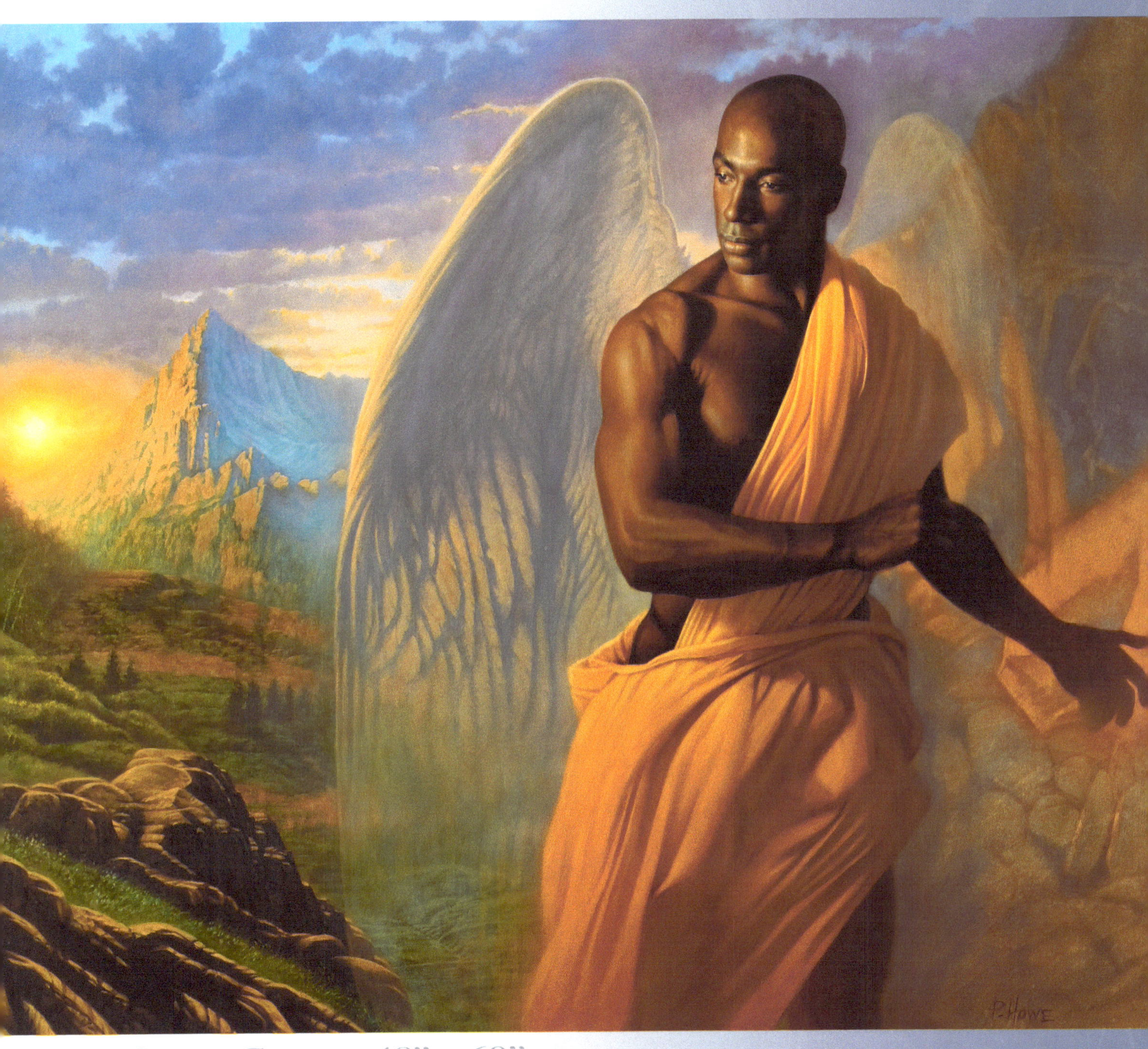

Oil on Canvas 48" x 60"

Comes the Dawn

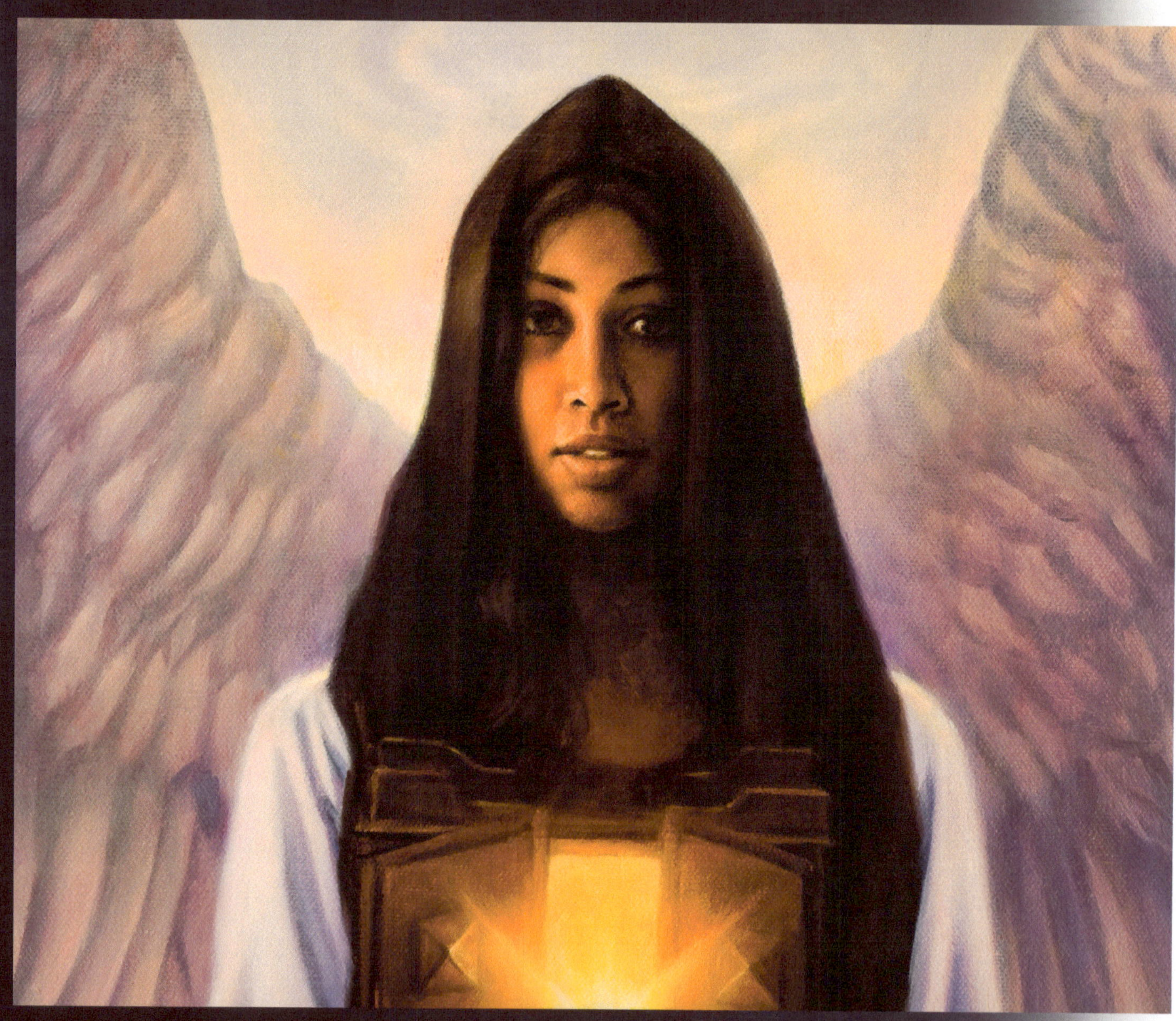

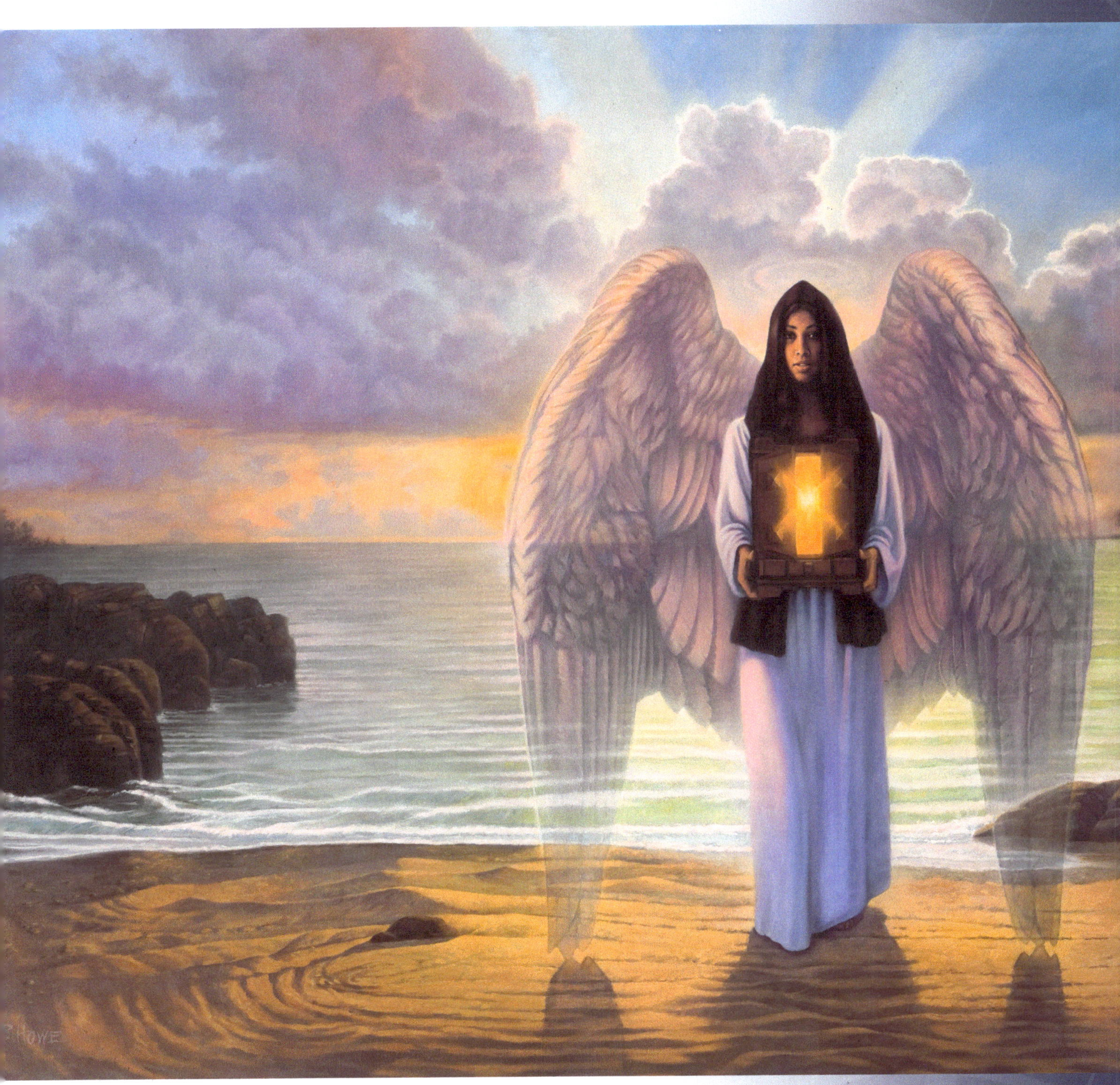

Oil on Canvas 42" x 64"

In a Golden Light

Oil on Canvas 32" x 44"

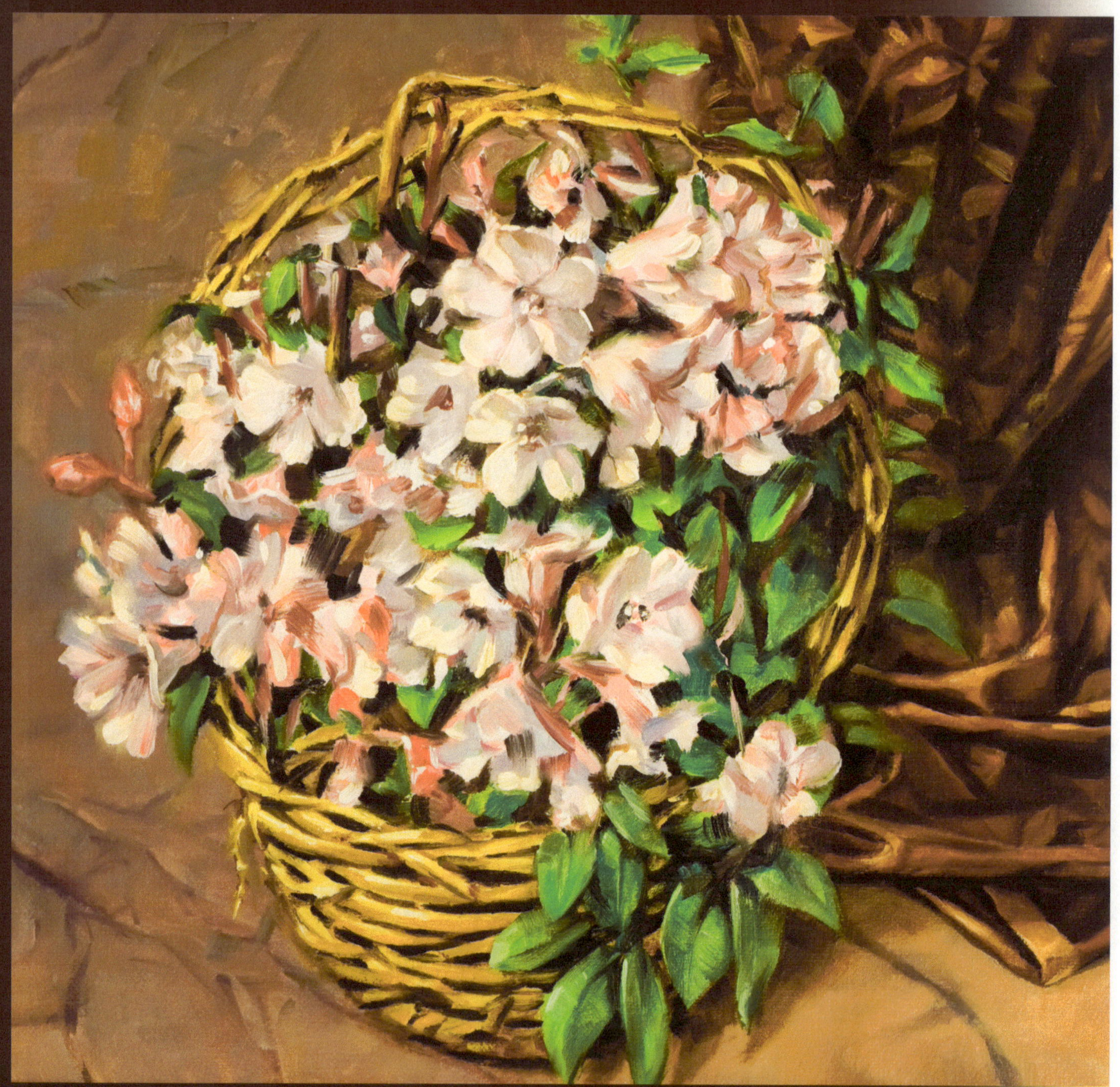

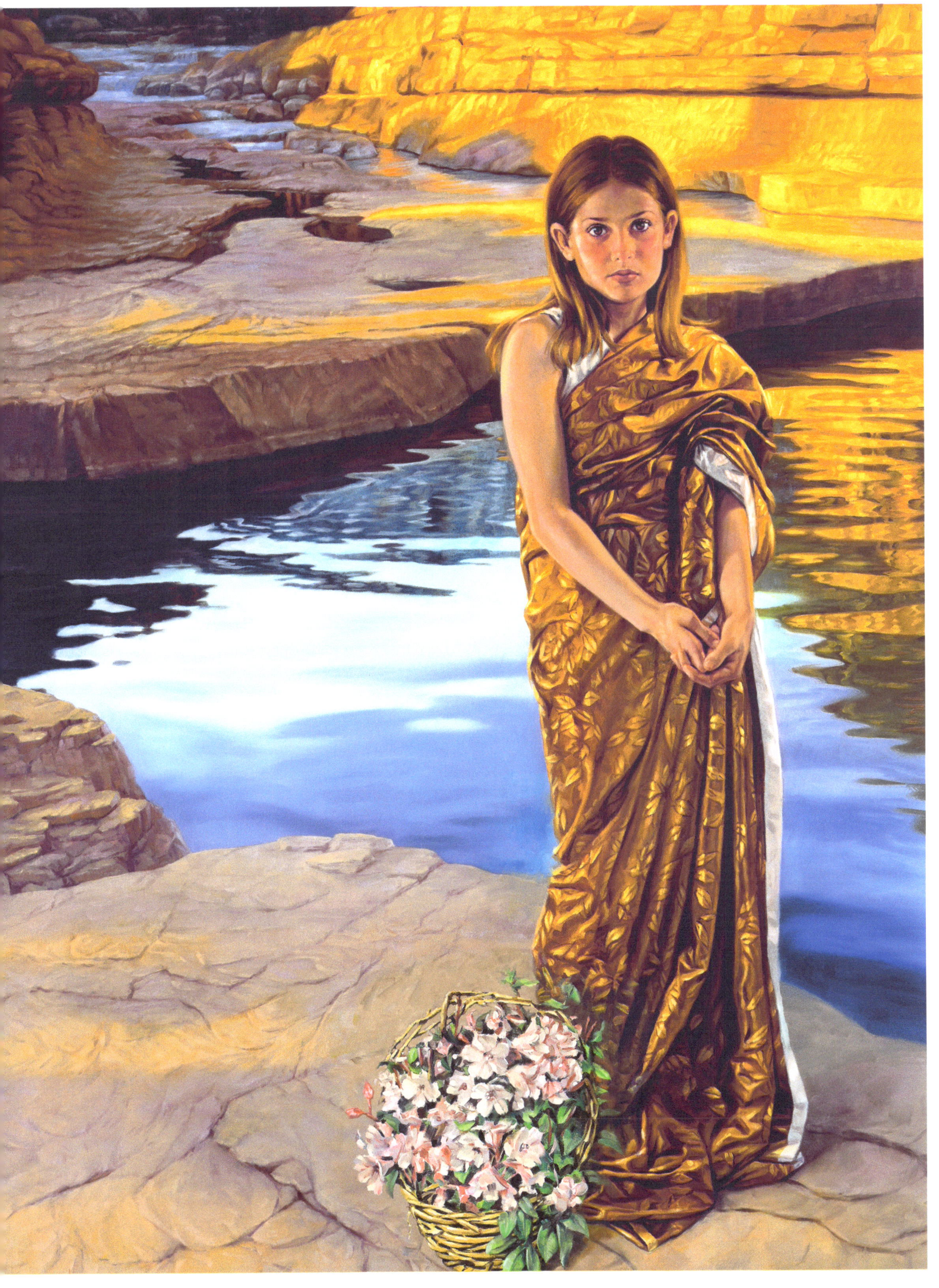

CONTEMPLATION

28 x 36"

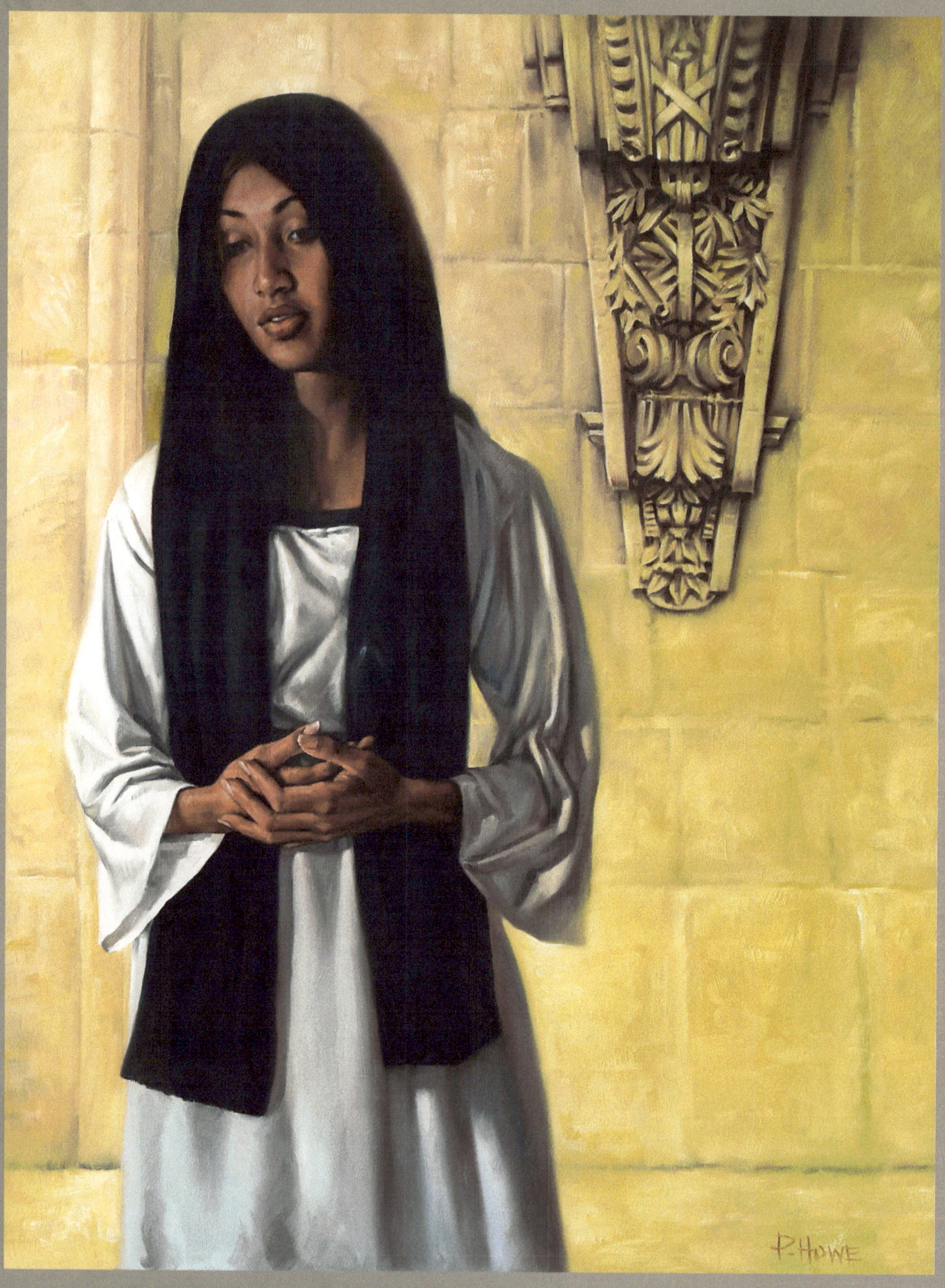

The Endless Waterfall

30 x 36"

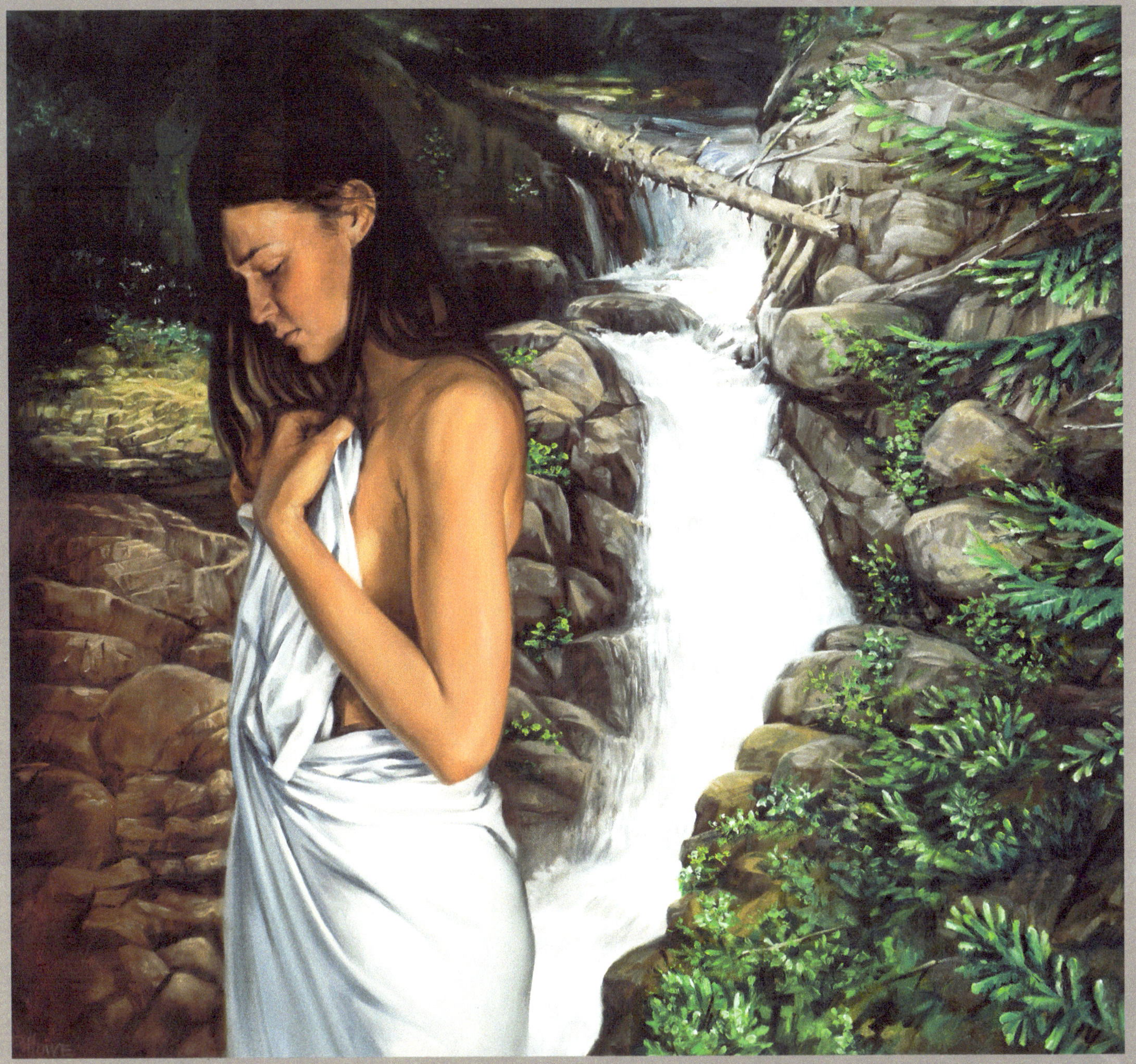

Follow the Light

40 x 54"

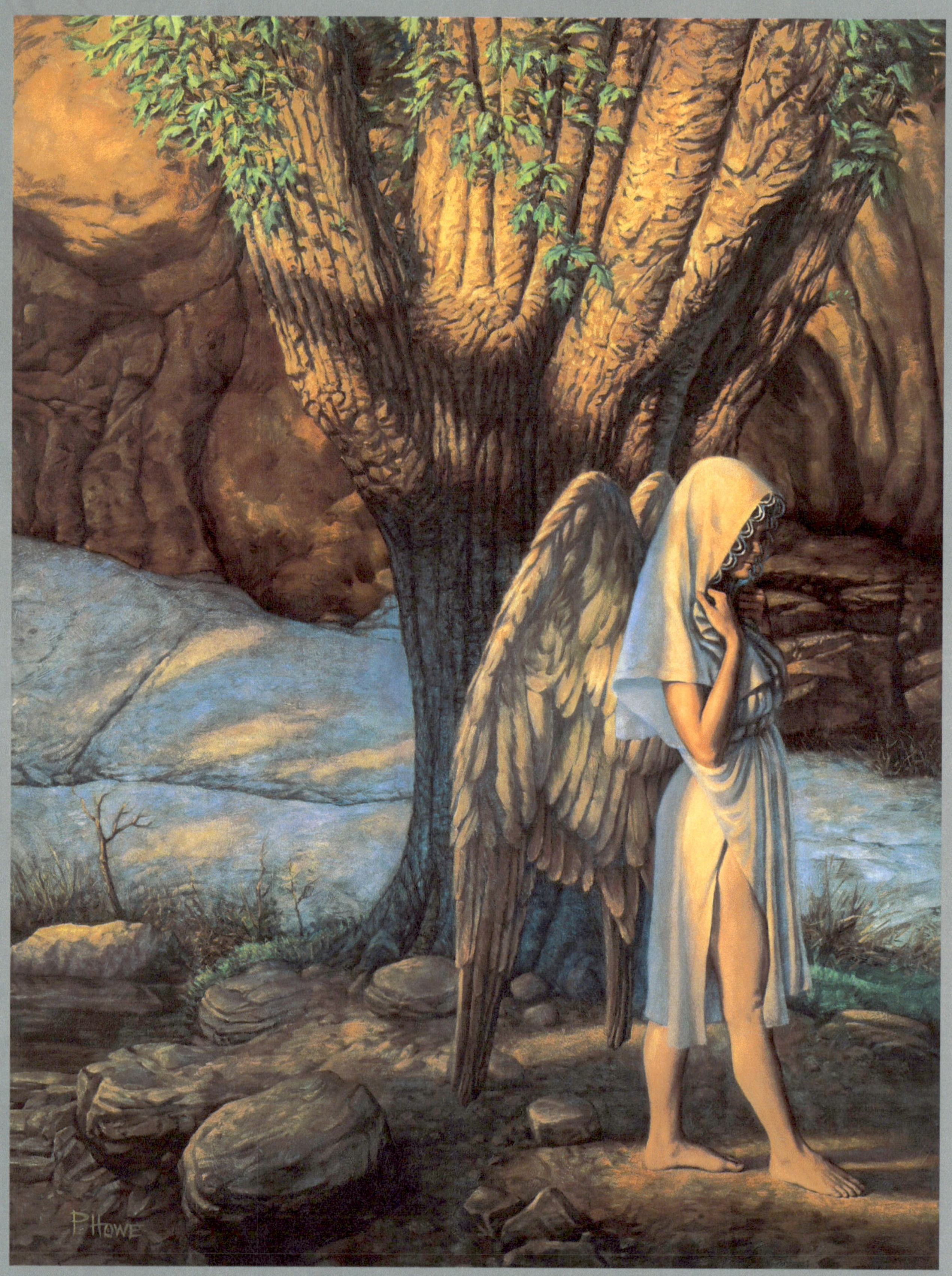

The Choice

28 x 38"

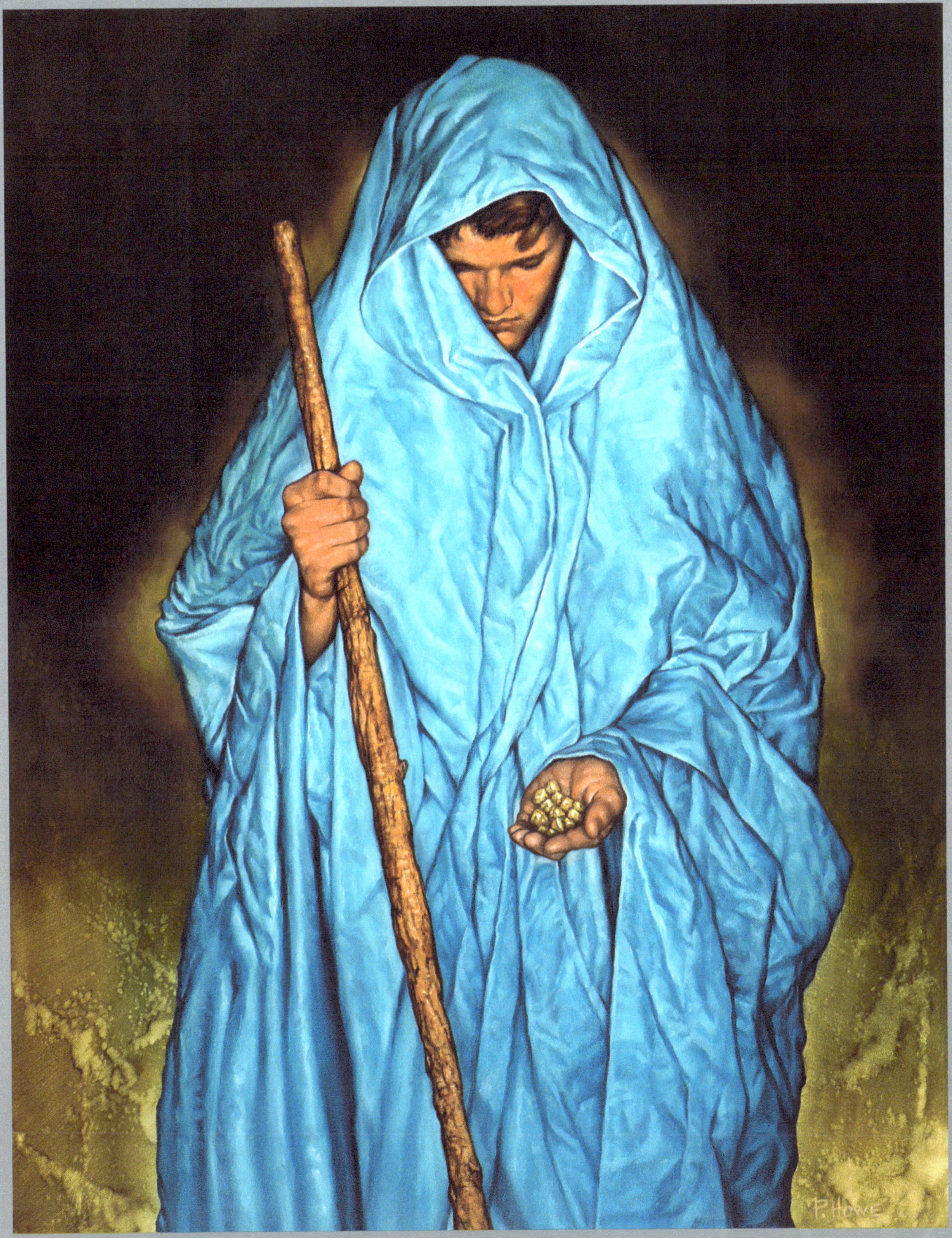

On the Road to Heaven

36 x 36"

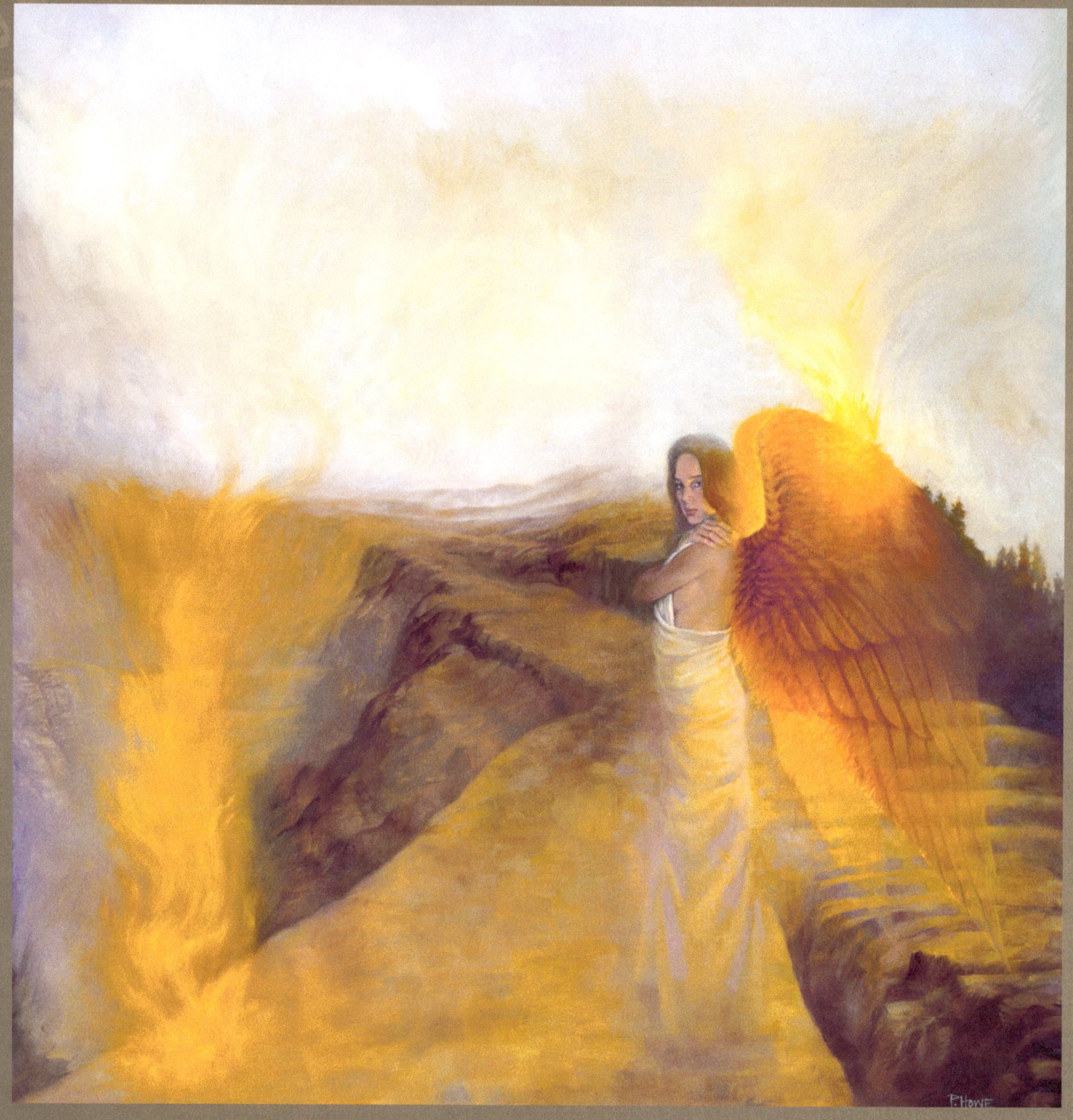

Time Passes

42 x 50"

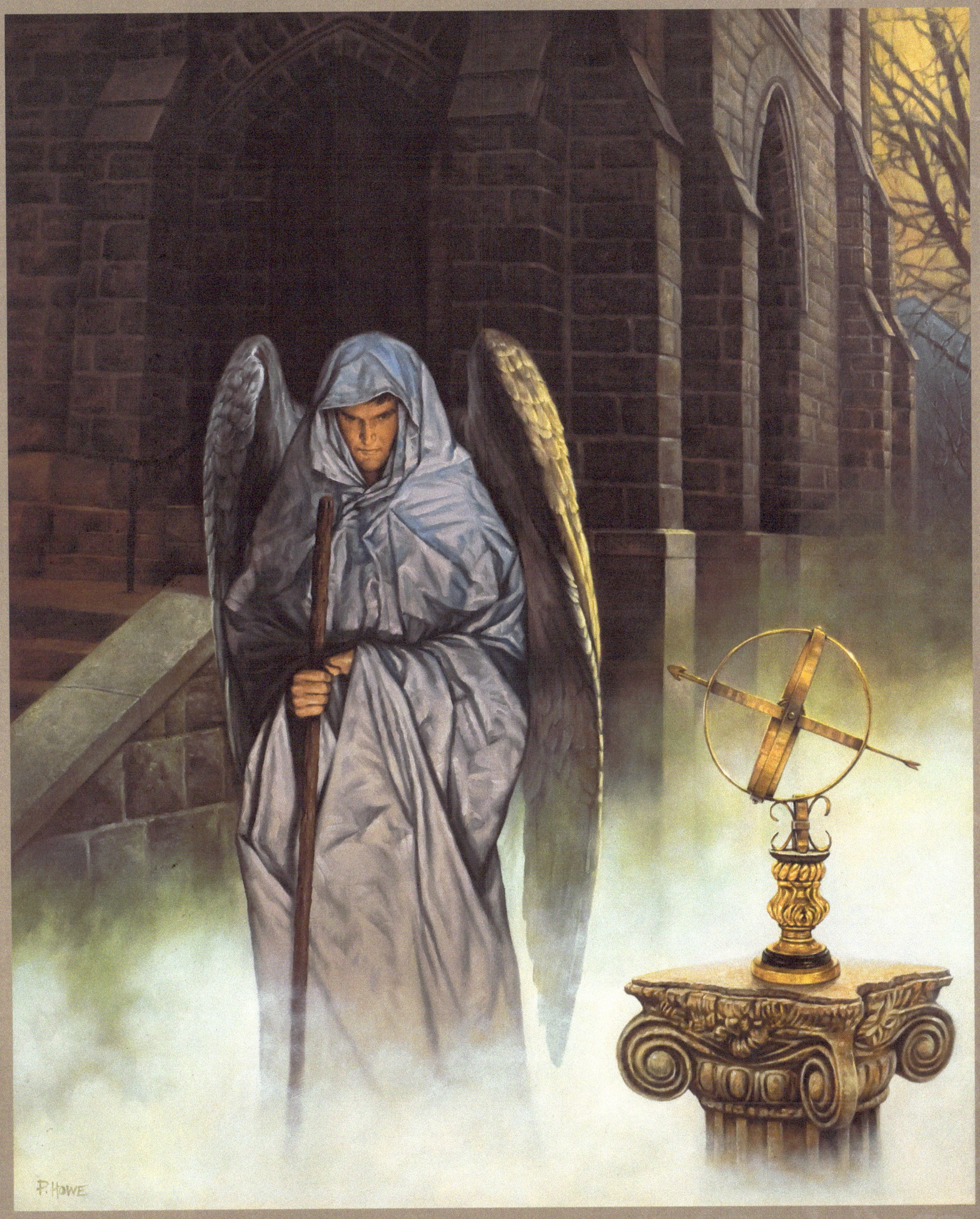

Oil Studies

Male Model in Robes

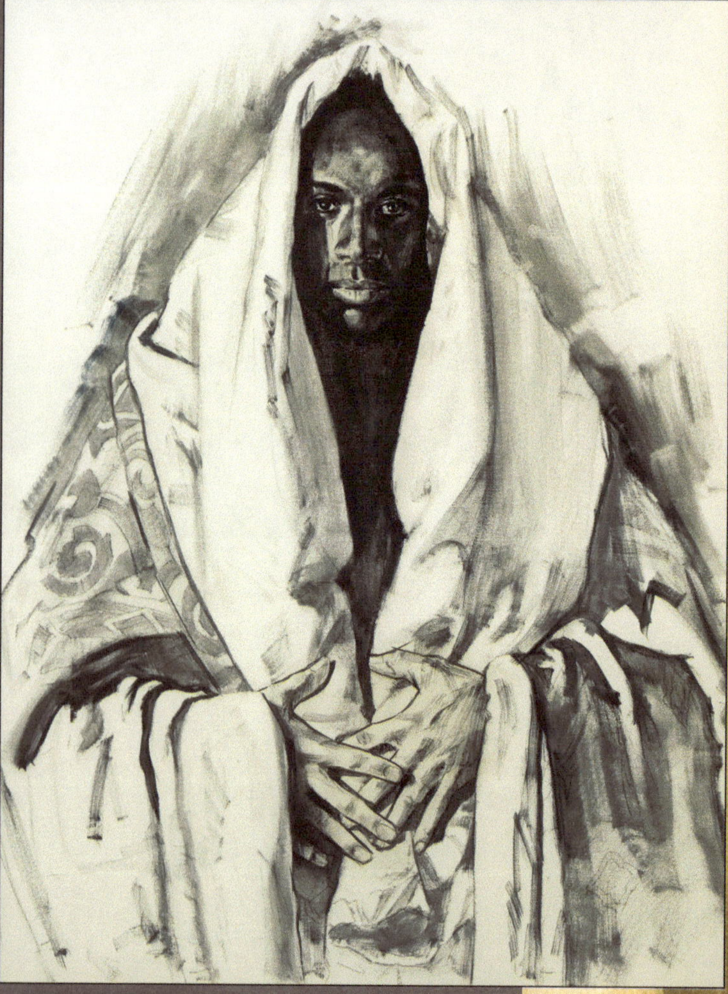

24 x 30"
oil on canvas

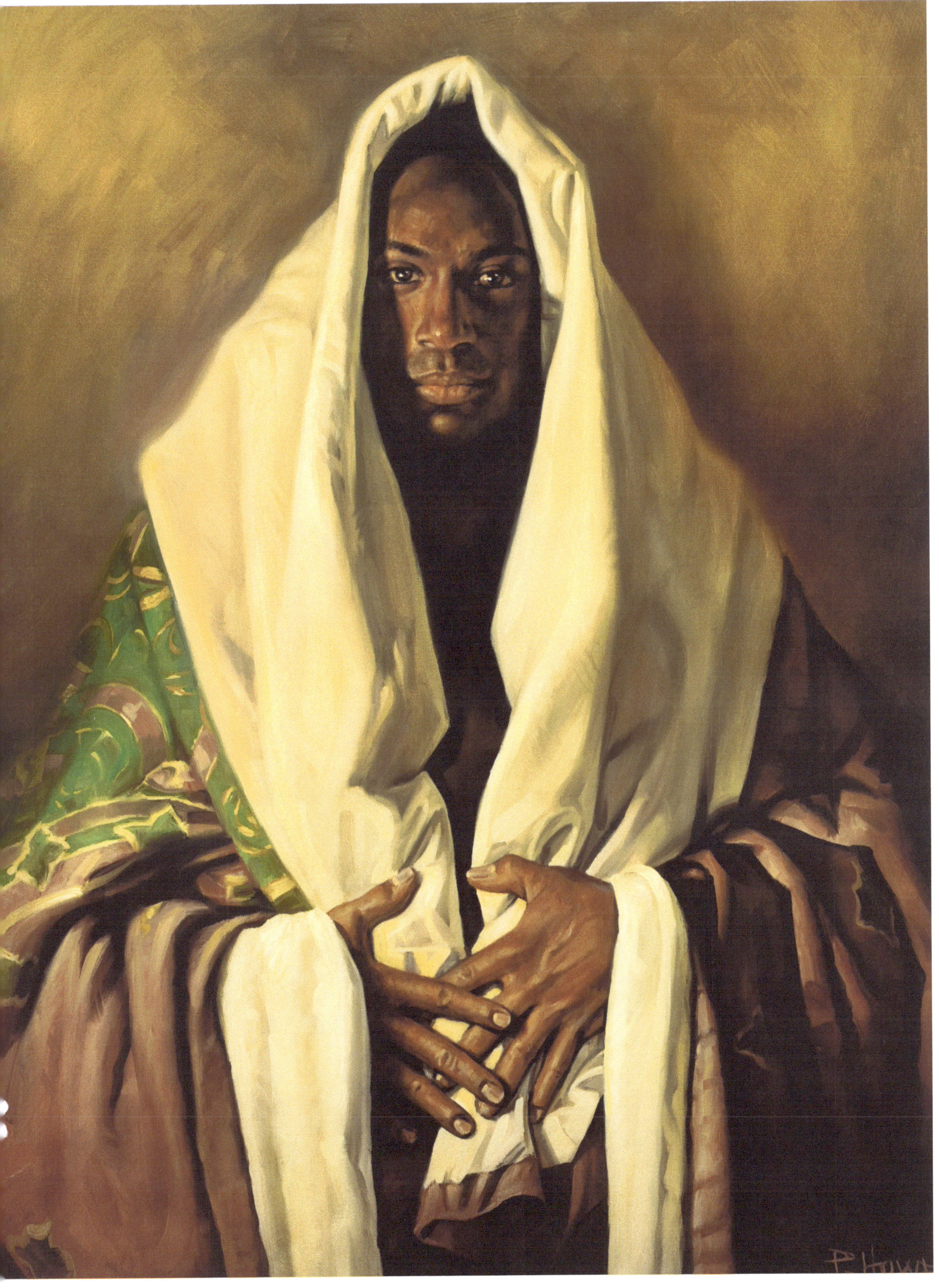

STUDY FOR FAR BELOW

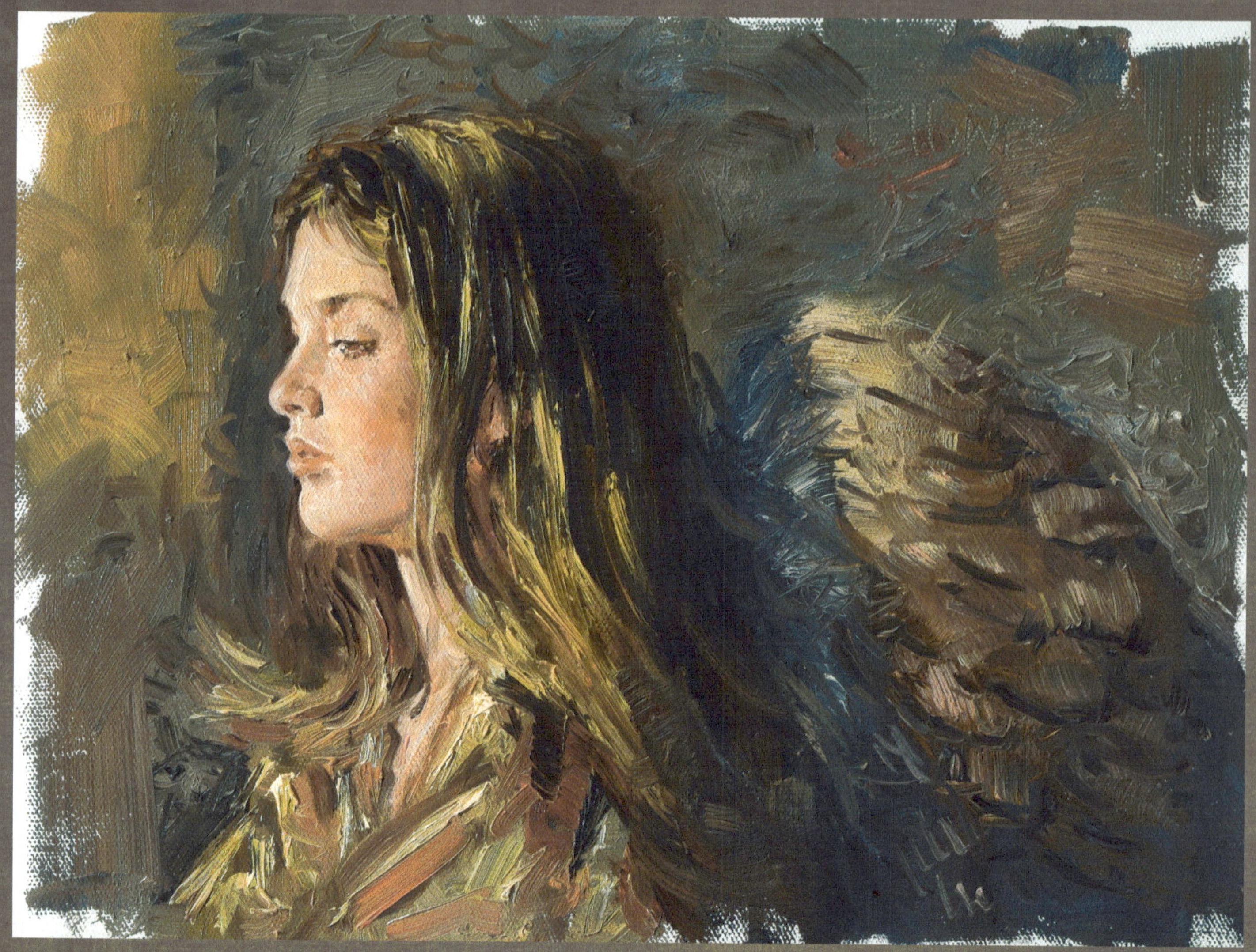

9 x 12" oil on canvas

4 HOUR STUDY FOR AT THE GATE

22 x 30" oil on canvas

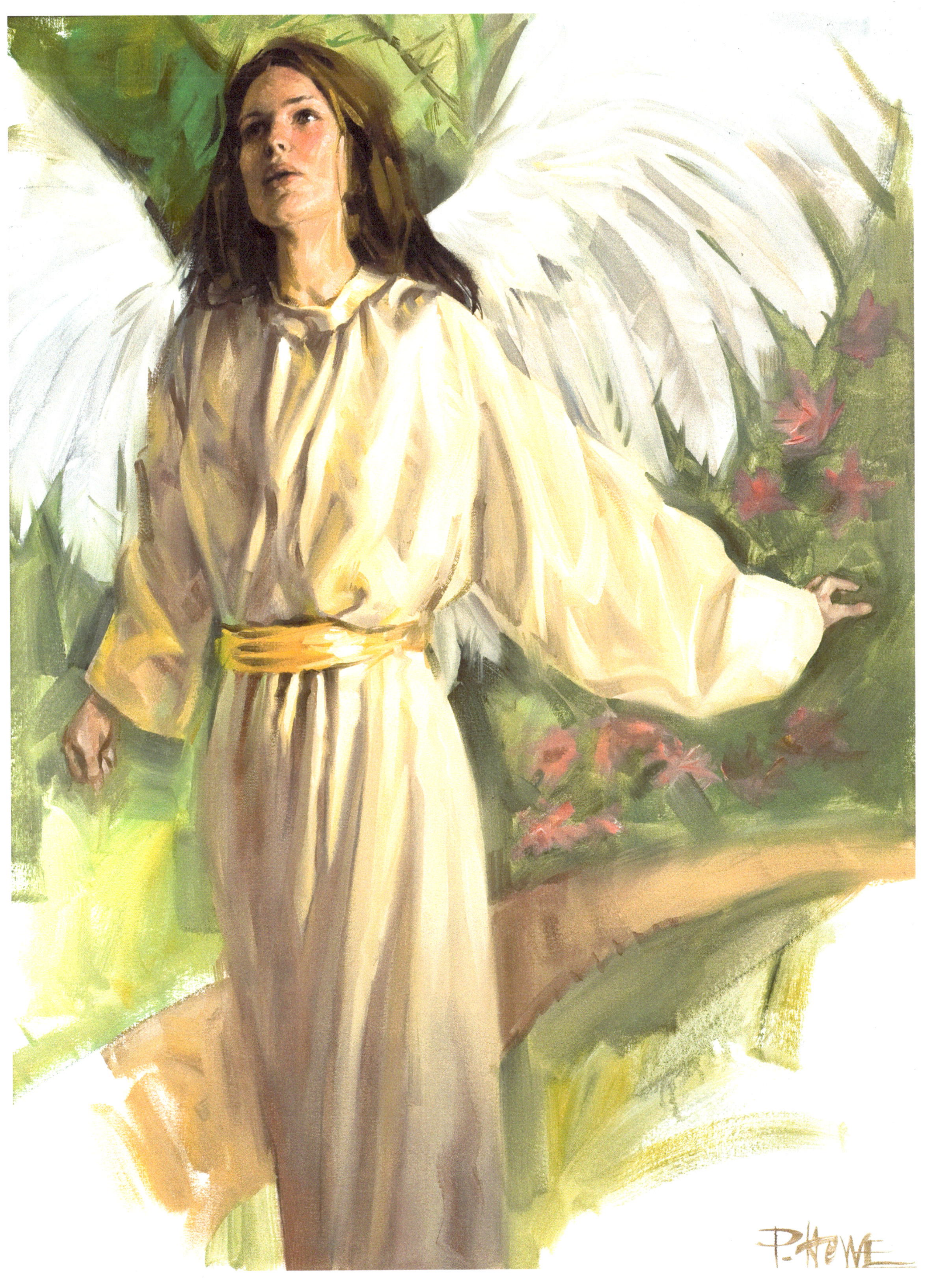
P. HOWE

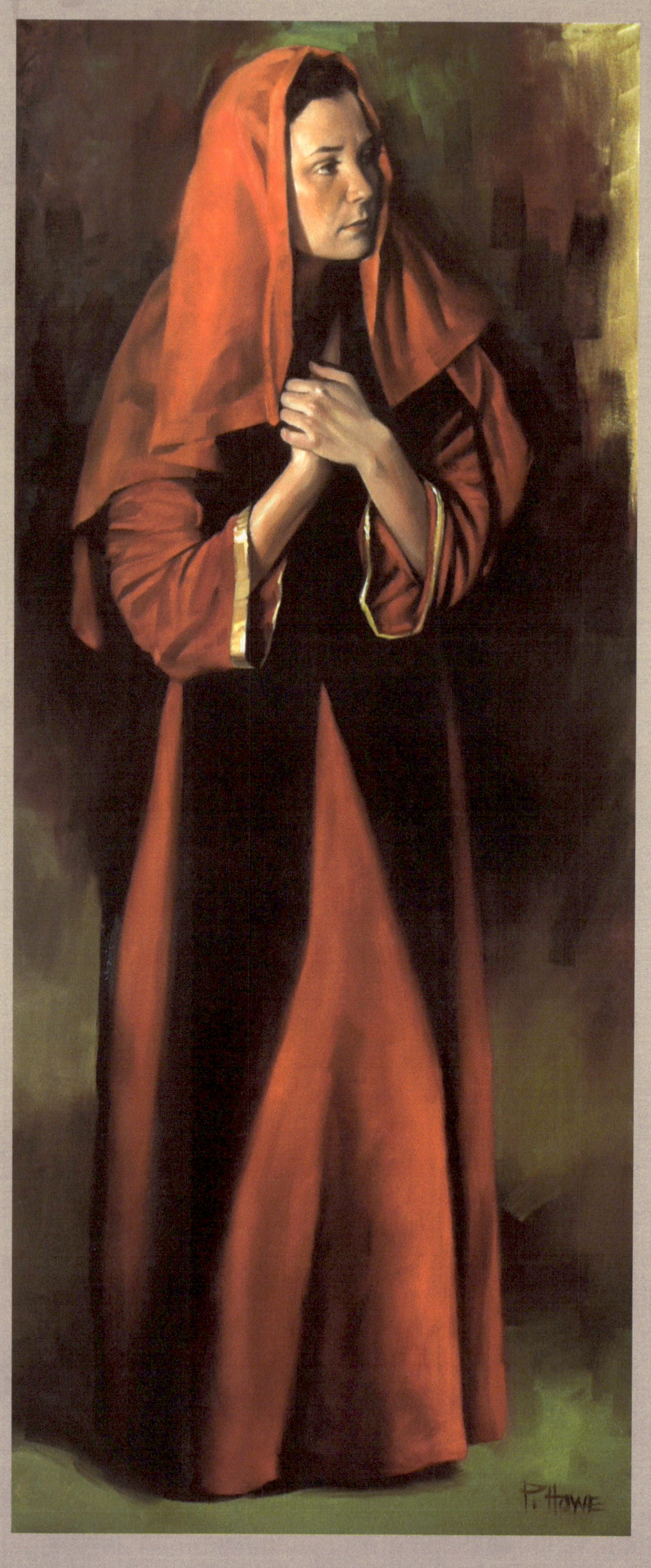

Model in Red Robes Study

22 x 40”
oil on canvas

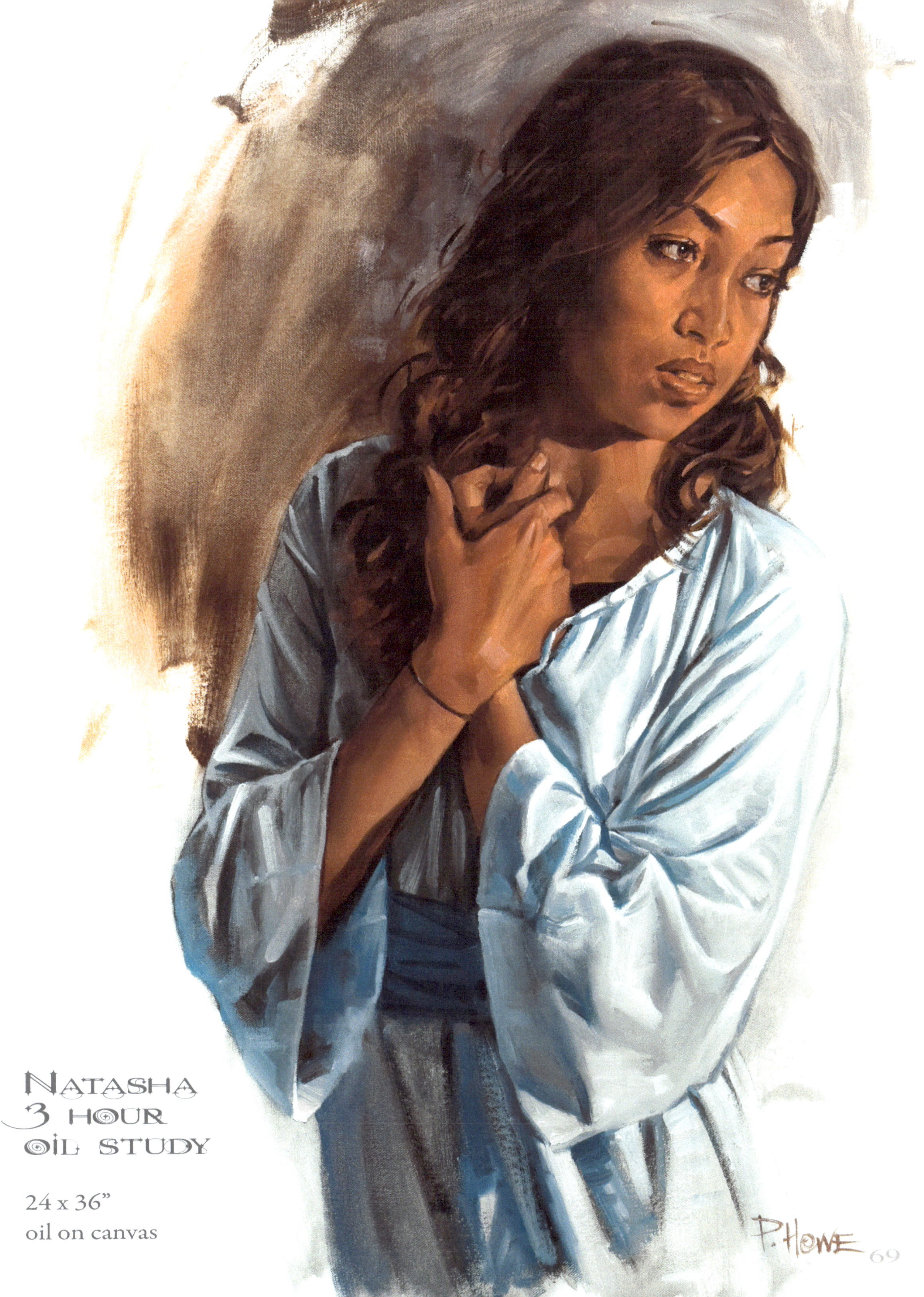

Natasha
3 hour
oil study

24 x 36"
oil on canvas

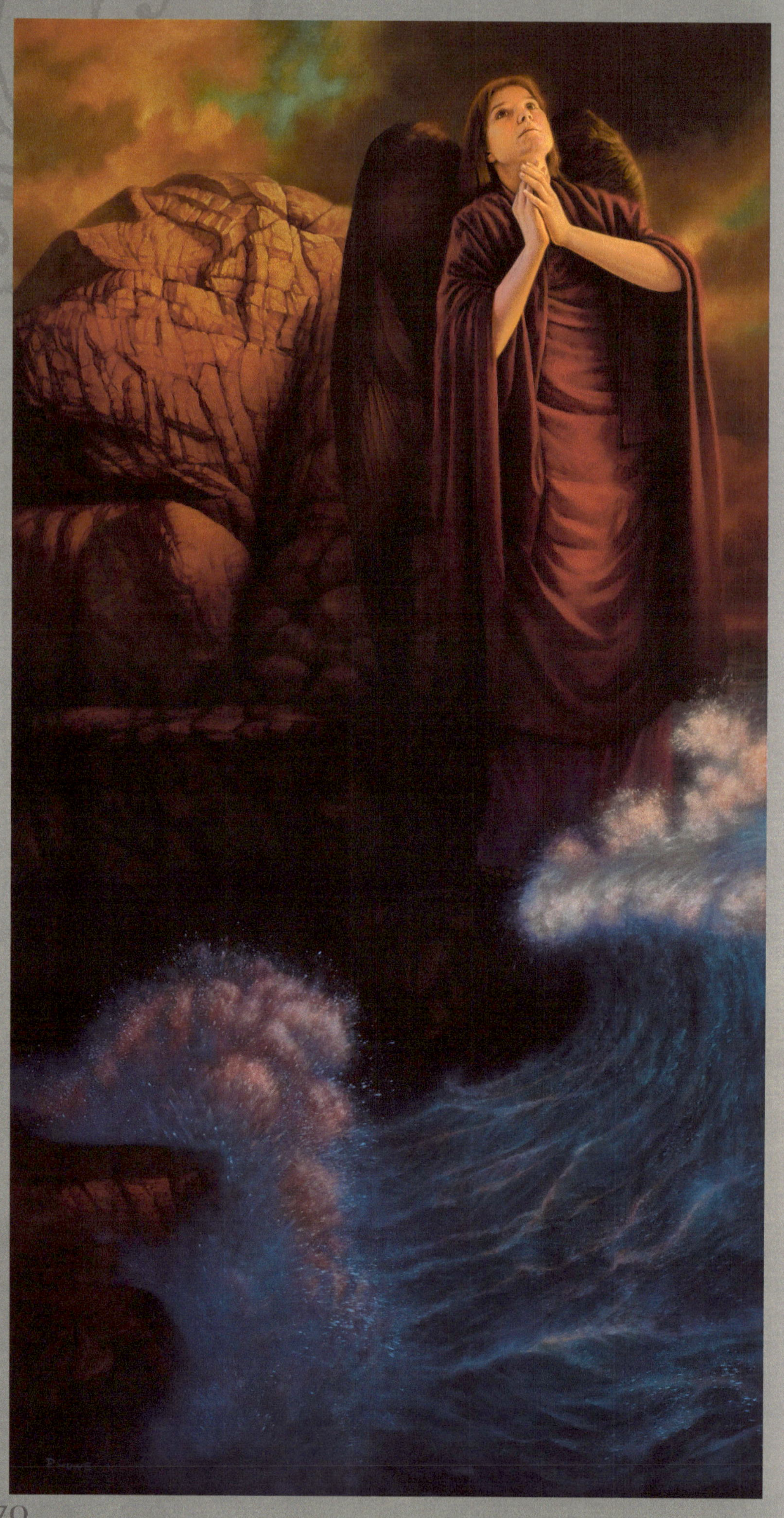

Incoming Wave

35 x 66”
oil on canvas

Study for In the Forest

24 x 36”
oil on canvas

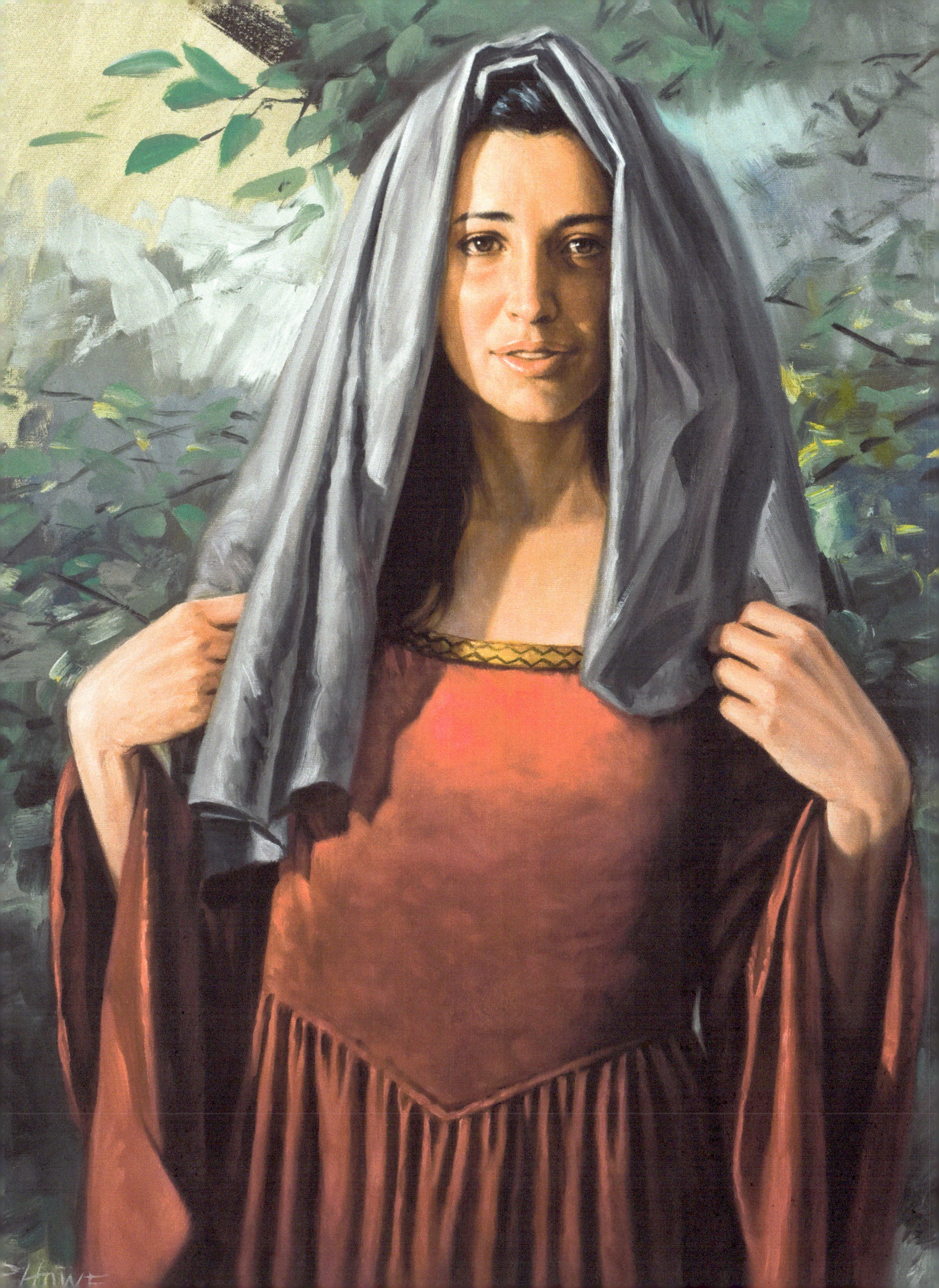
HOWE

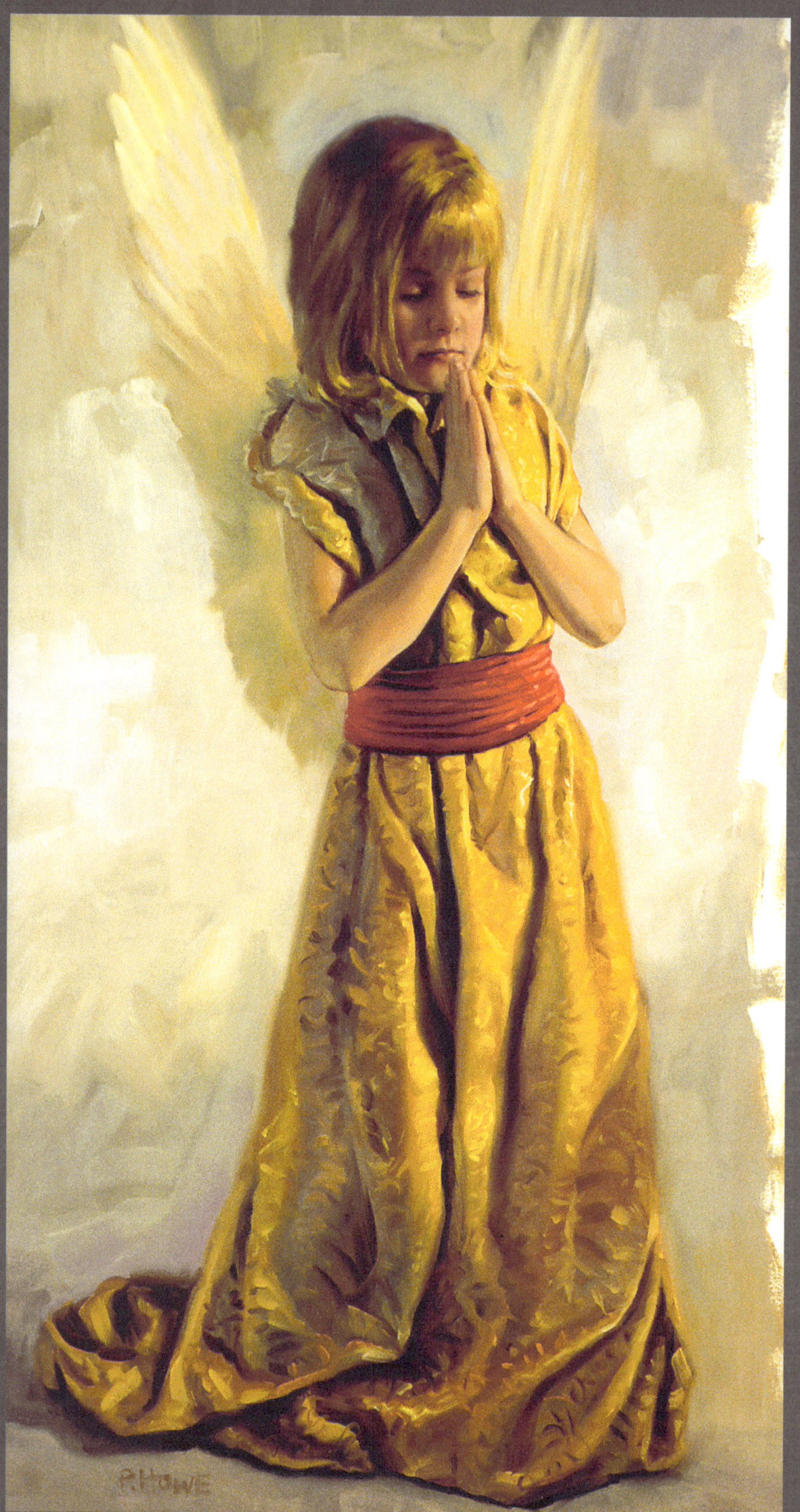

Child Angel 5 hour study

20 x 34" oil on canvas

Model in Purple Robes 4 hour study

24 x 36" oil on canvas

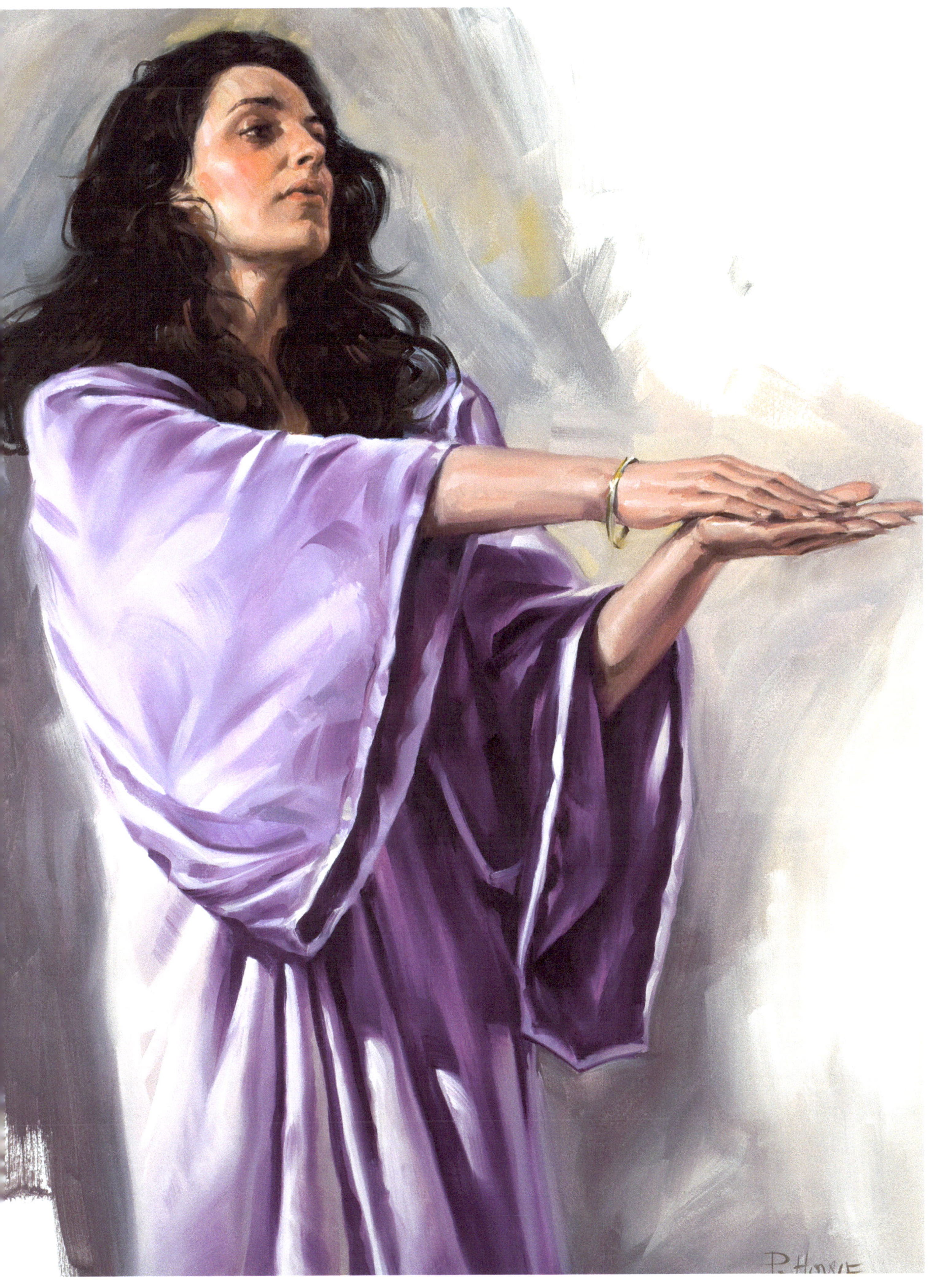

Study for The Boy King

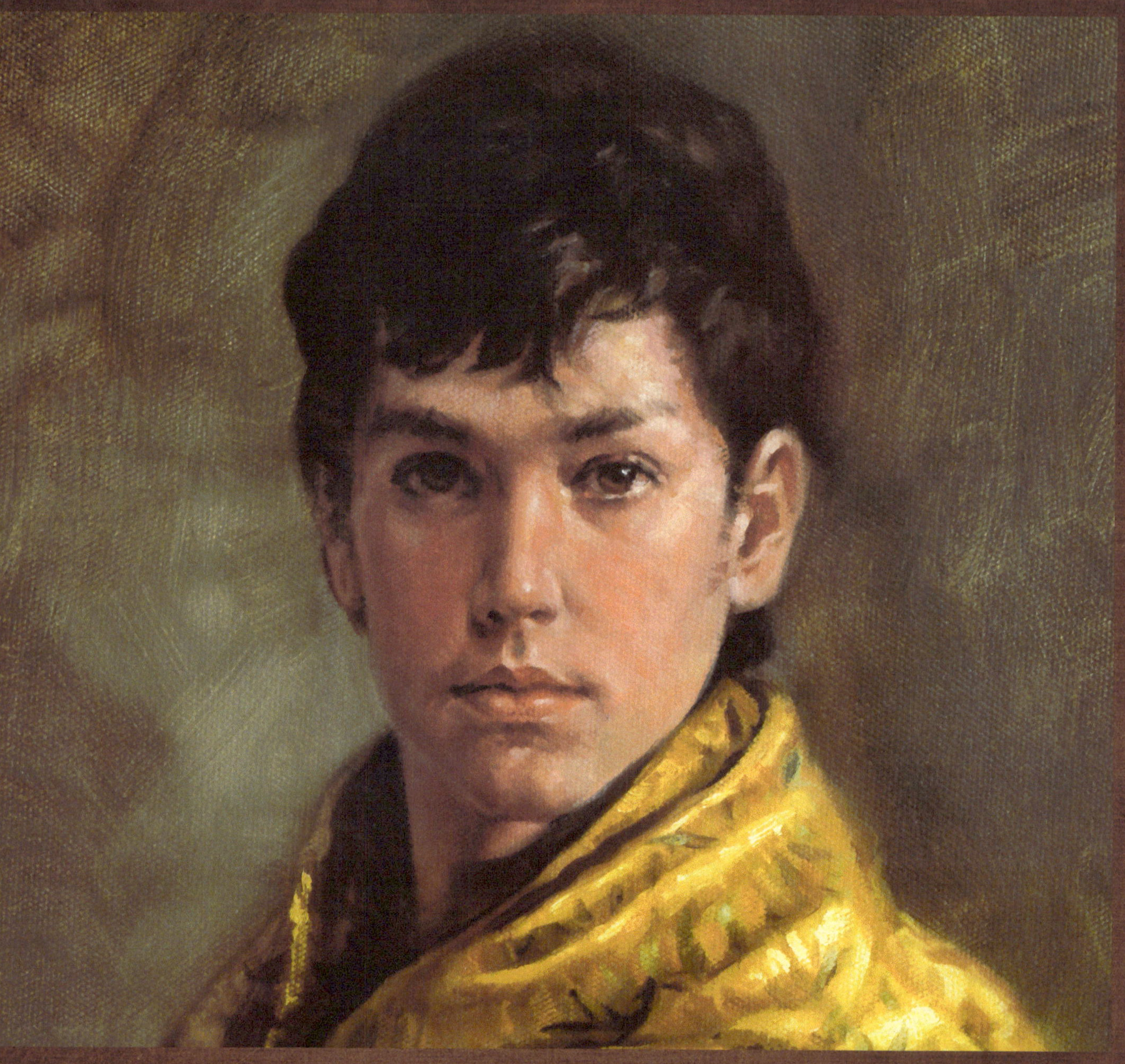

24 x 30"
oil on canvas

Study for The Tranquil Sea

24 x 36" oil on canvas

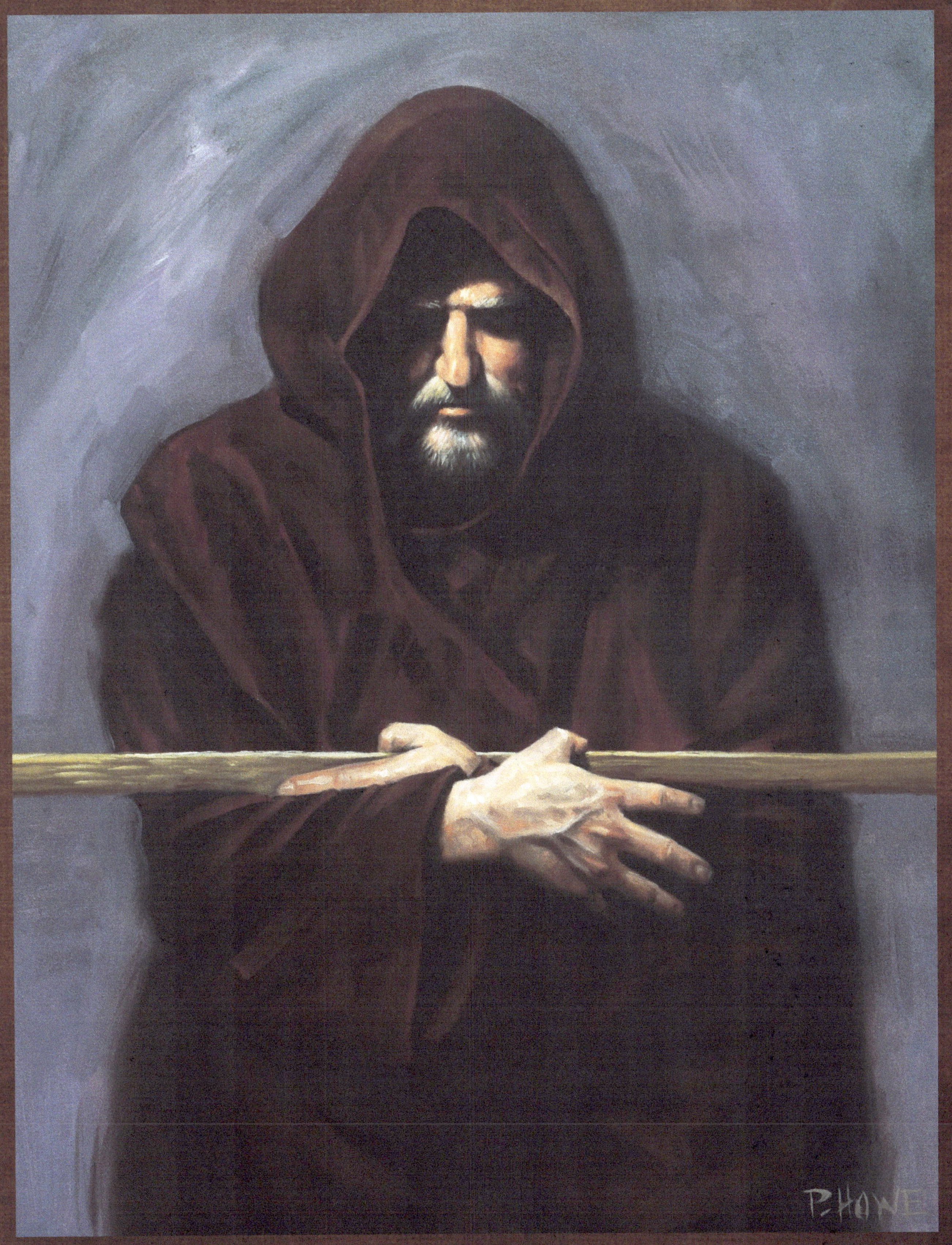

STUDY OF ALEXIS

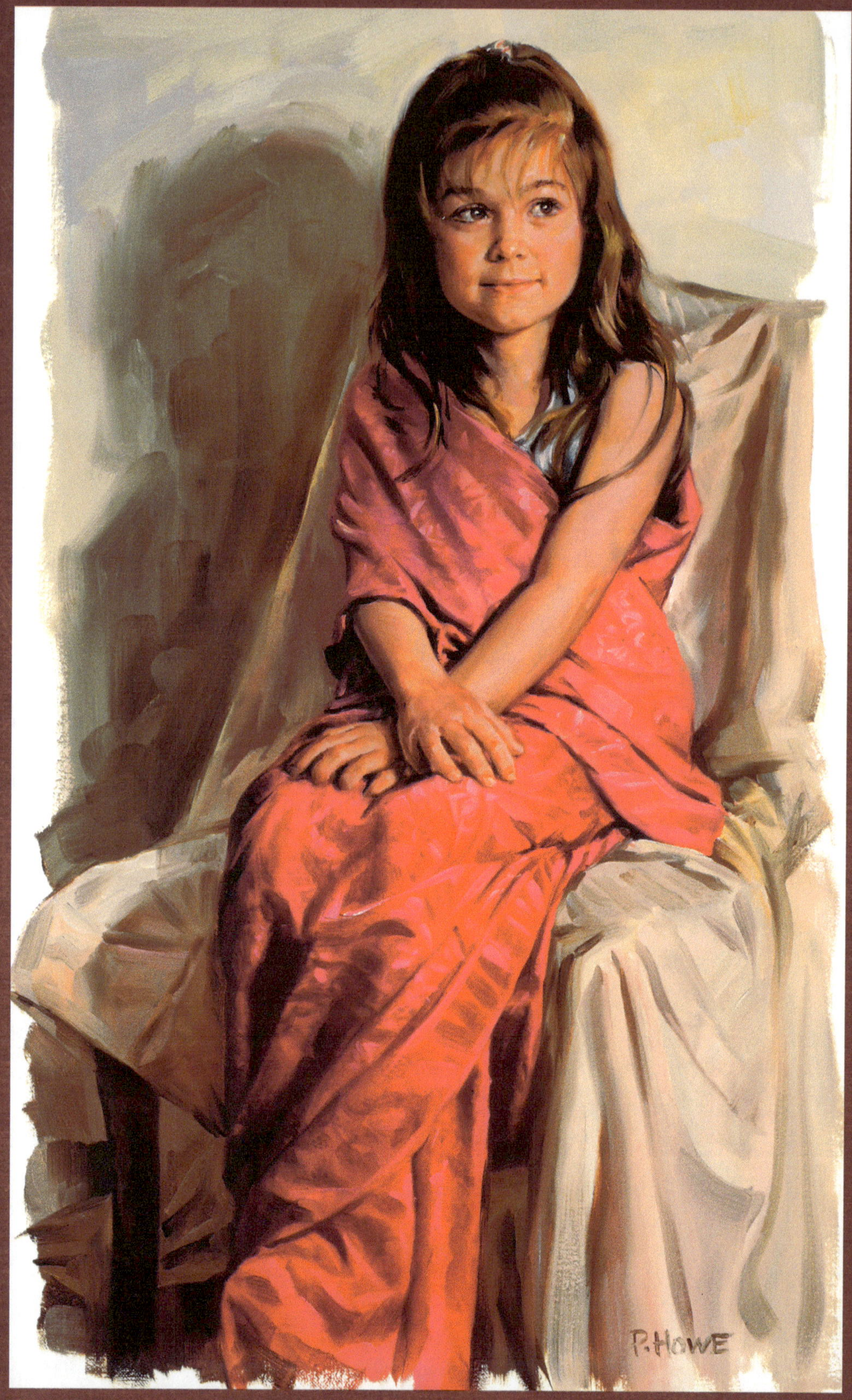

24 x 36" oil on canvas

THE ANCIENT DOOR

30 x 40" oil on canvas

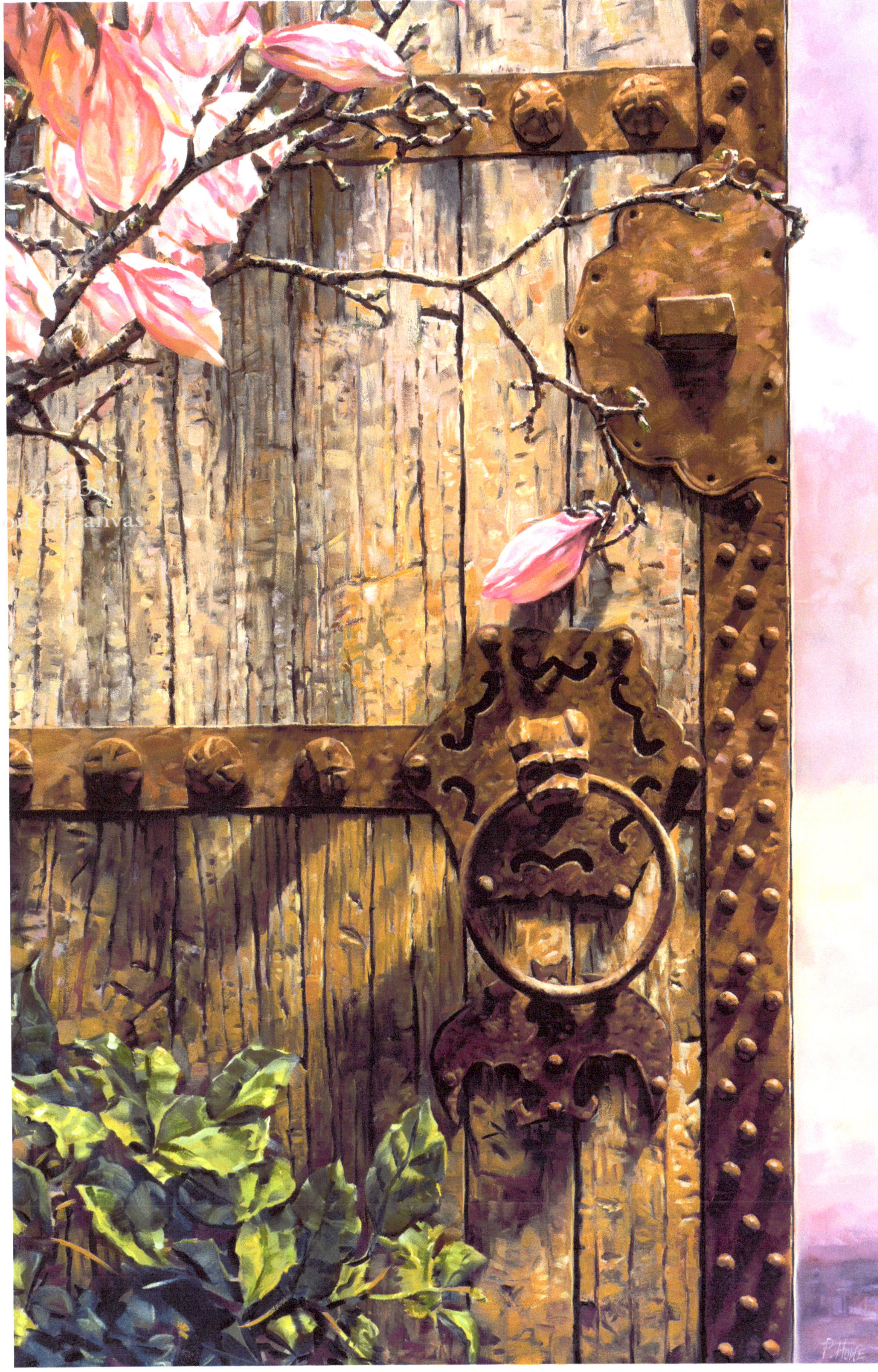
P. Howe

Small Studies and Paintings

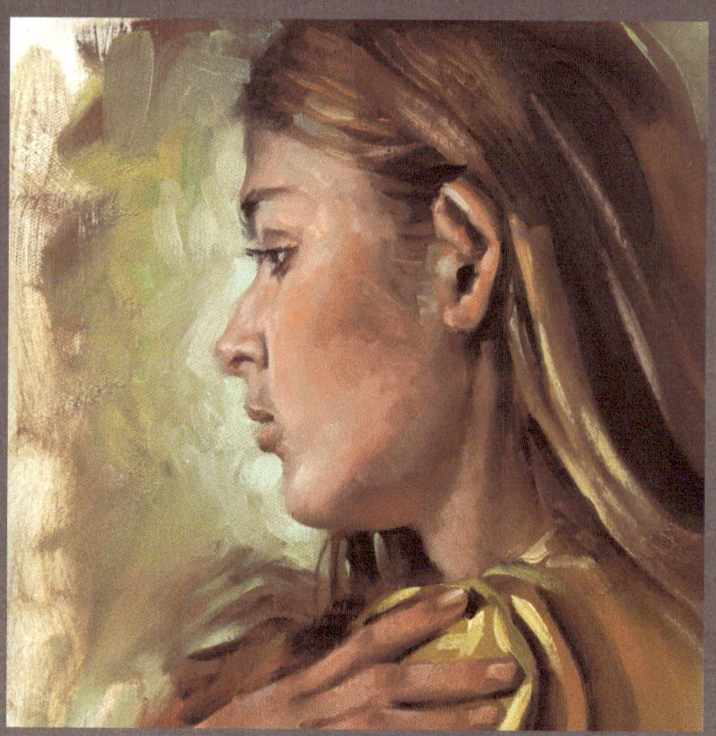

45 minute color study

8 x 8" oil on canvas

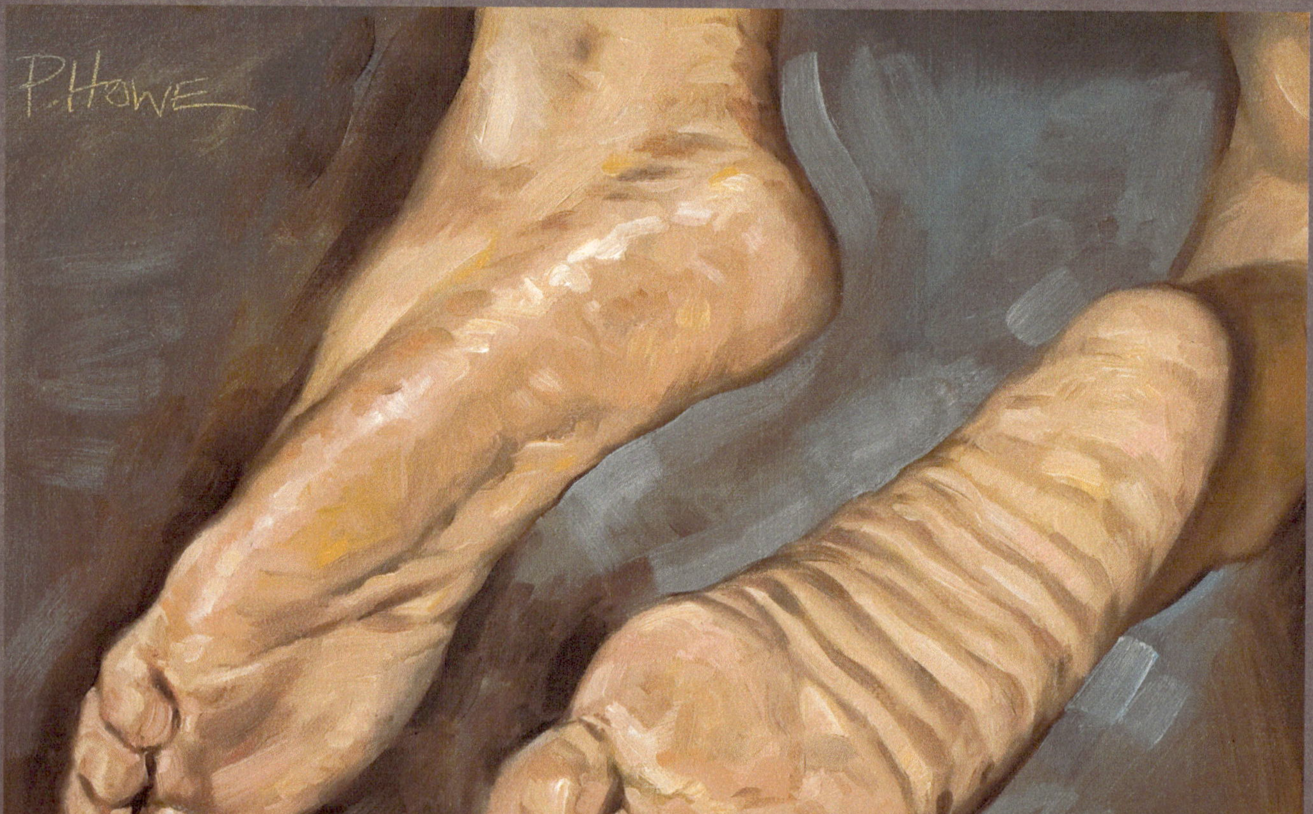

Model's feet sketch

10 x 14" oil on canvas

Model Study

14 x 24"
oil on canvas

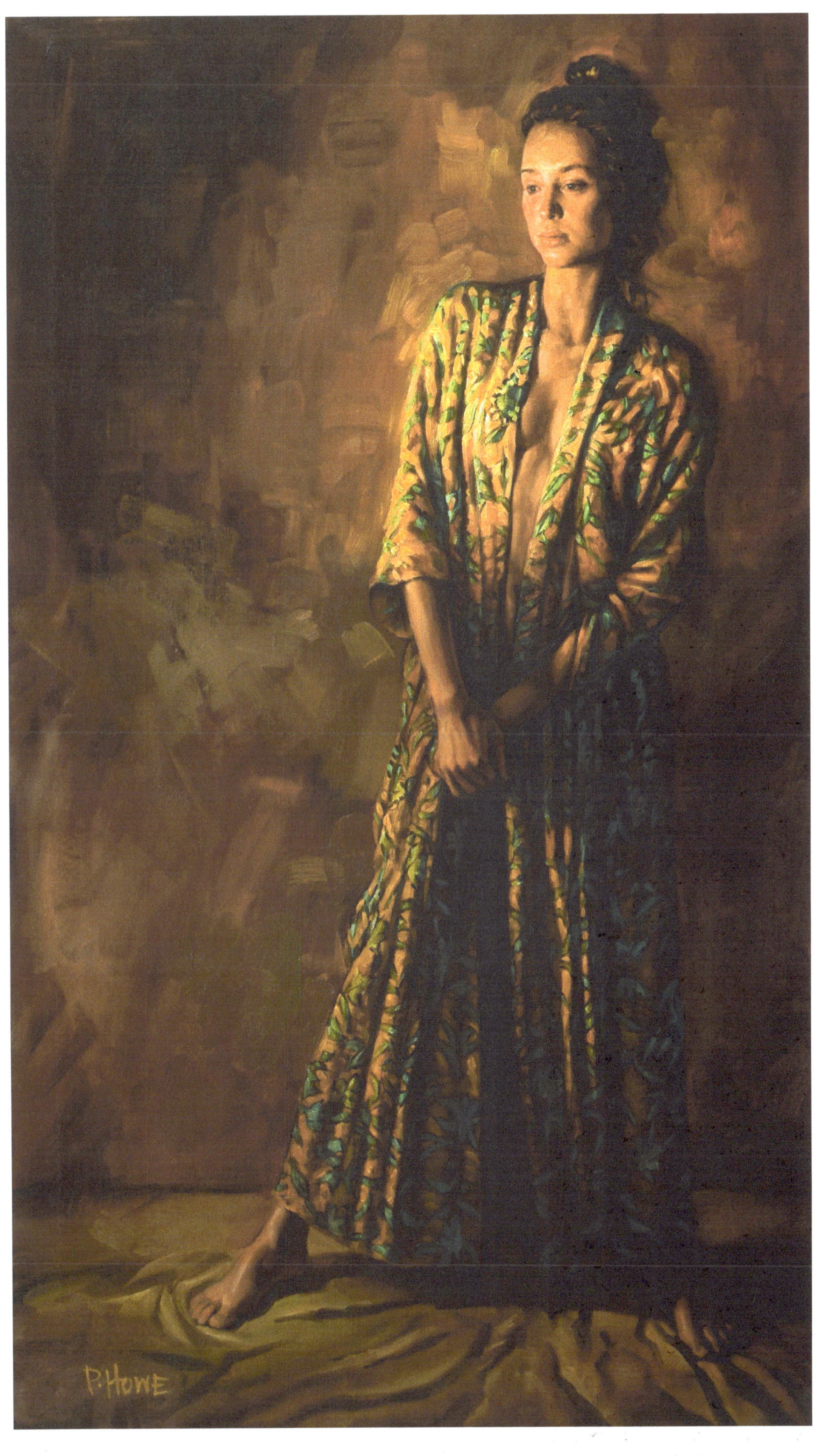

Child Angel Study for The Leaving Time

12 x 12" oil on canvas

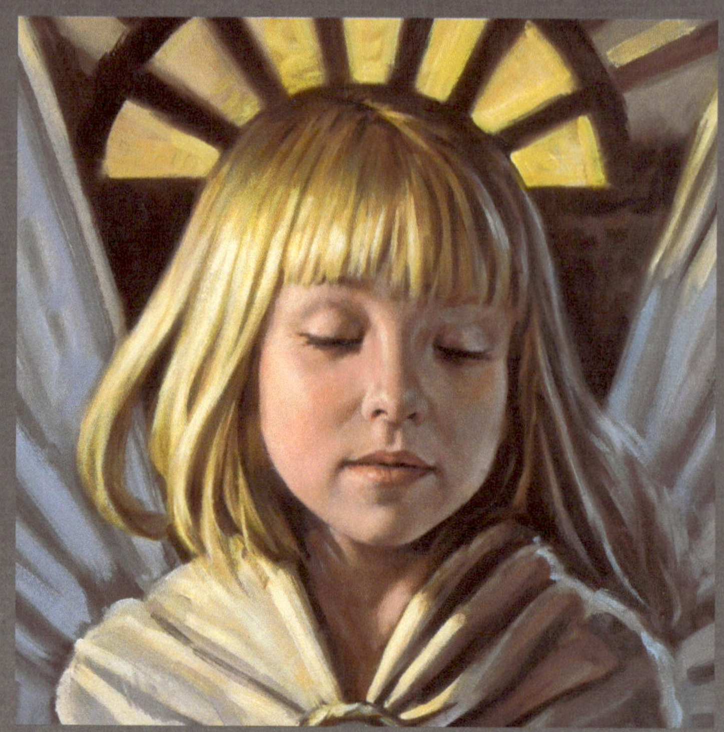

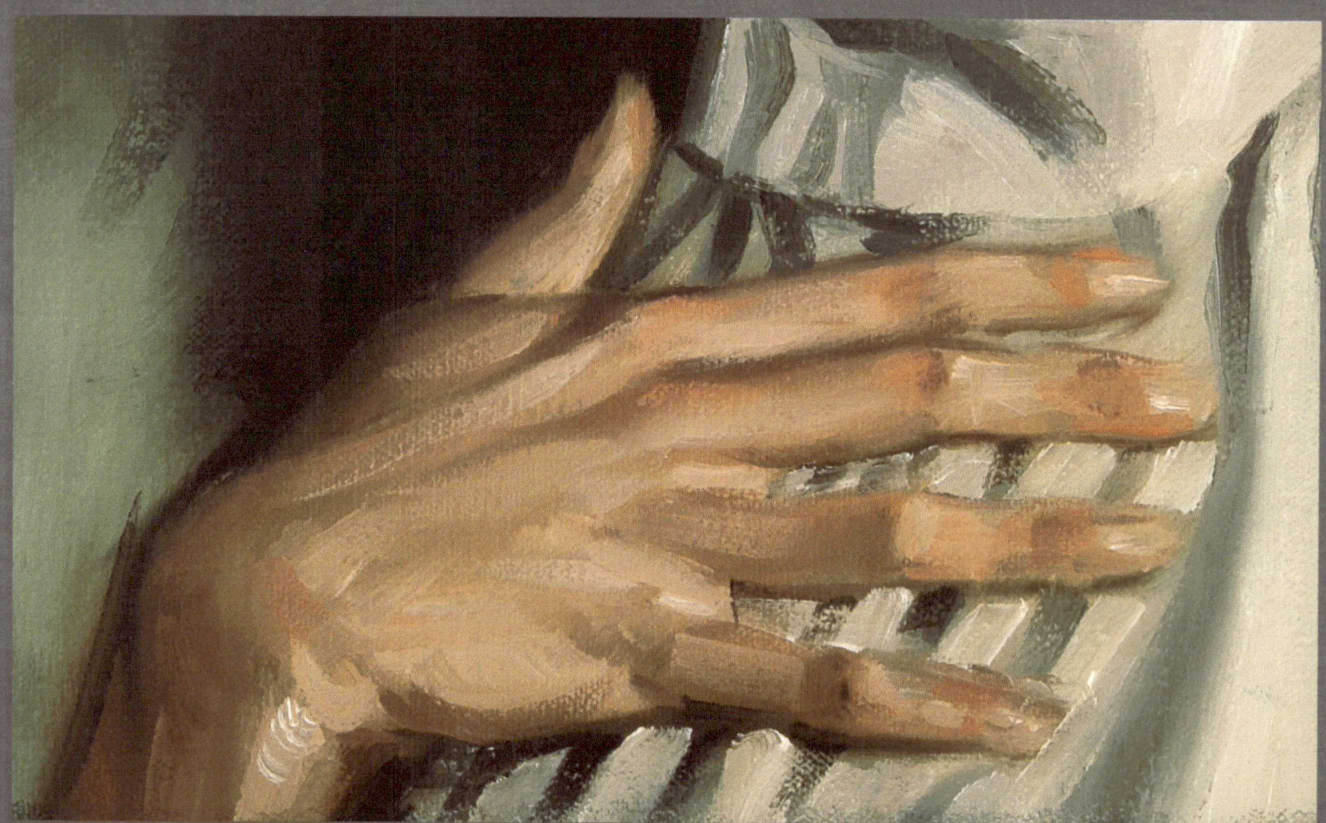

Model's hand sketch

10 x 14" oil on canvas

Man in Red Robes Study

14 x 24"
oil on canvas

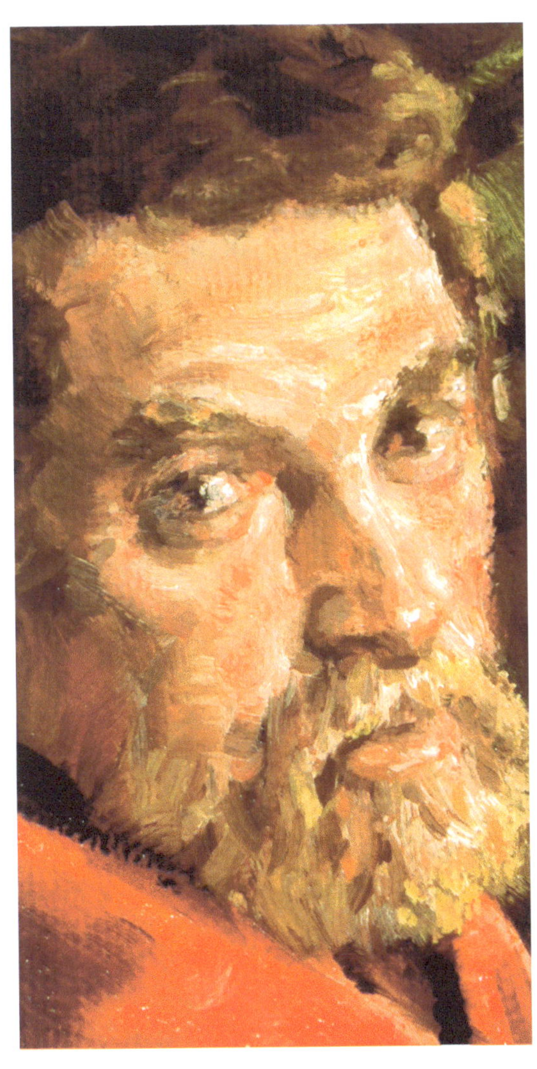

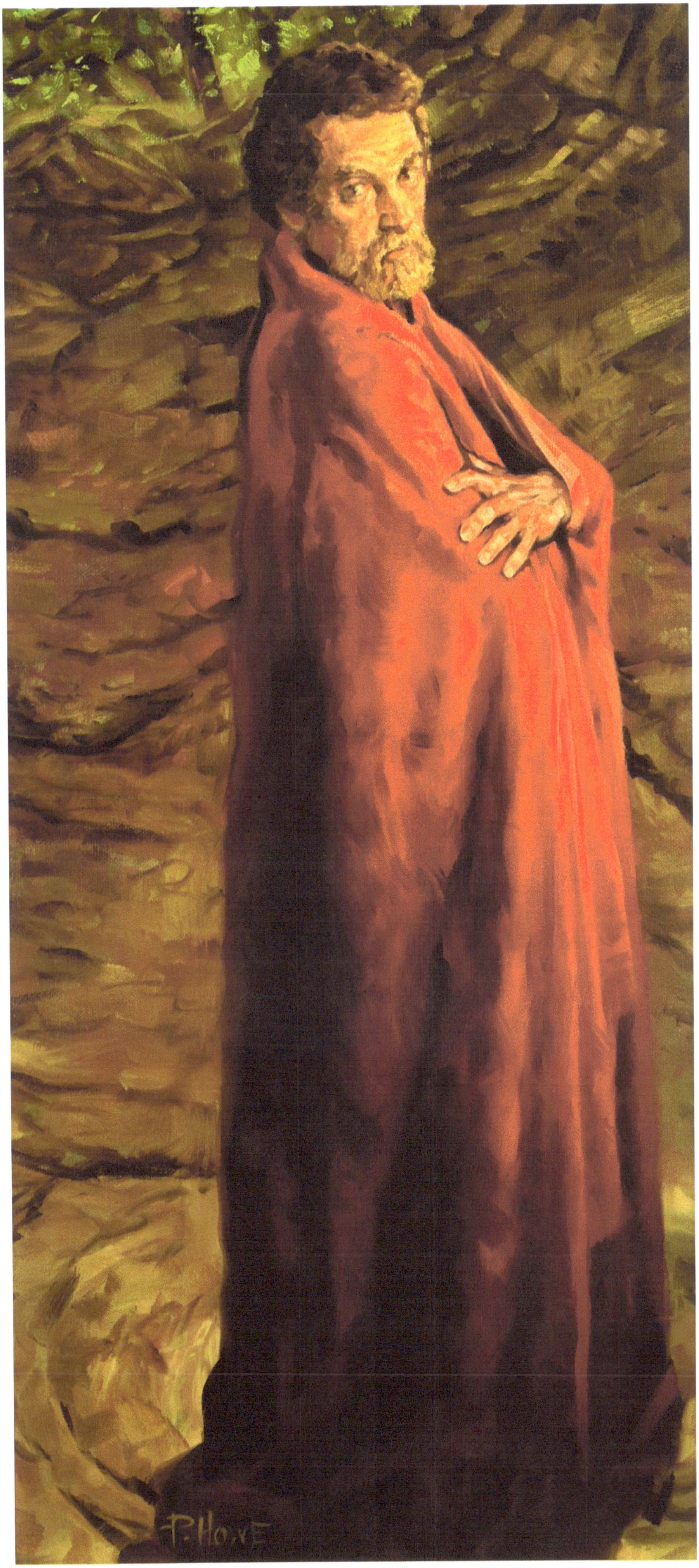

Figure in landscape study 1

8 x 10" gouache and oil on panel

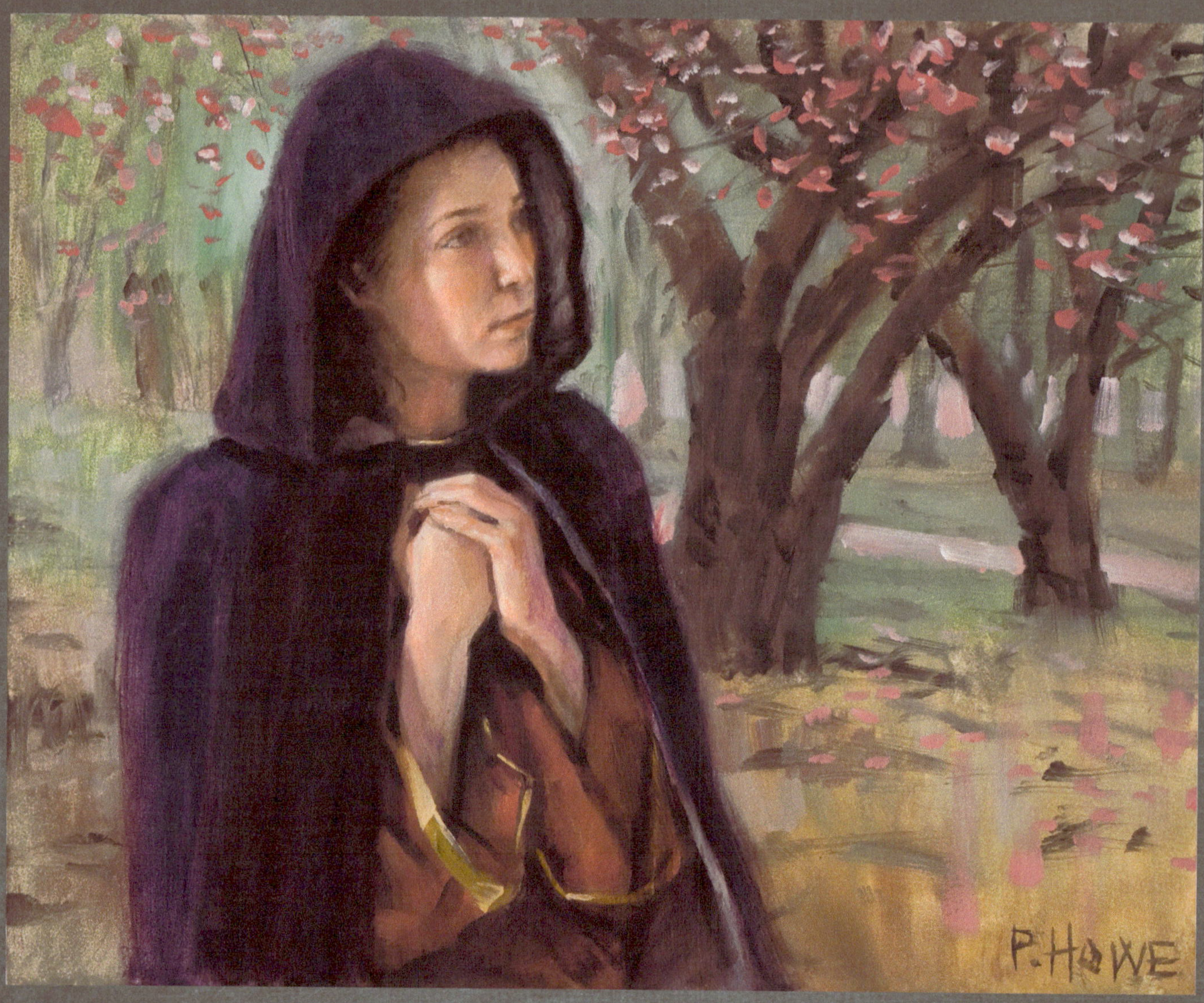

Figure in Landscape Study 2

8 x 10" gouache and oil on panel

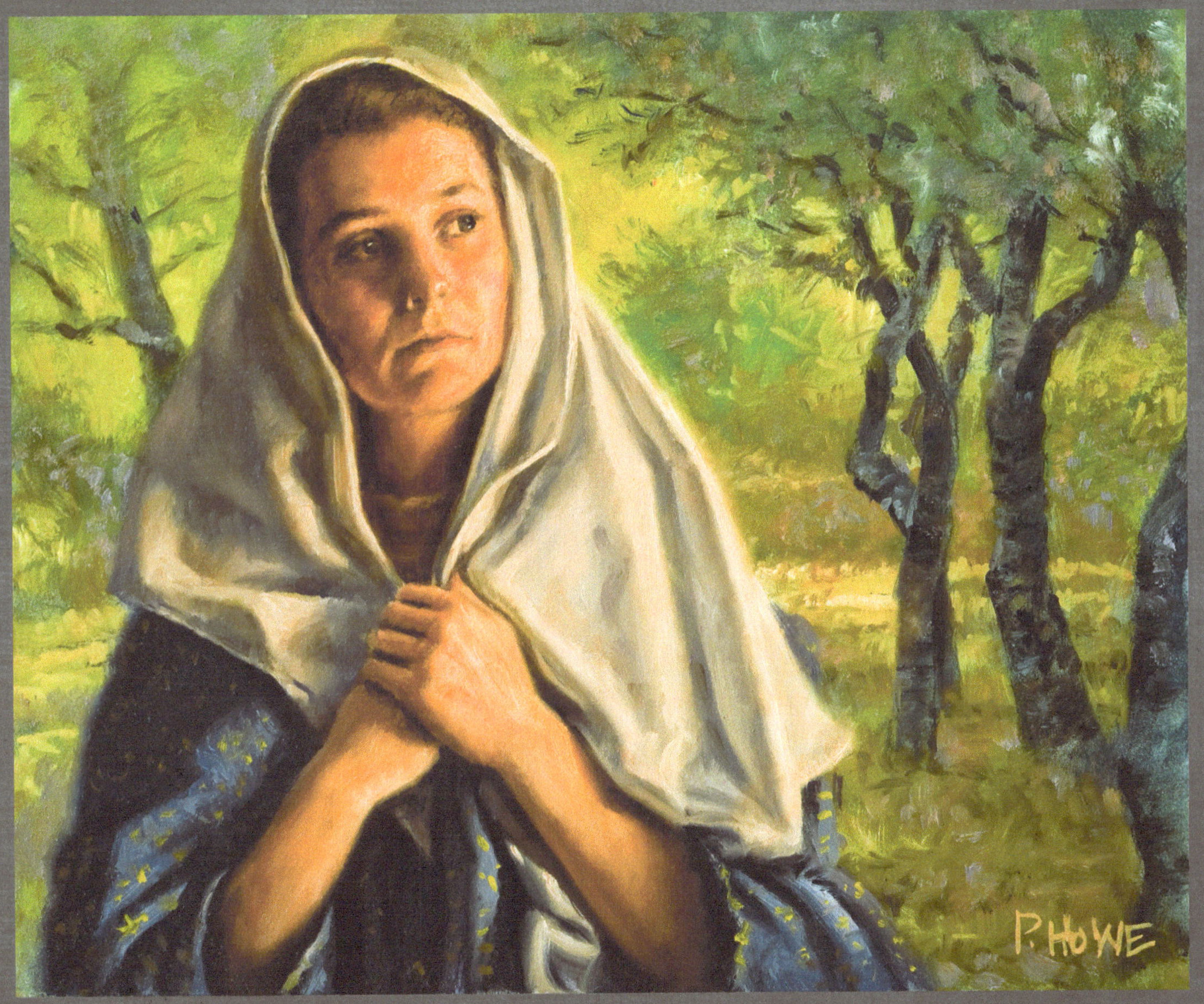

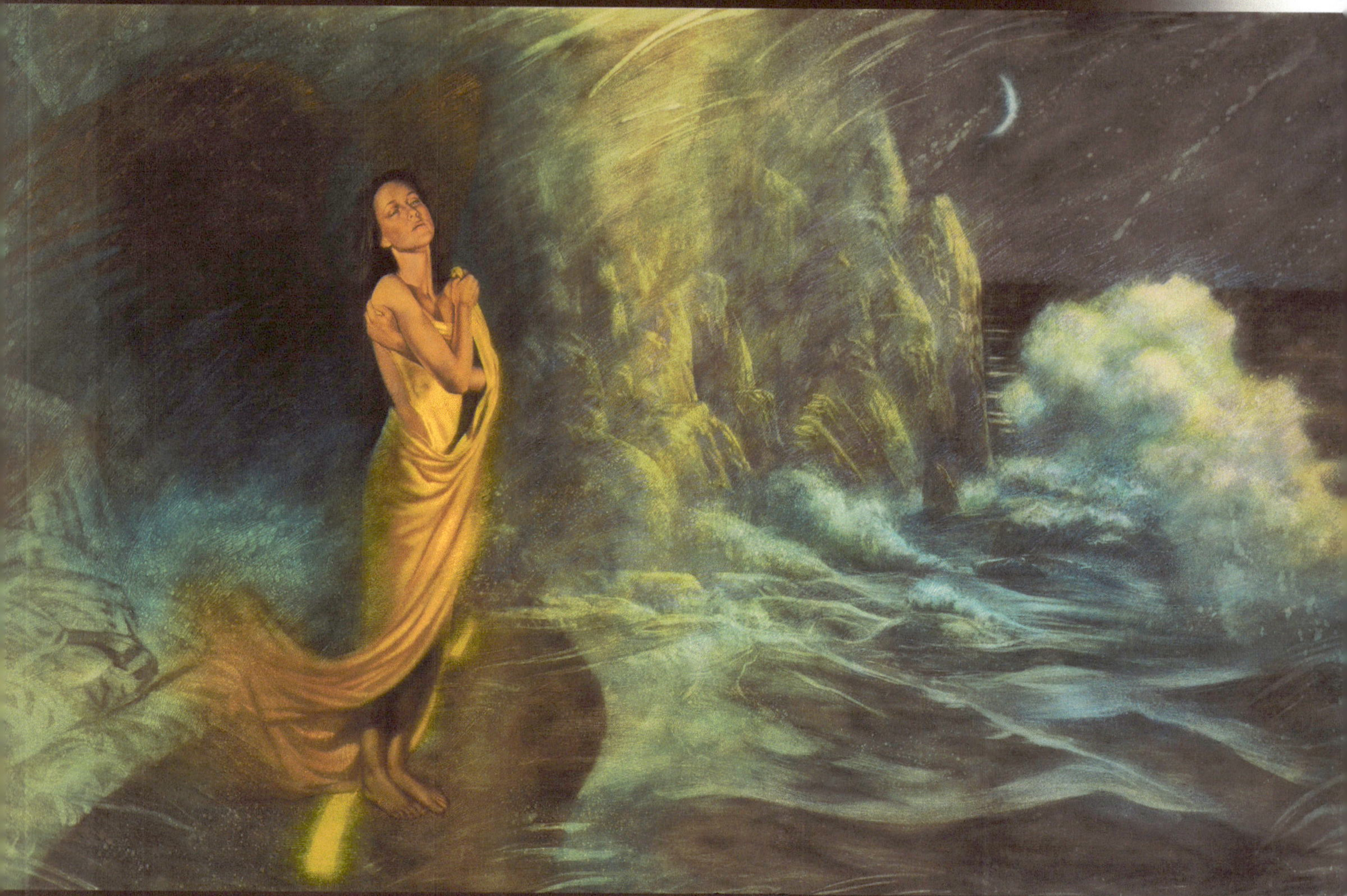

The Road

54 x 84"

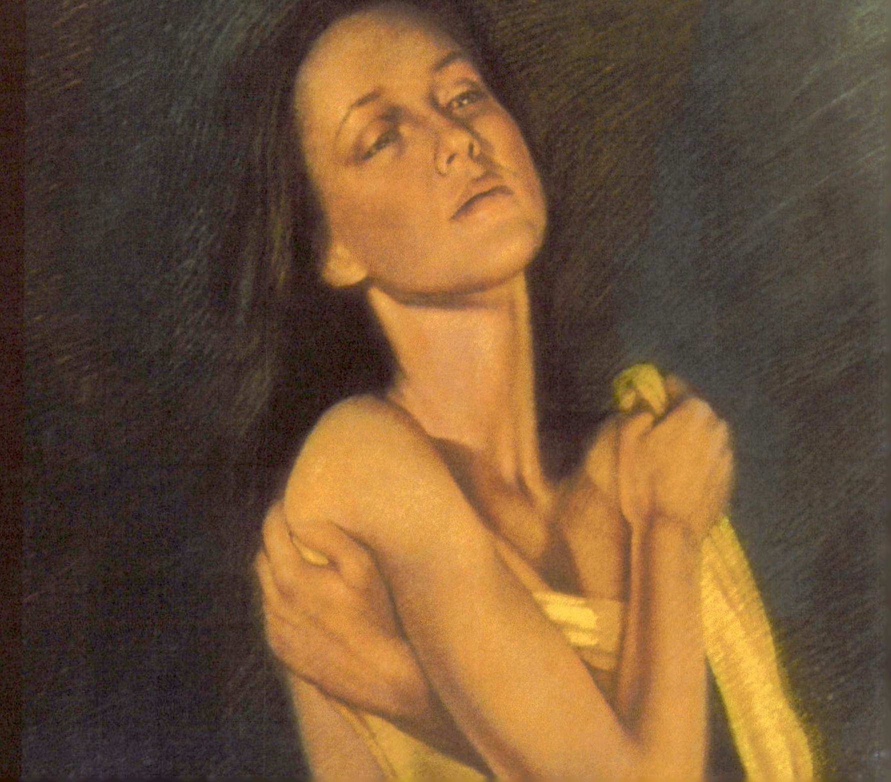

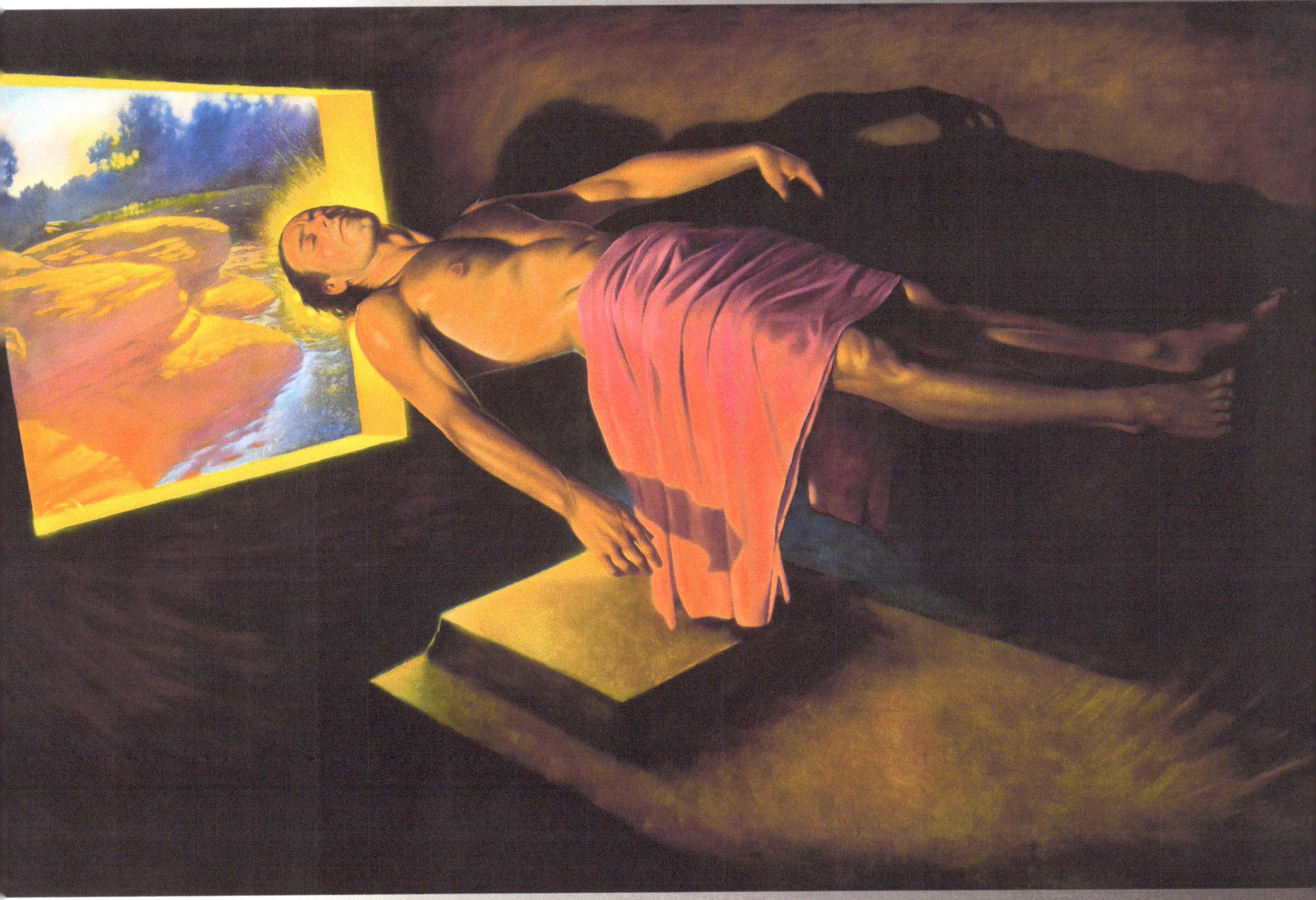

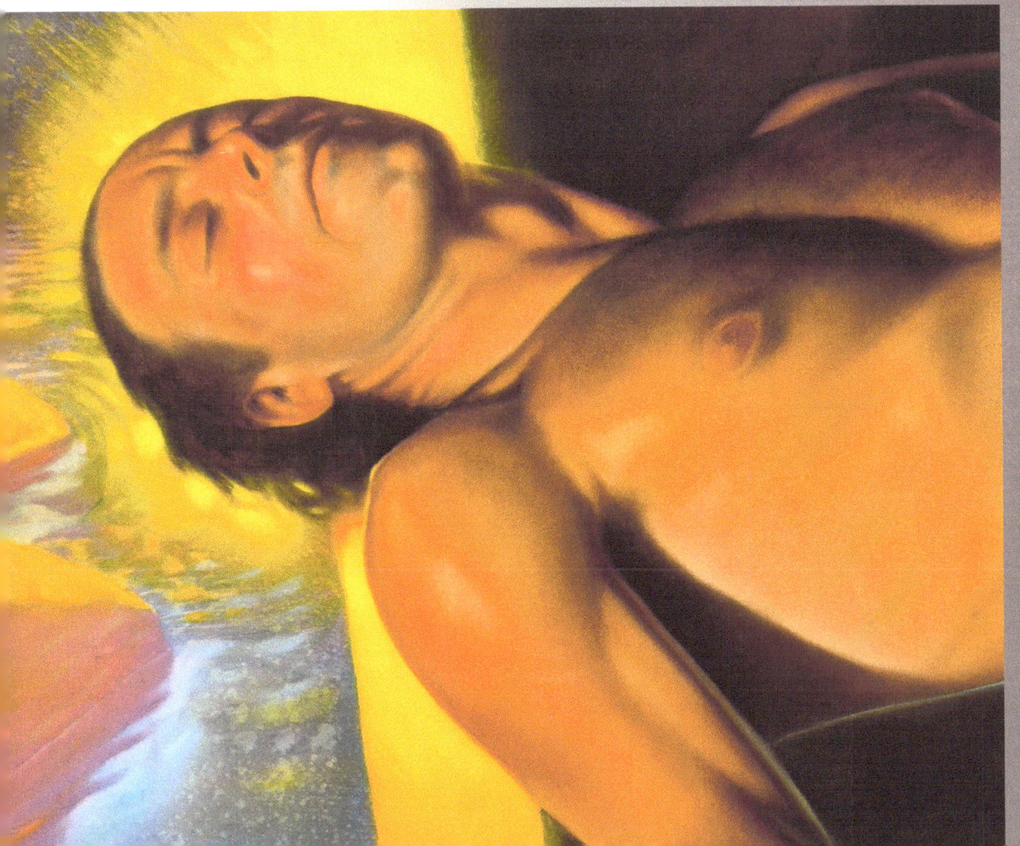

JOURNEY

60 x144"

Early Work

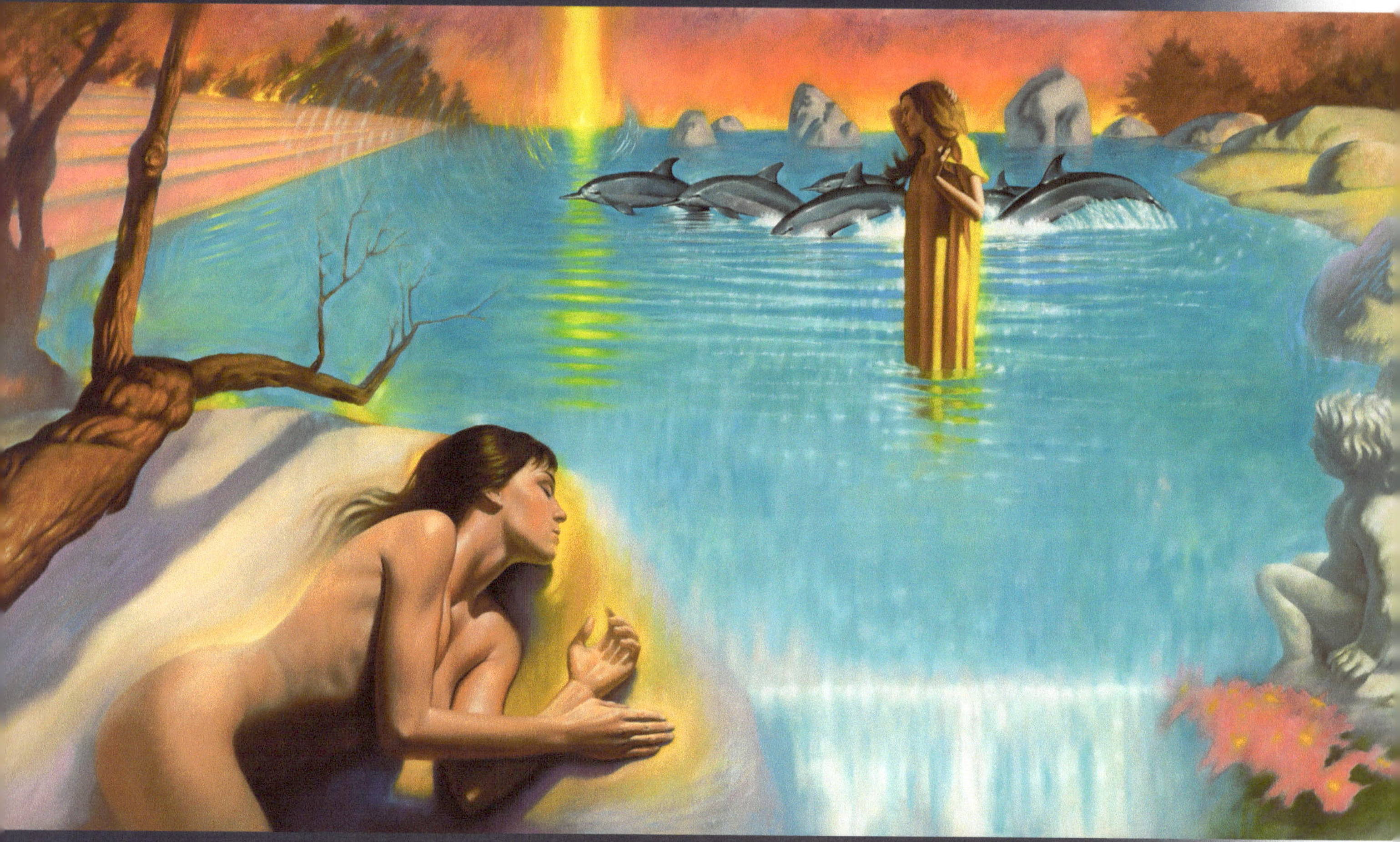

Vortex

60 x 120”

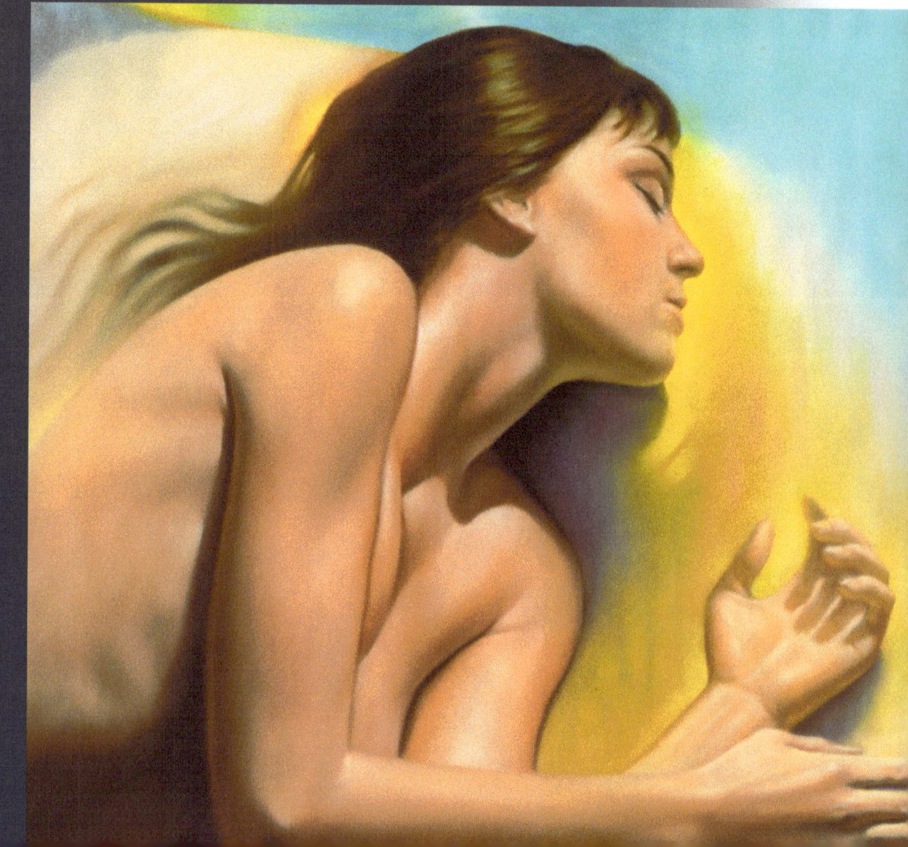

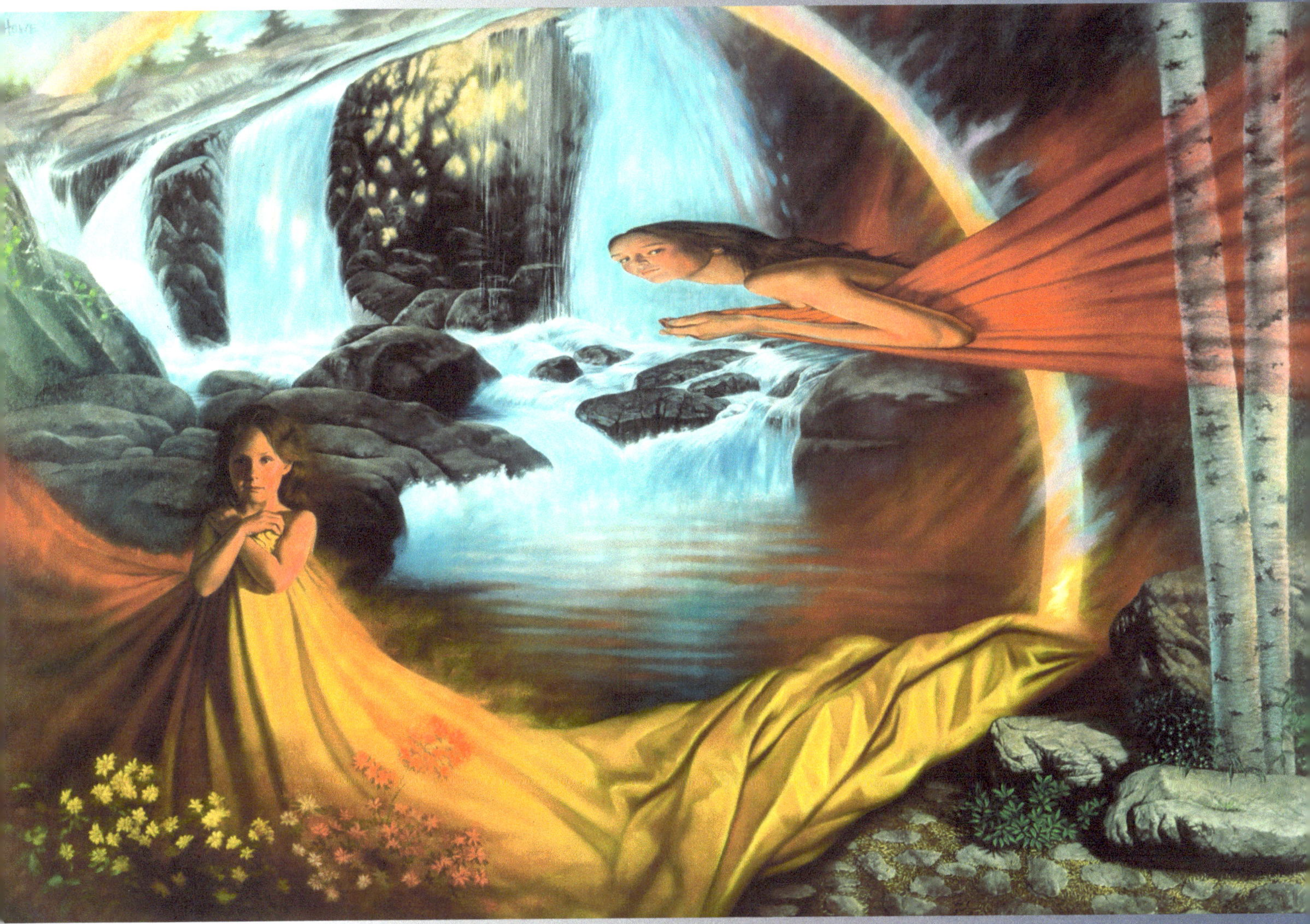

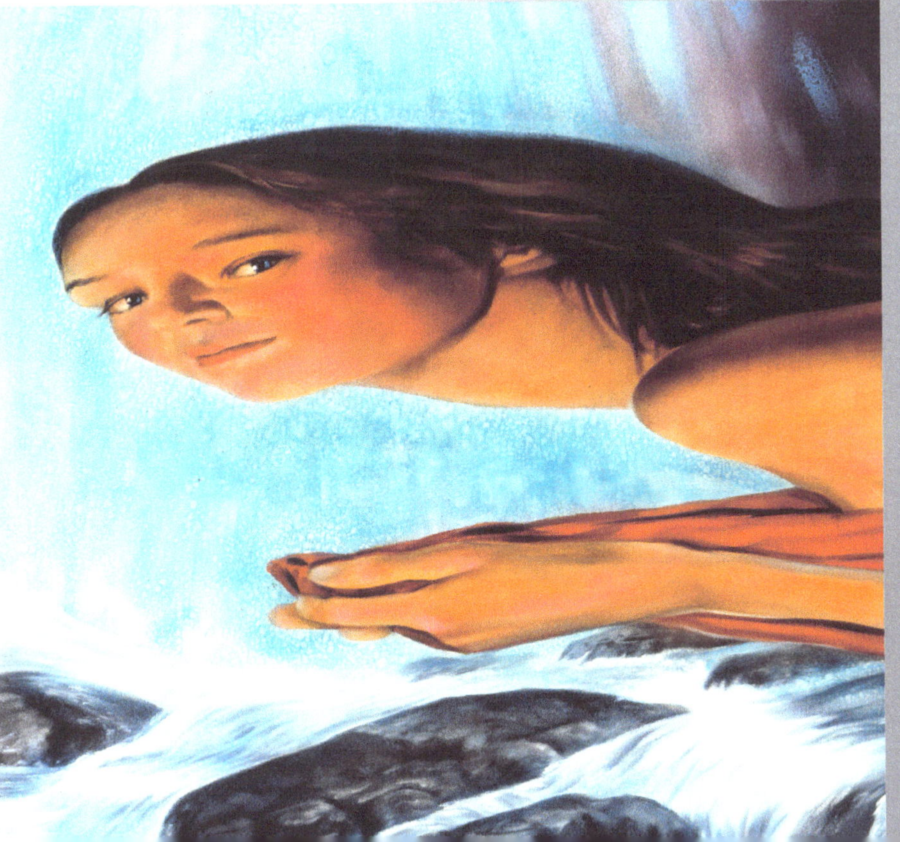

INVOLUTION

60 x144”

Figure Drawings

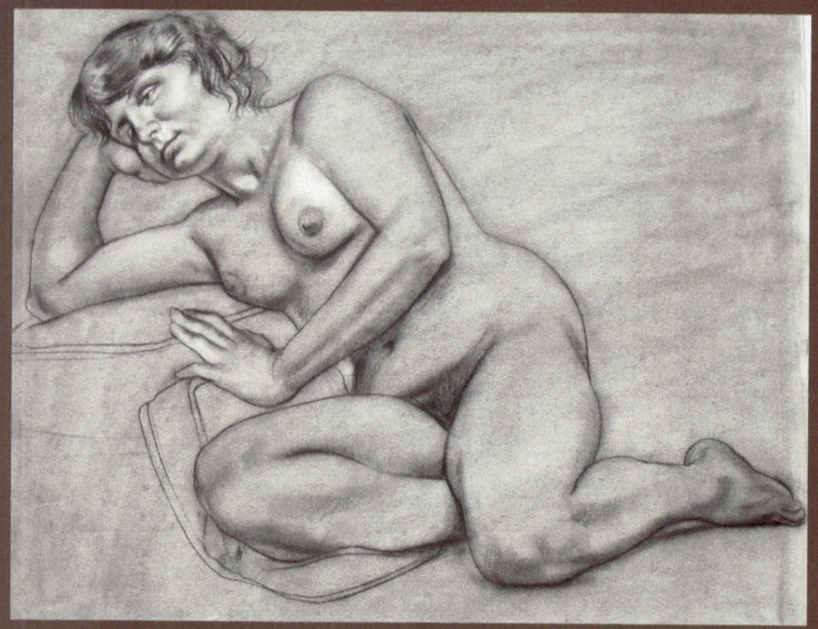

1-3 hour charcoal and conte life drawings

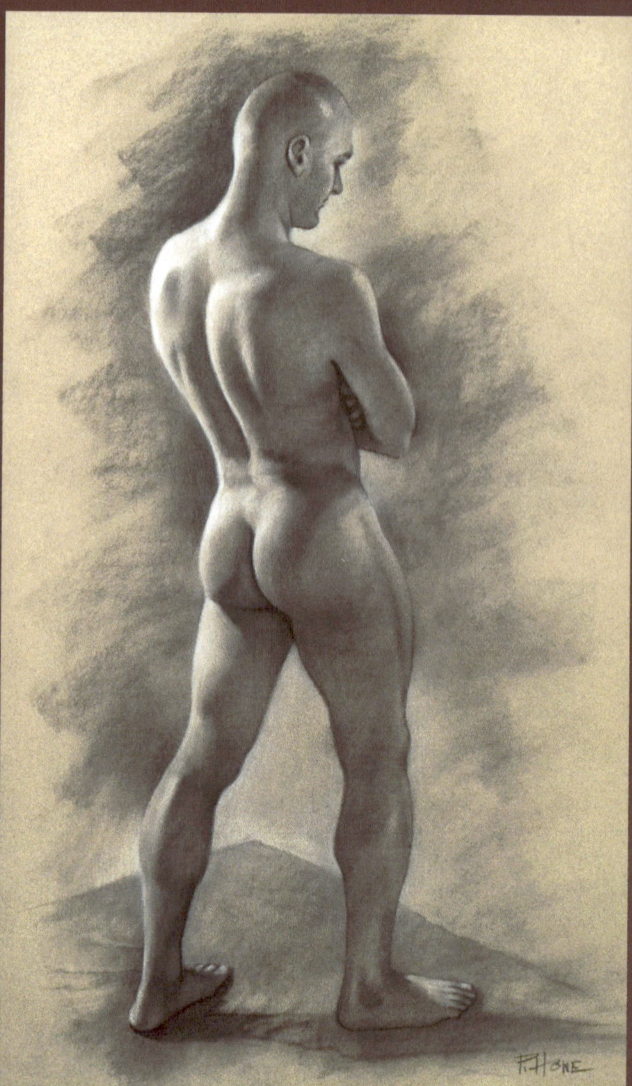

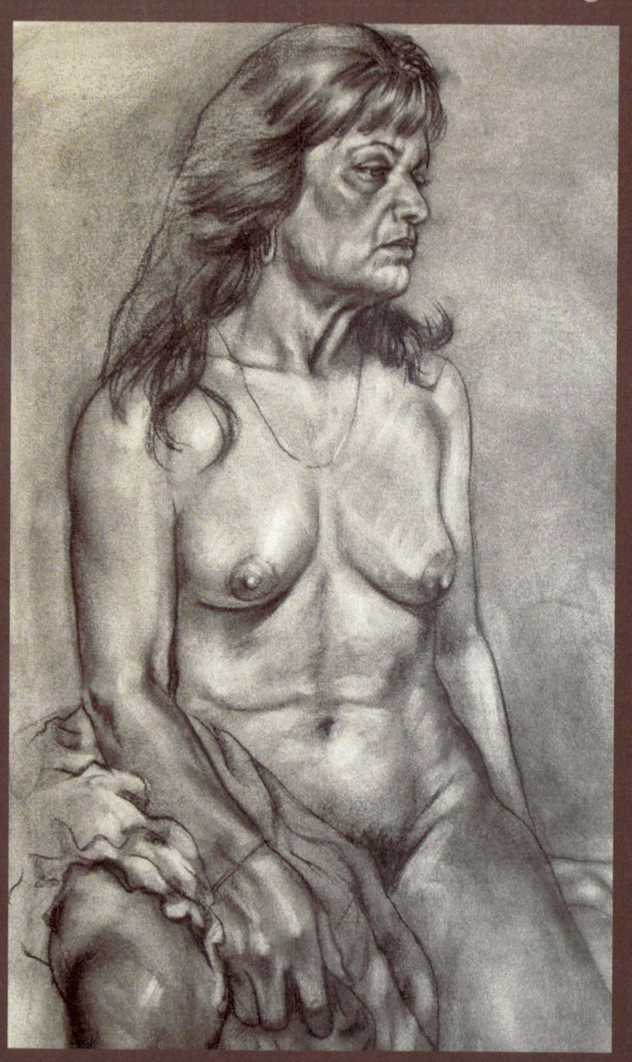

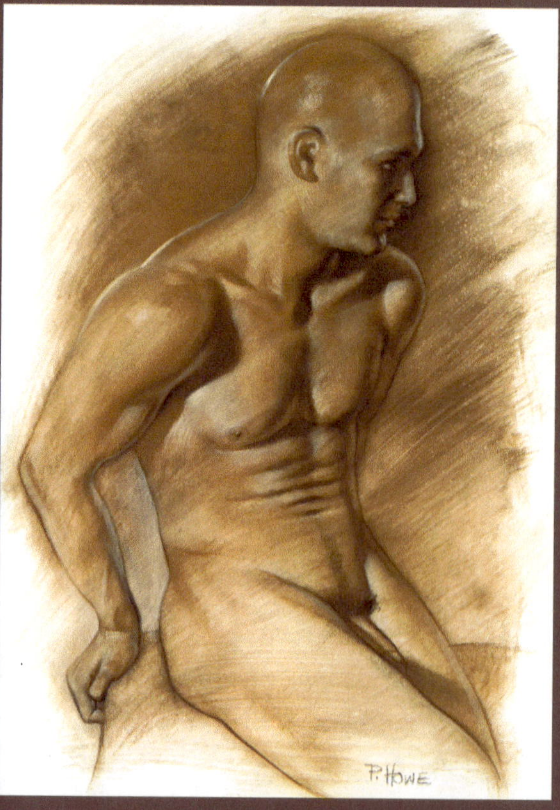

4 hour mixed media on paper 22 x 30" ---

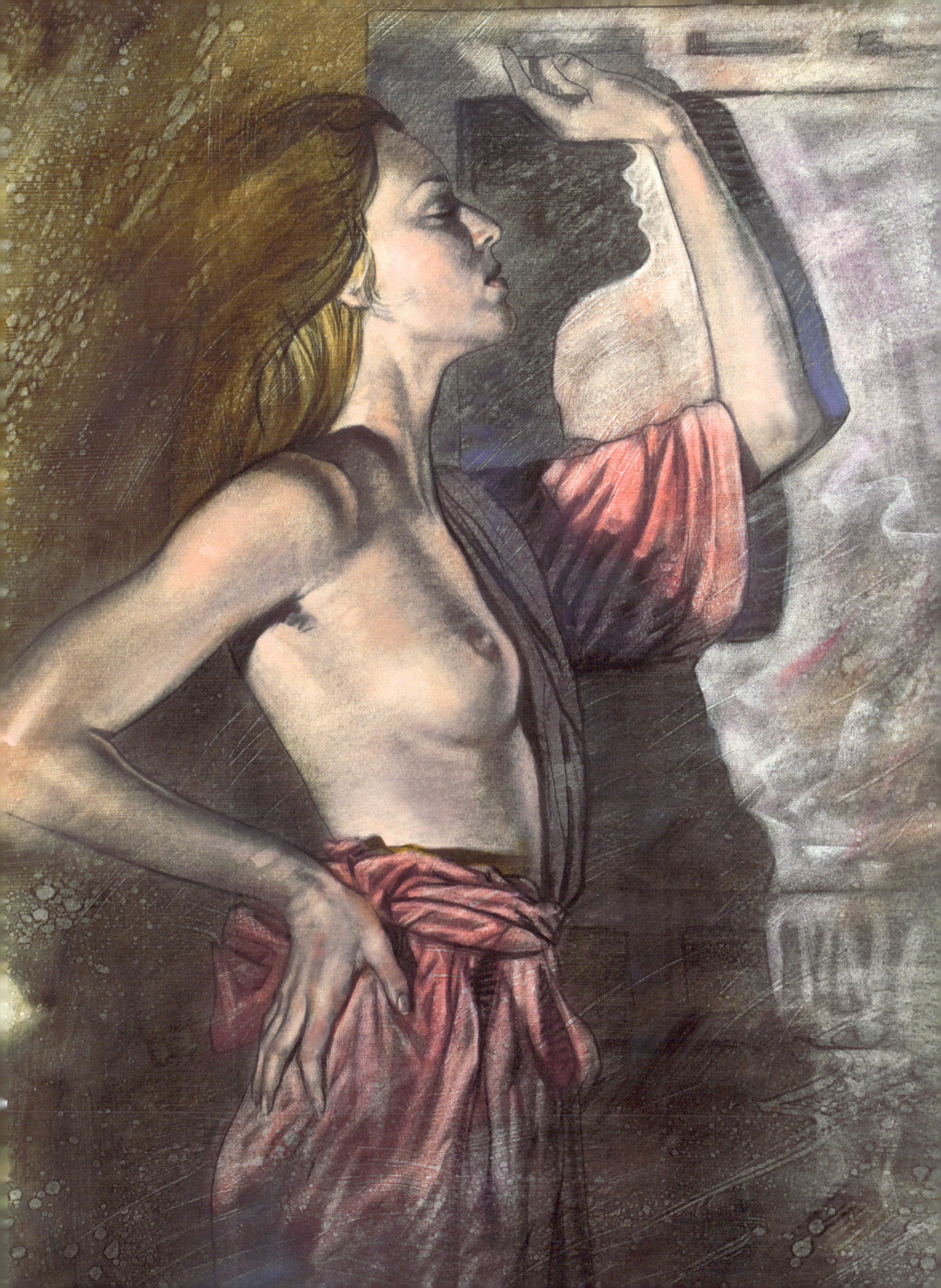

Back in high school, I realized the value of seeing professional artists' work. Much of my free time was spent in the library, reading up on as many techniques as I could find on illustrators like Rockwell, Parrish, and many others. I have learned from everyone, and still do, especially from students, who refresh my fundamental knowledge. The day I stop learning is probably when I stop experimenting, as each piece is something of a curious technical adventure in content, design, and paint application.

I feel we're all here to learn. So much of realistic oil painting comes from experience, sometimes trial and error, whatever it takes to get the vision realized. The concept, emotion, drive and energy it demands must come from each artist. Concerning technique, I hope these demonstration pages will help give insight to my own approach and a reflection of a narrative voice interpreted through paint.

AT THE GATE

4 hour study

22x30" Oil on heavy canvas (p. 67)

This 3 hour preliminary study was done for the larger painting 'At the Gate' (p. 40-43). For most studies, I paint more loosely than on my final work because there are no real restrictions. I have fun with the paint and can usually knock out a study in just a few hours, shooting for the overall feeling I will later invest in the larger work.

I usually start with a simple line drawing that I sketch out in pencil and then copy to a size that will fit into an opaque projector. Sometimes I draw directly onto the canvas with charcoal or light pencil, but my most accurate line comes from a bristle flat with either heavy paint, or just enough stiff paint to allow me to drag the brush in a quick drybrush manner. My goal is to get the line on as quickly as I can so that my momentum carries into the sketch.

Here I have used a heavy weight of cotton canvas. Despite what you may have heard, cotton canvas lasts just as long as linen, according to the conservators. Linen can cause buckling problems in moist climates. I usually use an acrylic-primed ground unless I want a smoother, oil primed surface. I always lightly sand the gesso before doing any drawing, then lightly fix it once or twice before painting.

I like rough canvas for some studies because it grabs heavier paint and pushes me to explore brushwork that would be otherwise hard to achieve. In general, if you want to do smooth, clean-edged work, consider a thinner weave of canvas or add more layers of gesso before painting. The finest canvas is portrait linen, but it is quite expensive.

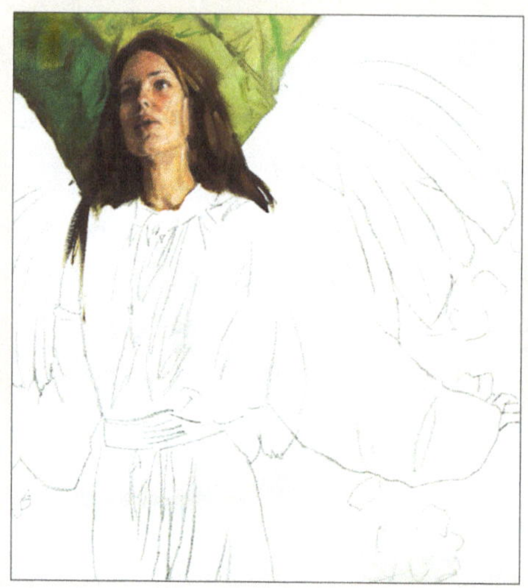

I immediately build up paint around the face and keep the thick strokes free and loose. Basically, I block it out, then pull the paint with smaller strokes to refine the underlying paint.

Most of the initial block-in was done with bristle flats for larger areas and bristle rounds to drag into those big areas to soften edges by scratching with the tip. I often draw with a clean tip, as you can see in the eye detail on the far right. The strokes for the hair are laid on quickly with drawn lines of solid color over the thick wet paint beneath.

If I used a sable or small brush at this stage, I would start fussing with the piece and that's not at all what the study is for. I get the paint on fast and finish in a few hours, then put it aside and let it dry, turning it away from me so I am not inclined to go back and give it details that it really doesn't need. In other words, I don't want to overwork it with fussy details and smooth strokes where the quality of the study is lost.

Some artists intentionally leave areas with a sketchy look, as in the wings here. I have to admit, it does give the work a feeling of carefree, effortless facility, but I try to not get too thoughtful about forcing that look. It can easily begin to look very artificial, as if painted for gallery sales and not for learning from. I prefer not to think about it at all and just paint, especially on these quick pieces.

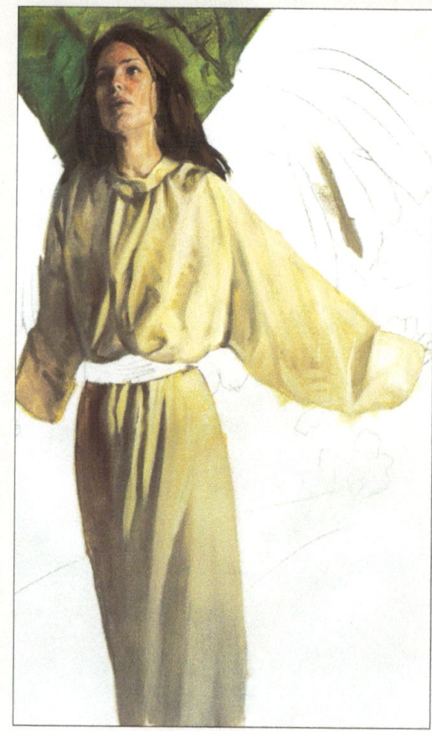

On some studies I don't use a drawing. I just block color in and refine it as I progress to realistic edges and values. After many years of painting tight illustration work, I had to retrain myself to loosen up for better overall effect with much more life to my figures, clothing, and backgrounds. I still have to occasionally remind myself that the look I want is painterly and not overly tight. If work is overpainted and too realistic or finessed, it looks stiff and boring to me, so I force myself to let go and try to maintain the realism that I enjoy seeing happen as the painting progresses.

For many years, to do this was a psychological block for me. I just didn't want my work to look that loose. Even though I often painted quickly and with some flair, I would go back in and clean up the edges. I know my painting improved after I spent years doing freehand figure work, like life drawing and sketching, which gave me the confidence that I could put down opaque paint and know that I can correct it as I refine it. Now, it's easier and more enjoyable to just paint loosely and not worry about losing some of the realism if the overall effect is a more interesting look or design.

It really helps me to think of my studies as quick, fun experiments to learn from, and my larger finals as more finished statements with a refined look.

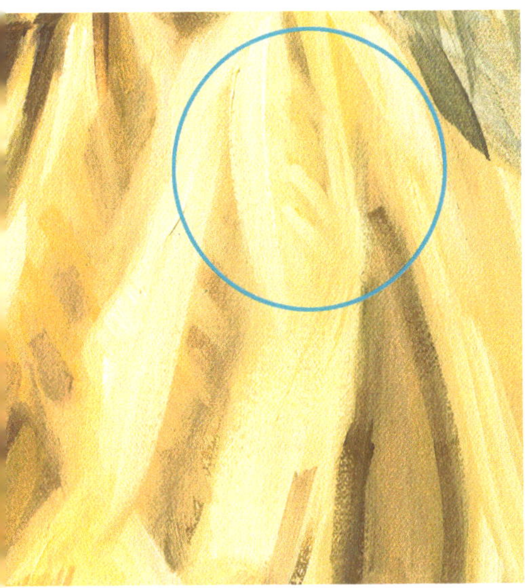

Directional Strokes- In the circles, you can see how well-placed strokes of oil paint follow the natural form of the hair and eye areas. It helps to put the paint down in directional strokes as this can further suggest a solid form beneath the skin.

Sometimes, the direction is hard to see, especially in smoother areas such as the model's cheek. Life drawing can help you see how light wraps around every part of the figure and any solid object in space.

Experiment with oil paint enough to learn how easy it is to find these natural guides. I can always smear the paint out or work over it if it's not right, since oil paint takes much longer to dry than other mediums. Knowing I can work with the edges of wet paint allows me the freedom to get the effects I like for faces and figure work.

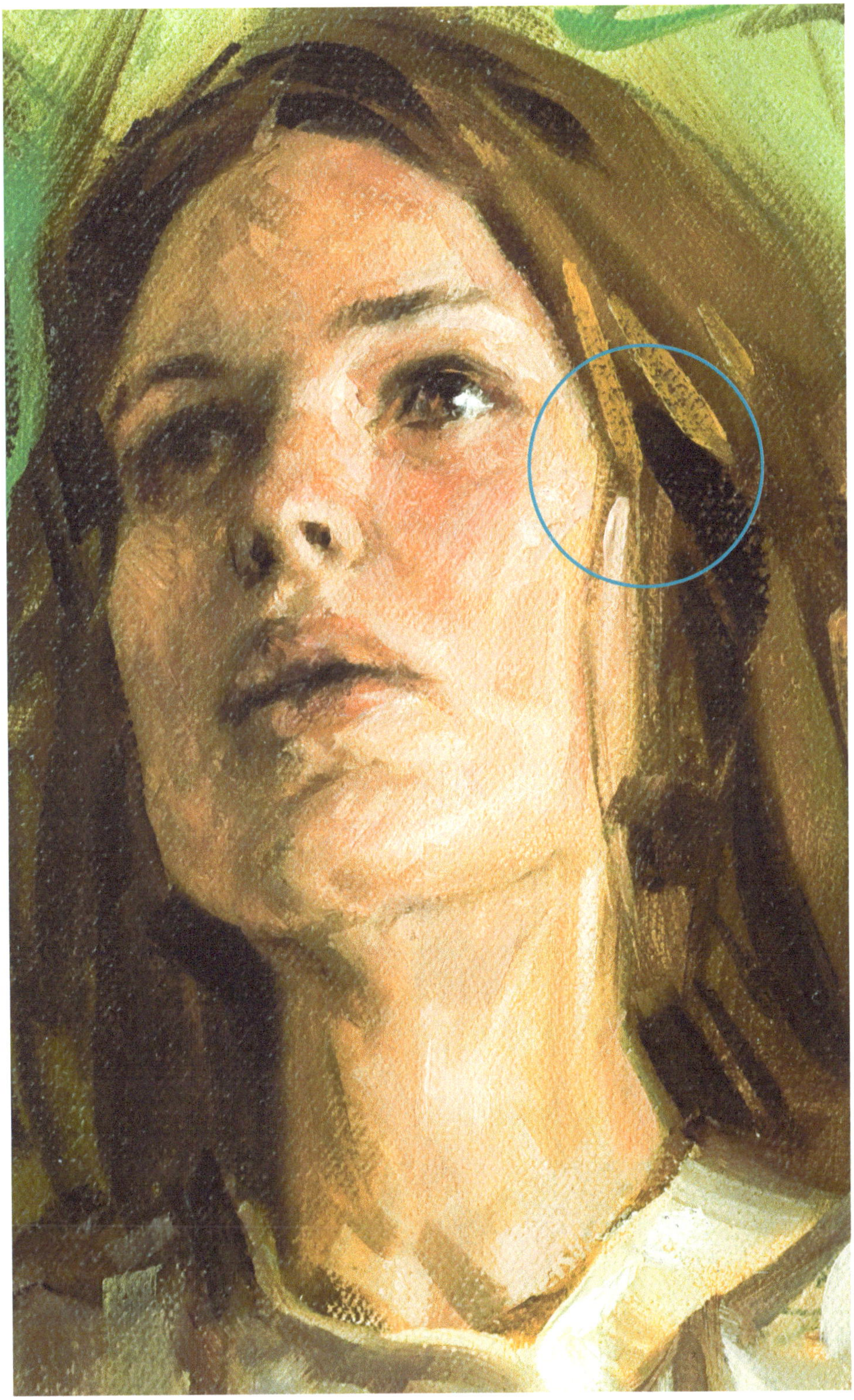

Right- an oversized shot of the final face. A lot of students have trouble mixing skin tones without making them muddy or off-color. Here's a good formula for a Caucasian skin tone base - mix a bit of yellow ocher into a small amount of white. I only use titanium white because of its mixing strength and clean color. Add to this off-white mixture a little cadmium red light or medium until the pile begins to flesh up in color. Add the red in small amounts as its covering power is pretty strong. A common mistake students make is to add too much red and then try to compensate by adding more ocher and white, ending up with a large pile.

If it's too red, add blue or gray in smaller amounts. If too orange, add a bit of deeper red, like crimson. Blue will neutralize this mixture and I often use green or a greenish gray to dull the color for some shadow areas.

Skin color varies as much as its light source, so study it closely for accurate transitions and density. A cooler background, as in midday light, usually cools the shadows as much as the light areas. Under warmer sunlight, such as in late afternoon, the color of the shadows can often go toward the complementary (blues, purple tones), while indoor warm light, like standard tungsten or candle light, has deeper warm shadows with little reflected cool light.

Studying photography can tell you a lot, but to get the best color tone that looks natural, especially in lighter skin, you can see much more color from life study. Since I often make up much of my skin color, I usually key it to the background tone. Here, the green is dominant, so the shadows have just a touch of green in them. I don't want to add too much or it will make the figure look sickly and artificial.

The Tranquil Sea

48x58" Oil on stretched canvas (p.44-47)

This piece was fairly clear in my mind long before I started the painting. Sometimes I do get images that just jump into my head, like music or a story concept. At other times, I have to sketch an idea out several times until I can get it beyond the abstract. Either way, I can see it in my mind and note it by doing a quick rough.

I like the subtle tones in this piece, and the boat sets a mysterious mood. The fog, of course, dulls the atmospheric effects down to a gray so that the overall values are more haunting and ethereal.

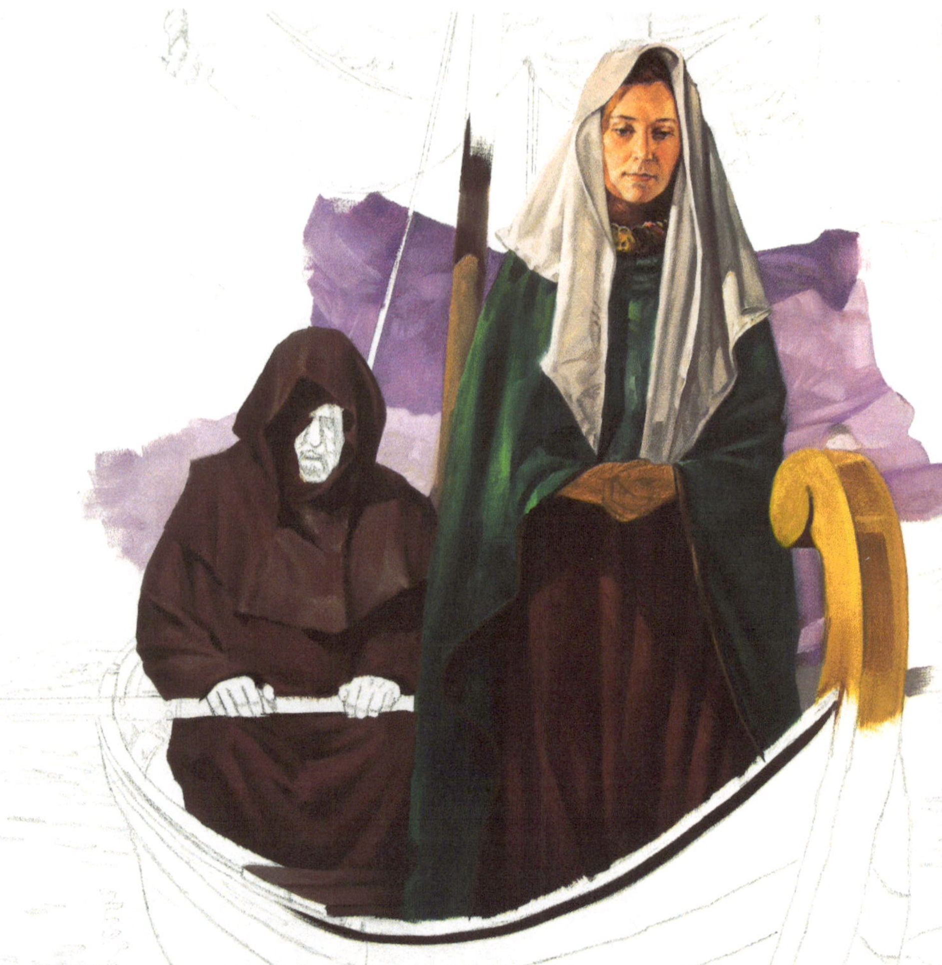

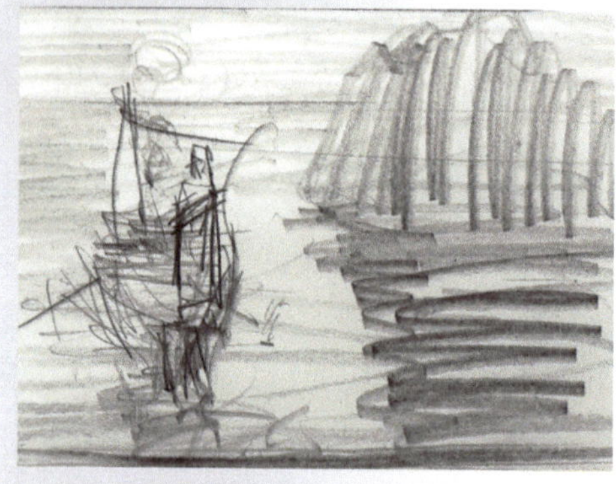

Above, the rough sketch. I remember the image came to me when I was sitting in a restaurant and I immediately sketched it out onto a scrap of paper.

Below, the pencil drawing I did to project onto my canvas.

My usual approach for large pieces is to block in sections with quick, accurate middle values and then refine the wet edges as I move around the piece. For accurate color, it's a good idea to cover the entire canvas with paint first, getting rid of the white gesso areas, so that it's easier to evaluate relative color. When you paint each small section first and leave white canvas showing next to the paint, the tendency is to paint too light because the white makes the paint look darker. Once you fill in the surrounding white, the early color will often look off. Even a simple wash of local color or using a gray-toned gesso will make it easier to match color throughout the painting process.

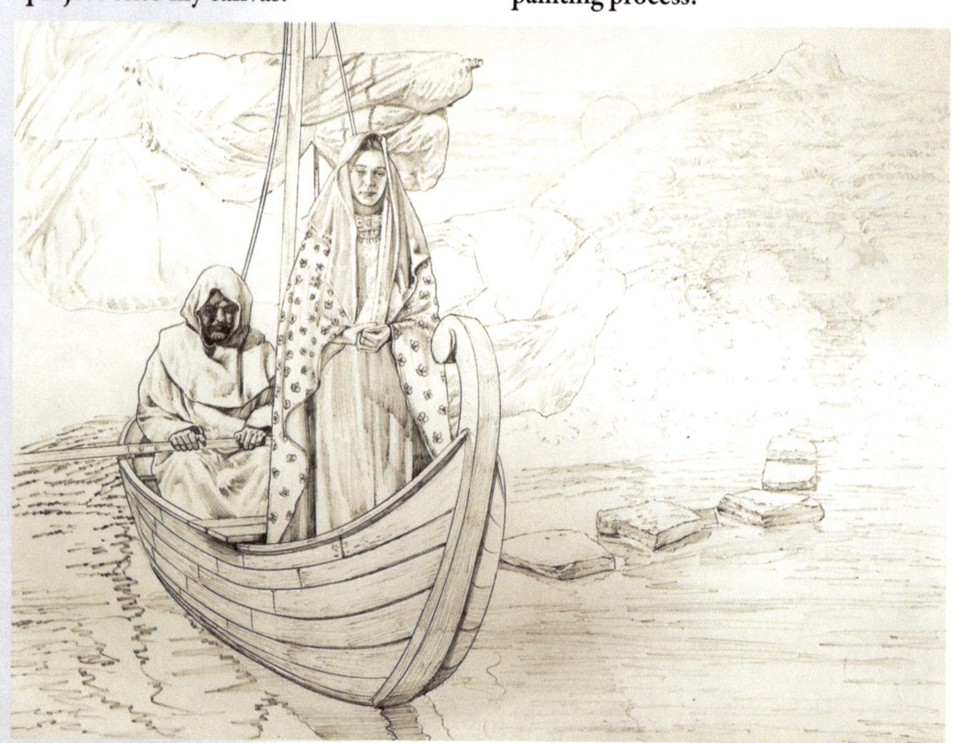

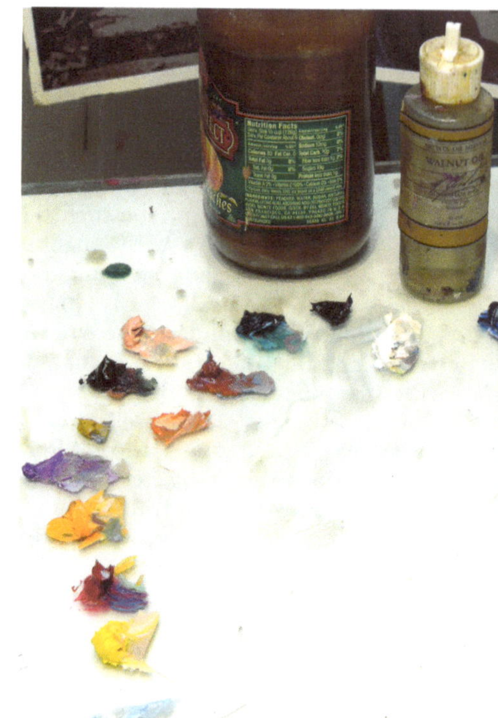

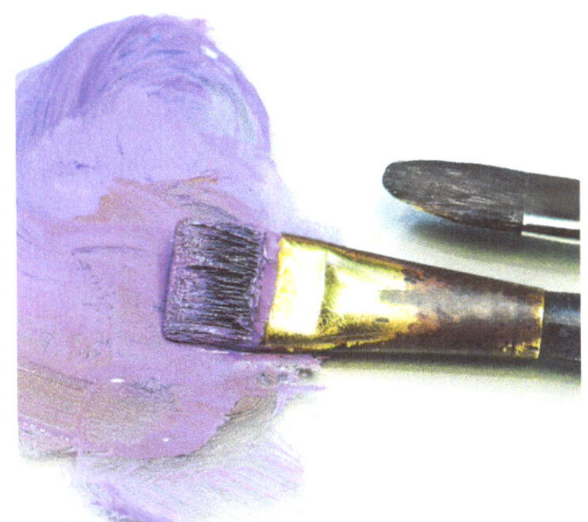

For the purple-toned background of the cloth, the palette above shows the mixture I used to gray down the violet and blue hues. I added a bit of burnt sienna to offset the cool color and tried not to over-mix on the palette, preferring to see the colors melt together as I laid out the strokes on the canvas.

Above right, the base purple tone of the cloth, the sky, and the ocher sail are all laid in quickly. Then the edges are tweaked and softened, here and there, and I let it dry. I tried not to overwork these base tones so that I could concentrate on the picture as a whole.

Below, my typical palette setup. I use a large glass sheet mounted to a white or gray board.

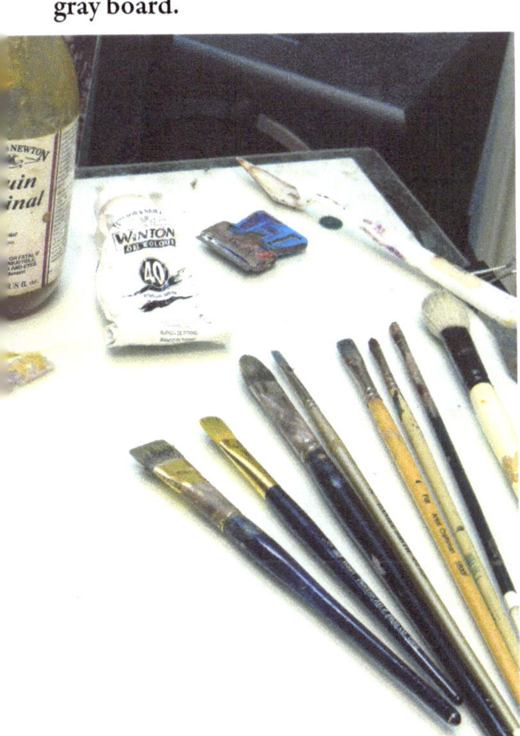

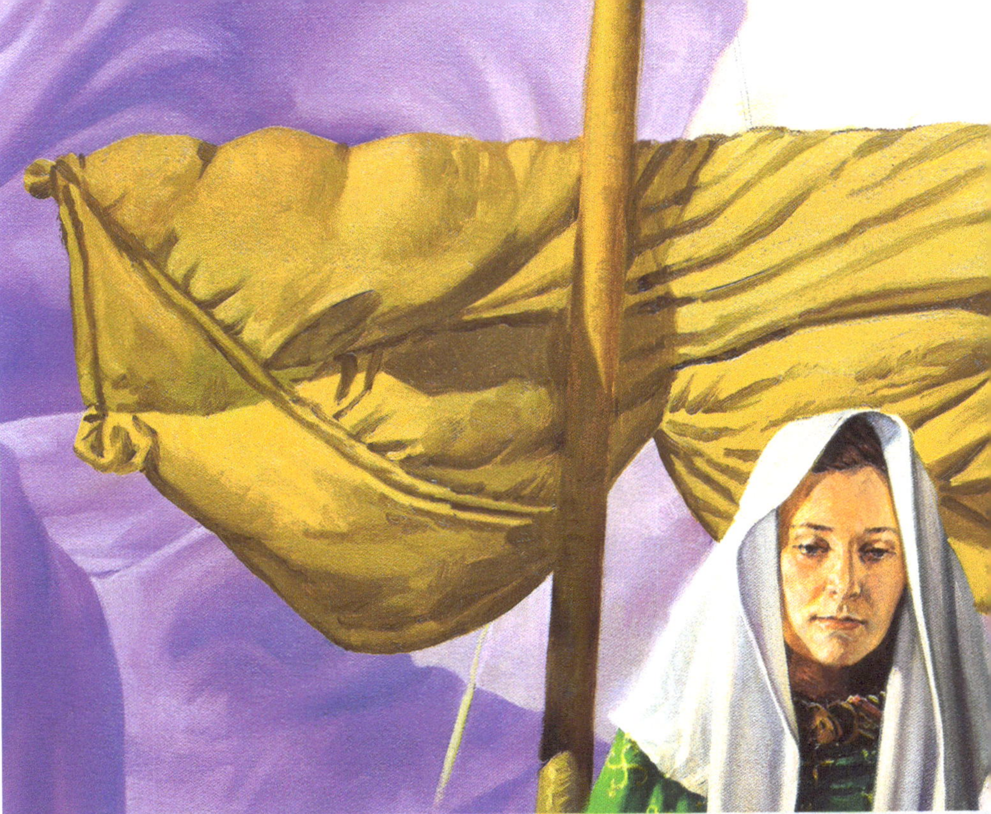

Above, the base sail color is a flat ocher, one of my favorite hues because it's a solid middle tone and very opaque. I added some burnt umber to darken the shadow areas, looking for blocky shapes. Next I added white into the ocher for some quick middle value lights, trying to keep the forms pretty basic.

Below, you can see the white areas of the sail and the cowl. Once this dried, I could easily glaze darker over this for a rich final look.

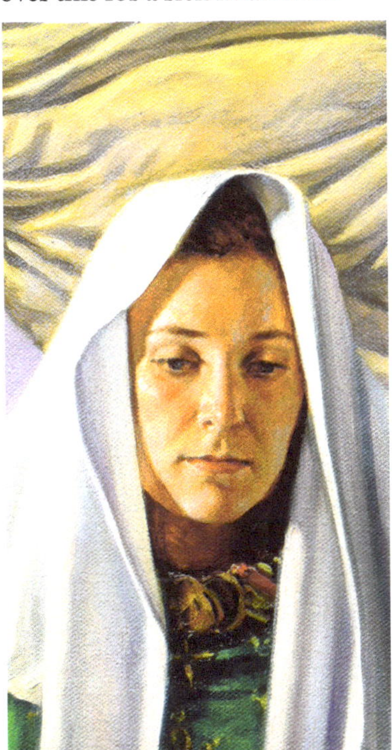

When I render hands, as in the example below, I try to keep in mind the tapered look of most female hands versus a blocky, almost squarish look for most male hands. A good bristle round will help draw out the basic shape- cylinders for fingers. Try not to think beyond this flat middle tone. Get the shape and drawing accurate and then paint the darker middle tones and next the lighter middle tones. Only after you have the hands looking solid just with the middle values should you add the highlights and shadows with a smaller round, even a sable, to accent the drawing and lift each finger off the underlying form.

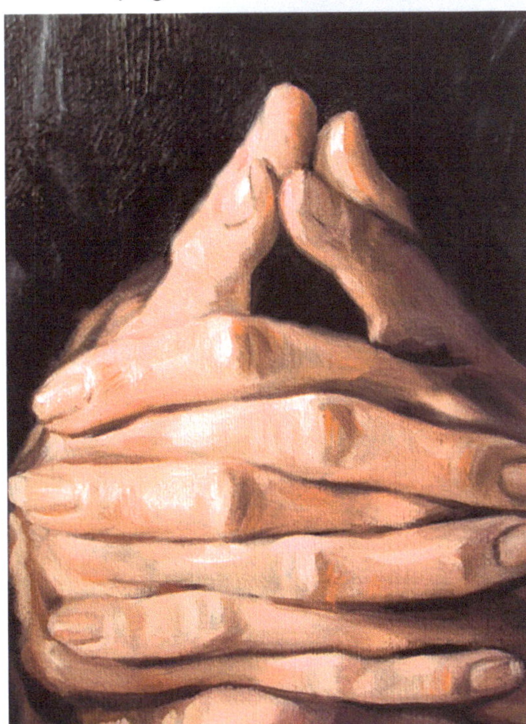

On the right, the boat and figures are just blocked in. I wanted to get the background green tone worked out before I concentrated on foreground edges and accurate color. Since the background hill is covered in a misty, dreamlike fog, I painted this area easily by working grayed down purplish tones right into the wet green and then pulling the paint into each area. Note that by using the sky color to tone down the background hills, this distances them, creating atmosphere. You can apply this effect to any landscape. I also used it to drop back the cloth and other elements throughout this piece, as you can see on the final, page 45.

There are times when I want the oil paint to stay wet for days, and other times when I want it to dry quickly. I can't always plan for this because I can only guess where I will go with made up backgrounds like these and I am never sure how long it will take. It's completely different from having a photo or a live model in front of you where you are guided by what's there, however stylized. I have done both, but for narrative work that has invented areas, like the boat, the land, the woman's patterned costume, and especially the water area, I just have to do a lot of logical guesswork to bring the painting to a convincingly realistic conclusion.

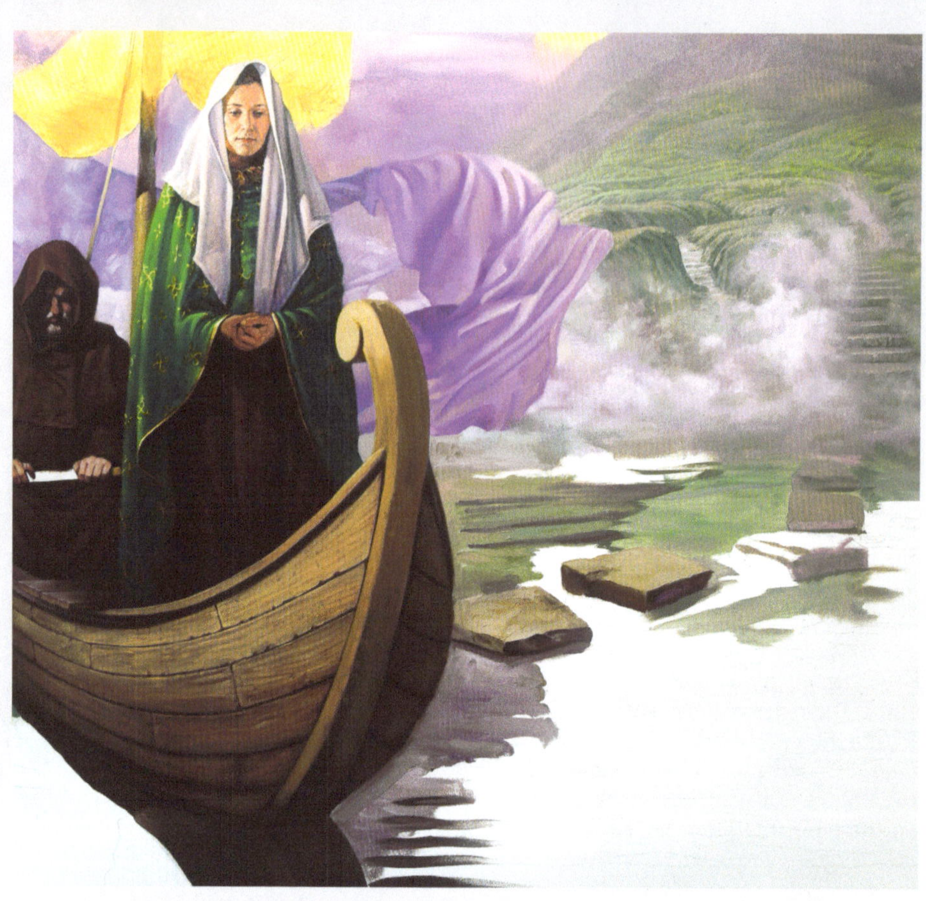

Block in of the background, above, and block in of the water, below.

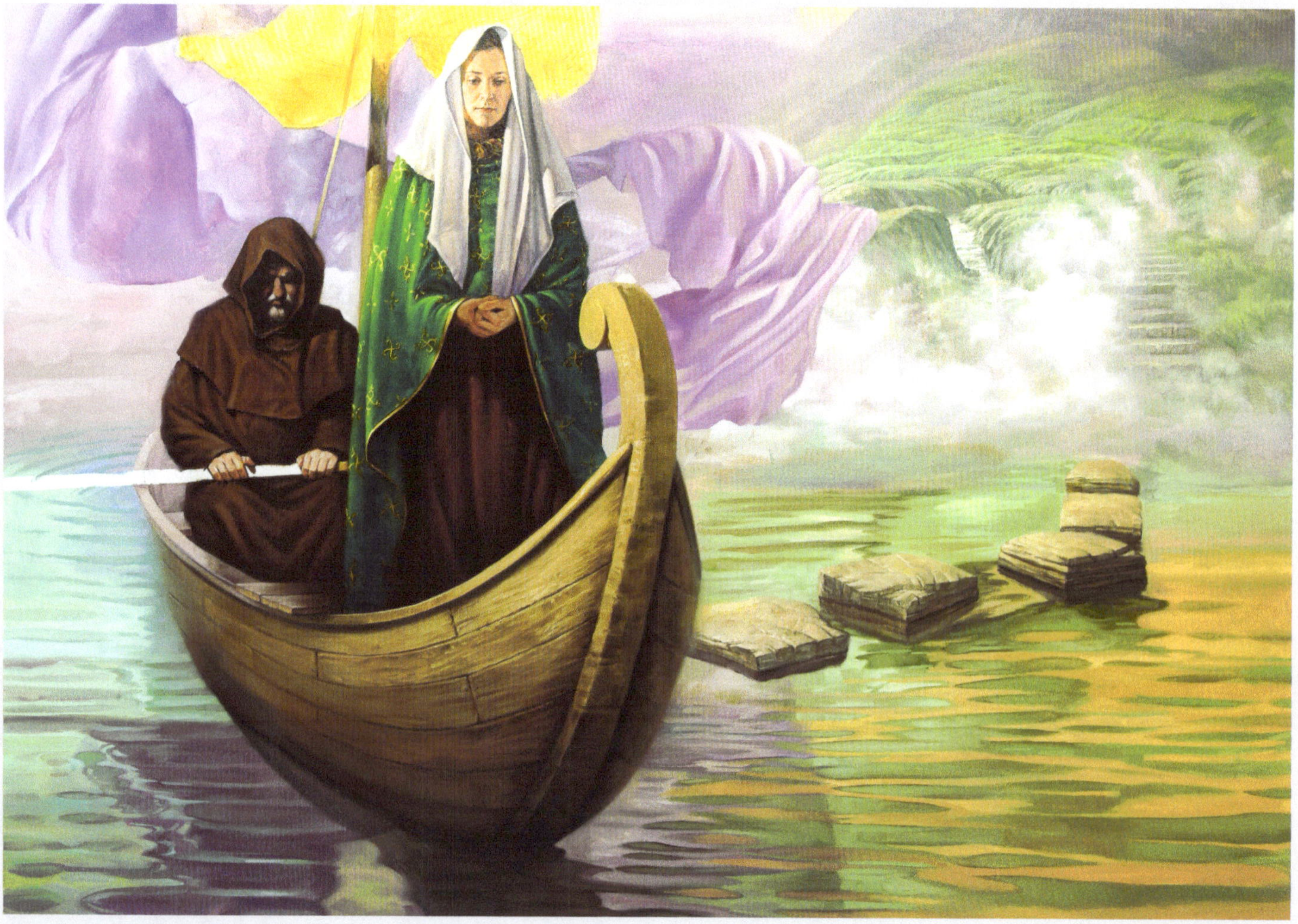

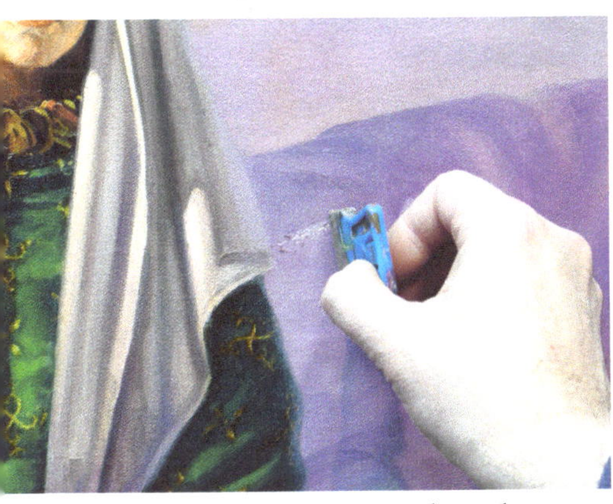

Above, if I get into an area where the paint build up is simply too heavy and I don't want to fight it as I redraw with color, I scrape off the caked oil with a dulled razor blade, taking care to keep the sharp end perpendicular to the canvas.

The lower left image shows the early stage of the rocks and the image below shows another color combination. I try to find a good base for the fog, guessing now and then, since I am making up this area. Once I feel the water has a nice surface look, reflecting the sky and boat, then I can relax a bit and start blending a few edges so that the area settles back to fit the image as a whole- not just nice water with a boat stuck on it. Everything should be harmonious for good tonal painting or some edges and colors will stand out and contrast poorly with the rest of the image.

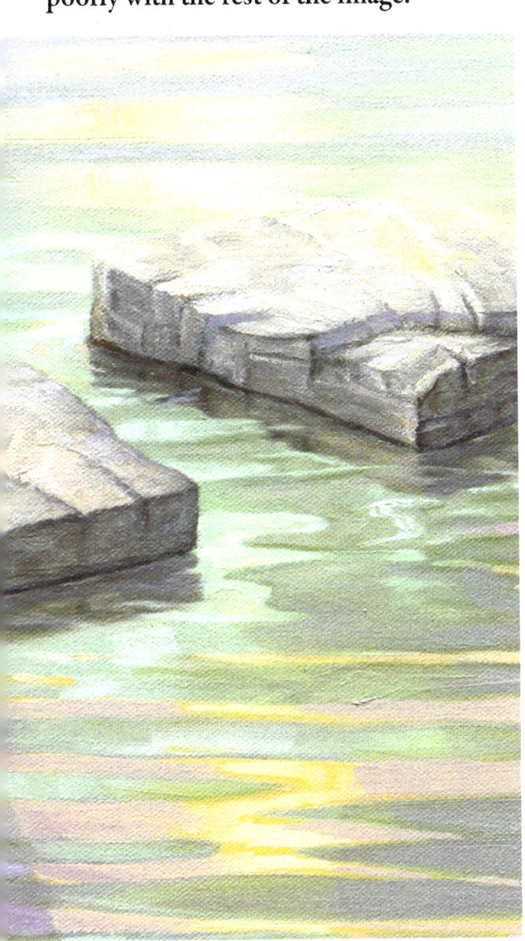

Right- To fade the water back and begin the fog, which will help set the boat upon the sea, I first covered the water area with a translucent green to kill the reds and unify the coloring, essentially graying down the underlying area. I added some Liquin medium to speed up the drying time and keep the color from going matte.

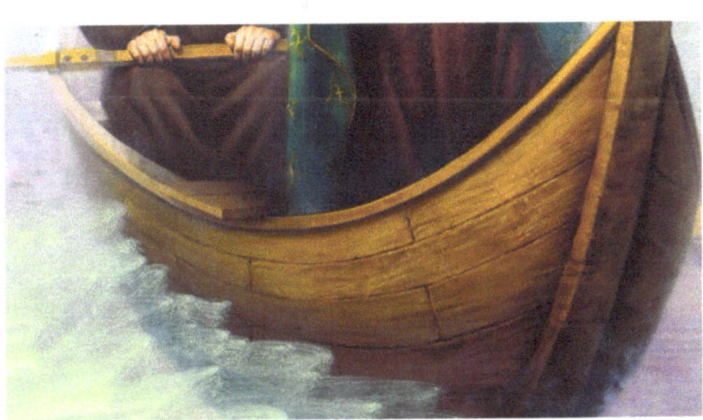

After the green set up and the paint became a little stiff, I dropped in strokes of opaque off-white, swirling the strokes with a wide bristle filbert. Again, I was guessing what to do and how far to take it, but logically I assumed the fog would be lighter and would create little misty swirls around the boat's hull, so I tried that first.

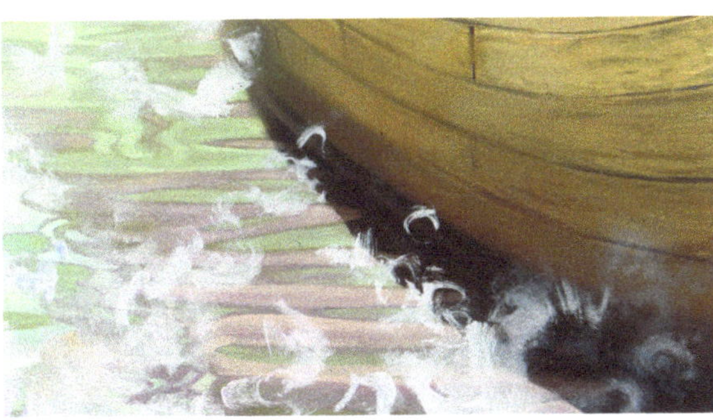

Next, I took a soft mop brush and smoothed out the curly strokes, then used a clean rag and pulled out some of the semi-opaque mist so that the boat would softly show through. I did this a few times until I had the look I wanted, but if it hadn't worked, I would have just smeared everything out and started over with the green mist.

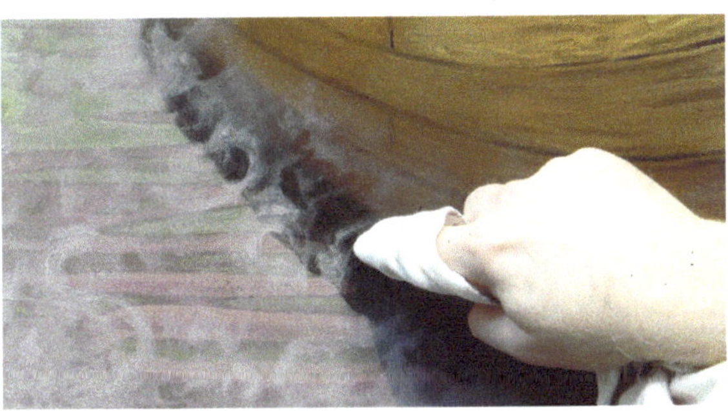

This fourth stage shows another pass with a bigger soft brush, in this case, a house painter's 3 inch brush, to drag over the stiffening paint. Once it gets tacky like this, I have to work really fast and the bigger the brush, the faster I work. Scratching at the swirls shifted the color just a touch until it started to suggest a believable fog layer.

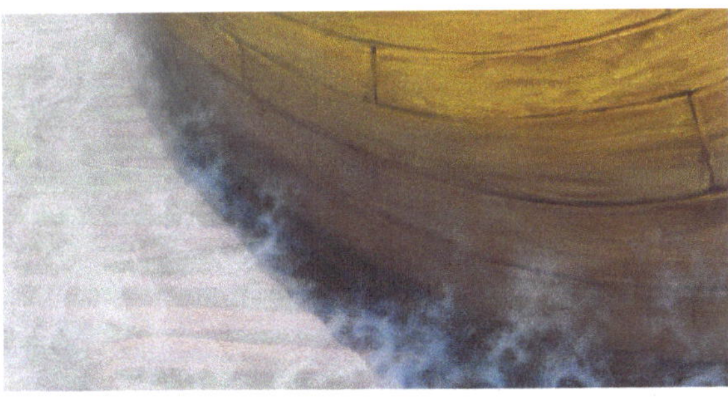

Lower right image, from the final (p.44-47) Note that the darker hull was glazed down a bit, which rounded it off some and set it into the water properly, allowing the soft fog swirls to come forward a little more. I also glazed some light purplish-gray over the entire water, just to push it back and make the fog seem believable.
All these stages combined resulted in the final look. I suppose I could have done this area another way, seeing it now in its final state. But when you make up areas like this, there's nothing to look at, so it's usually best to work in stages so you don't have to fight heavy paint layers in case changes need to be made.

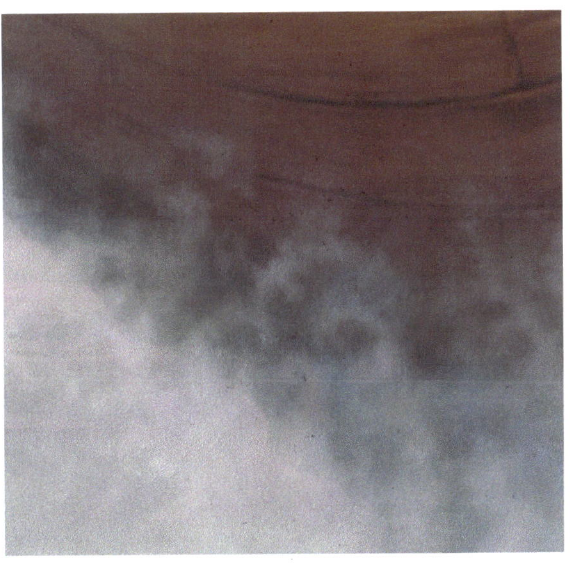

CAVERNA MAGICA

45x70" Oil on smooth canvas (p. 20-23)

This idea started from a recent trip where I saw the background tree lit up at night. The rest evolved from my imagination and a rough sketch that I transferred to canvas, see right.

This is a large piece. I wanted to try smooth canvas and keep the drawing pretty loose by using just black over my ocher ground, drawing the piece out freehand by using a bristle round. An advantage to larger work is that I can play with the spacing a bit. The feel of the larger brushes makes a big difference in the amount of opaque paint I can control.

I love painting landscapes of the Southwest. I have always had an affinity for the rocks and buttes there and have studied them enough to know the shape and coloring I like to employ in some of my work. In the background of this piece, I wanted to convey dusk or an early night scene with the last light shimmering over the top half of the distant hillside. I have seen this many times and it's always a remarkable sight. The coloring takes on a rosy glow in the warm tones and the shadows fall into soft purples and rich blues.

Since this setting is idyllic, I take liberties with color, shadows, and light, using the lines of the background shapes to force the viewer's eye back to the right, where the Angel is.

The vertical tree brings your eye back down from the top. Even the angle of the large left branch is aimed toward the figure, with the top area darker so that it fuses more with the background sky.

I knew I wanted a simple moon above that surreal waterfall and tried several different things but this low crescent was the only position that seemed to work, and even then I had to tone it down quite a bit so that it didn't stand out and jump forward in the frame.

So much of my work is experimental, especially at this rough-in stage, but that's what makes it so rewarding.

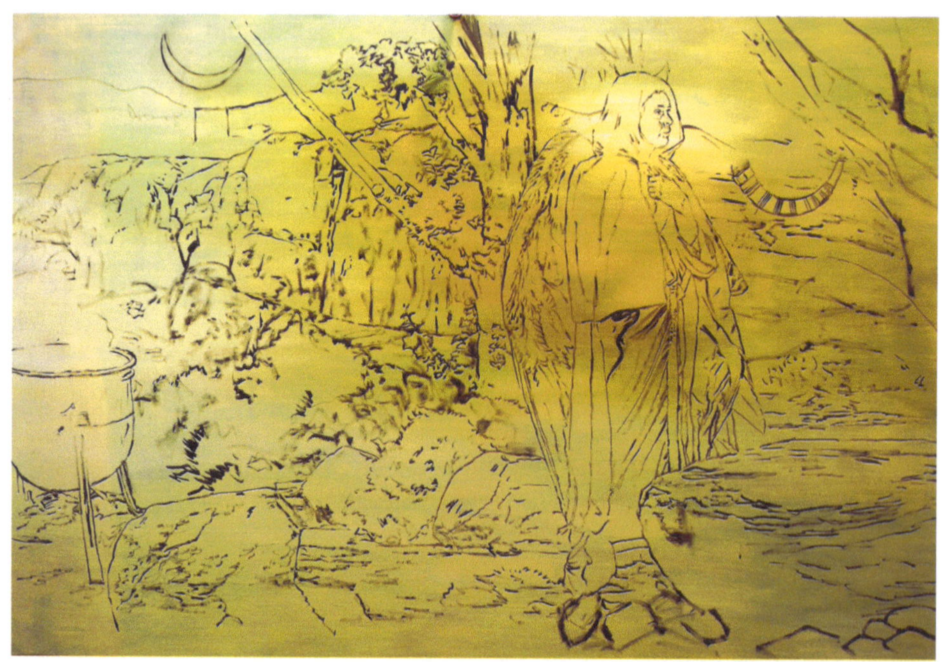

Above- A rough line drawing using alkyd black was used to loosely draw in the basic shapes. I prefer a bristle filbert or round brush with opaque paint that is thinned just enough to stroke out easily, but not so thin as to run down the canvas or show gray areas. I want the line to work for me, not to work over gray half-tones.

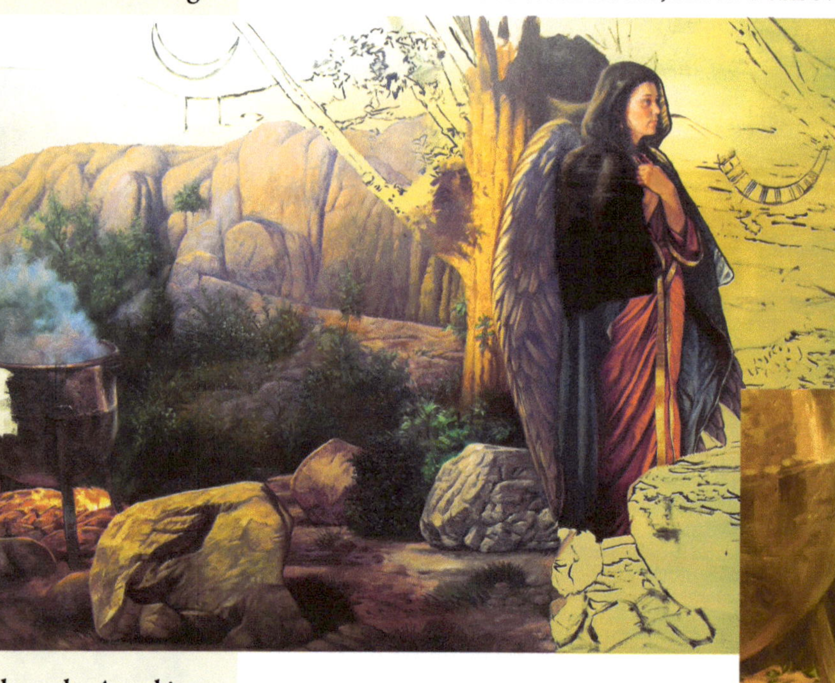

After working out the basic figure, I blocked in the left side to set the overall mood. Because of my illustration background, I've learned to work very quickly. Once the overall distance is roughed in, I smooth out edges and move on, knowing I can always return to refine areas.

To the right, note the basic block in of masses for the rocky foreground. This has more of a 'painterly' feel to it. It's a look that I'm sure some would think is more artistically in tune with advanced work. But I like the realism that I get by refining areas of wet paint like this. Without convincing realism, I don't feel that the image that is in my head is sufficiently rendered out to a satisfying degree. To me, this is more like study work, not finished art, but that is just my preference. I like all kinds of styles and respect any work that has something to say and is well handled.

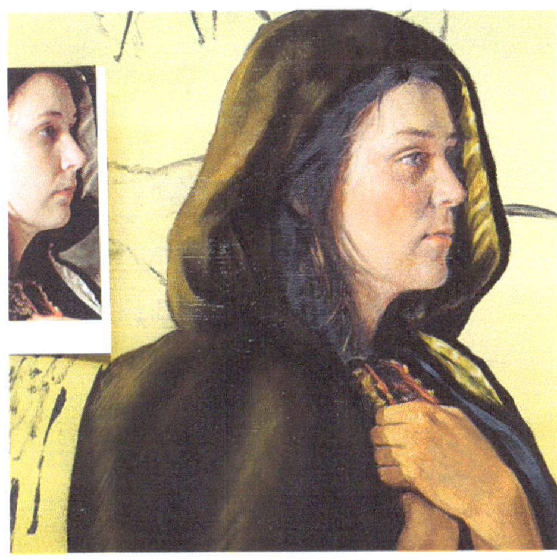

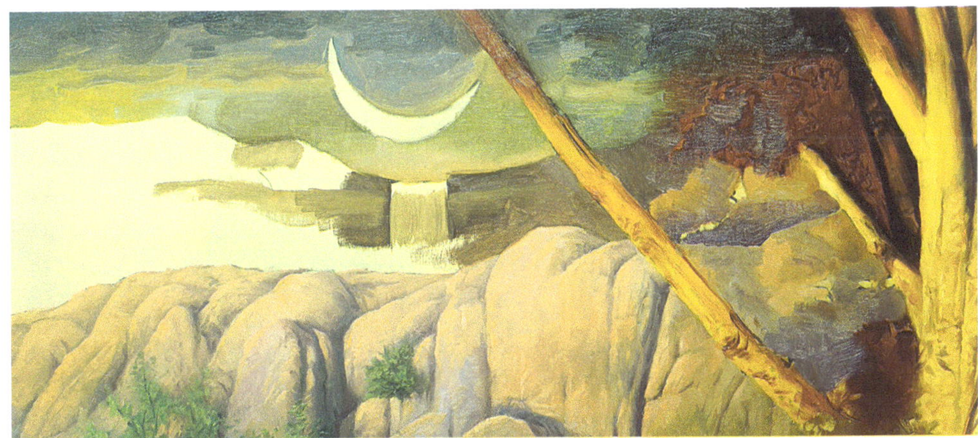

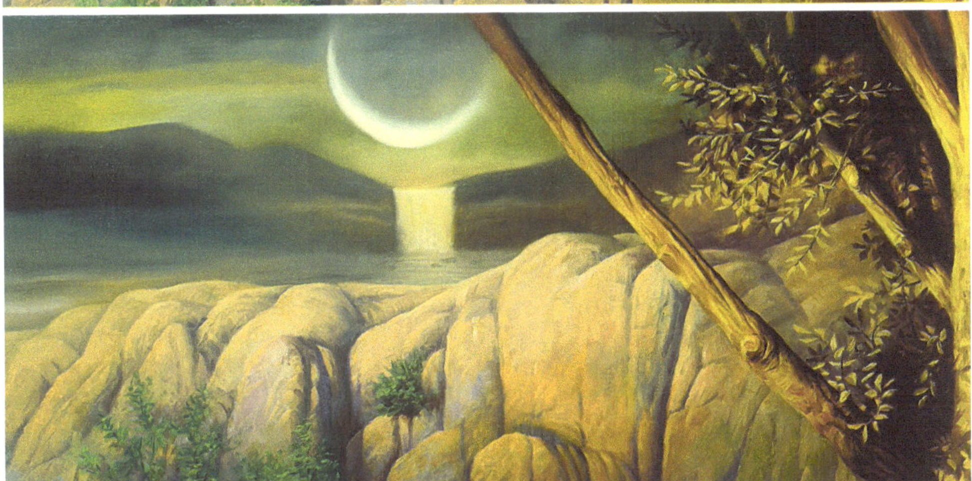

Good models are essential to my work, as is true with most realists. It is rare to find models who fall into naturally graceful poses. The little girl that posed for Far Below, on pages 4-7, simply moved into the light and held the pose long enough for me to shoot my reference photos. I want a guide to work from, but not to copy exactly, or the work will look stiff. My intention is to be creative, inventive, and not to copy photos or be a slave to a model standing before me as I paint.

Studies are fine and academic, but for my finished work, I try to open up my mind to a more spiritual connection with the image as it develops on the canvas.

Below, a close-up shot of my block-in stage for the foreground area and a few minutes later, to the right, as I begin to refine it just a bit, drawing into the wet paint and sculpting the masses. This stage is always fun and I am often tempted to leave it, but sometimes I want to see how far I can push the painterly realism.

Top, the sky area is quickly blocked in with heavy color and then, above, buffed out a bit on the smooth canvas. For the final stages, I went back in and tweaked a few edges and then color glazed or tinted to create the mood I wanted. (See final on page 21)

It's fascinating to watch how softened edges can suddenly make a dead area come to life, as in the tops of the mountains or the edge of the moon.

Lower right circle, you can see a color test, a glaze of burnt sienna over the ocher base. Once the middle values are down, I can drop color over these areas and test how far I can enrich the image, trying not to make it look gaudy or like an illustration. I'm after luminous color, not hot glaring effects, which look amateurish and fake. I glaze light to dark, but you can also 'glaze' lighter by using more opaque hues and the right medium, creating a fog-like result.

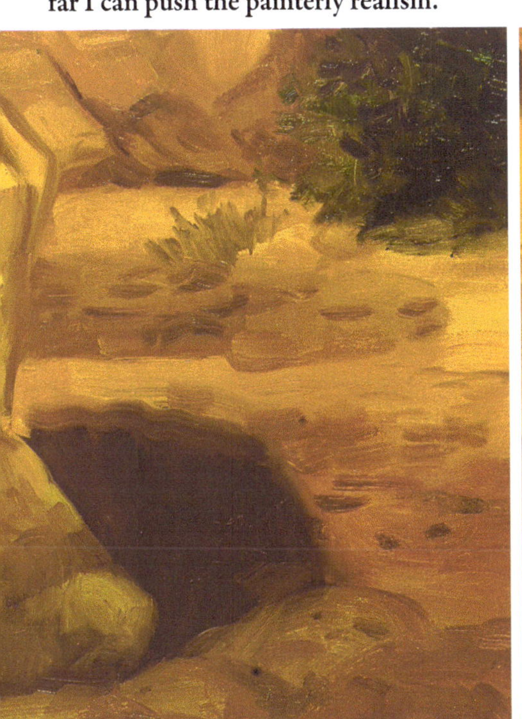

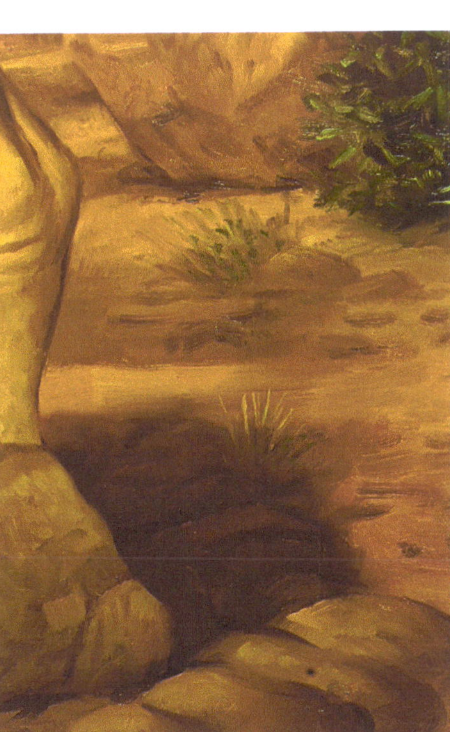

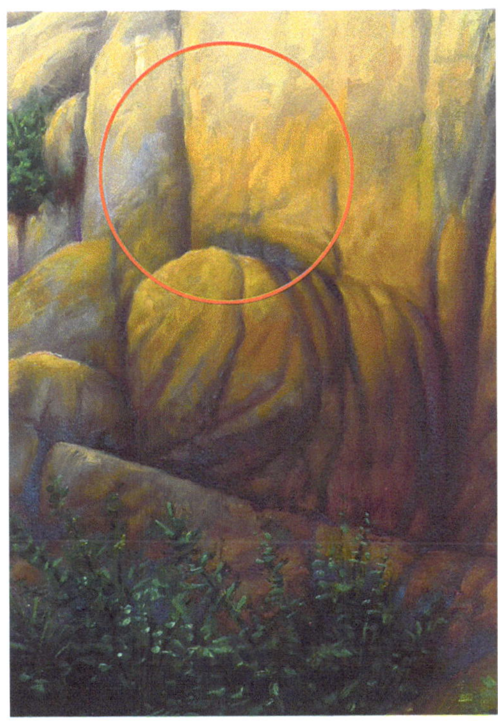

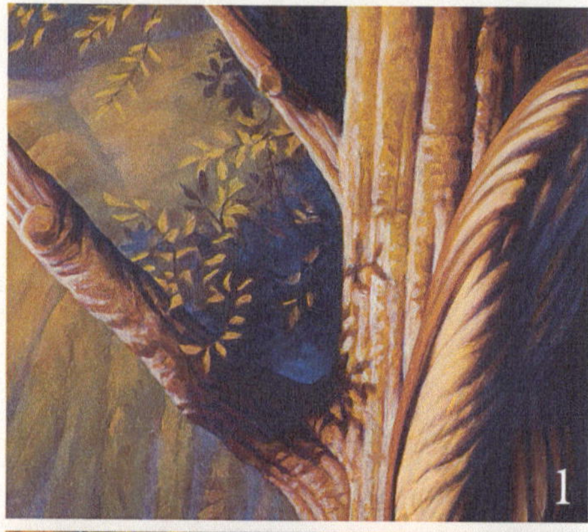

1

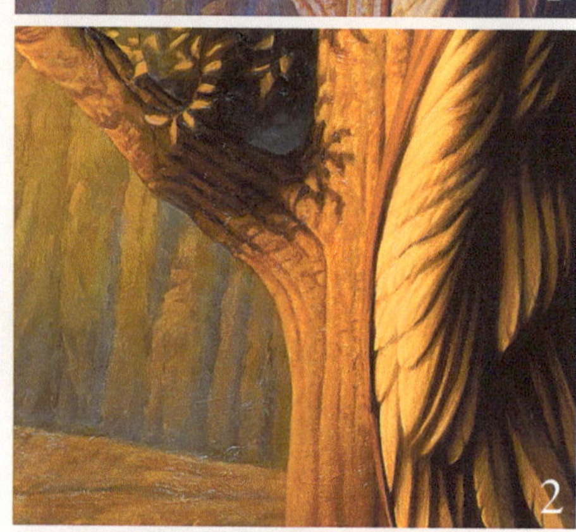

2

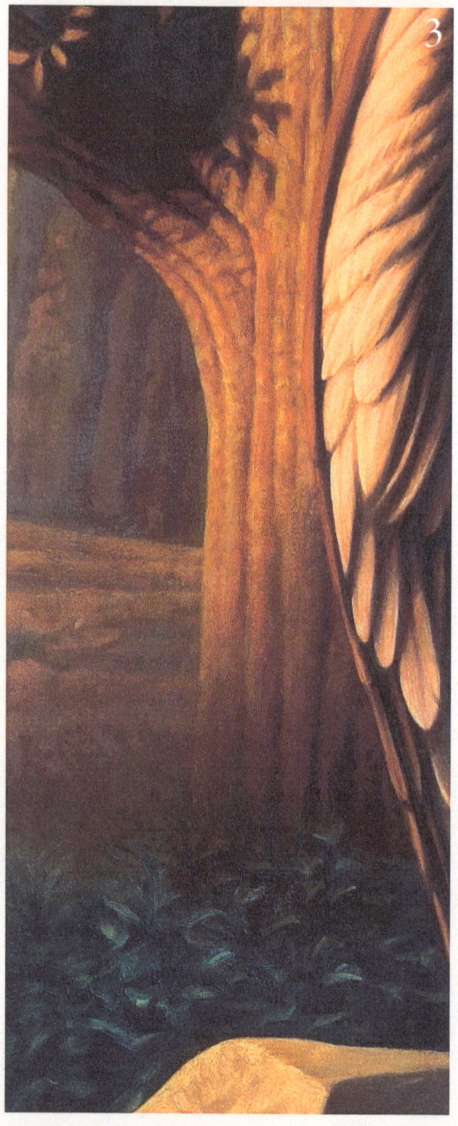

3

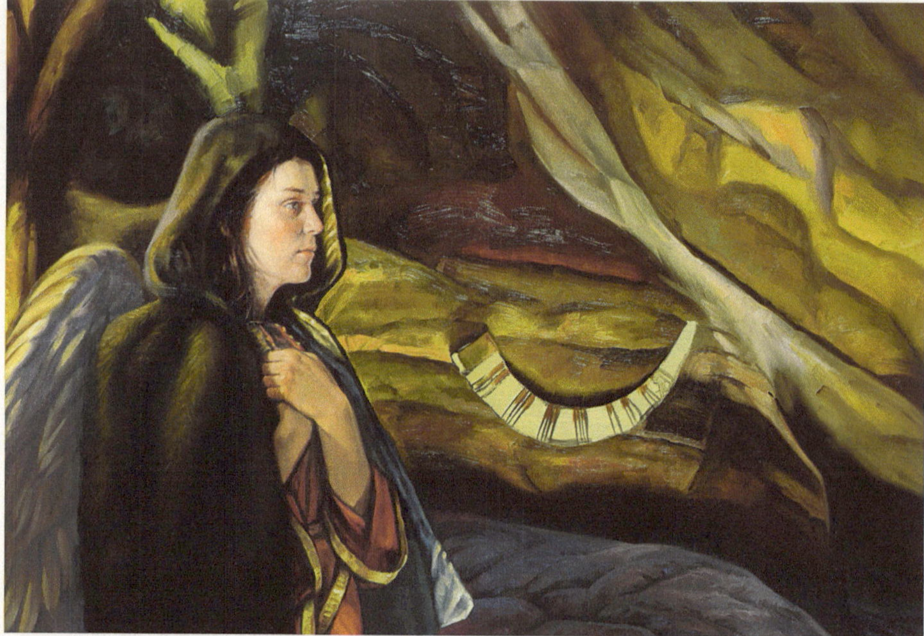

Left, three stages of the tree area. 1, the block-in stage, basic color, drawing, and reshaping of the tree with opaque paint that I let dry while I worked on other areas. Note the white edges that I later glazed over with semi-opaque color for stage 2. The lower left image, 3, shows the same area but with the final darker values, toned down to unify the painting. I used to prefer more contrast, as in the middle image, but now I try to refine areas to what I feel is a more sophisticated final look or mood by controlling subtle color shifts.

Above, the right side of the painting was quickly blocked in with heavy color and then the paint was pulled in the direction of the rock forms using an extra long bristle flat that is much softer than a normal bristle brush. Pulling one area into another sounds like it will just get muddy, but with some practice you can control the edges and color easily. I put down a lighter value and then glazed the dry base. This rich effect isn't possible with opaque color alone because it becomes a patina-like luminous oil finish.

Below, notice the white rock and compare it to the final on page 21. This was my first attempt and it looks too busy and out of character to the rest of the rocks and the landscape supporting it. The reason it is lighter than the final is in how I was preparing it, at this rough stage, for the more translucent color that would be applied in the final rendering. Sometimes, areas of paintings may not feel right. I don't know if that's artistic instinct or just common sense. It's like the wrong chord in music. To leave it would mean I didn't push the image enough. When I returned to that area, I scraped off the dry paint and blocked in a simple rock shape, making up a smoother rock to fit the image. In this way, I control the image and am not trapped by logic or reference to achieve believable realism.

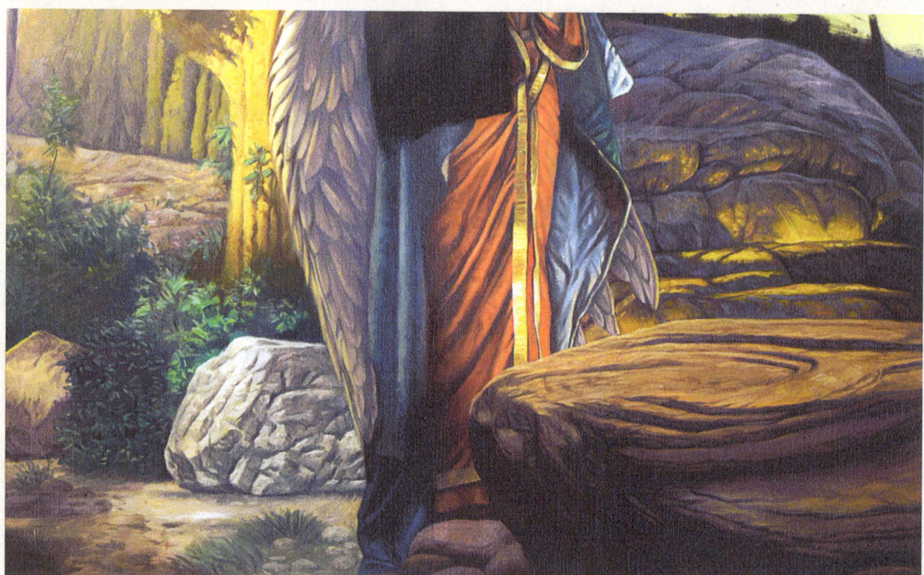

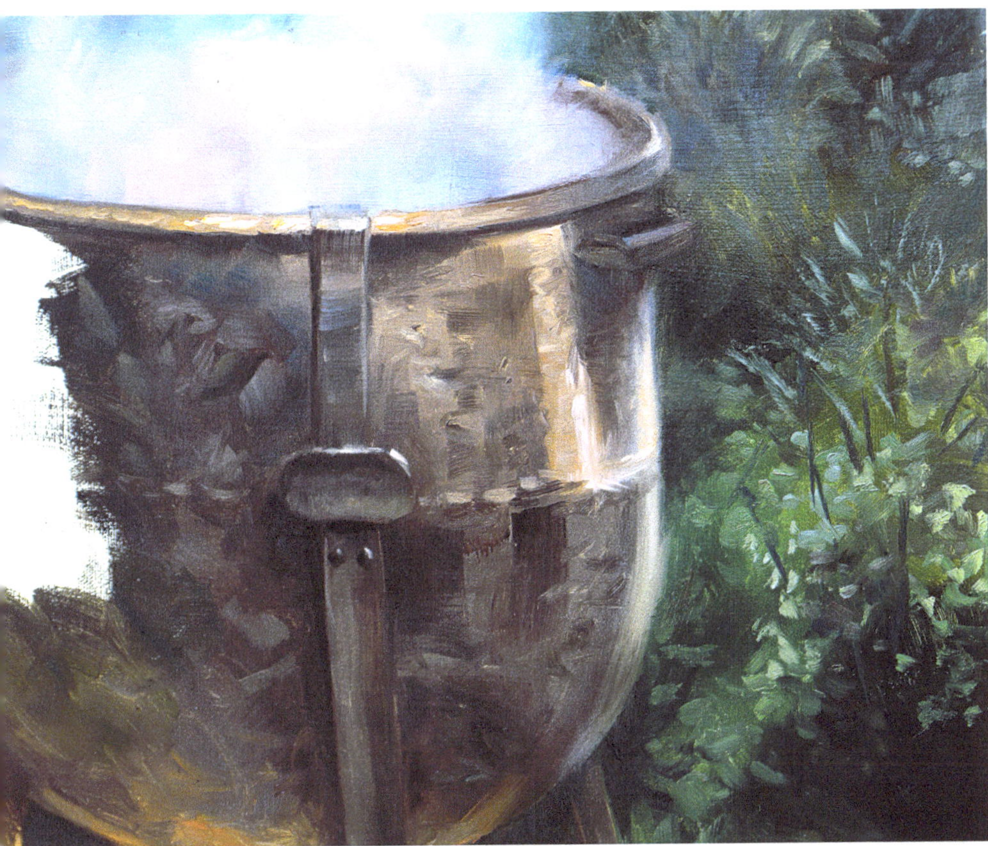

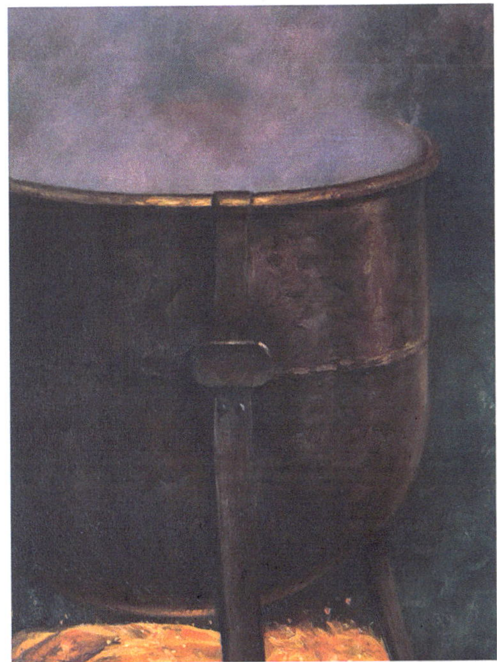

The cauldron at the top was fun to do. I try to think of intriguing, often symbolic objects to put into my designs that add meaning and support the concept. I enjoy painting much more if I am working on images that I feel I want or need to get onto the canvas. Adding the pot's smoke set a tone of mystery and gave the piece a more spiritual mood without saying pure fantasy. You can say interesting things without going so far as to force the work, leaving a bit of ambiguity for the viewer to interpret as they will.

Below- 5 stages of the pattern I worked over on the lower cloth base of the woman's robes. If you let the initial block in color dry fully, you can easily freehand a design over the dry surface, which I did here in white. Then it's just a matter of refining it and glazing darker.

The final head at the right shows the warm tone that I was after from the beginning. At times you have to be patient and let the paint dry, as I did here once I had the basic skin tones and brushwork done. The realism was there, just not the final color. Often, students will not want to wait, rushing to work over a half-dry surface. That can lead to an attempted look, rather than a professional finish. Nothing stands out more than brushwork that looks struggled or rushed. The right color can often only come after some experimentation. So long as the values are there, the realism will hold up. The coloring will enhance the final painting by warming or cooling the skin tones, backgrounds, and other critical areas that help set the feeling you want to convey.

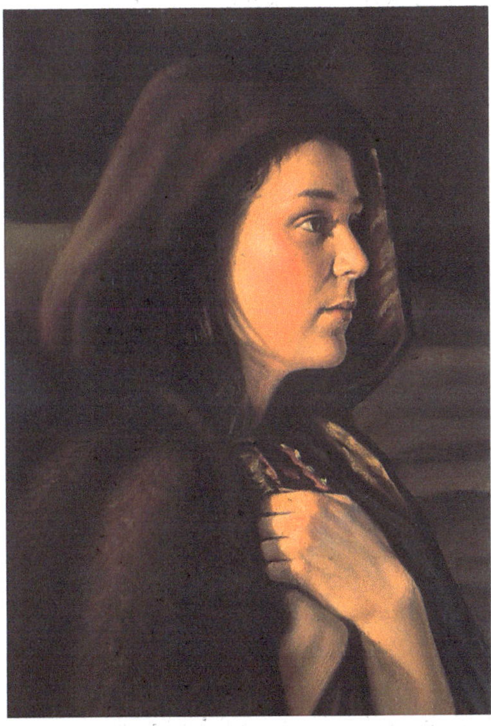

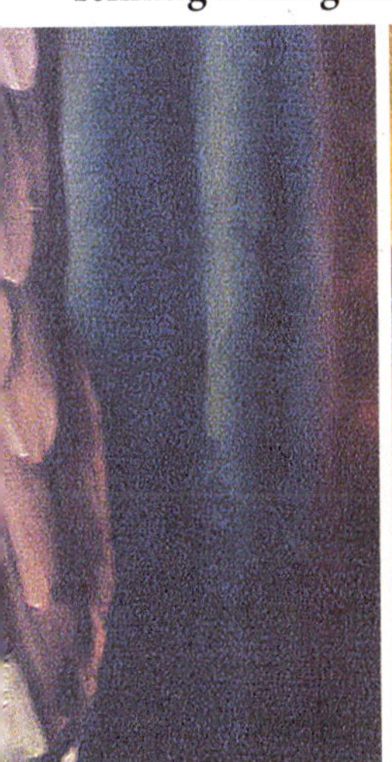

1

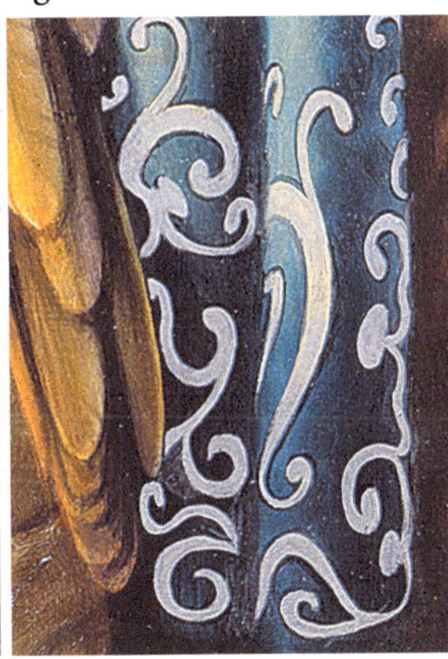

2

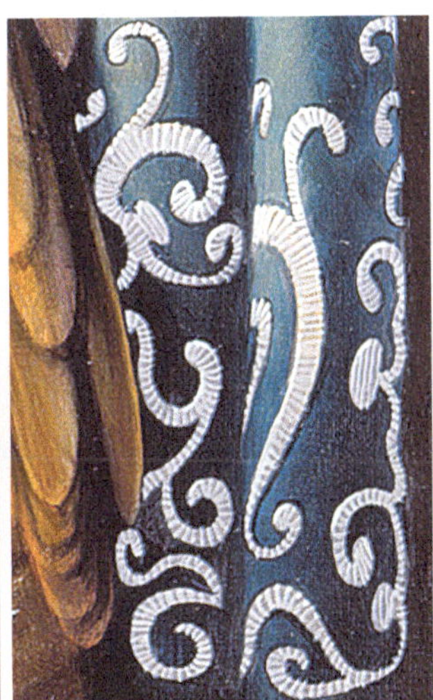

3

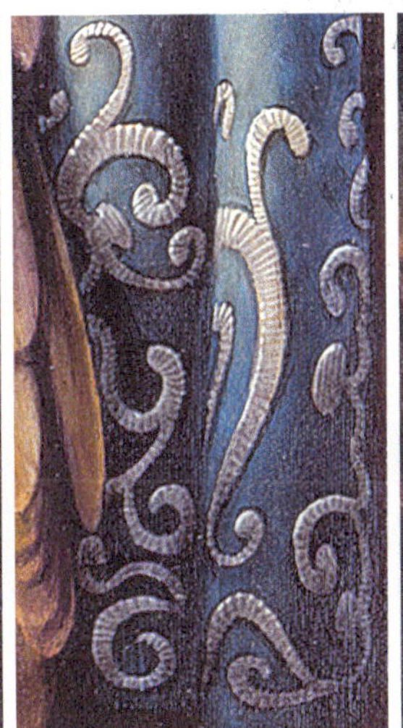

4

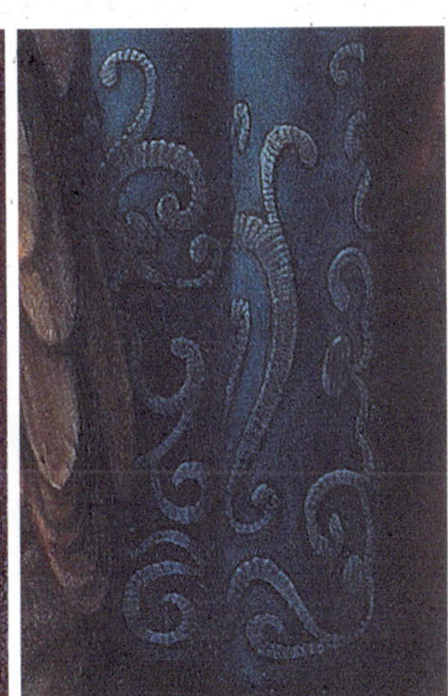

5

STUDY FOR IN THE FOREST

24x36" Oil on stretched canvas (p.71)

Like many of my studies, this is a preparatory piece meant to be a guide for a much larger painting where I plan to use the model in a forest setting. When I compose complex work, I often spend more time with the design and content than the actual painting. But for studies like these, I am more concerned about color and the technical approach than content. I have been told by a number of my artist friends that my studies are some of my best work, I suppose because the painterly quality shows more.

This piece followed a classic approach-first a loose drawing was done directly on the canvas, then lightly spray fixed. I used a thin oil wash of an ocher-gray tone to stain the canvas. (1, below) This dried thoroughly overnight. I often mix the thin wash using mineral spirits and a little Liquin medium, brushing it on with a 3" house painter's brush, then buff it out quickly. With studies like this, I will draw out several at the same time, coating each with the base color, enough to cover the white by staining the canvas with a nice middle-gray to paint over.

Next, (2) I blocked in the face and began to work into the area around the head, looking for edges to fuse to help control the focus as I see the piece start to develop against the base tones.

My studies range from a few hours to a day or two. This one took nearly 5 hours. I went back into the face to glaze a bit more color into the cheeks. The final study will help me with the larger work.

Above, three types of filbert brushes; sable, synthetic, and a soft long bristle. I used primarily the bristle filbert, as in the circled areas on this spread.

1- Over a dried wash, I lay in flesh tones.

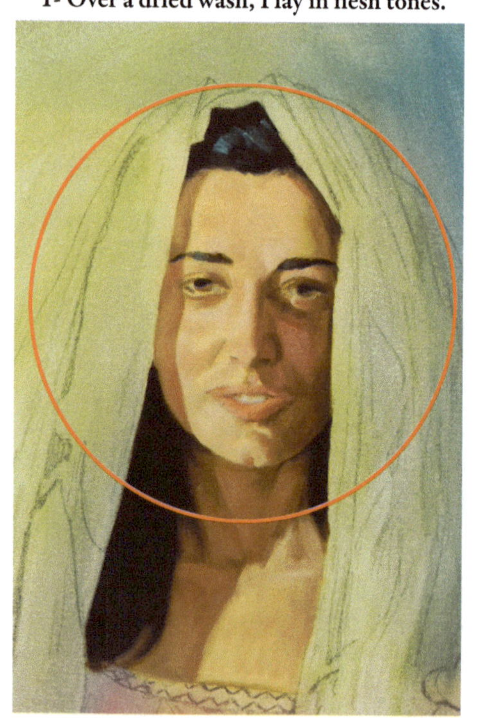

2- Color is built up with more opaque paint.

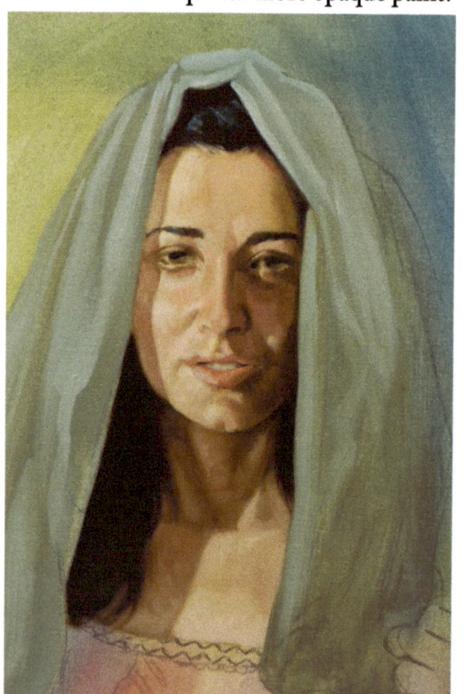

3- Darker features round out the face.

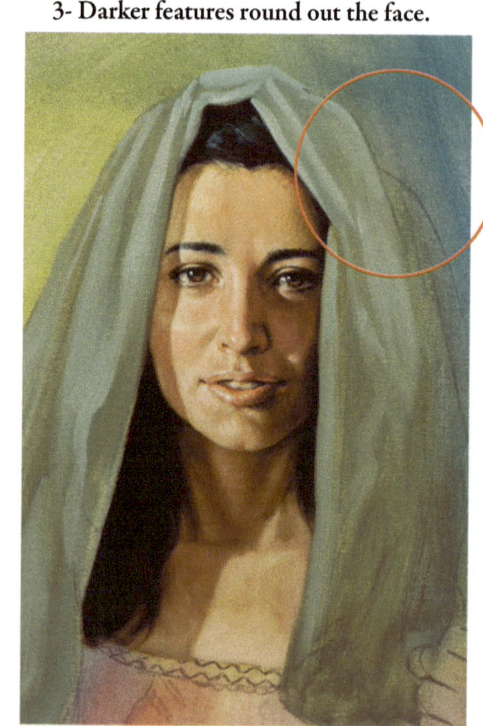

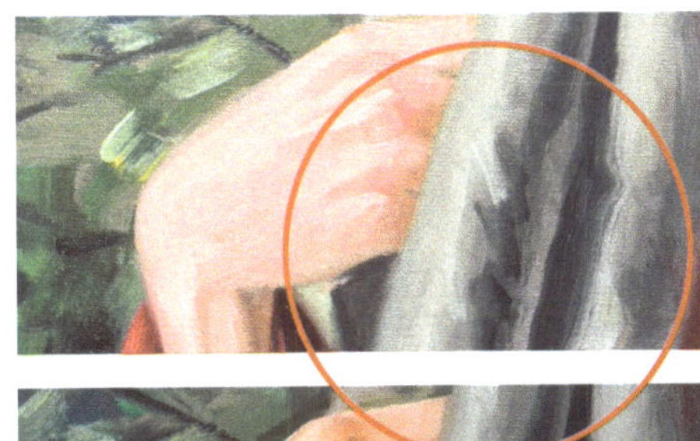

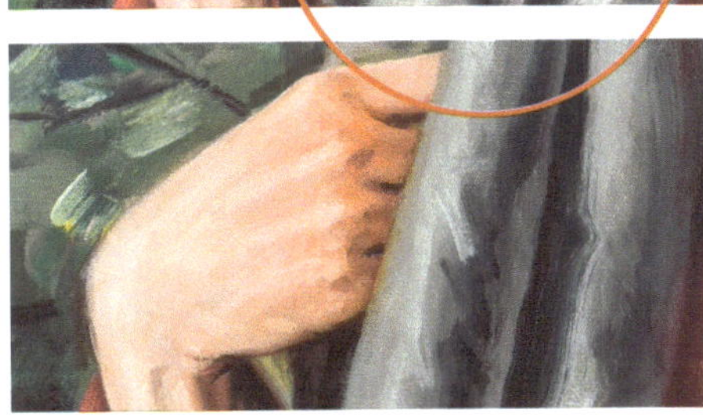

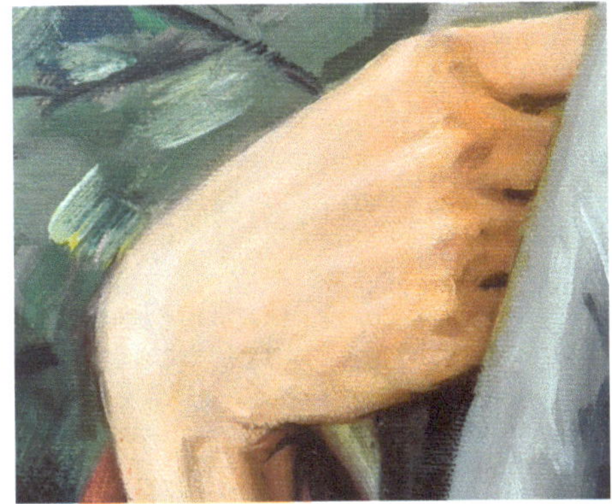

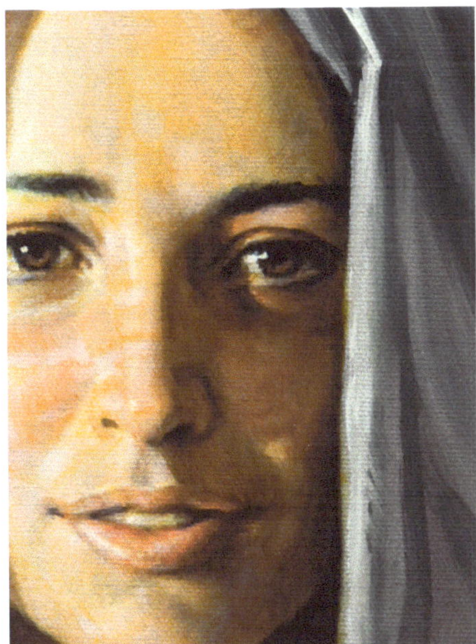

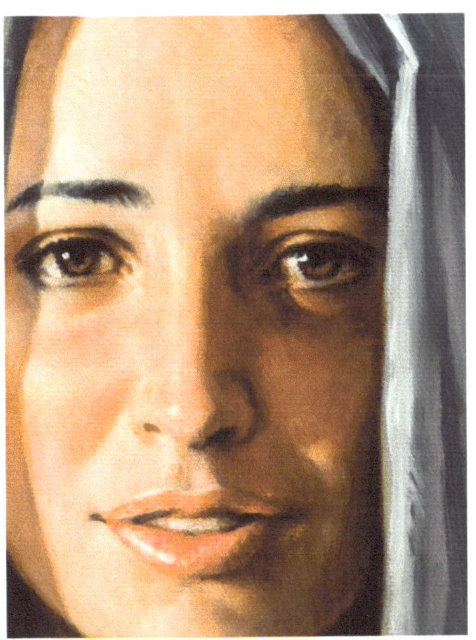

Above, these 2 stages follow the 6th stage, lower right. Here you can clearly see, on the left, the thin glaze of reddish-ocher coloring that I placed loosely over the dried skin base. Liquin medium works well for this because it permeates the underling layer of paint and allows me just enough working time to buff out the glaze and add some painterly effects, here and there, without losing the brushwork that I prefer.

I could have glazed from the initial drawing up, but pure glazing won't give me the look I want, or the texture, and it takes much longer waiting for each additional paint layer to thoroughly dry. The Liquin will dry overnight, usually even with impasto (heavy bodied paint) but I much prefer working 'Sargent-like' initially, and then simply color adjust the final layer. This method is quite safe, so long as I let the base layer dry completely, usually for a few days. It helps to work on other paintings concurrently, so I'm not tempted to go into the piece while it's still wet.

One of the surest ways to push oil paint into cracking is by applying fast drying glazes over thicker, slow drying layers. It can be done, of course, but unless you want your work to eventually pull apart, its best to let the underpainting dry thoroughly before adding another layer. Also, avoid temporary fixes, like retouch varnish to seal the underpainting. Varnish, like lacquer, dries to a thin brittle layer that will crack or flake off, especially on canvas, which flexes. A stiff, well gessoed panel is a much safer substrate for any kind of layered oil painting. You can see aging effects at any museum showing un-restored works.

Hands are not difficult to render if you think of them as 2 pieces- the palm is one unit, and the fingers (and thumb) as cylindrical extensions, each separate but linked to the palm section. Most hands will look right if you block in the base middle tone and then add brown or gray to accent finger shadow. The drawing must be accurate. You can add highlights to further round out the forms.

4- I work on the cloth, adding shadows first.

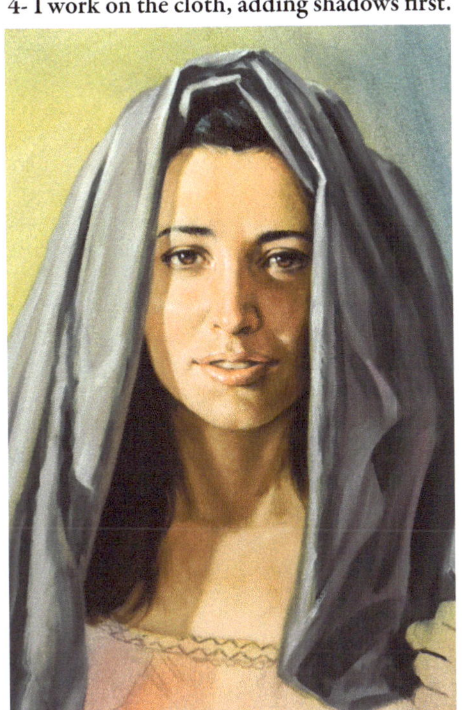

5- Background is roughed in, edges softened.

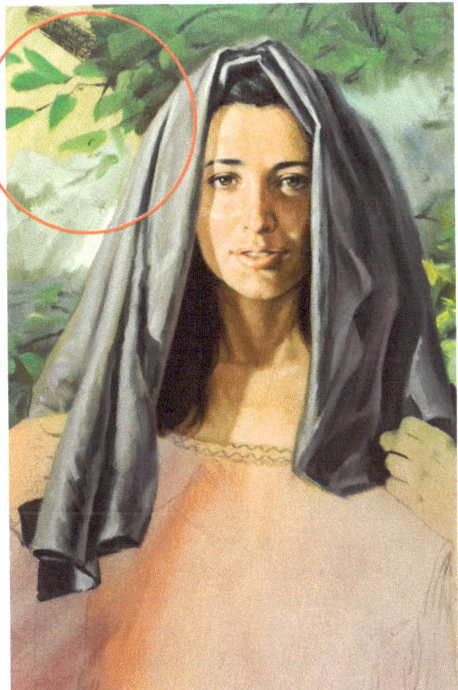

6- The prefinal head before glazing.

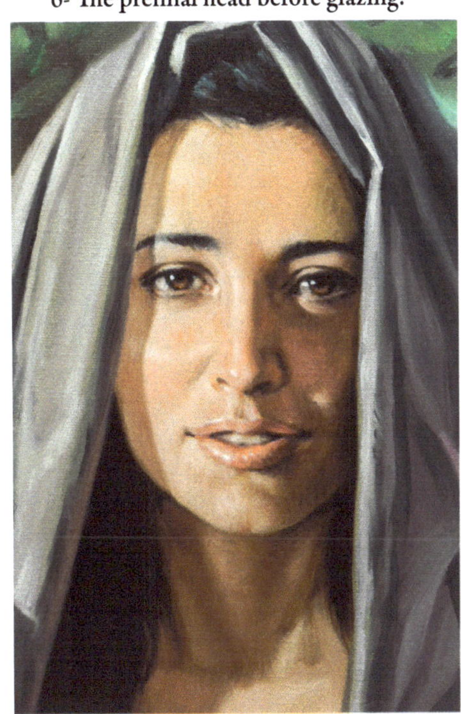

Sectional oil painting

48x48" canvas mounted to panel (p.4-7)

I enjoy doing realistic tonal images where the realism helps convey the mood and a sense of believable possibilities. To achieve this depth of realism and not let the painting process run astray while working on each area, I nearly always develop a full drawing or color sketch first.

There is a big difference in looking at something and following that as a guide to work from versus making up areas and achieving the same kind of realism. Since at least half of any of my spiritual works are made up or invented, I can't afford the luxury of experimenting too much as I block in the initial oil paint. The paint would get too heavy and create problems for overpainting. So I do whatever I can to prepare by developing a clean drawing and even a color study to work out the color and light effects and plan for 'lost' edges. Without planning, at least for this type of inventive work, you can end up with days of effort that look weak or unprofessional. This is a predetermined, well thought-out studio approach, not spontaneous painting. Even though I paint quickly, I still need to plan parts out ahead of time. This is the fundamental approach for most illustrators of realism as well.

Don't undervalue your instincts as a painter. We all have an inherent visual level of what is acceptable realism and what looks 'off.' My artist friends describe this as 'quality realism,' or work that stands out because of the ability of the artist to apply a high level of technique to achieve a realistic look. I prefer art that is not overworked or looks photographic and tight, yet has enough control to speak of the artist's ability and achieves a sense of realism that conveys the artist's vision.

I always aim for quality painting that falls between high realism and a painterly bravura look. The gifted artists and classic illustrators of the past had the rare ability to achieve a look of believable realism while maintaining fresh brushwork and a sense of mood, without overdoing or nitpicking their work. It's a fine line- when you take it too far, it looks overworked or amateurish, and if you don't push the realism enough, it looks fake or lifeless. Knowing what I am after, seeing it clearly in my mind, makes it much easier to transform onto a flat surface.

This demo shows one approach to achieve the kind of realism I prefer, an advanced technique that is challenging but fun to do.

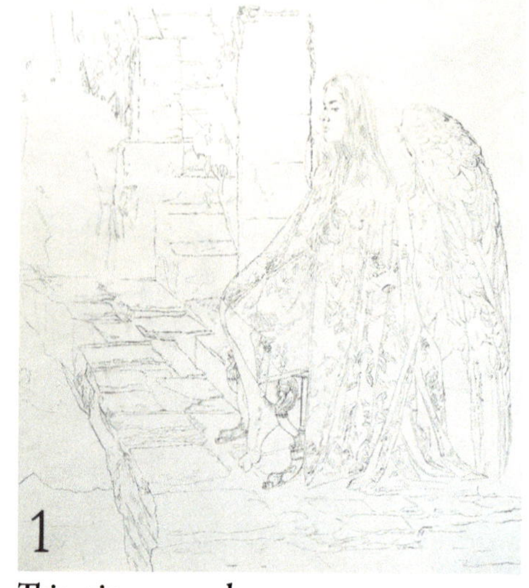

1

This piece was drawn out onto canvas, then fixed and mounted onto quarter inch masonite. At 48" square. it's a good size for me to work on the figure. I always calculate the size according to how big I want the important figure's face to be painted, in this case, around 5" high. If I could, I would do nearly every painting at least this large, if not mural size. My paint application works best for me with larger, thicker strokes, rather than using smaller brushes.

You can see the extent to which I drew this image out, more like for a watercolor. It really helps solve a lot of problems later on and locks it in my memory as I proceed with color. I think this stems more from my illustration background. My intention is to see the line just beneath the initial color, knowing I can freehand the drawing back in. But why spend that extra time when I can start with something accurate before my first brush stroke?

The model was a beautiful young girl who posed for me. The reference shots I took allowed me to expand upon the idea of her as an Angel looking down to Earth. There's more meaning to it, of course, but that is the essential visual I had in mind.

The background reference was minimal- an old black and white photocopy of an English garden shot that I had saved for 20 years. It's always fascinating when the design elements seem to readily come together after sketching out an idea, and the right model is found who fits the design.

I wanted a basic warm versus cool light effect and keyed the scene by the light on the girl's face. Faces are the one area I make sure to get good reference for. While you can sometimes fudge other elements, if you don't work out a good face, it will make the rest of the painting look weak. It's one of the reasons I like to work larger, to control the accuracy of the face without nitpicking it or using small brushes that can make it look overworked or fake. With many paintings, I do much of the central figure first, then build up the area around it to match that degree of finish.

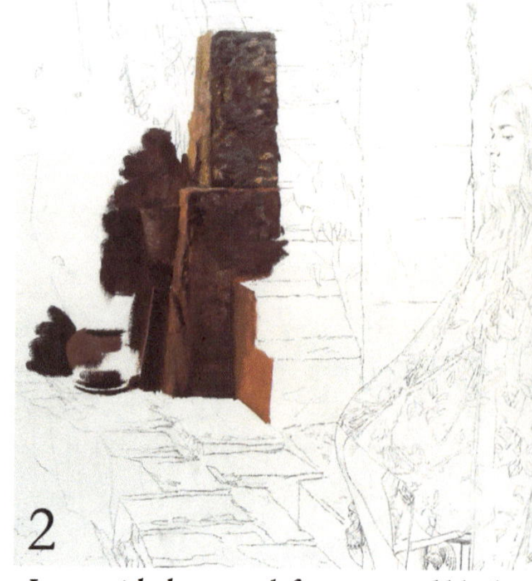

2

I start with the upper left section and block in the area with large flats, working opaque and fast enough to cover every area that I want to refine. I usually wash over the entire canvas first, to stain the white, but this demo shows an alternate approach, working in sections before finishing and unifying.

My goal is to put a layer of wet oil directly over each section so that I can go back and work the edges to achieve the sense of realism that I like. This allows me to easily throw relative planes in and out of focus. It is the fundamental principle of how we perceive realism today, in this age of 2 dimensional photos and videos. Our minds are attuned to accept this flat image as realism. To control the effect of realism, learn how to control edges, and understand how the eye and mind interpret this information.

In general, a hard-edge stroke against a softer edge behind it will give the illusion of realism in the same way a flat photo has areas of multiple degrees of focus, however subtle. As a painter of realism, you can command this effect and even push it further than any traditional photo. This is how some watercolorists achieve depth by flooding the paper with wet-into-wet washes (for out of focus areas) then work into drier paint, for crisper, sharp focus areas.

Oil is one of the few mediums where you can paint soft edges immediately for realistic results. You can also dry-brush, glaze, and scumble for effect, but I prefer the natural wet-into-wet approach for seamless blending. Many of my favorite artists of the past wanted an overall blended look where the illusion of lost and found edges gave their work a feeling of tonal realism to convey a subtle mood. It's natural for the oil medium. Despite what may seem daunting at first, oil paint is actually quite easy to use and the surface quality is unmatched if you want a rich timeless finish.

Some additives can help keep the paint wet longer for wet-into-wet blending. Most earth colors dry much faster, so adding a drop of oil of cloves to a mound of color can delay the drying time considerably.

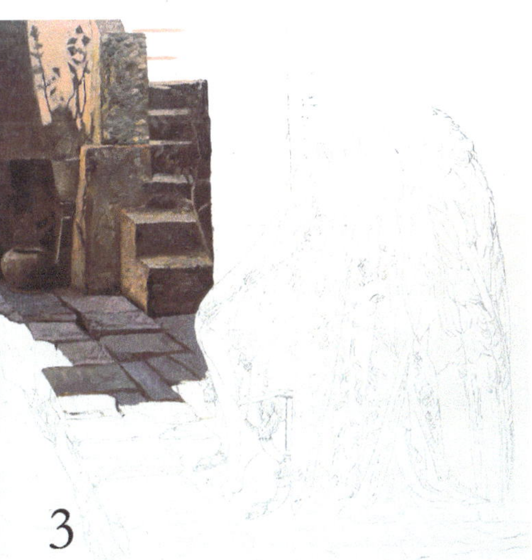

3

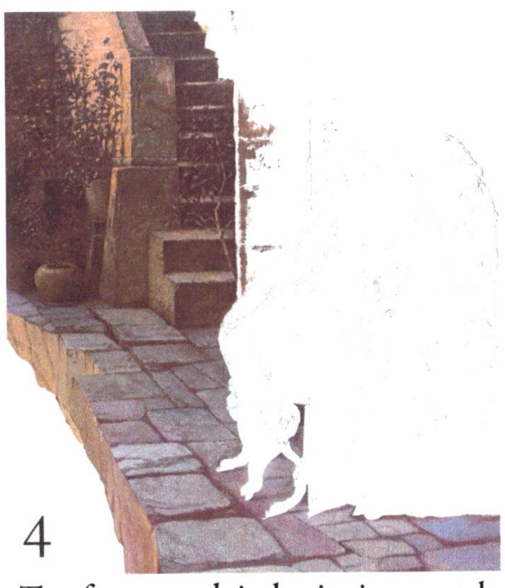

4

I am beginning to move the wet areas around a bit and get a feel for the color I want, how to handle the grays- warm or cool, and the edges- sharp or diffused. For a painterly look, I know that if I keep most of the painting in soft focus, then it will look more like a painting and less like a photo. I don't want my work to look photorealistic, that always conveys copying photos, which, to me, is a meaningless statement that shows little creativity.

I much prefer an illustrative flair, leaving brushwork here and there to give the work much more feeling. The softer focus block- in forces the few sharp strokes to come forward and snap into place. I know, for example, that I want the girl's head to come out of the dark tone around it, so I will make sure to keep her forehead plane crisp and light against the darker, softer focus area just behind her. You can adjust any painting with this in mind. Learning to control this effect is the key to realism for many portrait and tonal painters who want to give the illusion of greater depth. It really makes the painting look much more interesting as well.

I work my way down, from upper left to lower right, working fast with the intent that the entire canvas be covered with wet paint so I can refine the edges globally.

The simple background is the least important area which can be painted more freely than the Angel or foreground. Most artwork, especially landscapes and portraits, are more visually appealing if you keep the interest on the figure and let the background gray down or go out of focus just a bit, or a lot. I try to do this with every painting now,after years of painting every area in sharp focus. It's a lot more difficult to actually do, at first, and takes some study of what makes some pieces more interesting and visually appealing than others.

The great thing about being a realist is it's up to each artist to decide how far to push the effects. There are no set rules. It's in our mind's-eye that we determine what is pleasing and what is not.

The foreground is beginning to take shape and I feel comfortable with this first day of painting. When I come back to it, usually within eight hours, the paint should still be wet enough to work with and not become so sticky or dry that I can't do much with it. If the paint does get tacky, I will wait until it's really dry, in a few days, and then work on top of that with fresh paint. Either way, I work toward the same goal- to create an illusion of realism and keep the work looking painterly and interesting. The design and concept itself are, of course, the most important aspects, but I work that out long before I ever touch paint to canvas.

This approach is a bit more difficult because each area is fairly finished as I proceed into the next section. Nothing is transparent, so it's all up to my drawing skill to refine the opaque paint. If I get off, I redraw it as I progress, using opaque paint to freehand draw with color.

I made up the wings, which were a bit tricky. The warm light raking from the left side should cast a cooler shadow from the girl's head and highlight the top of the wing's form. Thinking ahead this way allows for a logical progression. It's always fun to figure out how a form is lit in three-dimensional space based on physics.

I learn something with every painting I do or see. There are no mistakes in art, just refinements. I don't think I have ever passed one of my pieces without thinking of areas I might paint differently or would like to improve. At some point, you just let it go and move on to the next concept.

There is a story about John Sargent who saw an early portrait he had done, prominently displayed in a museum. While his friends were admiring it, Sargent could not help but point out how he might fix certain areas that still bothered him from decades earlier. As intelligent as Sargent was, I don't doubt that he remembered every painting he did and just what, if anything, he would do to improve each piece. Simply put, I think it's in the true artist's nature to want to do better and better work.

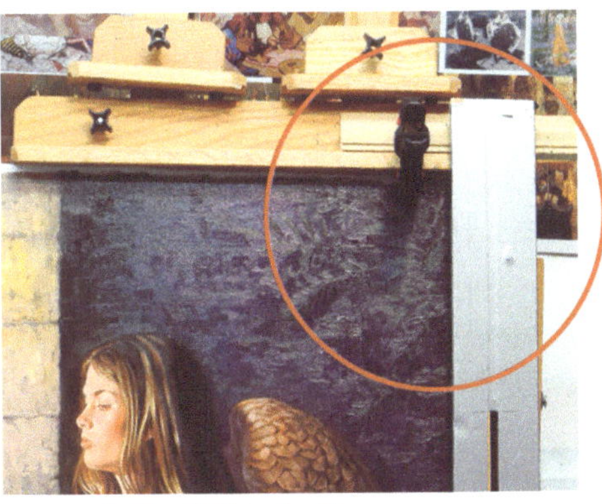

Maul Stick Support

For accurate vertical strokes, I use a long piece of wood that I mounted at a right angle to the top of the easel. This simple T-square slides across easily and is flat enough for my hand to rest on its taped surface. With this support I can noodle and tweak the paint below since my hand is raised above the wet paint. It makes it much easier to do detail work with finger pressure rather than my wrist. This support also allows my arm to rest.

I can drop a long vertical stroke down the length of the T-square or run a bar across two vertical posts I have on either side of my easel for accurate horizontal and angled lines.

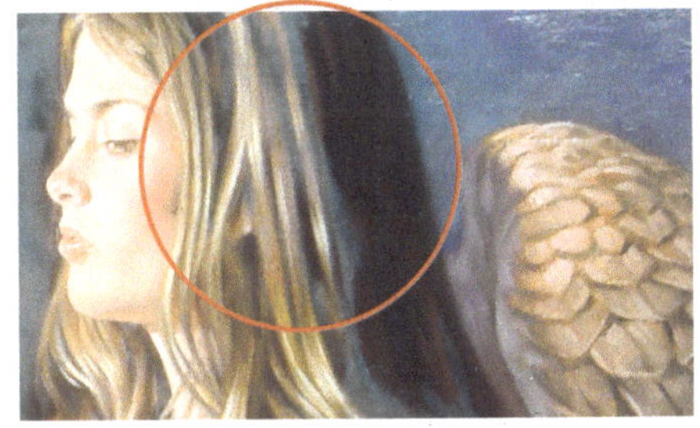

Working Over Matte Areas

If your paint is thinned out or you use umber as a base, it may dry too fast. To regain the shiny rich oil look essential for making critical color adjustments, you can use a medium that coats the area. I would avoid retouch varnish if you use canvas as it is a very fragile varnish layer that is prone to cracking. Any paint you put over this will also crack, especially in multiple layers.

Instead, I like Liquin medium, made by Windsor Newton. It penetrates the surface better than anything else I've tried and is quite stable. It sets up quickly and speeds drying, which most oil painters prefer. I also use WN's oil painting medium or mix my own. You can use linseed oil or walnut oil to coat over matte areas but they tend to run down the canvas surface and streak. Add a little stand oil for a bit more drag. Make sure the area is bone dry and use all mediums and extenders sparingly for greater longevity.

A Simple Approach

This method of wet-into-wet, painted in sections, is a more advanced approach because it utilizes opaque, not transparent paint. If the paint is too thin, it won't blend wet-into-wet. If it's too thick, it can be difficult to work into. I mix a middle viscosity, using pure paint from the tube and only thin it, as needed, with either walnut oil or mineral spirits, just enough to allow it to flow from my brush.

The ideal mixture by a quality manufacturer of modern oil paints is what comes directly from the tubes. Anything added to this will weaken the binder and thin the paint, but sometimes this is desirable.

If you want a simple approach, I will outline one here- 1, Draw out your image onto whatever surface you prefer. Canvas is ideal because it pulls and is an acceptable look. But panels work, too, so long as they are sealed well and gessoed properly. They are the most archival support because the paint can't flex, which eventually leads to cracking. 2, Work in the largest possible areas and keep the paint wet but just thin enough to still see some of the drawing beneath. Don't go for details at this stage. It helps to use the largest brush you can that seems just a bit too big for the area you are working in. It takes practice, but you can get more detail and a thin line by using a larger flat bristle or sable (or synthetic)with a crisp edge, than with a small round brush that doesn't hold as much paint.

3, Once the areas are fully blocked in, take a mop brush (see inset) or an extra long soft bristle, and lightly drag over areas so that all of the paint looks just a bit out of focus. This will happen easily, so don't overdo it or it will look superficial. If your paint is too heavy, the impasto will drag too easily for this method. If too thin, it will not drag much at all. So play with the paint viscosity to find the ideal thickness.

4, With a sharp clean flat, draw into this blurred area of wet paint using precise strokes. What happens is you are putting sharp focus strokes over a soft focus base. With some practice, you can get a photographic effect easily, if desired.

Why? Because, like photography, it's all about crisp edges versus soft ones. Studying photo prints and nature are a great way to see color and value, which is what realism is all about. You will see how color and value help soften edges and add to a greater degree of realism. 5, Finish with rounds or flats. You can draw into this wet area by applying more paint or use paint that is beginning to set up. This is a perfect time to add light touches.

6, Don't overwork the illusion!

Mop brush-

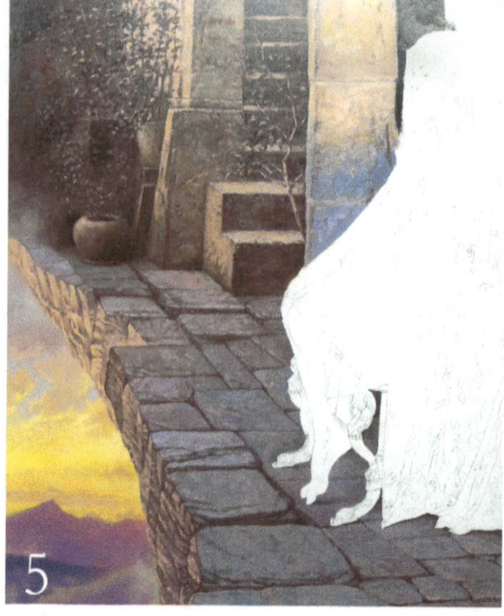

5

When you paint a sky it can change the entire mood of the piece. A good rule is to do the farthest background first, then work toward the foreground, keeping the background in softer focus than important foreground objects.

I did the sky at this point to tell me how much warm tone I could get into the left edge of the stones. You can see how the top, or farthest section of the stones, is slightly diffused and less detailed. Again, as it recedes in the distance, I usually keep it more blocked in and less worked over. The stones themselves are done with thicker paint strokes, using flats or filberts that I frequently employ.

The beauty of the filbert is that you can control its stroke edge by lifting the brush just a bit, blending it into the previous wet layer, much as a pen stroke can taper off to a thinner line. Similar brushwork is evident in works by Sargent, Boldini, Sorolla, and others who were able to produce work quickly with a full tonal range where the strokes seem to melt into the paint layer beneath, giving the illusion of soft focus realism.

Notice the warmer blue-gray of the top stone surface and compare it to the cooler purple in the shot for stage 6. When the paint was dry, I enhanced the color with a translucent layer of crimson, mixing the paint on the canvas and trying not to make it look too smooth or over done.

By dragging the paint over the rough strokes beneath, I was able to enhance the texture similar to how Whistler achieved his textured areas. Essentially, you create a heavy, rough underpainting with the initial coat. When dry, you drag in color and glaze here and there to enhance the foundation. I use this method with clothing, landscapes, or anywhere I want a heavy looking texture on the paint surface.

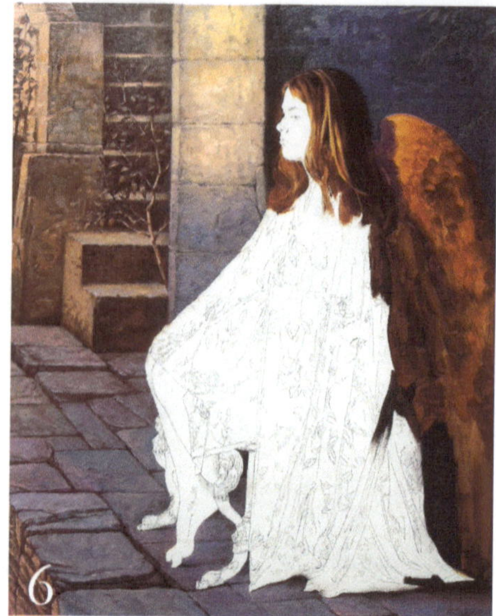

6

The upper right area was quickly painted in my usual manner of handling trees and bushes now. After many years of trying to paint trees in what I felt was the logical method, I finally realized it was much easier to block in the entire tree, or bush, in a dark mass first, going for just the shadows, not the middle tones. Then, painting opaquely and with confidence, I work toward the light, placing middle values right into the dark areas, and highlights into the middle areas. I know some artists who paint beautiful trees by painting around edges with all middle tones. They then add shadow and highlights in blocky areas, then blend these together. I really like seeing that approach, but for my own work it's not always right for the kind of subject I like to do.

With enough experience, I think most artists begin to fall into a pattern of technique that can be applied to most subjects. Don't overlook your natural strengths. I'm not as comfortable with trees, but figures, faces, and rocks have always been easy for me. Some artists do great landscapes but their figure work is lacking, and vice versa. There's no law that says you have to be able to paint everything well, just go for what you love to paint, subject-wise, and find what you are naturally gifted toward. Understanding color, edges, and other painting elements that help achieve greater realism will come to you in time, with practice, and a conscious commitment to seeing how nature works and how things fit together in a given space,

People ask me how to be a better painter. I never have a good answer, but I suggest it all comes down to looking and opening up your senses to appreciate everything around us. Study nature for edges and focus. You can achieve beautiful realism with an outline as well as with all edges soft and melted together. Above all, paint just want you want and your best techniques will begin to show in consistent work.

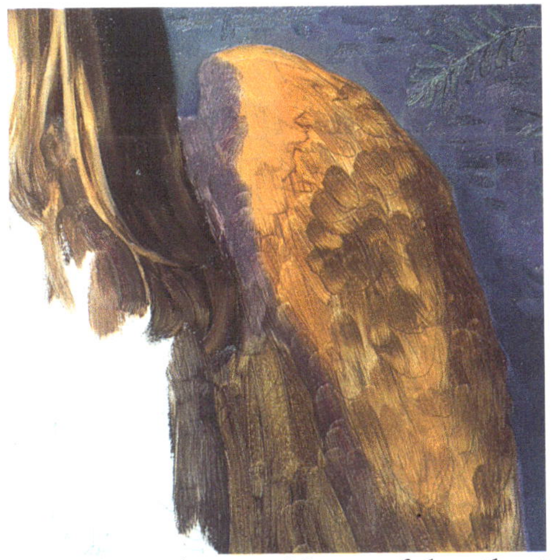

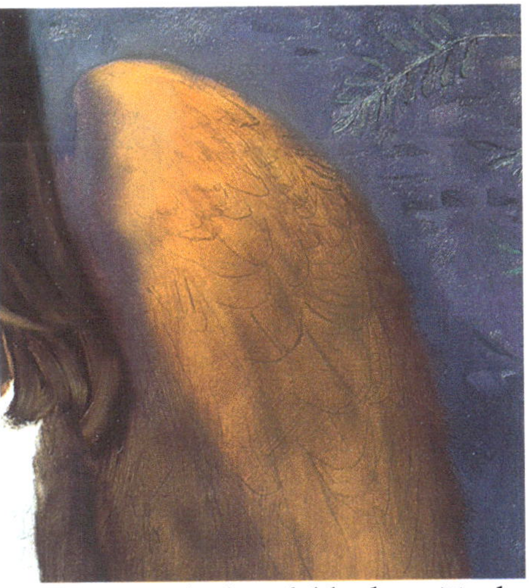

This shows the initial lay-in of the oil paint, quickly stroked or dabbed on. To the right, the same paint layer was dragged smoother by using a large bristle filbert that was soft enough to tug at the paint without pulling it off the canvas. In this way I can control the paint viscosity (thickness, heaviness) and therefore the opacity, and further set up my next thinner strokes directly into this receptive wet layer. I can push the edges, or focus, where I want, preferring a slightly out of focus effect that I can more easily sharpen up than if I left it with sharp focus (from flat strokes and a linear approach) which is much harder to force out of focus. I know if I control the focus, even minimally, I control the flow of where the viewer's eyes rest and that helps force interest to the more important areas, like the Angel's face.

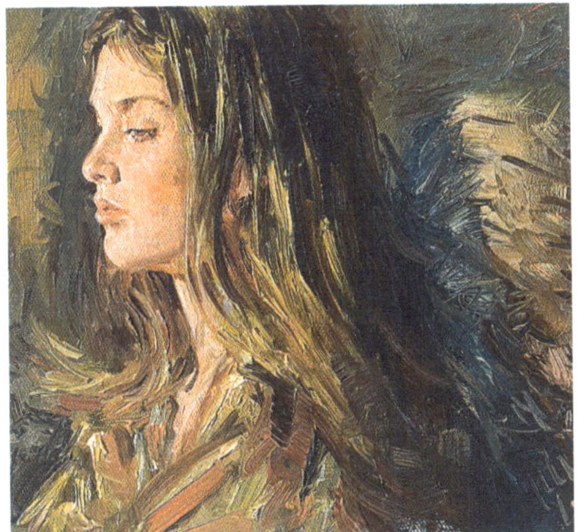

Here (and on P.66) is a one hour little study I did of the head and wings. I often do these sketches for two reasons- to help me test the color for the final larger painting, and to loosen up. Doing a fresh study like this, with no emphasis on making it look finished, can give you a new perspective on how to work with color and light. If I have been painting too tight or getting too concerned about color, or just bored with a painting, I stop and just sketch like this. The next time I go back to the full painting, my hand has loosened up enough that I feel more confident about continuing the work without fighting it.

Never paint timidly, it can look obvious if you attempted a passage rather than boldly painted it, even if it's off. If you put paint on and it looks unsure, it will convey weakness rather than mastery of the medium.

Try not to spend more than an hour or so on such studies or they will look overworked. This was only 7 inches high, so it went fast, and since there was no real thought behind it, other than the pleasure of painting, I could paint it a bit more freely than my normal work.

You can easily achieve effects with oil paint that rival watercolor if the paint is thinned in the same manner. Here, I used mineral spirits and just a bit of Liquin medium to add even more transparency and control. I mix this up first on my glass palette, then add color to the small pile.

This was painted in with a large bristle flat with detail control using the brush edge tilted here and there to quickly block in the gold and sienna coloring.

Normally, I go for more opaque paint, but some areas, like the cloth here, if drawn in well, can be simply washed in to use the pencil base as a value in the shadow areas. When you wash in areas like this, try not to tighten up. Paint loose and free, it's more fun and it's only meant as an underpainting anyway, so the detailing can come later once the paint sets up a bit. That's when I have the most control, when the paint is just tacky enough to pull the next strokes off the brush so that each brush stroke is grabbed by the underlying surface.

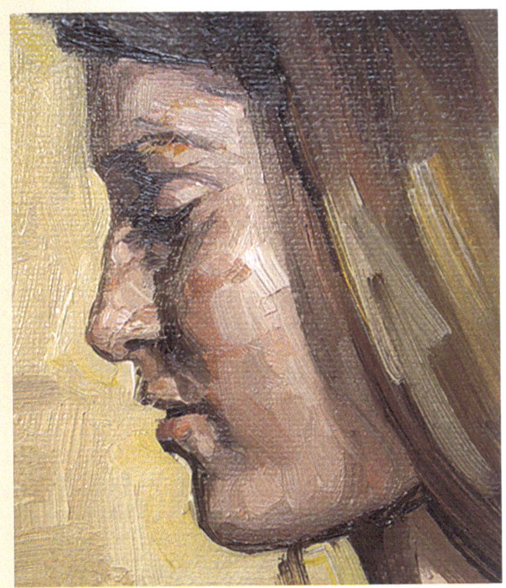

Thick or Thin Paint?

If you start with heavy paint you can quickly get into trouble with the oil being too slick or muddy and often difficult to control. I see this frequently in portraits where the image begins to look more like a caricature than the realism intended. While you can achieve some impressive textural effects, is it worth sacrificing control? I prefer not fighting the paint by building up from a wash base, then using heavier paint after I lay in the initial local color.

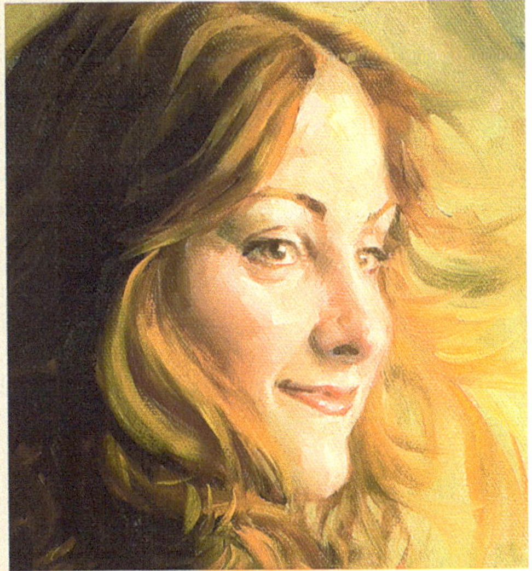

Brushwork Follows Form

You can enhance realism with brushwork that follows the natural curves and direction of form as light falls across objects in space. In both these examples, the strokes wind around and flow to help model the heads, or any form. This is especially effective for hair and muscle.

Above, this section shows a piece done entirely with the filbert brushwork I mentioned in stage 5. These are all tapered strokes that fade from the brush as they lift from the canvas surface to create soft edges.

Learn from Original Art

You can learn a lot from looking at the original work of most artists. The surface itself can not only reveal how the paint was applied, but why the artist chose to use it in certain ways to achieve a specific look. Contemporary art as well as 'old Master' work can reveal a lot about an artist's methods, insight, and even intent.

When I visit a museum and see a good realistic painting, (often called 'representational' work) I can almost feel the presence of the artist there describing how he or she did the painting and solved technical issues. Beyond technique, there is a residue of aesthetic worth in some art that encourages me and inspires me to work harder to achieve the effects I want. And, more importantly, to create a body of work that may inspire and move others.

Students often review an artist's or illustrator's work strictly by the images they see in print or even online. You can learn from this, but the information measured from books or other small reproductions can often yield the wrong intent. In this book, I wanted to include several full page close-ups to show technique because it is much more instructive, for those who may be looking to study surface quality. Most printed images are reduced down, which visually makes them look quite a bit tighter. Original oil color is richer and, if any glazing is used, that quality can be lost in print. I often glaze or patina my final layers of color and that radiant quality of light shining through the oil paint surface can only be seen in the original oil, even as much as I would like to see it in my high quality fine art prints. The closest I have been able to reproduce it is to photograph the art with a slight raking light to enhance the painterly look, but that top layer of color will still be reflective, not translucent, to the camera's lens.

Try this for a real eye opener- on your next museum trip, put on a pair of enlarging glasses that magnify what you see and you might be surprised at how much more you can study the work. It can be instructive to look at masterful work with what is basically a magnifying lens, and see how the brushwork, the glazing, and the surface were handled. These are clues to the artists' techniques, but also to what was in their minds as they developed their craft and placed it on canvas for the world to see.

Great work resonates the artist's intent as well as instructing you by showing off individual techniques. I've been in front of a few pieces and sensed the energy of what it must have taken to create the work, both technically and emotionally. Let the work take you in and it may teach you the secrets of its technique.

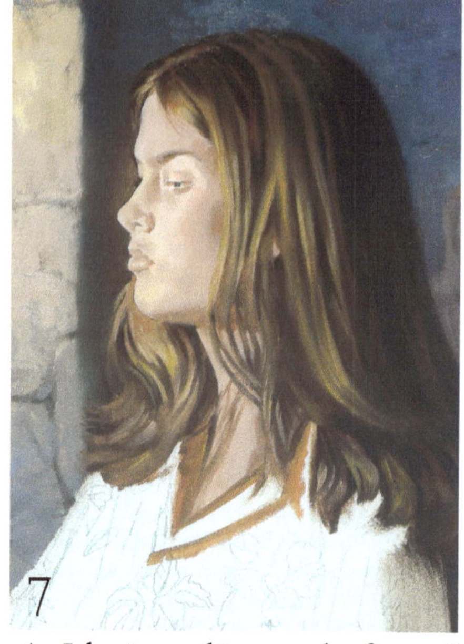

7

As I begin working on the figure, I quickly block in the head in base color planes and put on enough color to suggest the hair. It's important not to work too long on the face values (lightness or darkness) before matching it against the dark of the hair. The skin may look too light when you drop in the surrounding area. To work wet-into-wet is my goal here, so I want to blend the skin into the hair while it's a larger mass rather than wait and try to get the same effect with dry paint.

A good way to understand wet-into-wet effects is to work in smaller sections right up to the next wet or dry area. In this case, the full head is one section, so I worked up to and into the background around her head. I painted enough of the gray back in to blend with the surrounding tone. It's much easier to paint into a unified area, like the gray behind her head, than to try to paint up to the hair edge. If you soften each edge area, it will keep it from looking like it's pasted or stuck on. This is really important to give the work an overall unified look.

Let's say, for example, that you want to paint a hand against a blue sky. Paint the blue sky in first, not too smooth to give it some character, and just up to the edge of the hand. Then paint the hand in until it looks fairly finished. At this point, no matter how well the hand is done, it's still going to look cut-out and flat on the blue field of the sky. For some that may be a desirable look, but how do you make the hand look even more believable as if it 'lives' with the sky or belongs in front of it? You lightly blend the edge of the hand, usually the shadow side, into the wet paint of the sky. If it looks too soft or fake, you can always re- sharpen that edge with a few flat strokes. It's tricky to do at first, since the flesh color of the hand contrasts with the blue of the sky and where they meet can turn gray, but it can be done with enough practice and patience.

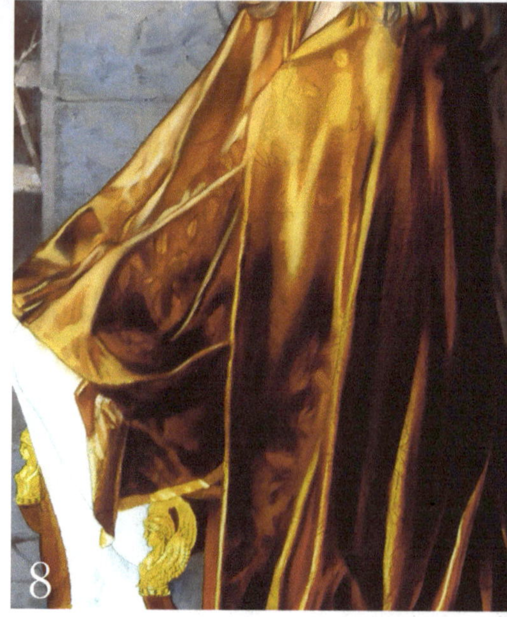

8

Perhaps the best approach to paint convincing cloth is to paint the larger masses in first and then refine them until they look right but have no pattern details. Then leave it alone to dry. I used to try to paint right into that wet area, but it's much more effective to paint details over the dry surface. I know artists who even redraw with pencil or ink over the dry areas, then paint into that. My approach is somewhere in the middle, by freehanding the pattern with a detail or flat brush, using thin opaque paint, and then blocking in the pattern color and refining that. If I mess up with my design, I can always just wipe it off and redraw it with paint over the dry surface. If it had wet paint beneath, I would have to smear it out or blend it together and that can result in a muddy passage that I would have to clean up.

If I was after strict photo-realism, which I have done on some commercial jobs, I would use every method I can think of to get the pattern just right. I feel it looks better to be a little loose with the drawing, conveying more of a personal touch to help set the mood. I feel this is what the Pre-Raphaelites often overlooked, allowing finicky detail to dominate a painting and losing sight of the overall effect. Stiff, detailed realism using tiny brushes looks much too tight, more like photo copying than painterly realism. It's something almost anyone can be taught to do, yet the real mood and meaning are often sacrificed for superficial detail.

I would much rather see a great illustrated piece by someone like Dean Cornwell, who was able to convey emotional scenes with a bravura style, than any tight realist work that suggests the emphasis is on technique, rather than what the piece is supposed to be about. My ideal painting is deceptively realistic, convincingly so, but not overworked, yet has, upon closer inspection, a fluid network of strokes to keep the surface interesting and non-photo like. It's paint, after all!

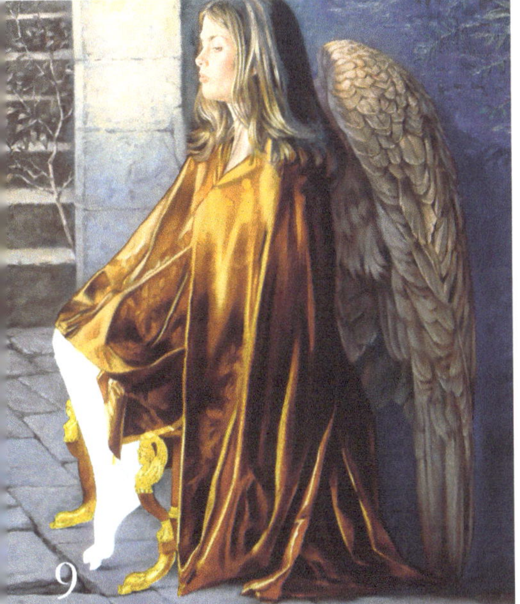

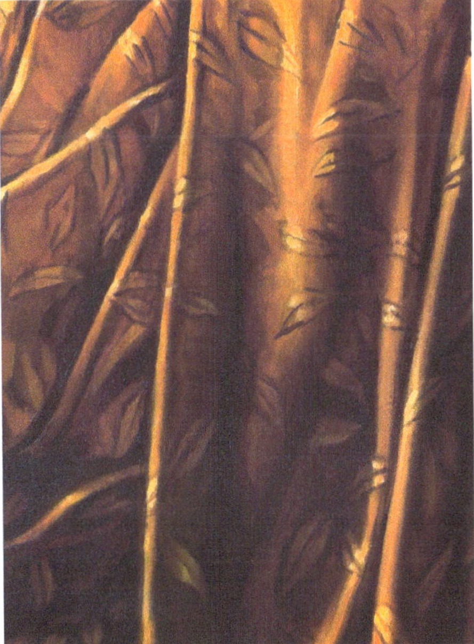

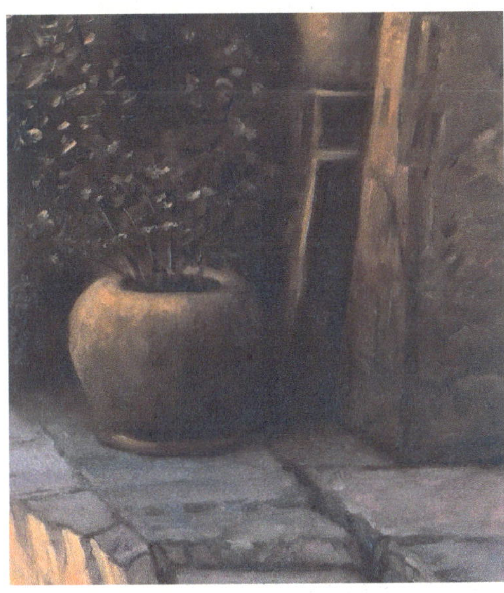

Above, most of the painting is moving along well. I am about 4 days into it and the background is fairly dry so I know I can soon work over it with more color. The leg area is a separate section that I can paint in any time, but the white of the canvas is bothering me, so I block it in with a middle flesh tone and then move on to the background to fuse the color into the leg edges.

At this point, I considering glazing, or what I refer to as a 'patina' layer of translucent color to enhance each area. It doesn't take much color if the original values from the initial paint layer are close. In the foreground rock, I pushed the blue-gray tone more toward a light purple shadow by adding crimson and purple in a very light veil, always trying to keep in mind my original concept coloring and fighting my old tendency to make the color too hot or acidic looking. I don't want the final art to appear illustration-like either. I really try to keep it on as high a level of sophisticated 'art' as I am capable of, both in thought and technique. As much as I love great illustration work, there is a look to it that says 'commercial art' and it's one I keep separate from my fine art.

Even though my work has a narrative quality, I always try to make a statement and not paint a meaningless picture. If I shoot for this goal, I will know that I did my best to keep my aesthetic intent intact.

Final feet and chair details

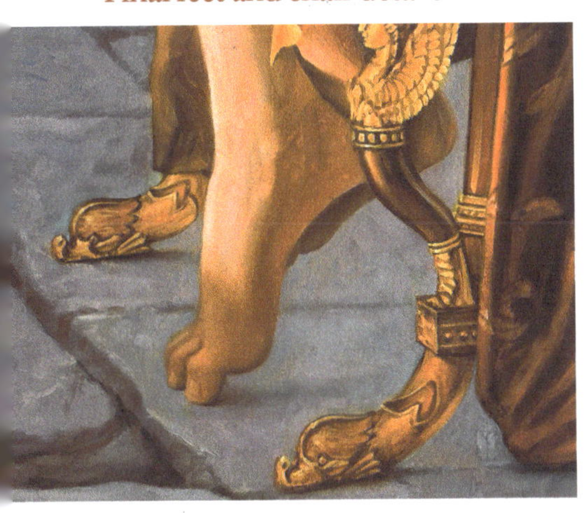

The shot above shows some of the cloth blocked in now, just before blending or fine-tuning it. I chose a simple pattern that suggested leaves yet did not overpower the general flow of the cloth. In lighting this area, my concern was to give a nice sheen to the brown cloth base. Wherever the detail edges fell into the same highlight areas, I applied a similar highlight to the detail. If you don't pay attention to these little things, it will often look off. You can be off color but not value. Ultimately, it's the color harmony that tells your mind when full realism happens and that reaction is instantaneous. It is an amazing ability we humans possess.

One of the reasons I enjoy painting realism is the correlation of the visual experience that is both psychological, logical, and emotional. This is a direct reaction to how anyone views your work. I'm sure you have seen someone in a museum or gallery who walks up to a painting and immediately either smiles or makes a face. They react to the image with an initial response that is totally visual and without reasoning. It's only after they reason out the purpose or value of the piece that they may come to a final conclusion.

For my own taste, I gravitate toward those rare images that excite me. The best ones, the ones that stay with me, make me think. They draw out emotion like great music. Listen to your own voice when you get the chance to see quality work, not to someone trying to sell you a piece or what you might have heard about the artist or the artist's work. Open your senses to what it may be saying to you, even beyond what the artist may have intended. A great piece will call to you and may even transfer some of the artist's emotion.

When you touch people with the images you create, then you have done something. If your work is well crafted and original in scope, then you may also reach an audience who appreciates quality.

Adding final color glazing

This final area has been darkened by glazing over it, when completely dry, after about two weeks. I first toned it with a rich pass of blue, then another of burnt sienna which thins out to a beautiful rich reddish brown that is quite translucent. Doing a color chart will show which hues are more translucent than the opaque colors, and their respective drying times. Transparent hues are noted on the tube labels and on manufacturers' web sites.

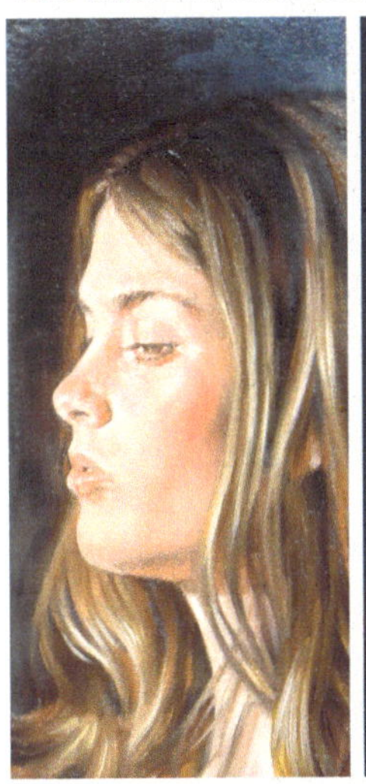

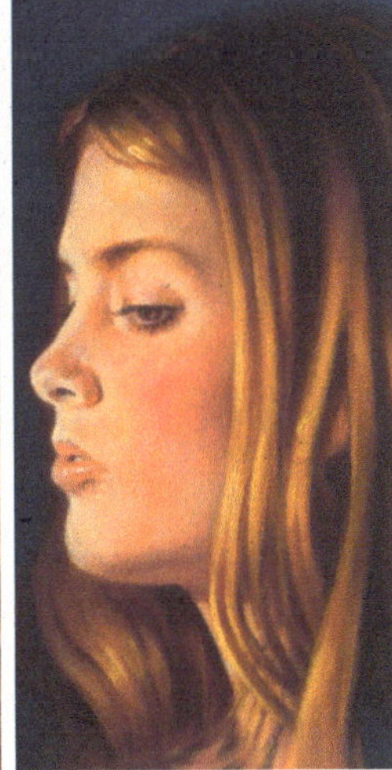

Comparing the left face to the final on the right, you can see how effectively a few layers of darker glaze add a rich tone to the skin. The deeper coloring now looks more like the sun is hitting her face and wings.

Sometimes I think of glazed areas like warm sunlight or cool shadows-translucent and effective. I like to push these effects a bit without going overboard. It's in this refinement that glazing helps enhance a rather dull piece, bringing it to life. It's one of the reasons I still prefer the finished look of oil paint, since the effect of glazing is the oil, caught like amber upon the surface.

AT THE GATE

48x70" oil on mounted canvas (p. 40-43)

This fairly large piece was done on canvas that I mounted to a panel by securing the overlapping canvas areas in the back with 1/2 inch thick fir strips. Then I gessoed it with 4-5 full coats, letting it set for a day before doing the drawing. I fought this surface a bit as it was super absorbent from gessoing the canvas after I mounted it to the panel. This gave it more of a fresco quality, great for washes, but I prefer the paint to stay on the surface more where I can control it. In the future, I will remember to gesso first, then mount it and add another layer of gesso if needed as a final coat before drawing on the surface.

For larger paintings, I usually start by doing a clean drawing and projecting the sketch either by shooting a slide to use in a slide projector, which is the sharpest and cleanest projection, or by using an opaque projector, which can go soft (blurry) at the edges, so keep the image in the very center of the plate. I make sure to get the image squared up properly, which is really important. The easiest way to do this is to draw in a box and, when projecting, square the box to the proportion of the canvas edges. If it isn't squared properly, the image may shift or skew, which will make any figures look disproportionate. I can always redraw them with paint, but that defeats the whole idea of working out the design ahead of time. I much prefer this to the old grid method of transferring the drawing, which, for me, is less accurate and outdated.

I used plenty of mineral spirits to wash over the base color tone and kill the white (1). This wash also helps set up the opaque paint to come, giving it more tooth to pull against the brush, so I have much more control in wet-into-wet areas. Since all solvents are toxic to varying degrees, a big wash like this would be an unsafe approach if you are allergic to oil paint. Turpentine is stronger than mineral spirits, but I like MS. There are new safer 'solvents' on the market but they feel greasy under my brush.

Alkyds, which dry fast and are safe to use with oils, make a great alternative, but are thinned with MS. Acrylics work well for underpainting and are water-based. Recent studies suggest that oil may not adhere well enough to acrylic (plastic) to use it for underpainting, but I think it's quite safe if you keep it thin and lightly scratch it with fine sandpaper before applying the oil. I would avoid the new 'water-based' oils.

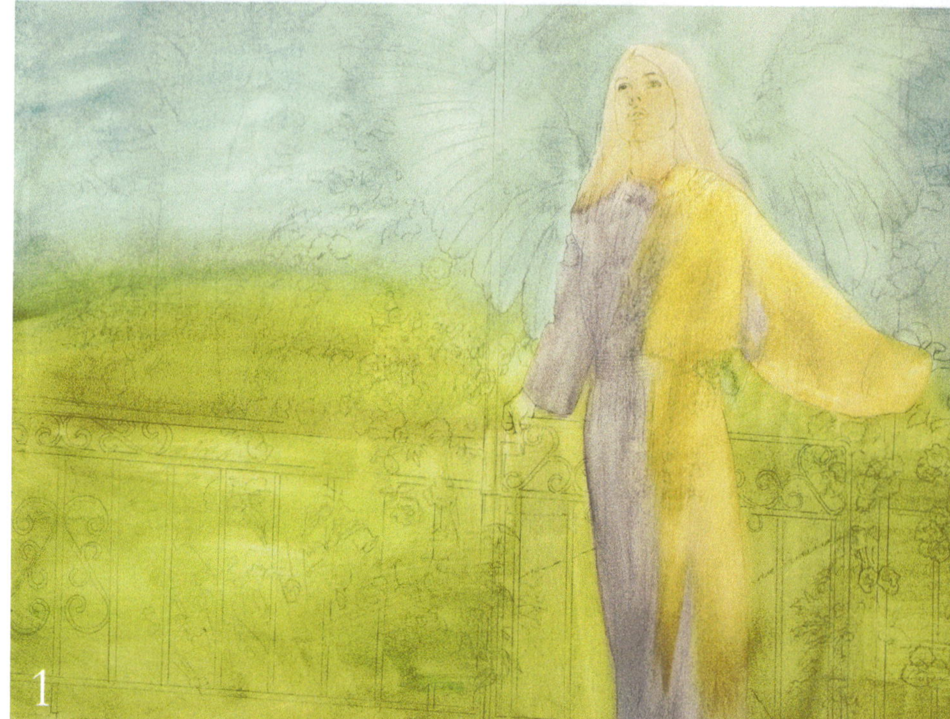

I enjoy painting fog, it's such a natural atmospheric affect that enhances the mood and grays the colors so you can play with the focus quite a bit. I try to employ any effect to give my work the feeling I like, falling somewhere between realism and a surreal approach that, hopefully, suggests something more spiritual in content.

Fog creates a similar effect to what atmosphere does to landscapes, building up layers of thick moisture (mist) that diminish color and value as it accumulates in the distance.

In 2, below, the left area shows my quick block-in of the farthest background trees. I could have done the far trees first and then overpainted them when dry, but I like doing as much work as I can while all the areas are wet, so I can model the tree form against the background sky or bushes.

The idea, especially for atmospheric effects, is to take the background gray and dull the colors, to make the entire area recede and let the figure come forward. I made up most of this area so I can push the design until I am satisfied.

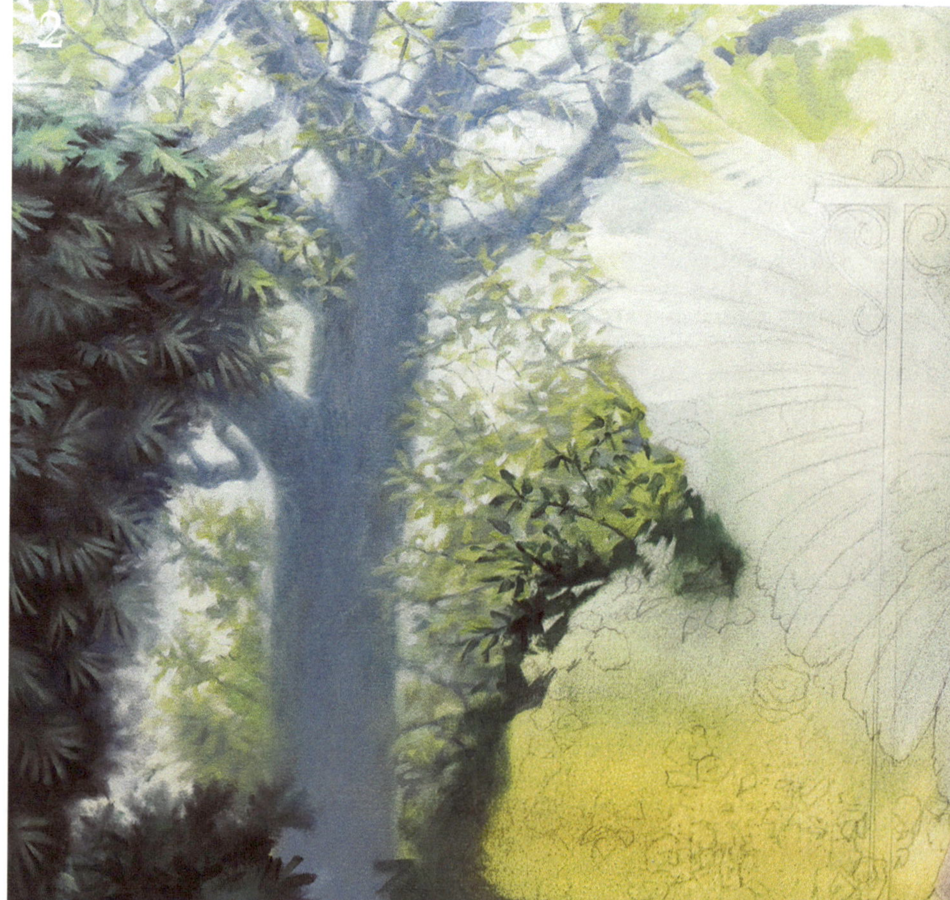

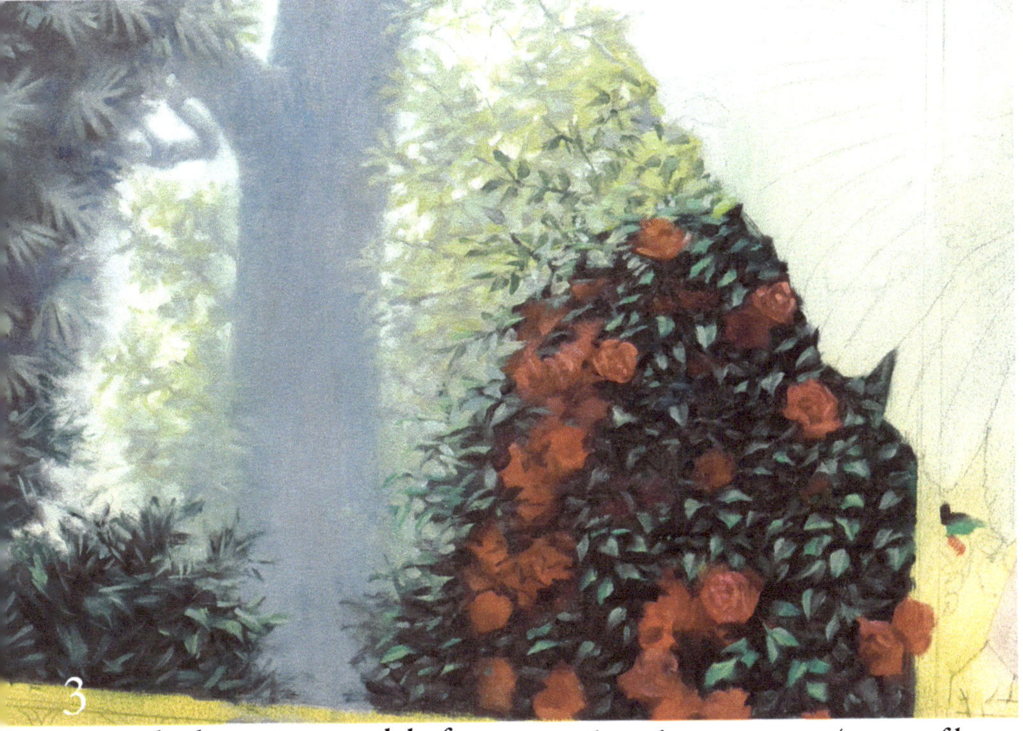

3, I am slowly moving toward the foreground area, trying to keep a soft focus to the background plants and yet maintain some realism. I know that once I get the fog layer over these darker tones, the whole image will drop back a bit and feel more like the painting I have in my head.

Below, I blocked in the red mass of the right bush and pushed the background much farther back. In nature, warm hues tend to come forward while cooler tones recede, but I have seen some nice work with cool foregrounds set against warm backgrounds.

On the right, you can see 4 stages of how the bush developed, starting from my block-in at the top, then a smeary mass of dark tone. In the third image I begin to drop in some of the leaf shapes with even heavier paint. The lower right image has a bit more refinement with some base color for the flowers now. If I had a clear photo or something to look at, I might just go ahead and finish this area, but I know the tone will shift as soon as I get the white fence blocked in. Sometimes, you just have to be patient and stick with the painting plan as it unfolds in front of you.

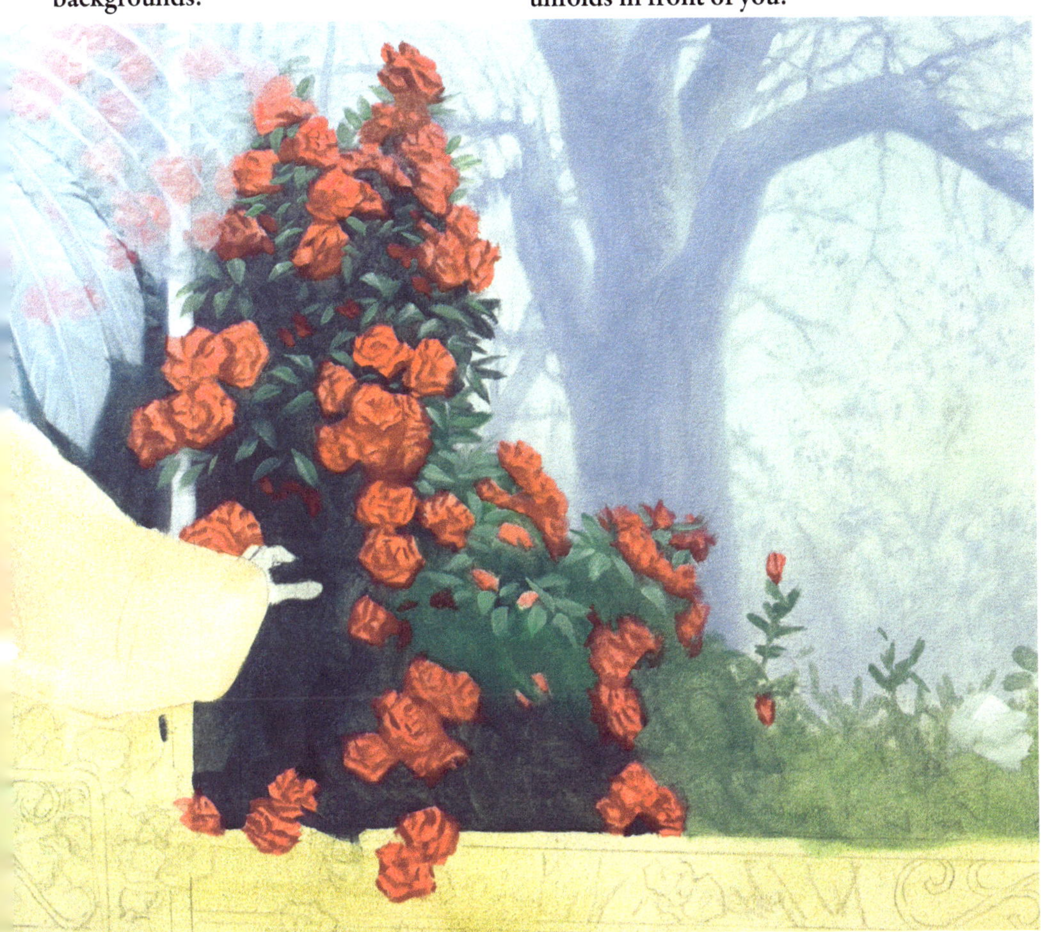

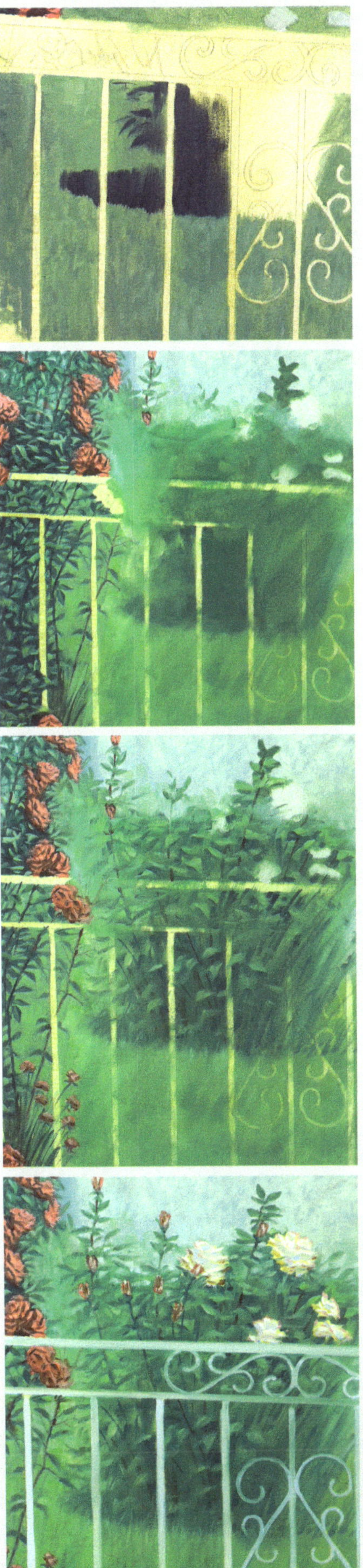

Maul Sticks for Support

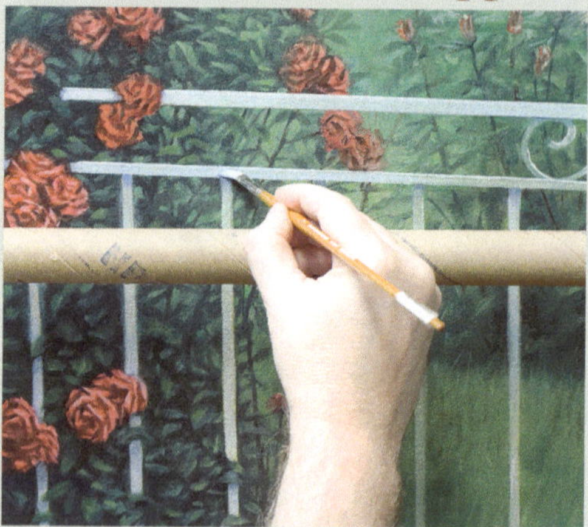

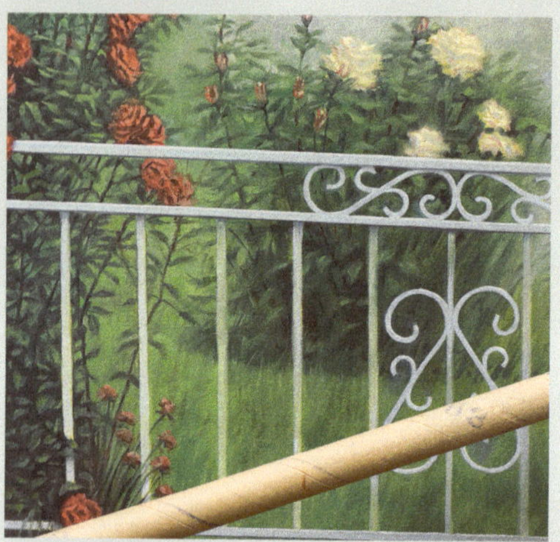

Above, one of my cheap maulsticks made from a sturdy cardboard tube. I built 2 vertical wood beams with screws mounted every 2 inches or so to hold the rod ends. The two vertical supports stand to the sides of my easel. Any straight tube, mop handle, or dowel rod will work, so long as it doesn't bend too much in the middle.

Below, my vertical T-square that hangs from the top of my easel, essential for clean vertical lines as on the fence here.

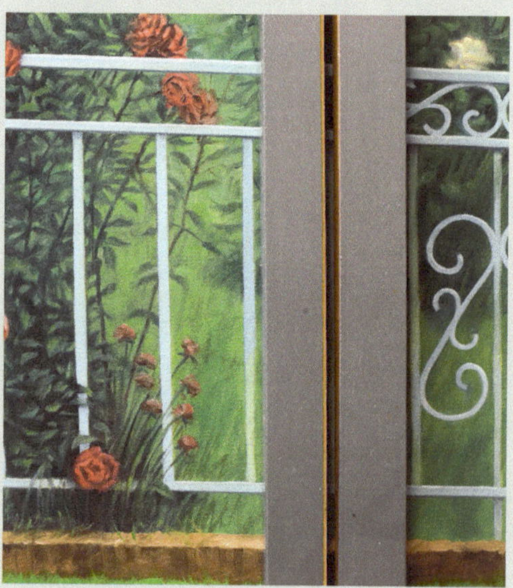

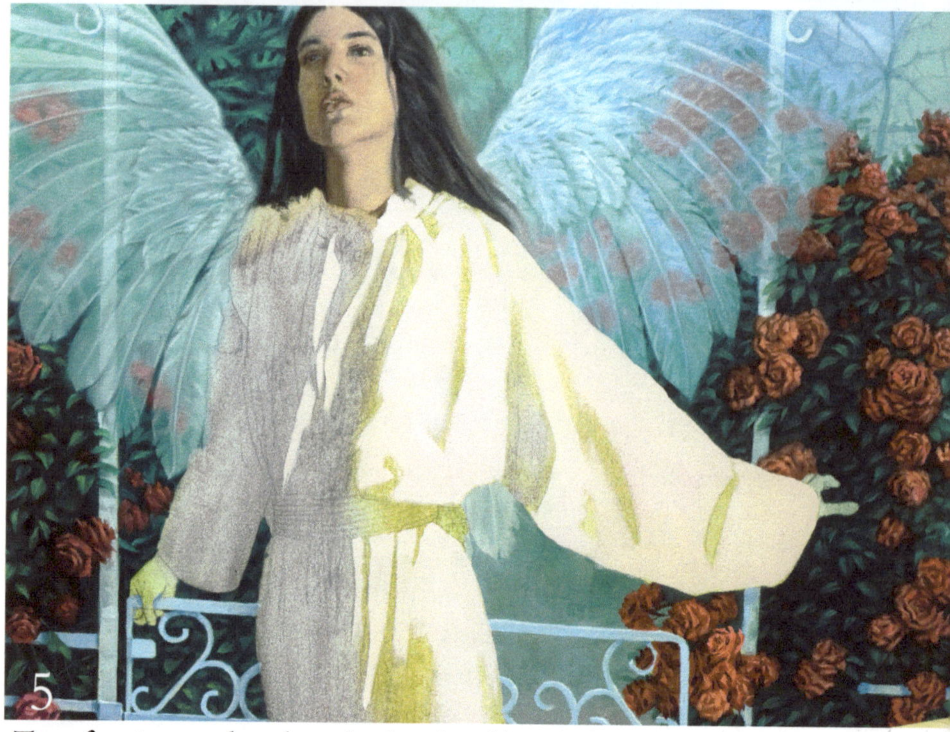

These four images show how the Angel and her clothing developed from my initial gray wash. I first blocked in the highlights, above, and made sure to use heavy enough paint so I could work into it at my leisure without worrying about the base color drying by the time I finished stage 7.

I usually do any figure work just after the background block in, since it's the most fun and defines the painting. But in this piece, I did the figure last so that I could get the clean sharp edge of her white robes to stand out against the softer background gray tones. In the final, I still softened the off-white edge a bit.

Blocking in the middle tones came next, 6, then the shadows, all painted with a large bristle filbert loaded with heavy color. The use of an oversize brush sped the block-in to under an hour before I tweaked the edges with a round bristle brush.

This figure is 33 inches high, which makes the painted head 4 inches. Any smaller and I would want to use small brushes. At this size, I can still use filberts and maintain more control over the fluid brushwork.

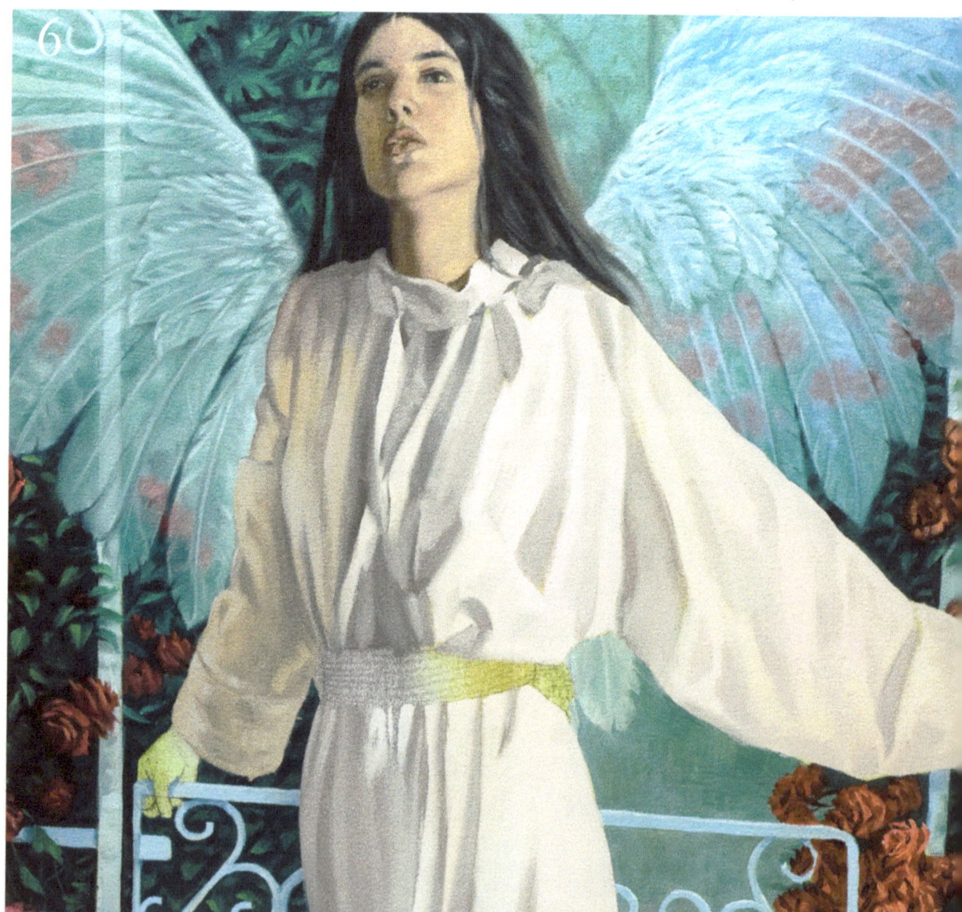

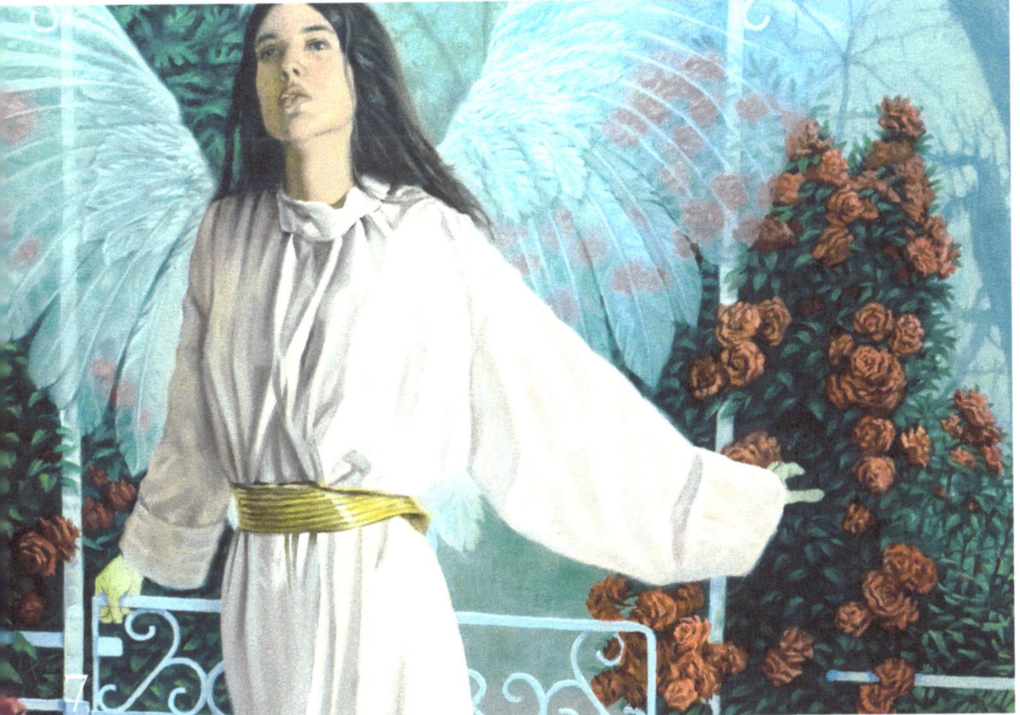

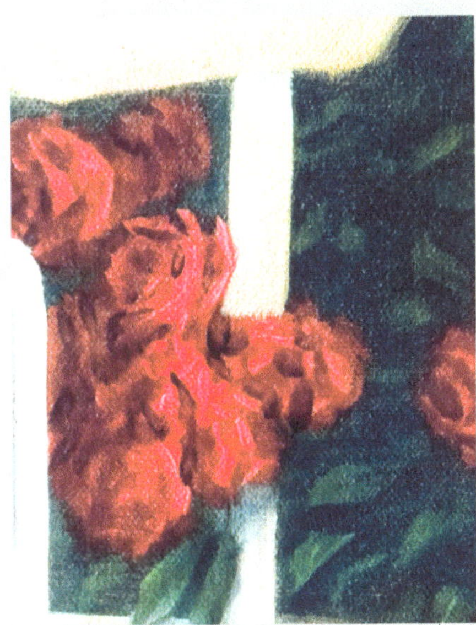

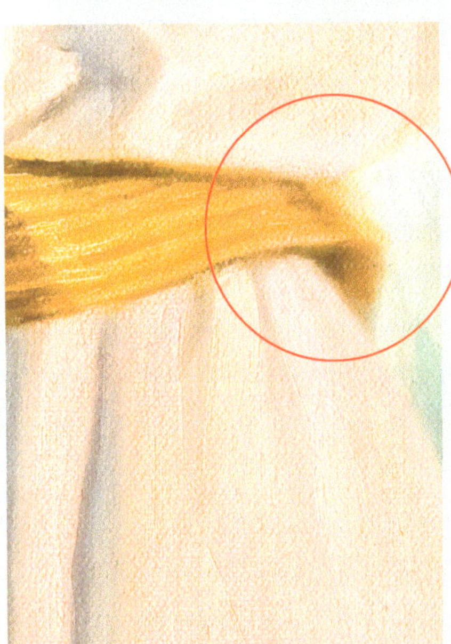

Stage 7, above, shows the smoother areas where I scratched at the whites and off whites and blended the edges into the background so the figure doesn't look like she is pasted on. I used to blend sections with a soft brush, but now I prefer to take a thin bristle and simply scratch from one area of wet paint into the adjacent one. You can use heavier paint with this approach and there is more control, leaving the kind of fresh illustrative look that I prefer over too smooth of surface. It all blends in when you stand back a few feet. You can also look at the overall effect in a mirror or study a quick digital shot.

I know my final color will have a rosy warm tone over the white base of the clothing, so I try to bring up the values (the light and dark) and not worry about color just yet. I have to make up the final color anyway, placing my model into this blue-green setting, but that final color will come from a few glazes over the white.

The last stage brings the painting closer to the vision that I had when I first imagined it. Below, in the final, I softened the wings, glazed and enhanced colors, and pushed that diaphanous quality that conveys fog and suggests a spiritual look.

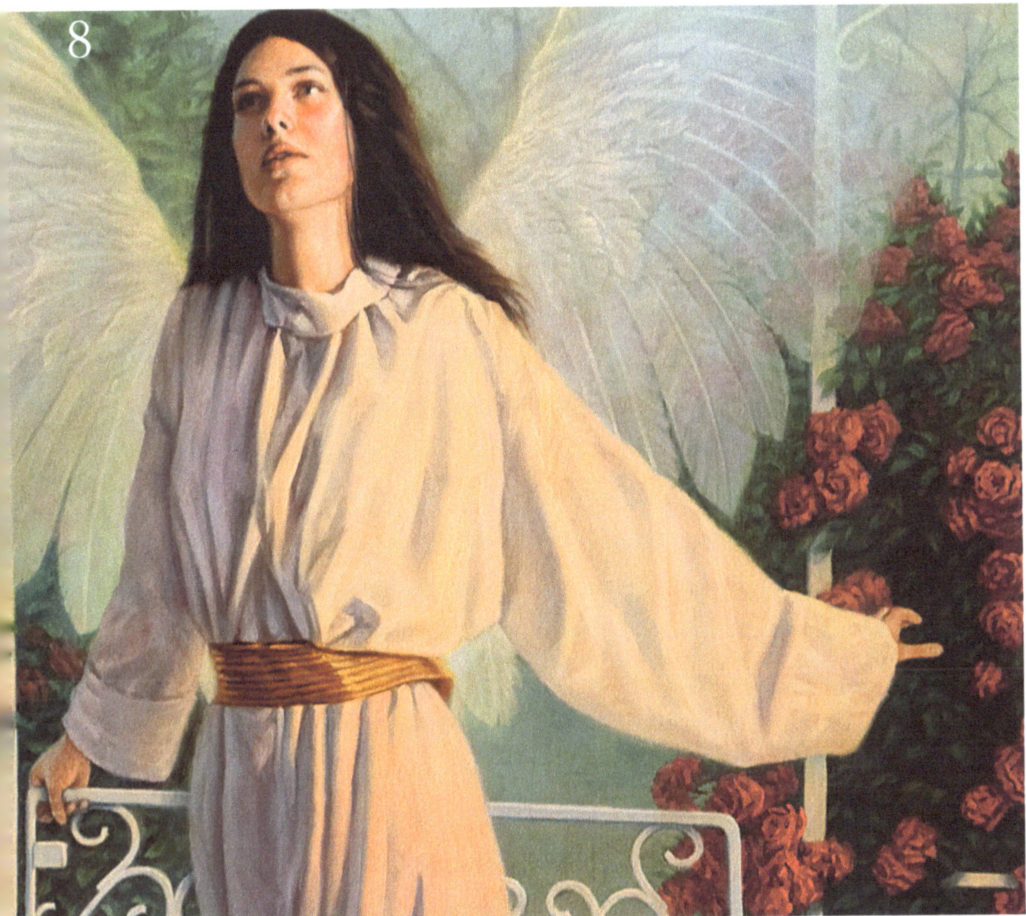

These two closeup shots show the final glazing used over the base color areas of opaque paint. You can see how effective the warmer tones are now, even in the gold belt.

The heavier weave of the canvas grabbed each glaze well, although I would have preferred a smoother weave in the face area, even though I put on additional gesso for her skin. The canvas texture can look enhanced and I prefer not to have a rough look in the skin areas.

Note how the red flowers come to life a bit more and the soft edges fuse better because the coloring has less contrast around the greenery, the edges of the gate, and especially the robes where the warm tone meets the greenish gray. (see circled area)

Male Model in Robes

24x36" Oil on canvas (p.64-65)

Compare the final to these stages and you can see the logical progression of how I applied the oil paint to achieve a degree of realism and depth.

1 and 2, I started with a dry-brush oil drawing that was used as my underpainting, letting the drawing dry completely before applying color. I do sketches in black or brown alkyd or oil in a drybrush manner because it forces me to use the brush more precisely, to put down just what's needed while trying not to overdo the sketch.

In 3, I have developed the head and blocked in the base of the robes. The color is too cool at first, but I know I will probably tone it toward a warm pinkish cast, as in the final. I much prefer to glaze over white or light areas rather than paint them all opaque because the subtle quality of a glazed oil is much more interesting and tends to look jewel-like in the final patina layer than with just opaque color alone. Opaque paint is reflective while translucent oil looks like captured light. I try to utilize the best of both techniques.

In 4, I am ready to add some final brown tones in the background area, then warm up the whites to unify and harmonize this study. I will also add subtle shading to the model's face, which will give it more depth and enhance the realism.

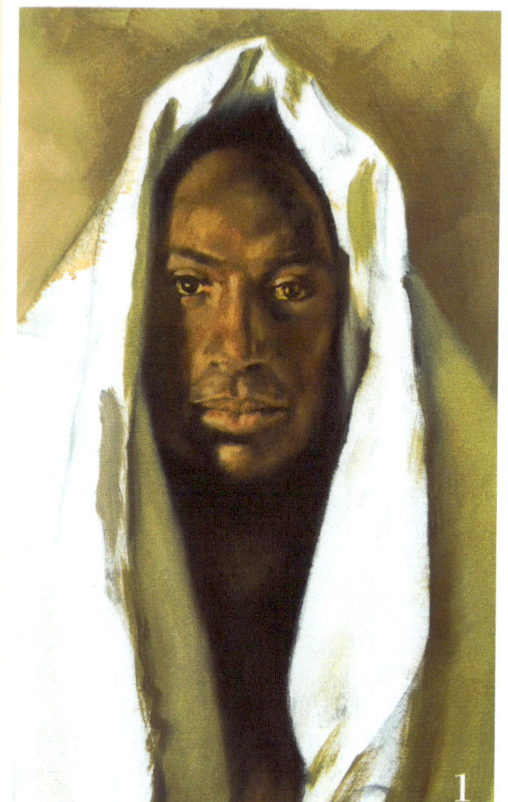
1

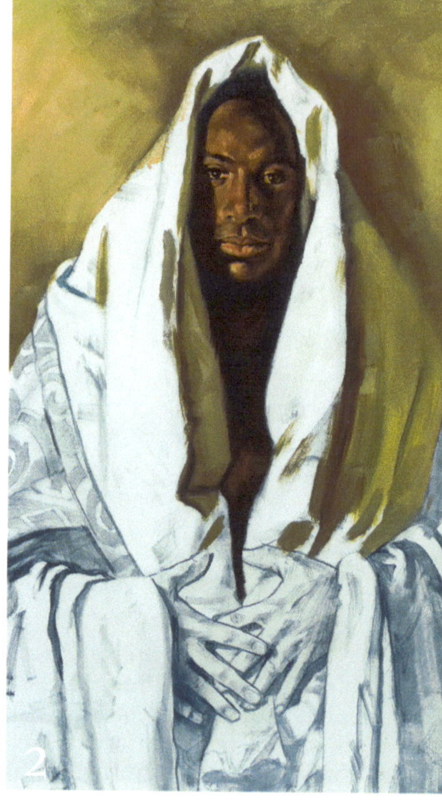
2

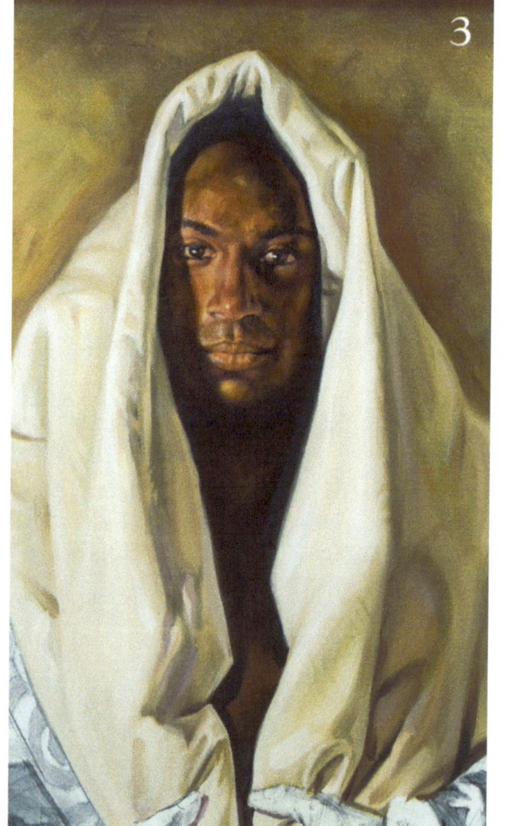
3

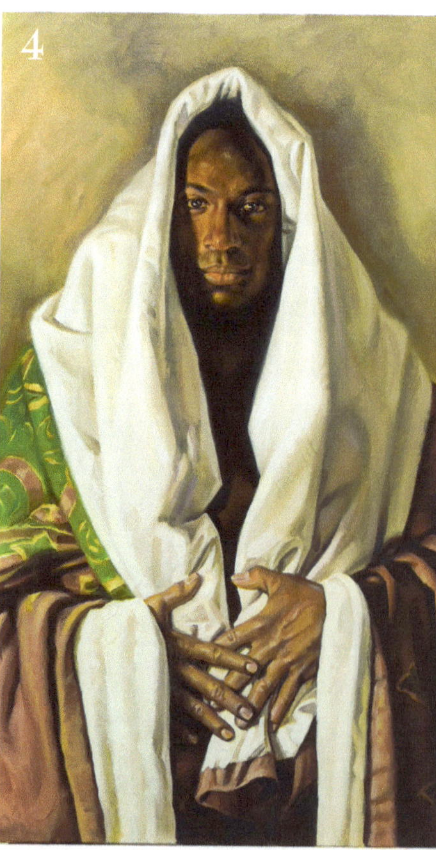
4

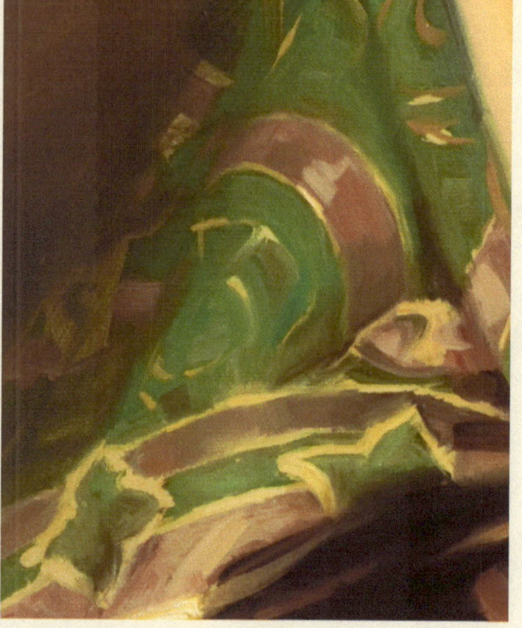

On the left, in contrast to how I handled the cloth in Far Below, p. 5, I used a more direct opaque approach here. This method is less accurate but has more life in its subtle wet-into-wet transitions. The basic procedure is- paint the largest mass color first, in this case the green middle-tone, then the reddish-brown area below it. I added a few shadow green strokes and then began to rough out the color for the stripes. Once the stripes and patterns felt right, I added ocher to the edges of the red stripes. When the base colors were all blocked in, I begin adding highlights and finally pulled the brown background into the wet cloth color to push it back.

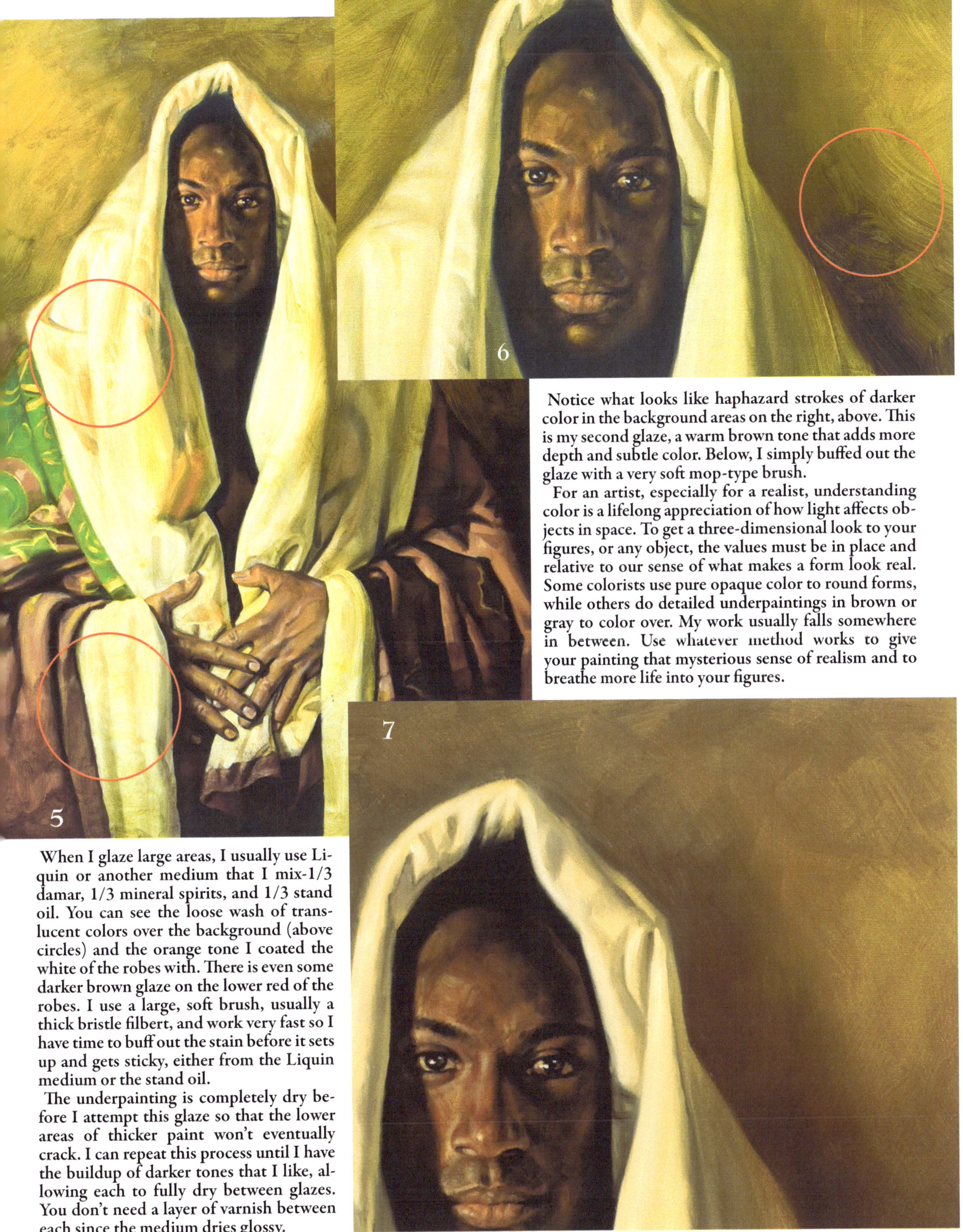

Notice what looks like haphazard strokes of darker color in the background areas on the right, above. This is my second glaze, a warm brown tone that adds more depth and subtle color. Below, I simply buffed out the glaze with a very soft mop-type brush.

For an artist, especially for a realist, understanding color is a lifelong appreciation of how light affects objects in space. To get a three-dimensional look to your figures, or any object, the values must be in place and relative to our sense of what makes a form look real. Some colorists use pure opaque color to round forms, while others do detailed underpaintings in brown or gray to color over. My work usually falls somewhere in between. Use whatever method works to give your painting that mysterious sense of realism and to breathe more life into your figures.

When I glaze large areas, I usually use Liquin or another medium that I mix-1/3 damar, 1/3 mineral spirits, and 1/3 stand oil. You can see the loose wash of translucent colors over the background (above circles) and the orange tone I coated the white of the robes with. There is even some darker brown glaze on the lower red of the robes. I use a large, soft brush, usually a thick bristle filbert, and work very fast so I have time to buff out the stain before it sets up and gets sticky, either from the Liquin medium or the stand oil.

The underpainting is completely dry before I attempt this glaze so that the lower areas of thicker paint won't eventually crack. I can repeat this process until I have the buildup of darker tones that I like, allowing each to fully dry between glazes. You don't need a layer of varnish between each since the medium dries glossy.

The Old Conquistador

24x36" Oil on stretched canvas

Technique using multiple glazes

My good friend John was playing around with some costumes I had when he put this helmet on and I asked him to pose in a direct light for a chiaroscuro effect. You never know where the next painting idea will take you, that's half the fun of being creative. I had no real interest in doing this sort of piece, but seeing the light on John's face and how he fell into the pose was enough to peak my desire to paint it. Portraits can either grab you or bore you, and the few I do are usually friends or models I like- faces with real character and sensitivity.

I started this piece by doing a simple but accurate drawing, only around 5 inches or so, then projected that onto a stained and dry canvas panel. I put on the base values first, using this as more of an underpainting. I moved into local color only after the initial dark base was completely dry. When you isolate stages like this, you don't have to worry about the paint pulling or washing off with overlying layers.

This piece looks like it has a lot of detail, even in the oversize blowup to the right, but it was painted fairly quickly, just about 12 hours total time, using bristle rounds and then smaller brushes to move the paint around. It's a straightforward approach that always works.

Right, the finished painting. Note the darker overall tone due to glazing after stage 6.

1
Pencil drawing over a pre-toned canvas.

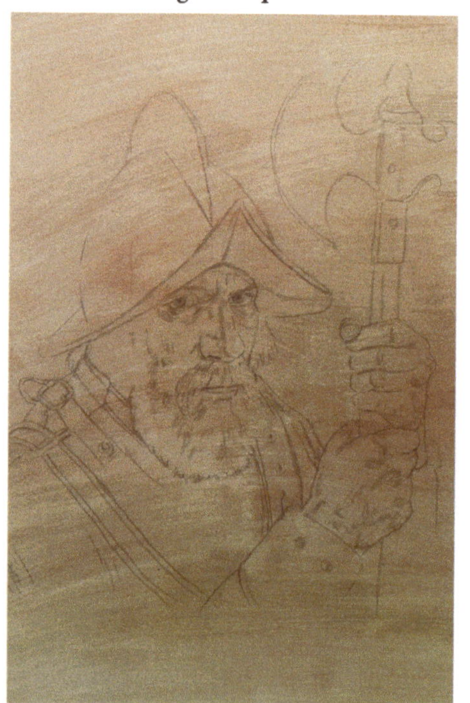

2
Burnt umber used to redraw the shadows.

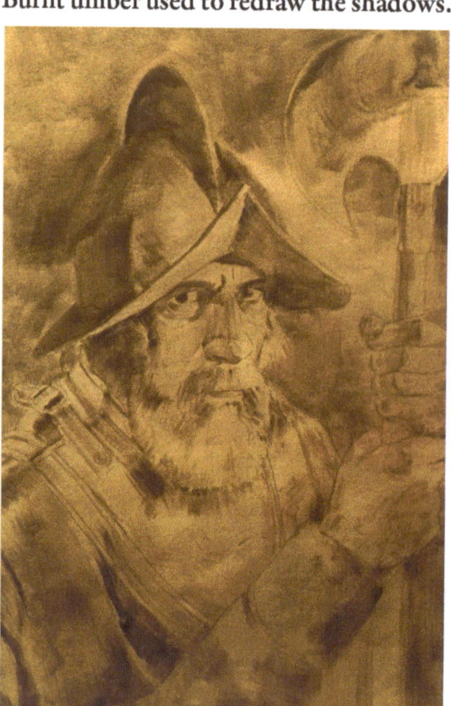

3
Black shadows added and highlights pulled out.

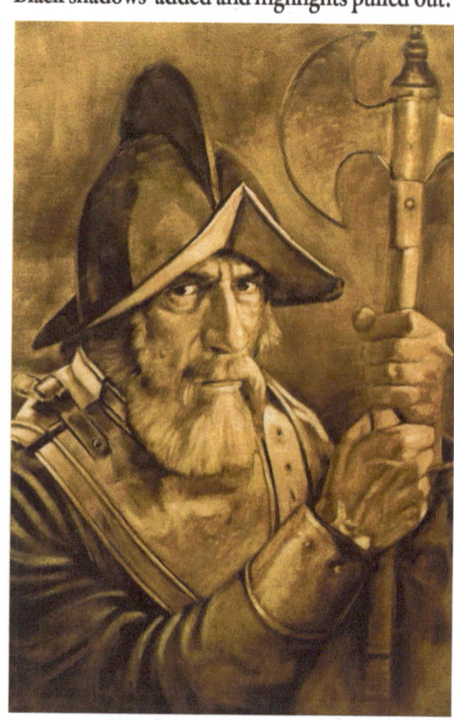

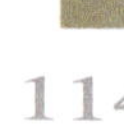

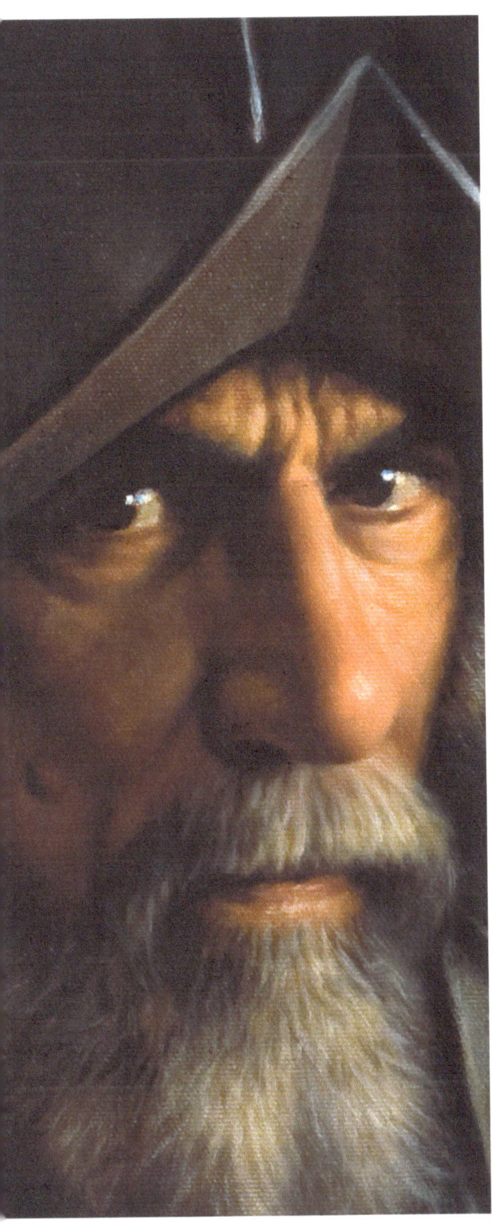

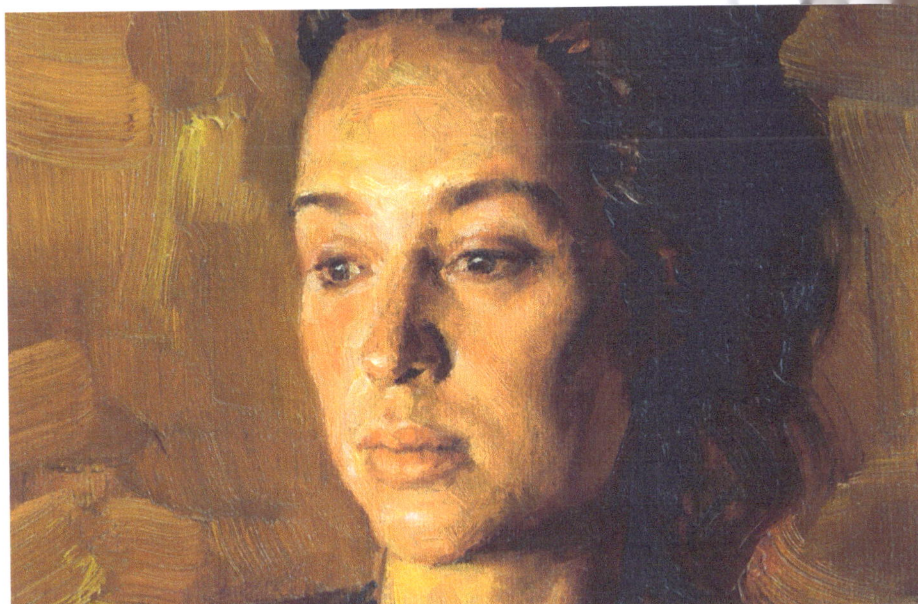

The head, above (from p. 79) is painted only around one inch high, yet it's interesting to see the strokes blown up to get a feel of controlled brushwork. I know that my tendency is to push thicker paint in the direction of the forms, following the curve of the woman's cheek or the horizontal plane of the forehead. Some artists follow a more 'impressionistic' approach by placing small strokes of graduating color and value to blend one edge into another. You can also softly drag one wet area or let the work dry, then drybrush with a minimal amount of semi-opaque paint to create a soft edge. A blow-up like this can help reveal ways to rejuvenate your working methods by revealing how to place color or adjust edges.

Left, a closer shot of the final image. Note that the final is much darker than stage 6, below. I glazed over the painting with 3 or 4 passes of burnt sienna, a deep red, raw sienna (not ocher, it's too opaque for thin glazing) and black, with some blue mixed in to add to the depth. I simply kept darkening the shadow areas with thin translucent layers until I felt I had reached sufficient density to make the face look more three-dimensional and the lighter areas show some glow in the skin.

You can't get this sort of depth with just straight opaque painting, not even with color contrast. You can get a beautiful opaque look, but not the full depth. By adding patina layers, the final glazing really enhances the overall rich color density and enhances the realism.

A close variation to this technique is taking small brushes and laboriously working over each area as if it were a tight watercolor or gouache rendering, but this can lead to an overworked look and can be very time consuming.

4
The first opaque base color is added.

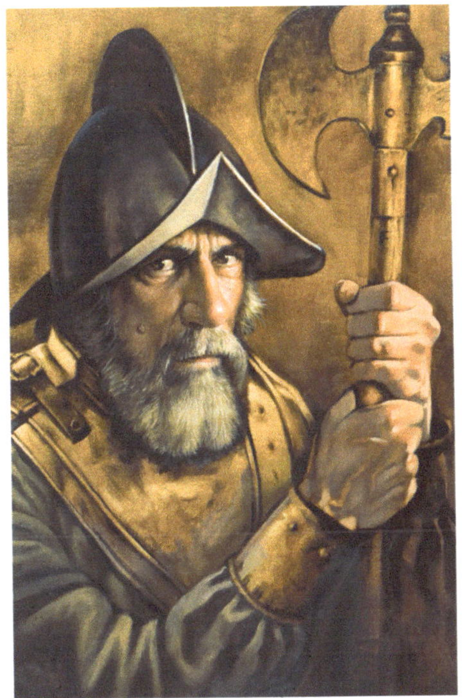

5
I refined edges and added more color.

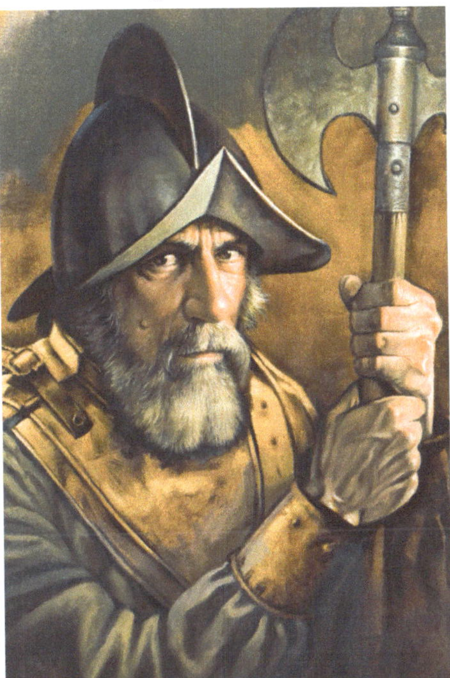

6
This stage is ready for the darker glazing.

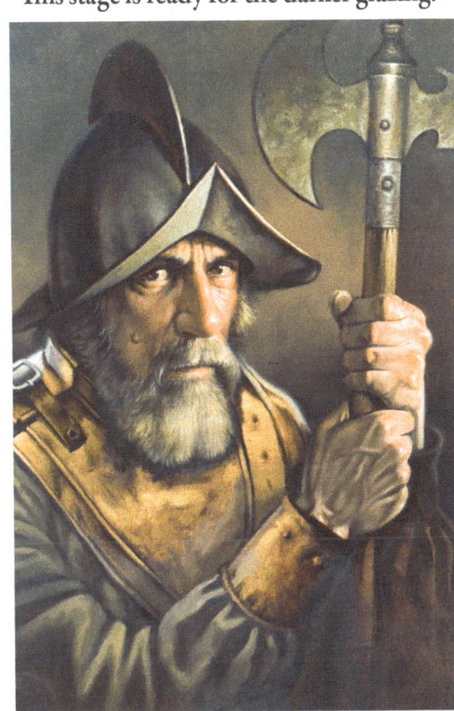

NATASHA

3 hour study using fast drying medium

24x36" oil on medium canvas (p. 69)

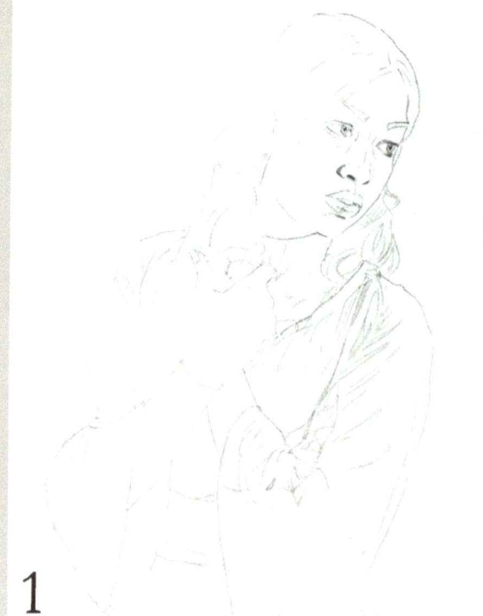

1

1. I projected my drawing onto a loose sheet of acrylic primed canvas, then stretched this onto standard 24 x 36" stretcher bars. I prefer a simple outline over a tonal drawing as a base because you can see the line through a fairly heavy wash.

I always spray the pencil drawing with one or two light coats of fixative and let this dry for at least a half-hour. (Avoid breathing any spray. Spray outside if possible.)

2. I tried a fairly new medium, Galkyd, made by Gamblin, to help make the oil washes more translucent and dry much faster. I know if I can get the paint to thicken up a bit so that there is some pull to each stroke, then I have much more control when I work the detail areas. The Galkyd, for my use here, worked well, but dried much too fast for my normal use. This is just a quick study, so I tried to work as fast as I could, sticking with flat brushwork and accurate blocky strokes.

If you mix up your own medium, try adding a bit of stand oil and 1/4th damar varnish. This will give your paint additional pull, or drag, so that the paint you put down will be pulled off the brush easier and will dry with some gloss to it.

You can see, in image 2, how the head was blocked in and the feeling of a watercolor-like wash was achieved by floating a soft house painter's 3" brush over the initial color. Into this, I simply stroked more direct solid coloring and built the head into a three-dimensional form.

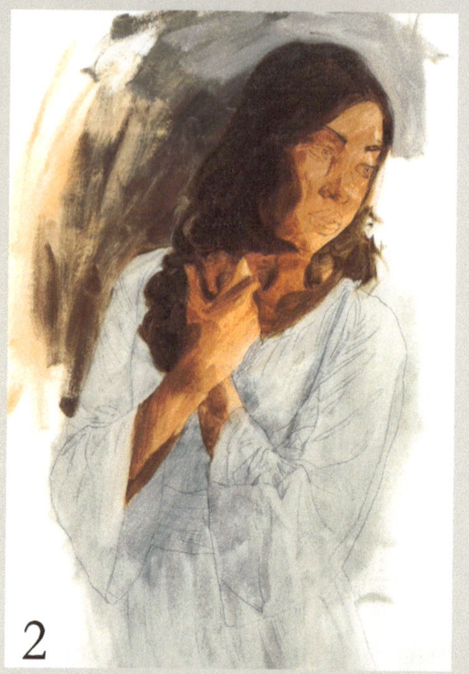

2

Above, you can see the quick washes of Galkyd medium thinned with mineral spirits and then quickly built up with heavier paint. Since the Galkyd dries so fast, I have to make sure the strokes I put on are quick and accurate. My pencil base helps guide me without controlling me to such a degree that the piece looks stiff or photographic. This piece is not about details and finessing, just a color sketch to loosen me up. It's an experiment in handling whites and edges.

For my larger pieces, like the Angel paintings, I often start out with no medium and use only mineral spirits to thin the paint with, or add extenders, like oil of cloves (very sparingly, just a drop or two) and walnut oil to the faster drying earth colors. Burnt and raw umber, yellow ocher, and other earth hues, dry much quicker than most oil colors and usually leave a matte surface that must be matched when painted over. This surface can even absorb the next layer of paint, so I tend to seal my first wash or underpainting with Liquin medium once it has thoroughly dried.

Using a medium at the start can help speed up the drying time of the initial underpainting and leave a glossy finish, whereas turpentine and mineral spirits leave a matte residue. So the use of Galkyd here has a purpose, but forces me to work quickly before the paint sets up and is so tacky that I can't do much with it until it dries completely. Galkyd can dry so fast that you don't get much working time, but many artists prefer oils to dry quickly so they can paint over them even faster, sometimes within hours.

Adding Japan and especially cobalt dryers will chemically speed up drying time dramatically, but both additives can cause surface problems that lead to future cracking.

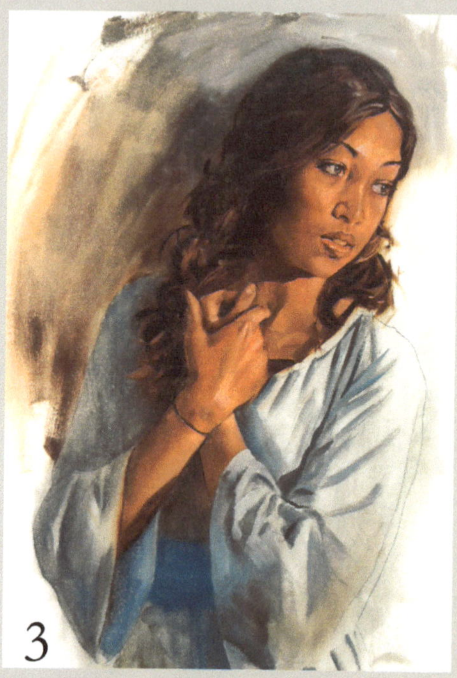

3

In 3, notice the effect of the harder edges against the softened wash; sharp focus against softer focus areas will make those sharp planes stand out much more, simply by contrast. For example, if you want your figure to really come forward against any background space, keep the background on the soft side. The sharp edges will visually stand away from the softer background. Use the softer edges (rounded forms and diffused areas like hair) to melt or blend into the background just a bit more to help seat your figure in the foreground.

Study photography and impressive painters like Sargent and Zorn to see how much they used this principle for great effect. This adds much more interest to an otherwise dull piece and keeps the work from looking too photographic or photo-copied.

One of the reasons I became an illustrator was a respect for those gifted pros who really knew how to handle oil paint. I learned from the classic fine artists of the past, of course, but the great illustrators influenced my technique the most. Some, like Sundblum, Abbey, Leyendecker, Pyle, and Cornwell, had real flair, a very rare ability to put down paint with what looked like effortless brushwork rarely matched today. Rockwell had exceptional color skills and handled opaque paint as well as anyone. By studying their work, I found that a more painterly approach suited my narrative pieces best and far exceeded any modern fine art. Even though the imagery was commercial and sometimes trite, the technique was still masterful.

It's all a learning process. Every study or painting I've done has taught me something, especially when I make mistakes. I try to learn more about the craft of oil painting from every artist I meet who understands how to manipulate paint.

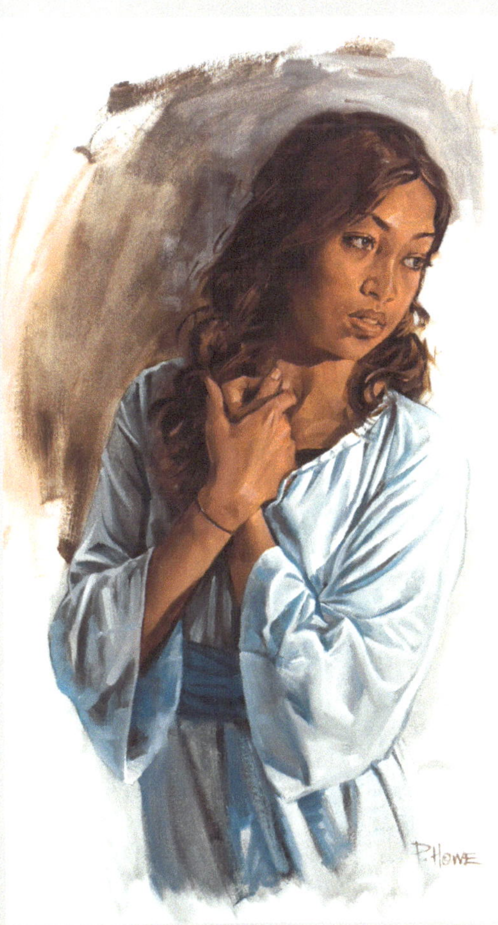

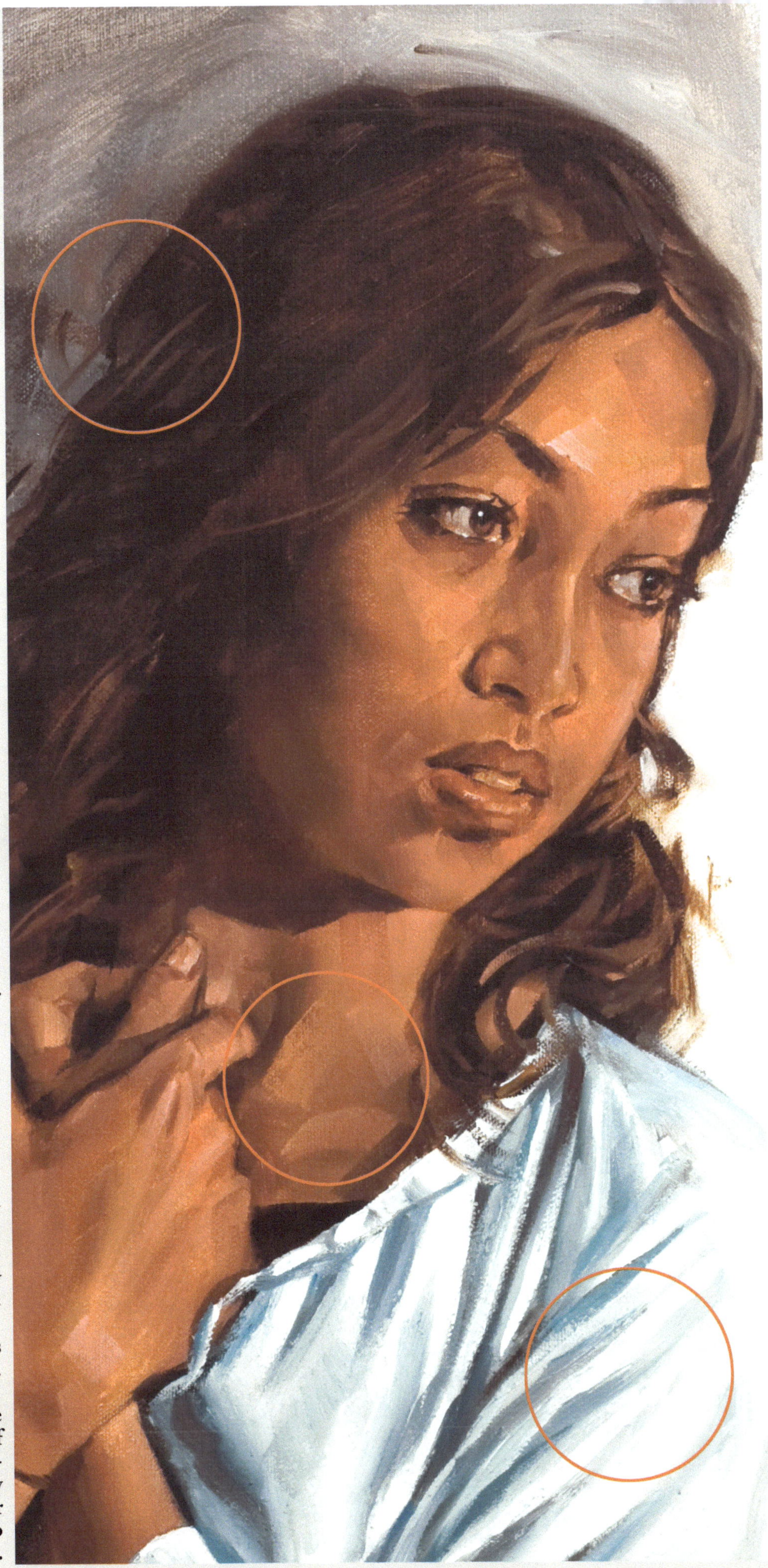

The final study, above, (P. 69) was done in 3 hours. I usually don't work quite that fast, but the downside of quick drying additives (siccatives) or mediums is that, once they are on the surface, they speed drying to the point where you either have to work fast or let the paint dry and then work over the dry paint, using it as an underpainting.

I much prefer a wet-into-wet overall look for my more finished pieces, working in sections that I bring together over a period of days, not hours. The Galkyd medium seems more suited to artists and illustrators who prefer working in multiple quick-drying layers, not slow blended areas.

In the top circle, you can see the initial brown wash of mineral spirits mixed with the fast drying Galkyd. This area set up in about 30 minutes. Without the medium, it would have stayed wet for at least a few hours longer, although slick to paint over. The medium made the normally slow drying oil more receptive to over-painting by making it tacky so the new brushwork pulls off in nice sharp paint strokes.

Middle circle, the more opaque passages are easier to handle, like drawing with color. I used bristle flats to lay on heavier strokes.

The bottom circle shows the more opaque whites used to clean up the muddied area of my initial brown wash. This area had stiffened up by the time I reached it, so the heavy white went on easily. But another half-hour or so and the underpainting would be too tacky to work into, especially if using sables.

Sail Away

48x60" Oil on stretched canvas (p 50-51)

This painting took several days to complete and turned into more work for me because I tried some new techniques to achieve the luminous color in the sky, the water, and overall warm light. It's a fair sized piece. Working this large helps in the detail areas to achieve some realism without resorting to tiny brushes and nitpicking the image.

Below, the original drawing was transferred to my canvas as a tracing by blowing up the drawing on a copier in reverse and then adding a thin chalk layer to the opposite side, smeared with bestine. When I applied pressure to the canvas, which was pinned to the wall at this point so the canvas stayed flat and firm, the drawing was transferred. While it is time consuming, this method sometimes helps to get my original drawing down a bit more accurately, even though I tend to change things as I paint. On this piece, however, I stayed true to the original sketch.

This piece is one of a series of Dream Images that I enjoy doing because the theme allows me some freedom to create a world where there are no boundaries, no real world physics to inhibit my imagination. I can push color, defy gravity by having objects float, and even bend forms, as I did in the cloud mass, to give the background a surreal atmosphere.

I like adding design elements, like the floating cloth that flies freely above the woman on the couch. In most of my work, I try to keep some of the concept hidden, even mysterious, so each viewer is invited to interpret the paintings in their own way.

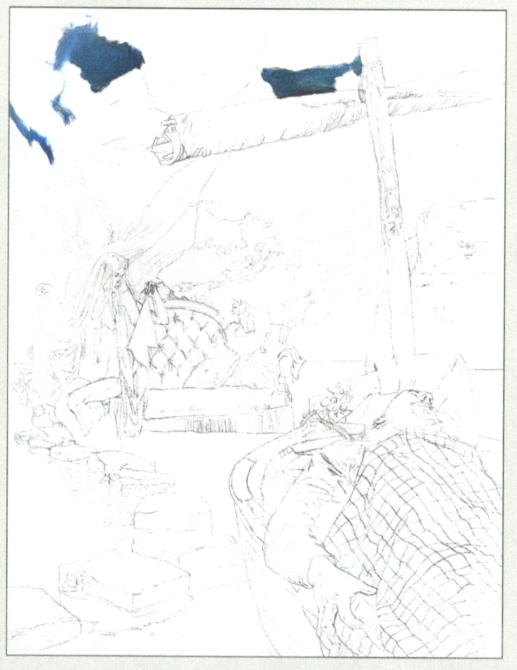

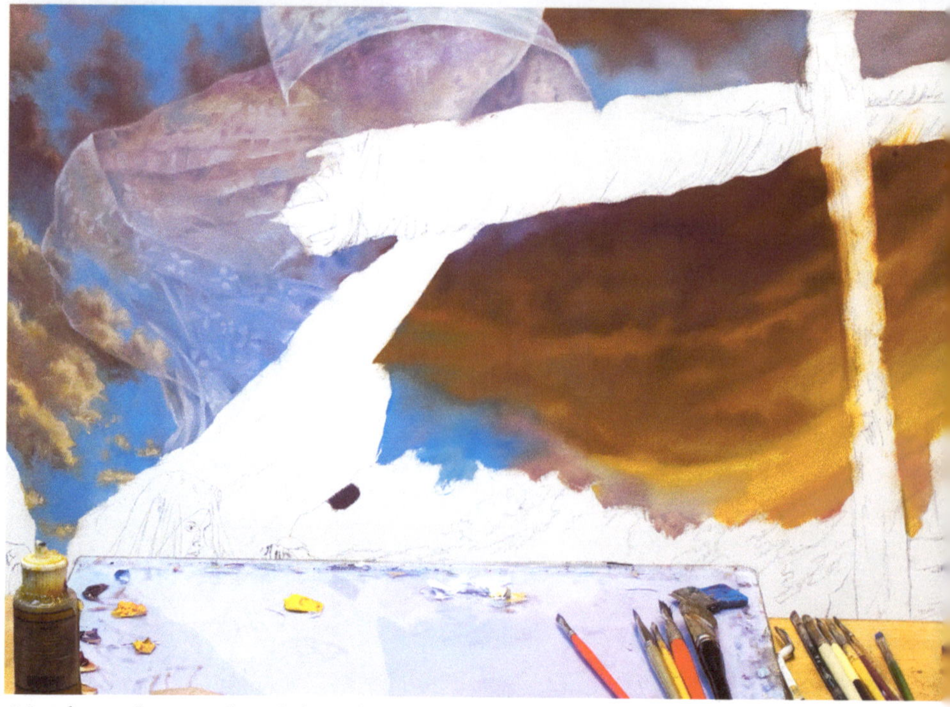

My glass palette is placed directly in front of my painting because I want the same light on both the palette and the canvas. This allows for more accurate color matching, especially in skin tones and sky areas. It also keeps me from turning to the side hundreds of times during a painting session simply to mix paint on the palette.

Above, note the sloppy area around the unpainted mast. I am not concerned about trying to keep my work clean, at least not at this stage. Since I paint with opaque color I know I can always paint over any area as I move toward the foreground, redrawing as I go. I prefer keeping the background loose at this stage, concentrating on the overall mood of the piece, dominated by the fluid sky.

Even though this is a fairly large piece, the woman's head is less than an inch high, making the full figure only around 5 inches or so. I can paint small if I have to, but the canvas tends to create problems if I don't add a smooth layer of gesso ahead of time to help smooth out the skin tone areas.

Below, this shot is a good example of how I lay on initial color in a loose but accurate direct method. When I was first learning how to paint, I found only a few books that attempted to show another artist's technique. Hopefully, some of these demos will help answer questions about my approach, such as how to build up paint layers, the block-in stages, glazing, and overall color tone and mood. (These are the main questions visitors ask about my site demos.) Beyond technique, a strong design is essential to lead the viewer into and around the image. Before starting this painting, I spent a few days working through the design, moving elements around until I felt it had a solid composition.

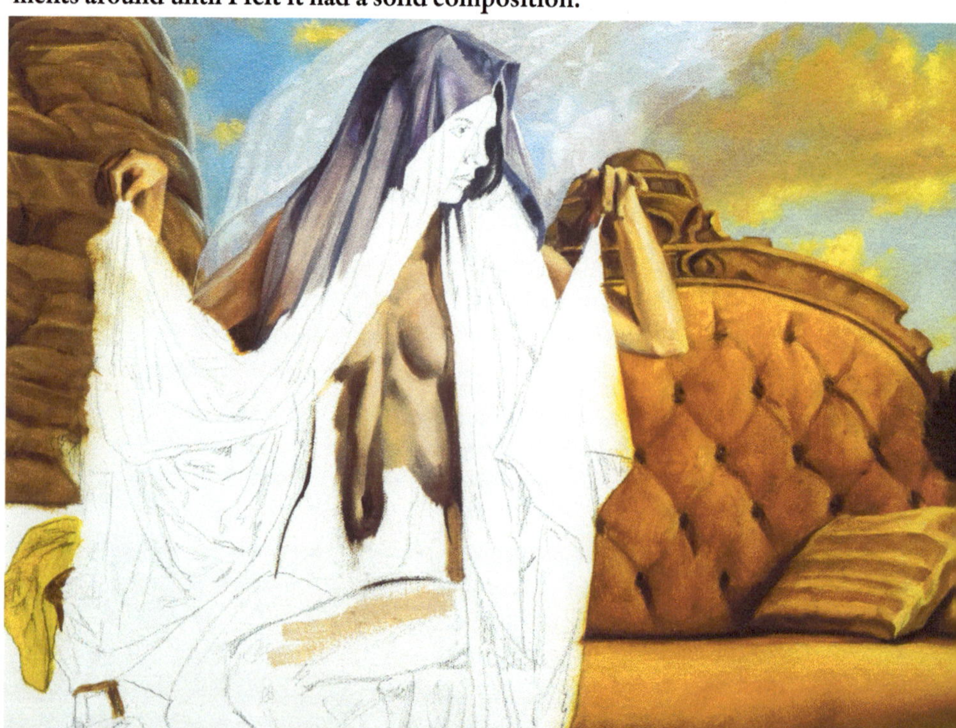

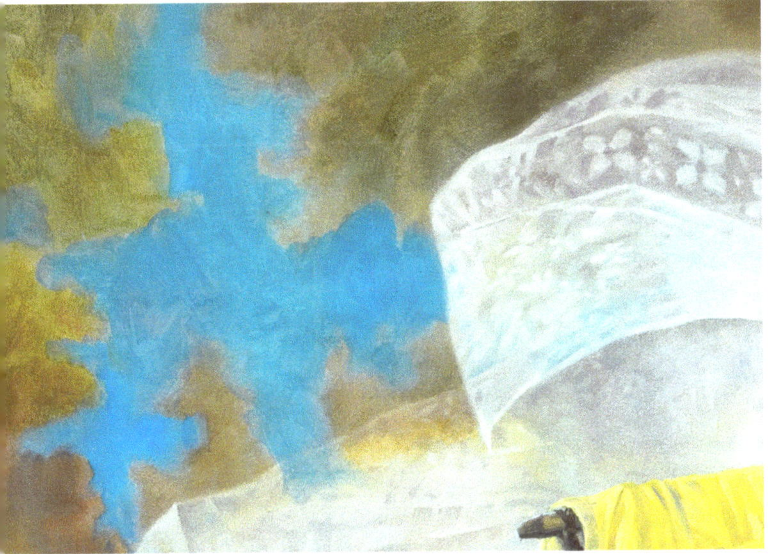

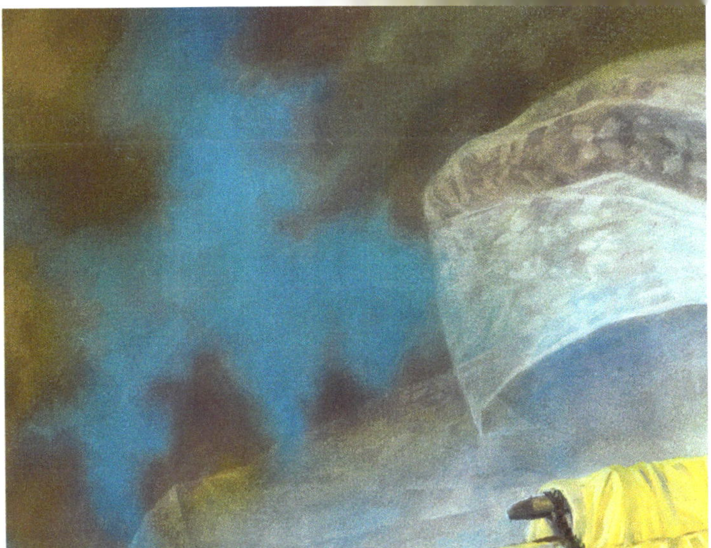

The cloud mass on the image above is the same as the one to the right, which has been buffed and blurred out with a mop brush. A small soft house painter's brush works just as well, so long as you pull in the direction of the cloud forms, guiding one mass into the next. You can layer on effects like this over and over. A good medium really helps, not only to speed things up dramatically, but to thin out the paint and make it more receptive to the blending. Don't use just mineral spirits or turpentine if you plan to work with multiple layers of paint, they can remove the underlying layer and leave a fragile matte film that is the dried residue.

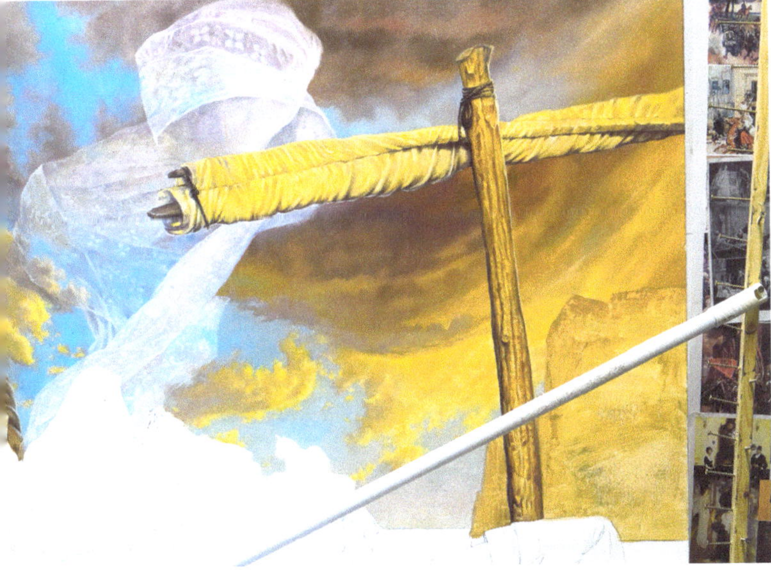

Above, note the maulstick I have attached at one end to a vertical wood beam with nails screwed into it. I use this quite a bit when I need to steady my hand. I can make nice diagonal lines or just rest my painting hand against it as I hold my free hand to guide the stick angle. I have a collection of cheap rods now, from old tripod legs to this broomstick handle, which has a hole in it to help grab the nail. Whatever works!

Most of the sky at this point is blocked in so I start developing the sail and mast area. If you think of a background as one mass to complete first, then the middle ground in front of that, objects like the mast will naturally come forward for several reasons. Color variance, sharp edges, the linear effect of the shaft and cross beam- all force the sail forward to break away from the background. Stacking elements like this is a fundamental approach to realism with greater depth and interest. I try to use whatever design tricks I can to enhance my work, like the softer floating material drifting just behind the edge of the sail. I try not to go overboard with too many unnecessary elements or the work will lose impact by becoming too busy, distracting the eye, rather than guiding it.

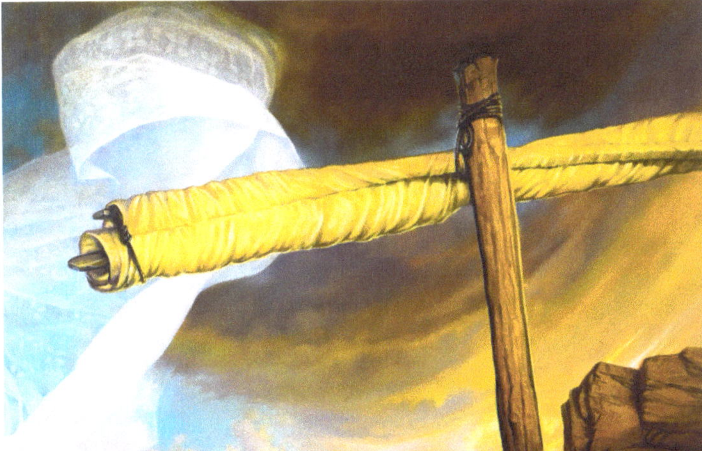

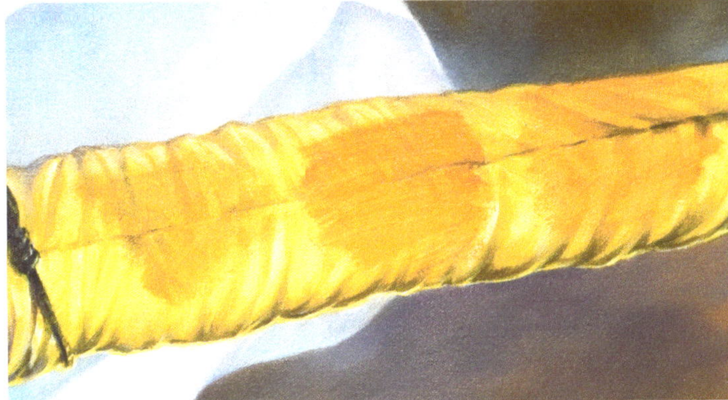

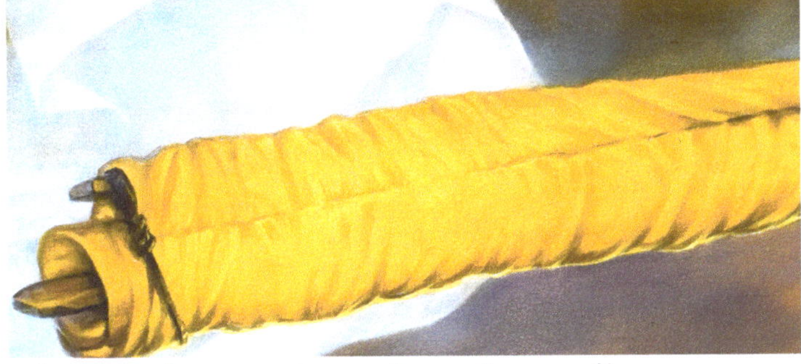

Above, the three mast images show a closeup of how a test glaze was applied over the dried ocher base color. If you work quickly, you can wipe off the test color and use the hue that works best.

The lower image shows the full glaze, buffed out smooth to give a richer tone overall.

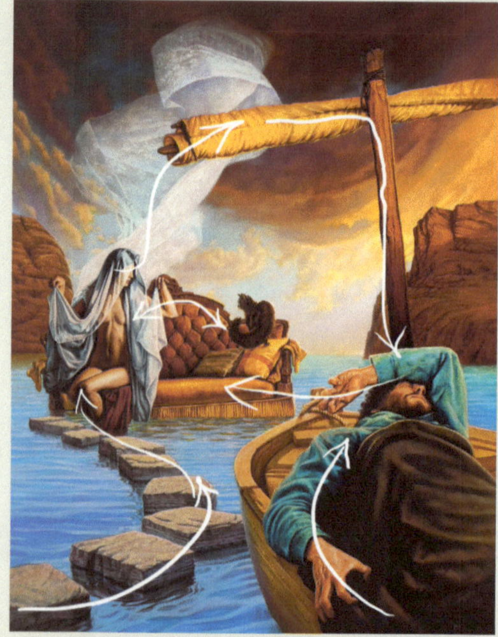

For my larger works, I spend many hours testing different compositions until I feel there is a strong enough design to control the viewer's initial response and lead you into the image. On this piece, the dynamic push toward the woman on the couch is buffered by the cross arm of the mast and the sky bending down to push the visual path back toward the man's arm and around again to the cat on the couch. By darkening and blurring areas, like the right side of the mast, they fade more into the background and become less of a pull away from the center of interest.

Beyond composition, there are those elements that suggest spiritual and dream connections that are designed for each viewer to interpret however they choose.

Below, an extreme closeup section showing the cloth pattern and the glazing effect over an impasto base. This has a similar feel to how Whistler achieved some of his interesting textures, dragging or glazing over a dried impasto underpainting.

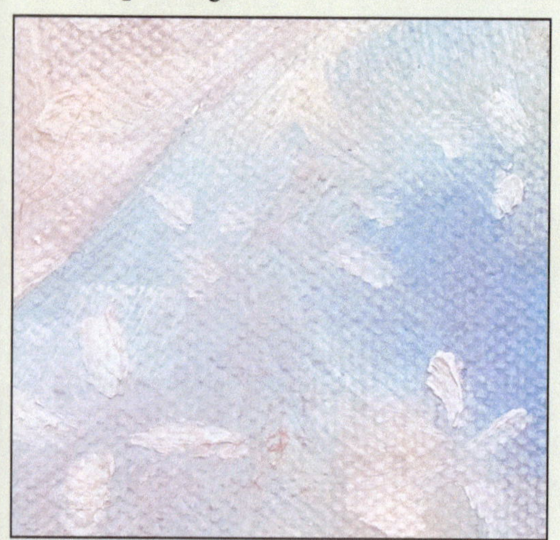

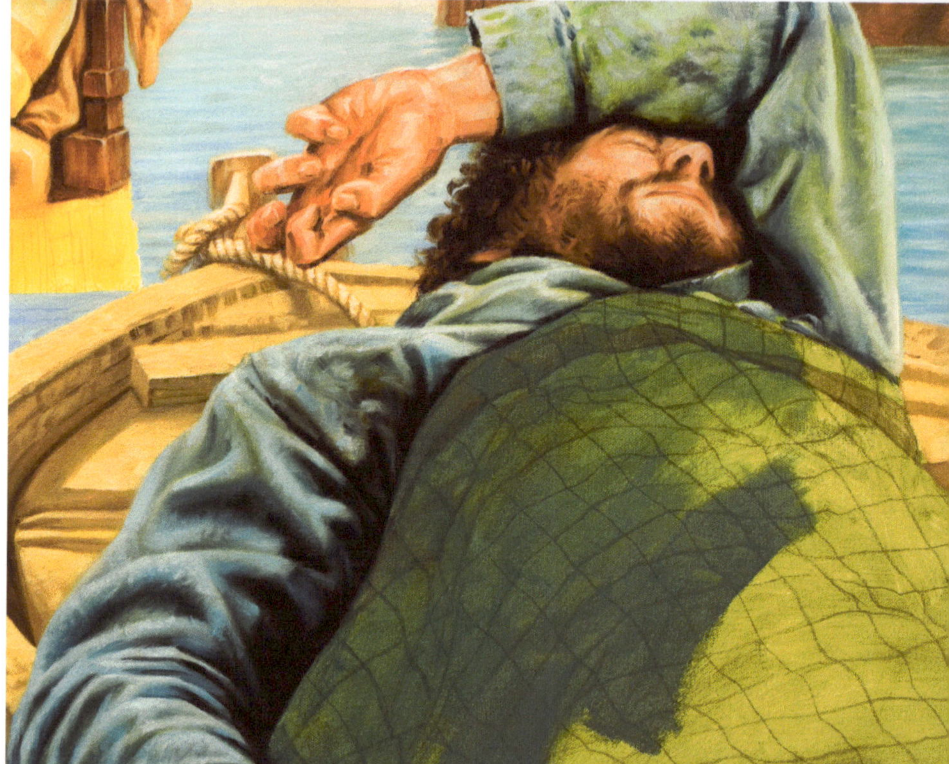

Above, the rough blocked in color for the lower figure is based on local color for each area: reddish-pink for his skin, middle blue for the shirt, middle green for the blanket, etc. If you start with the middle tones, it's easy to adjust them lighter or darker from that base mix of color. One of the nice features of oil paint is that if you mix enough of the base middle color (local color), you can add black or the complementary color to it for darker shades, and add white or light hues to it for lighter halftones. It works best with opaque paint and reflective material, like skin, cloth, and other solids.

Below, some of my experiments with the floating rocks. I tried a number of effects, pushing them to look more interesting, a process that can be fun but sometimes difficult when making up such areas. They finally evolved back to basic rock-like stones and I fudged them enough to give them the realism that I prefer. I wanted them in the design to help lead the viewer back to the woman. Compare these tests to the final rocks on page 49. In the end, I settled on a natural look, with a warm tone for the sunlit areas and a cooler gray tone for the shadows.

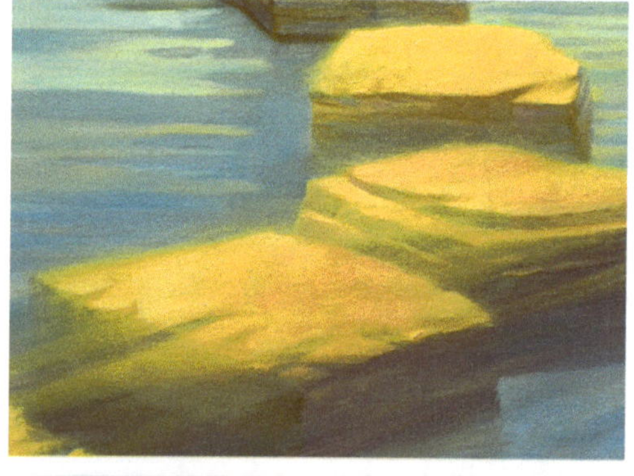

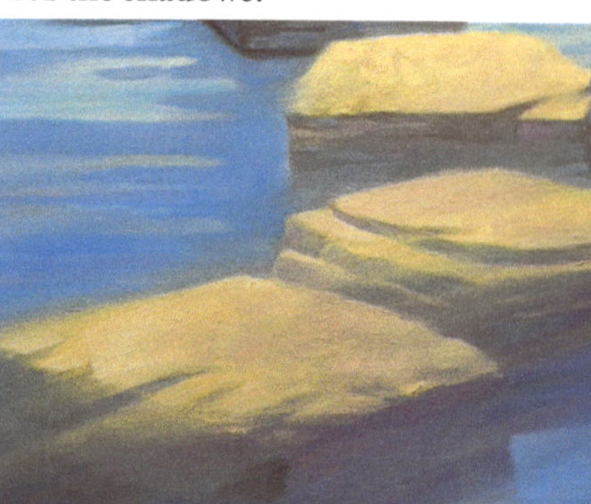

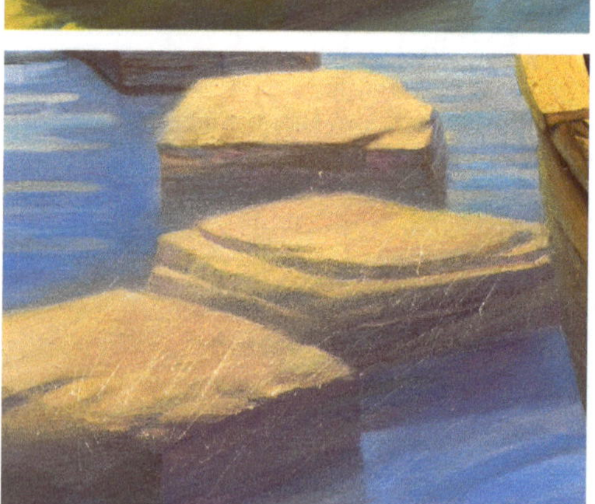

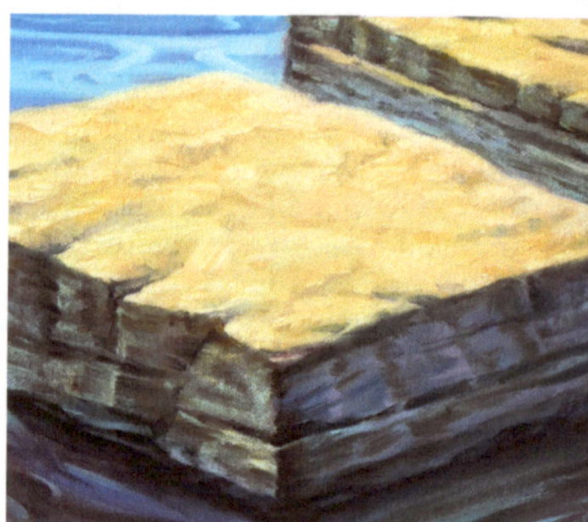

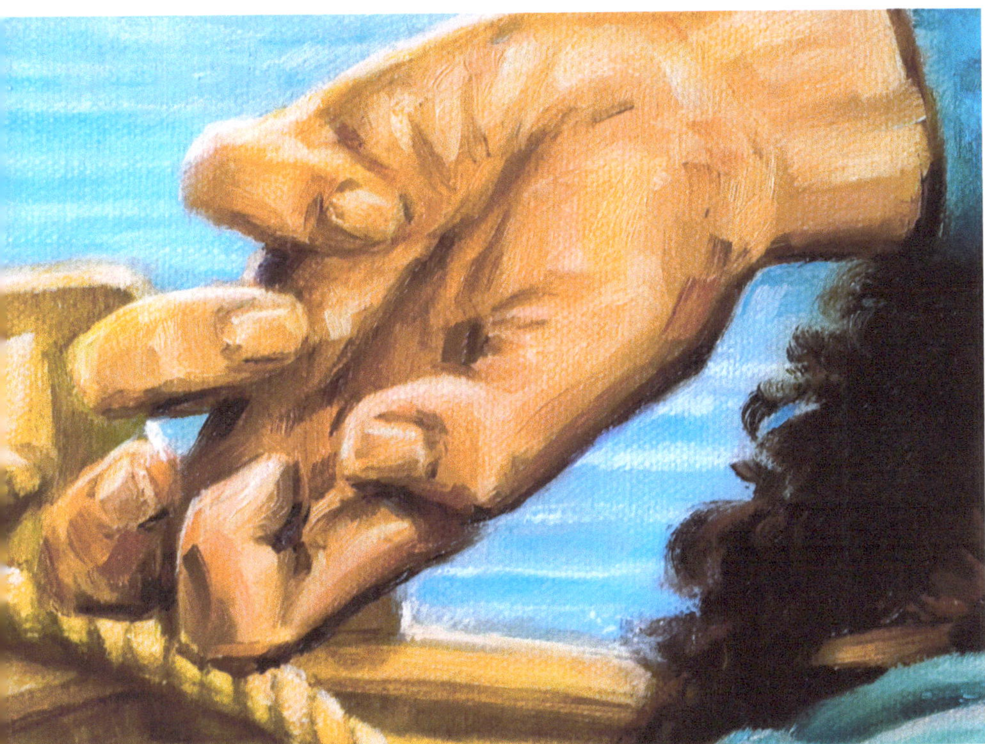

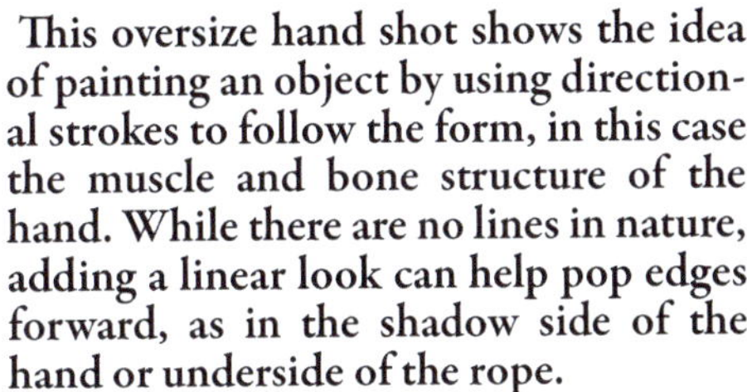

This oversize hand shot shows the idea of painting an object by using directional strokes to follow the form, in this case the muscle and bone structure of the hand. While there are no lines in nature, adding a linear look can help pop edges forward, as in the shadow side of the hand or underside of the rope.

Right, three stages of the rocky precipice; a thick block-in, then refinements with 1/4 inch bristle flats. Note the middle tones first, then the shadows. The final color was enhanced with a rich burnt sienna glaze to suggest sunlight hitting the top of the cliff.

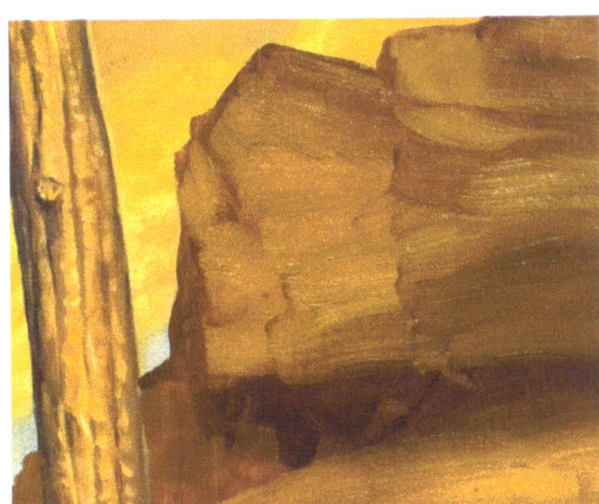

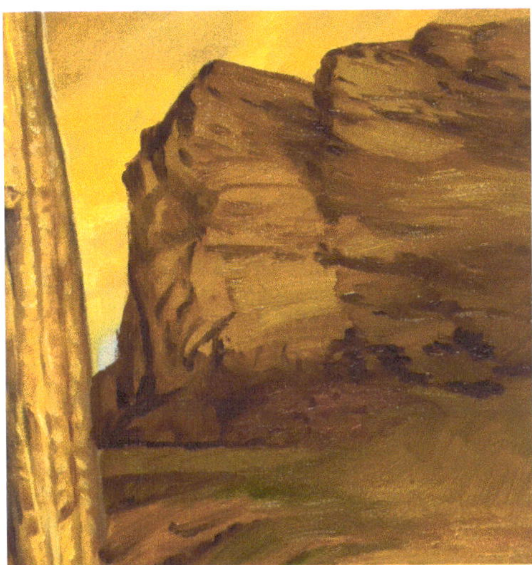

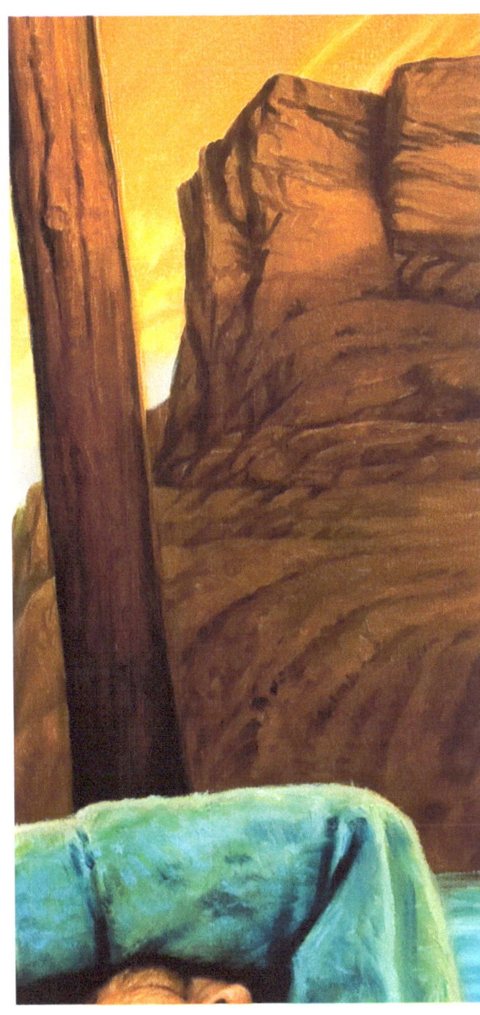

Below, the fully developed woman and couch. I painted her skin tones the same way I would with a larger figure, but did everything on a smaller scale, using a few small brushes in these areas only. Once the base tone was roughed in, (see previous spread) I let this dry thoroughly and then glazed up or down from that middle value. Think of sunlight hitting form and it's easier to anticipate where glazing can enrich color.

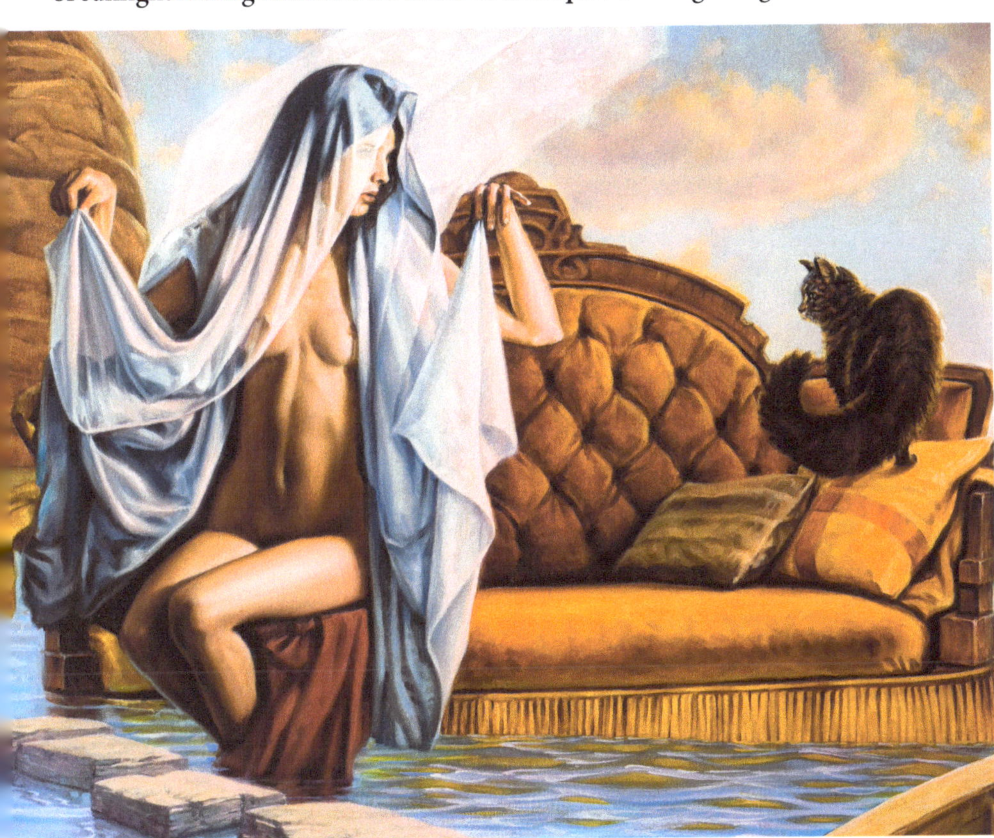

Study in Red Robes

22x36" Oil on canvas (p. 67)

Brown underpainting technique

I have received numerous questions regarding this study by visitors to my site, philiphowe.com, especially from artists who live in Europe and India who have asked about my underpainting technique and how to keep it realistic. I apply the same principles used with direct painting, I simply use fewer colors, keeping the base color in the umber range mainly because it will dry quickly and still result in a rich look. I do most underpaintings in just a few hours, adding alkyd or oil white into the umber wash and quickly building up the figure into a solid form. This dries overnight, ready for final color. (image 4)

Umber, or sepia, is a natural middle tone base color for most figure work, but burnt sienna (reddish-brown) or even cool (blue-gray) underpainting works better in some cases. For landscapes, an effective approach is to do an underpainting in reddish browns to offset the variety of greens found in nature.

Similarly, on this piece, adding white into the wet burnt umber resulted in a nice warm gray which will look more blue (cooler) when the warm flesh tones are placed over it.

In 5, you can see how easily the red color is laid on once the underpainting is fully dry. I use a medium to thin the paint to a translucent state and help it flow as I build up the surface with richer, more solid color.

Below, if you hold a flat brush at this angle and work horizontal to the canvas, pulling the brush in the direction of your hand, you can lay on oil paint with squarish brushwork that stands off the surface and gives crisp edges without dragging the paint into the underlying area. It takes some practice, but once you are comfortable with it, the results can be very painterly and bold, as on the closeup at the far right. (See circles)

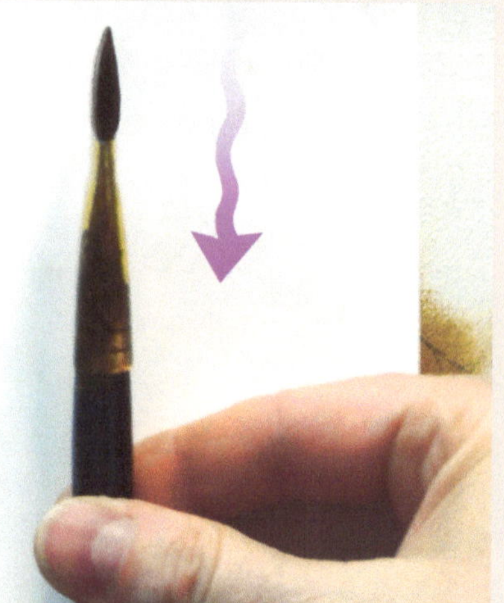

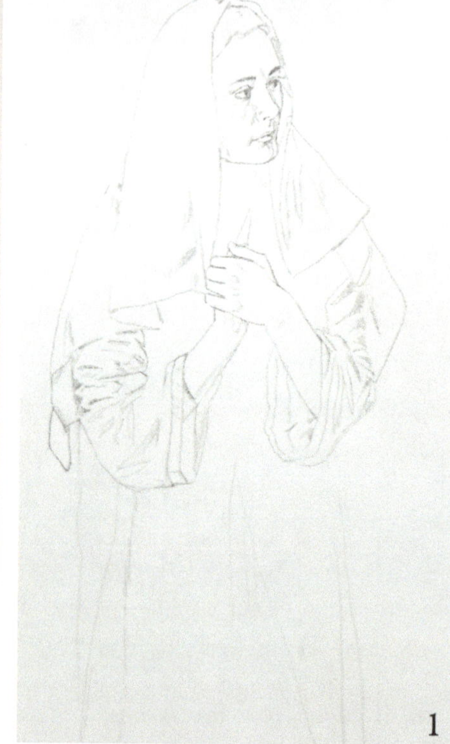

1

1- I prefer to project the sketch for two reasons- I already did a clean drawing on paper so why freehand it again when projecting it is much faster and more accurate? The other reason is that it's cleaner to place a thin pencil line onto the slick gesso than to try to draw it out from scratch. Any erasing will only smear the pencil. If you have to erase, try a kneaded eraser and roll or dab it, not stroke the pencil line, to minimize smearing.

Below, a closeup of the head underpainting with alkyd white mixed into the burnt umber to speed the drying time.

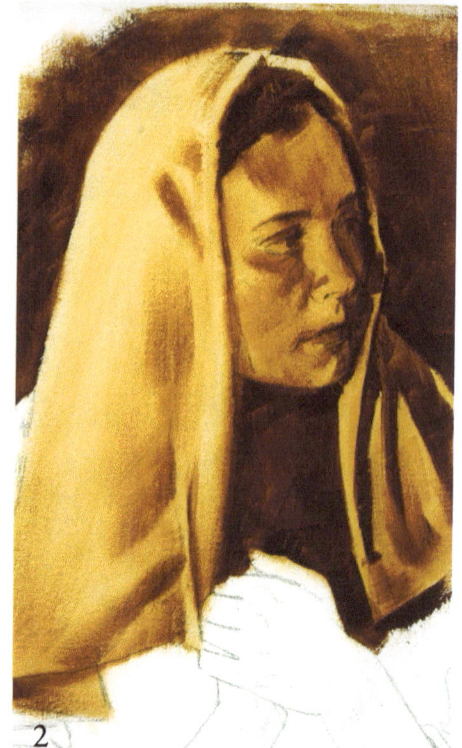

2

2- The quick wash of mineral spirits with a little Liquin added to the burnt umber oil color. Once this set up a bit, I added alkyd white into the mix and worked on building the form. White added to translucent umber will cool down the color, turning it to a warm gray-brown that is an ideal underpainting for Caucasian skin tones.

Below, the finished underpainting is ready for color to be applied over it. Combining Liquin with the alkyd white assures that the painting will be completely dry overnight.

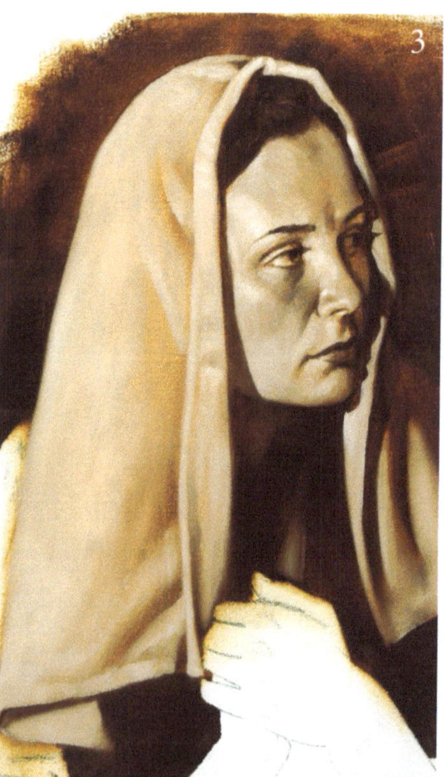

3

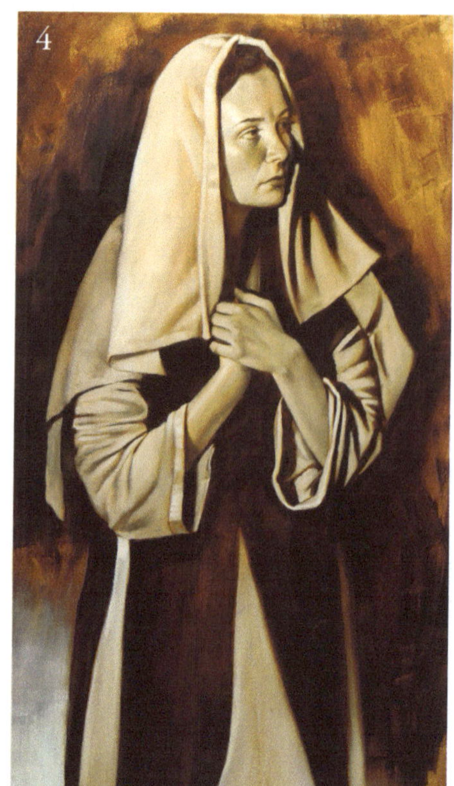

4

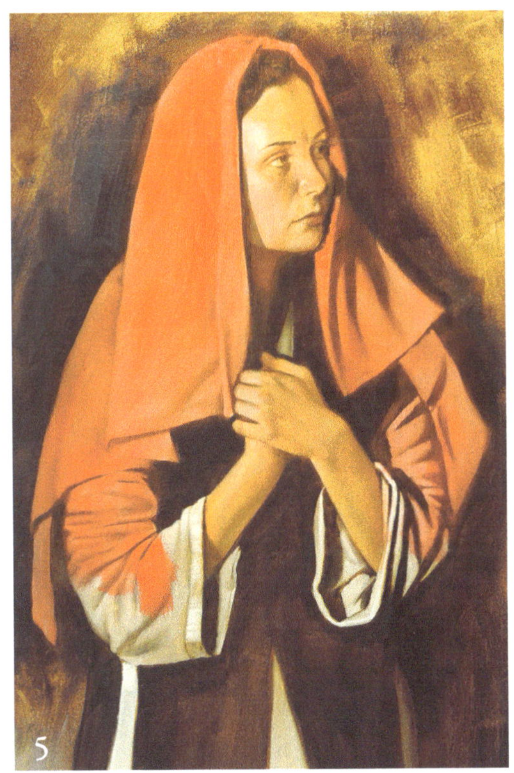

5

5- You can see how the reds contrast subtly with the underpainting gray. On the sleeve, the translucent red is very quickly painted on, allowing the underpainting values to show through. Burnt umber, an absorbent clay hue, dries matte, as can be seen in the upper left. The Liquin I used on the color layer brought back this area

6- By the time I worked my way to the bottom of the painting, the face area was beginning to get tacky. This gave me more control over the final subtle coloring in the cheeks and around the eyes. But I had to work fast before the paint became too stiff, in about an hour..

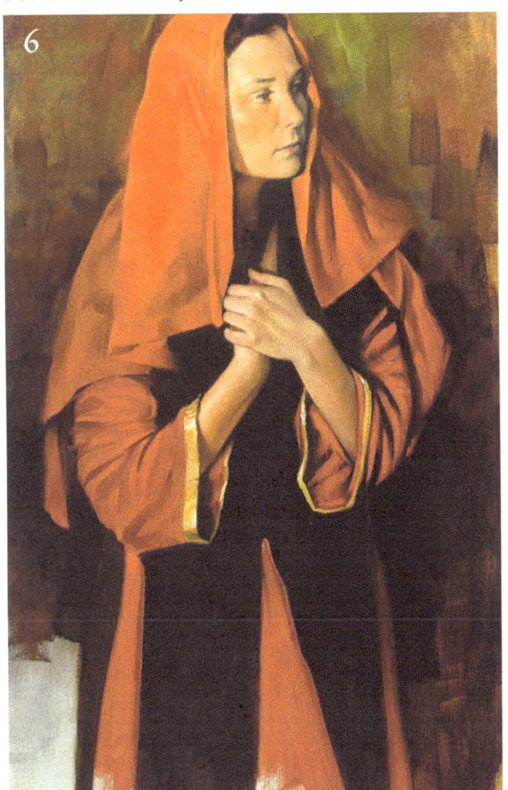

6

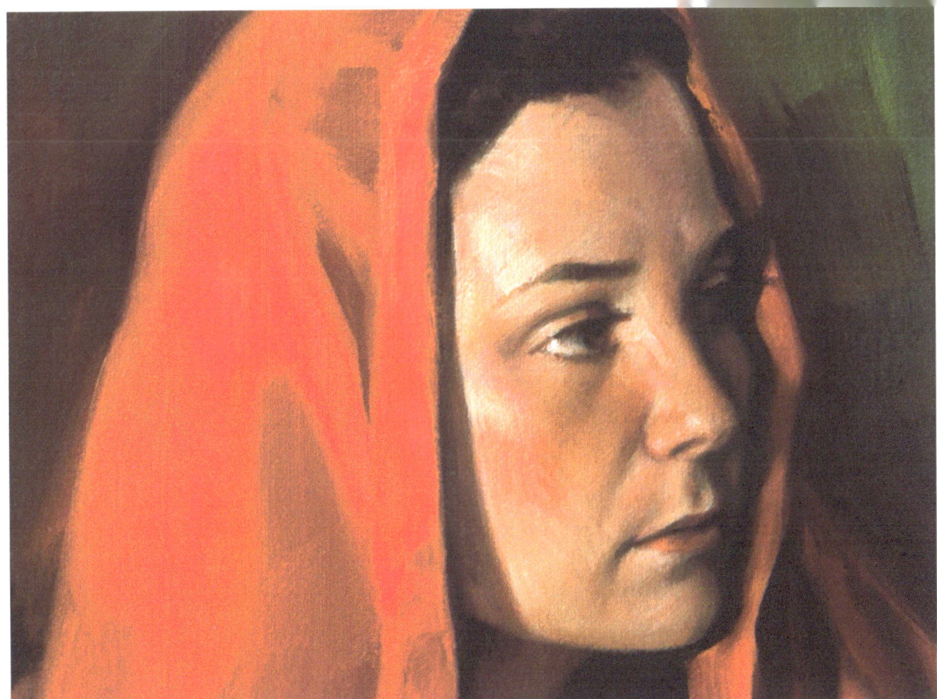

The final head, above, has a nice combination of painterly strokes with some flesh color that doesn't look green and sickly, but rich and alive. The combination of the brown underpainting and the pink and ocher coloring over top of it gives the skin a more believable tone without making it look chalky or flat. The gray showing through is from the underpainting.

Below- I like illustrative brushwork, which probably stems from my illustration years using gouache and acrylic in a direct, opaque manner. The advantage of working this way in oils is, of course, that if edges are too crisp, I can easily blend or fuse them into adjacent areas.

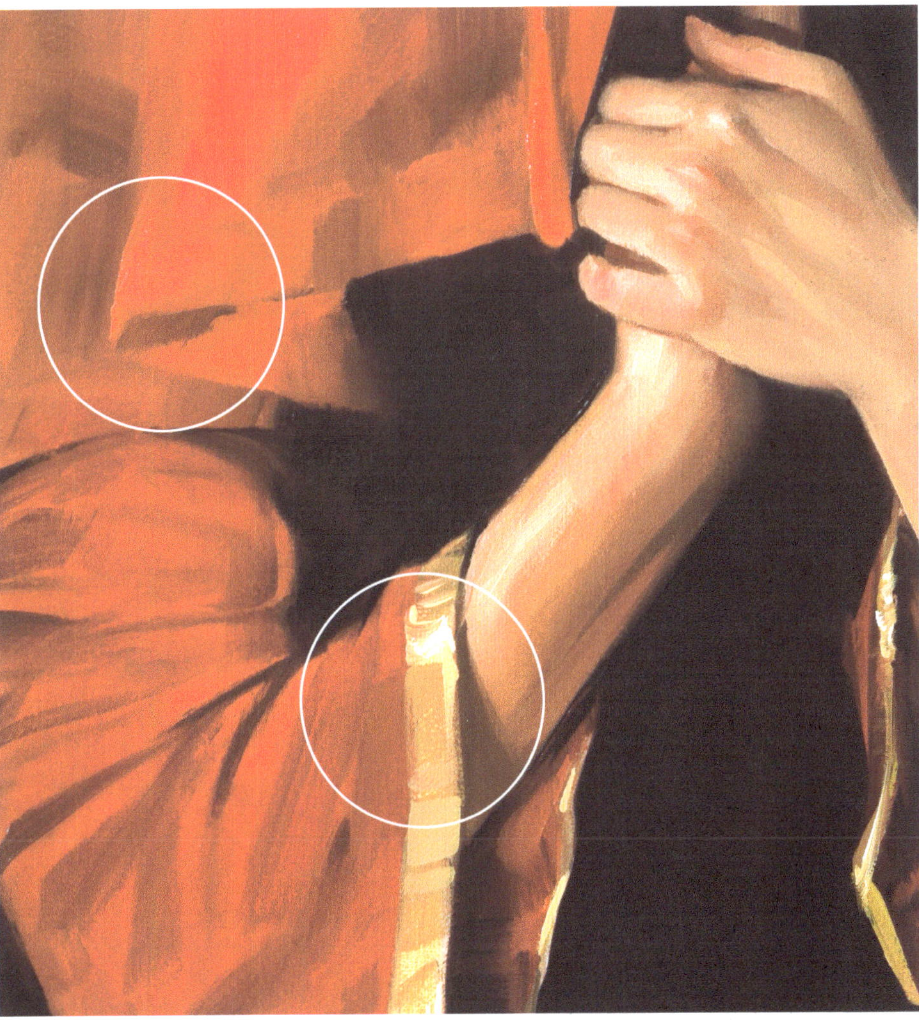

Morning

40x48" Oil on mounted canvas (p. 53)

Gouache underpainting technique

Gouache is a water-based medium with a glycerin-glue binder that many illustrators use to create realistic work which can rival oil paint for reproduction. Since it is water soluble, unlike acrylic, gouache can be reworked indefinitely by simply re-wetting the area or overpainting. It is not usually used on canvas, but on paper. I don't recommend this method unless you mount the canvas to a board and keep it very rigid, as I did here.

Like watercolor, you can wash on gouache, which has a natural tooth because the pigment is not as finely ground as watercolor. This leaves an ideal surface for oil and pastel. I freely washed the entire canvas using a wide house painter's brush and a white plate full of generous tube color. I concentrated on getting a base underpainting. A standard spray bottle was used to mist areas and then buff them into each other wet-into-wet, a unique approach similar to using oils with heavy washes, but more flexible.

Once the surface was covered with dried color, I began to pull out highlights, rewetting areas with a little water and pulling sections up with a dry rag, paper towel, cotton swab, or small brush. This is subtractive painting. It yields a beautiful result that leaves a tint or stain of the underlying color, like light hitting a three-dimensional object. It works best with chiaroscuro lighting- directional light of more contrast than soft light where the middle tones are more unified.

This can also be done in oils using enough solvents in a wash effect that can be buffed or sprayed, splattered or scratched for effect. I know a number of illustrators who do a very detailed pencil drawing that they spray fix, then color over with oil washes or glazes for a realistic look.

Below, my very rough sketch showing the abstract movement that started the concept for this piece.

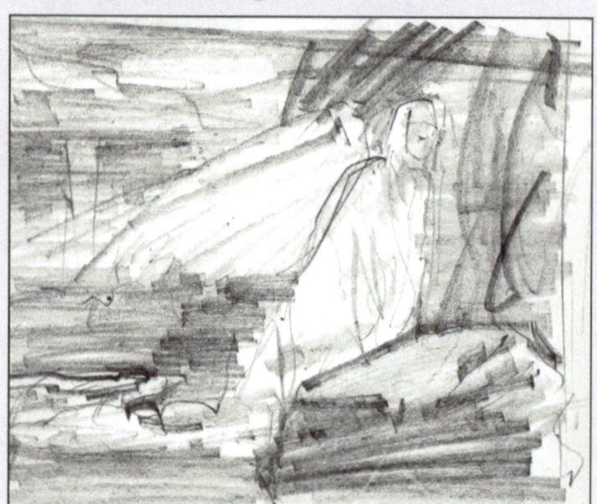

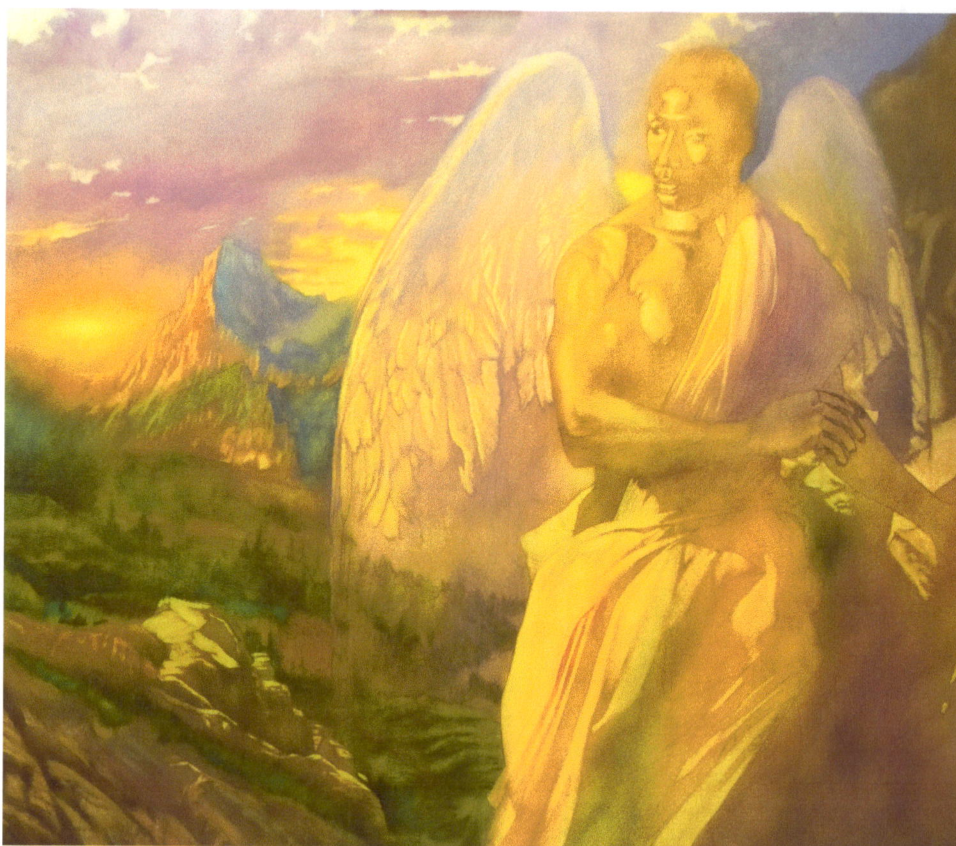

Above, the fully washed-in gouache base that is ready for a light spray of fixative and then the oils over this foundation. I have spoken with a couple of conservators that I know who said that this method is quite sound, very permanent, more than acrylic because the oil will bond with the gouache base better than oil over plastic.

Below, four stages of how the rock area begins to come to life a bit as if light is raking over it. The oil layers over the dried gouache glaze the color with a darker buildup. I can always go opaque if needed, but the idea here is to create a luminous image that suggests cascading light. Note the upper right image (2) with whiter rocks where I went back in with alkyd white to tweak the underpainting opaquely.

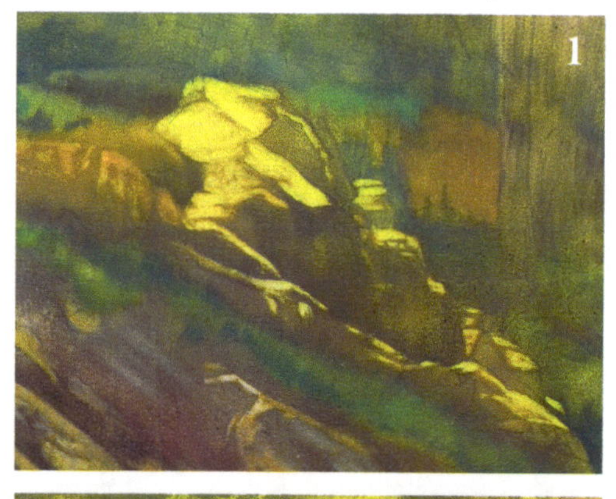

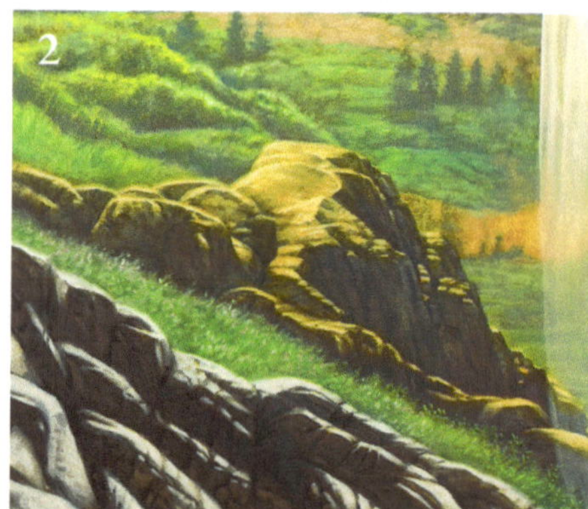

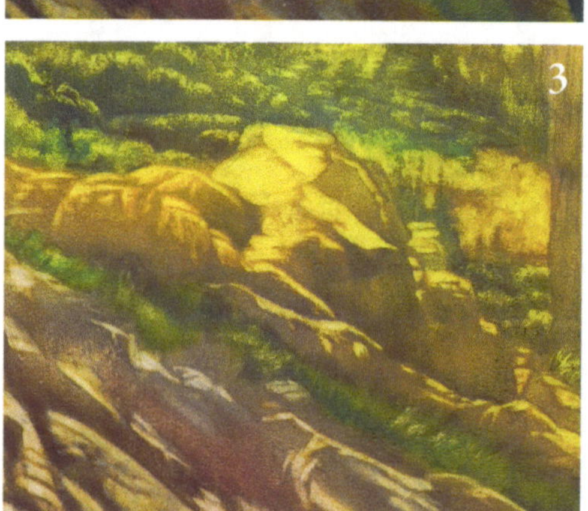

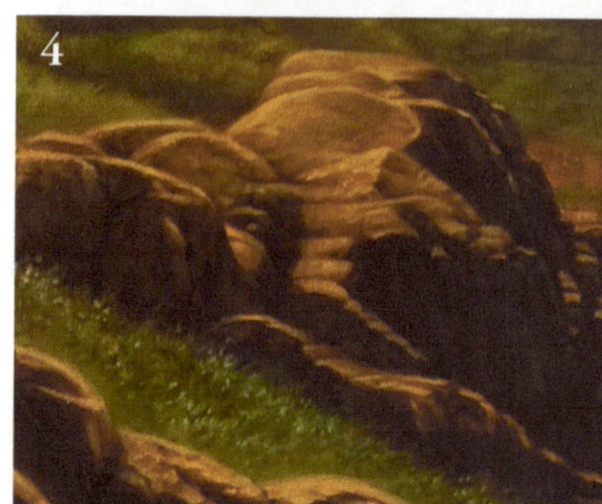

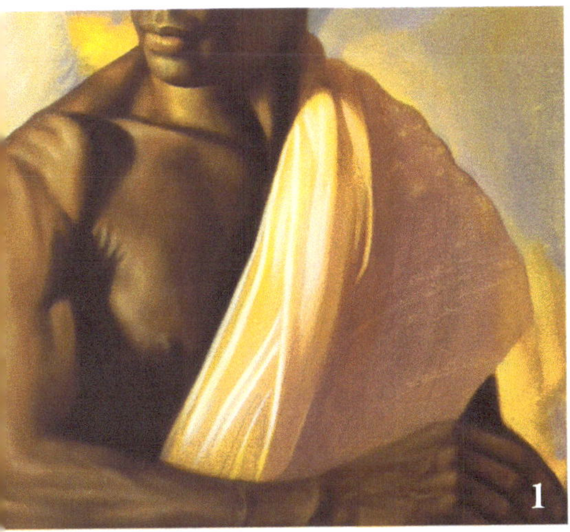

1

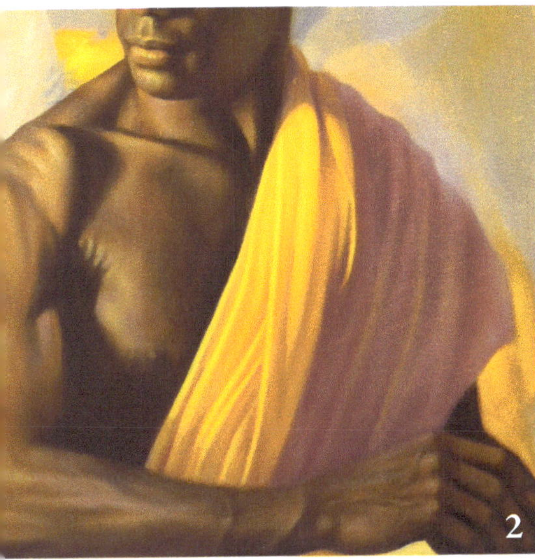

2

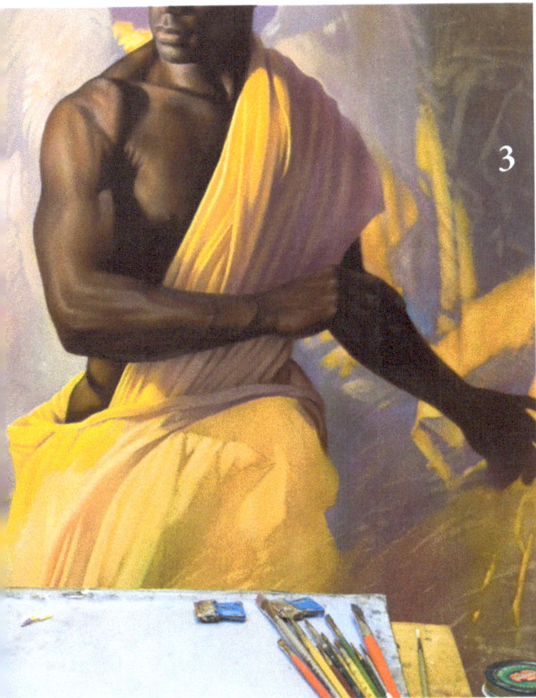

3

On the left, the 3 photos show the progress of the yellow robes after I worked in oil over the gouache base. The top image shows the darker layering of color for the shadow areas and the opaque whites I repainted, then let dry so that I could glaze pure transparent color over the highlights.

When working with translucent color, avoid the cadmiums, ochers, umbers, darker blues, and red earth tones, as these are all opaque colors. The siennas, crimson, phthalos, and many processed colors are more transparent. Don't use white, it will opaque and tint down any color. A good medium can also make most colors translucent but for the purest color, stick with hues labeled as 'transparent.' There are a number of ideal colors available now made by companies like Dan Smith, who have hired chemists to develop their own brands of specialty colors, like golden browns and pinks, unique hues that are quite stable.

For the yellow robe, I used a gold-toned hue and freely coated the area to give the cloth a rich finish that I could not achieve with opaque paint. This is one of the reasons that I don't use heavy impasto to begin with, as coating an area like this would look too rough and unfinished, more like a Whistler effect and not what I want for this painting. I prefer not to fight heavy texture when I am pushing realistic effects that may be best achieved with a smoother finish and built up in layers. Some of the best work I've seen has rich heavy impasto, but in every case, the artist had something literal to work from, a model or photo to follow. With my work, I invent enough areas that the heavy paint would just lead to a loss of realism and, for me, that means it wouldn't convey the mood that I strive for.

Below, the finished robe area with softer edges and a deeper, richer tone overall.

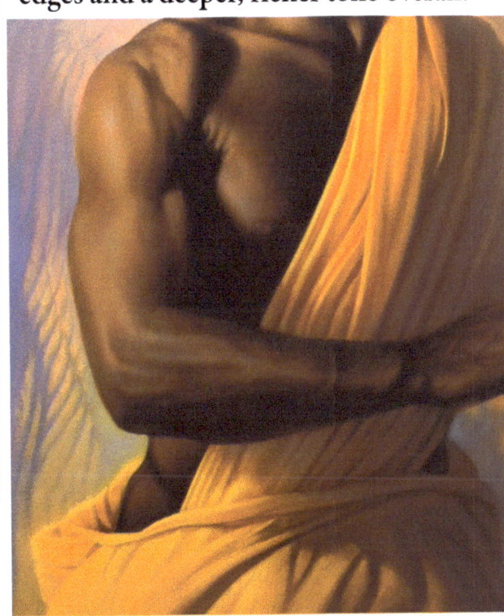

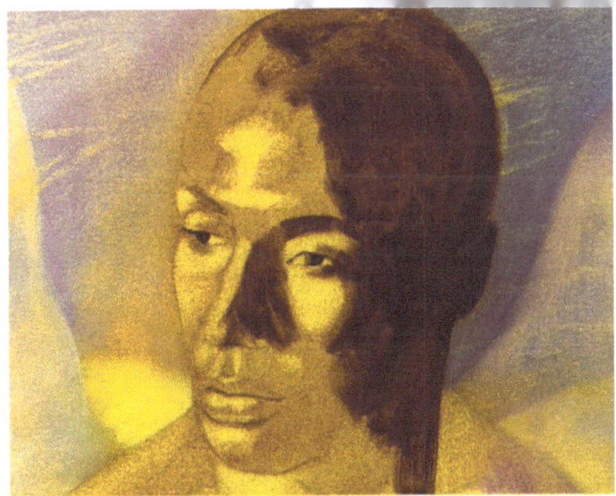

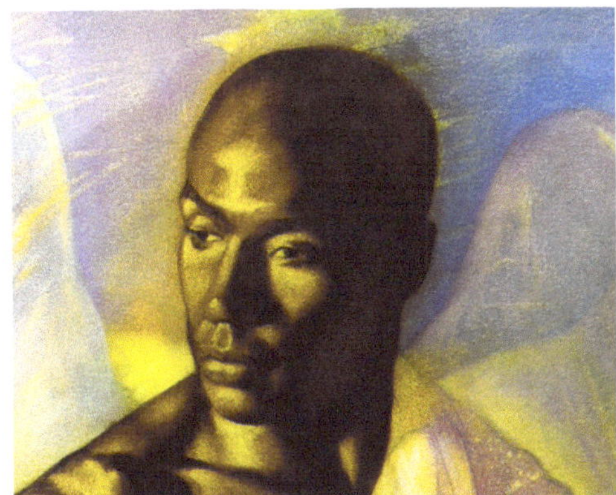

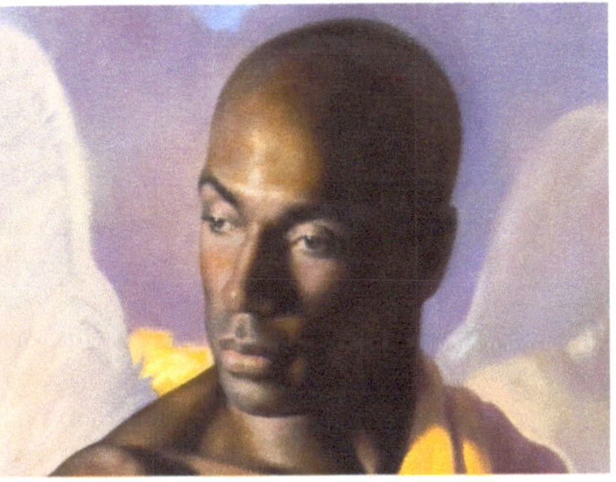

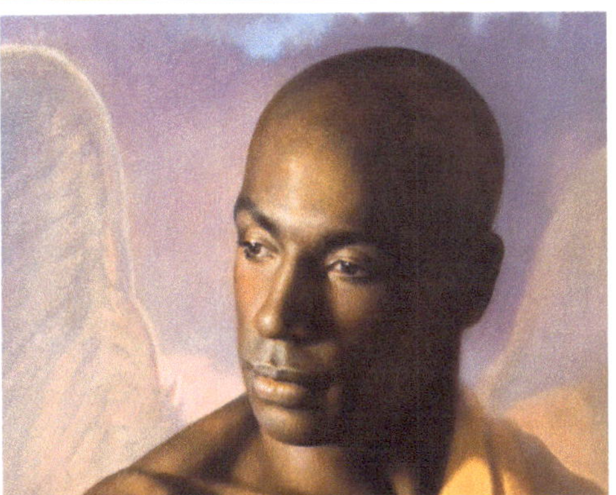

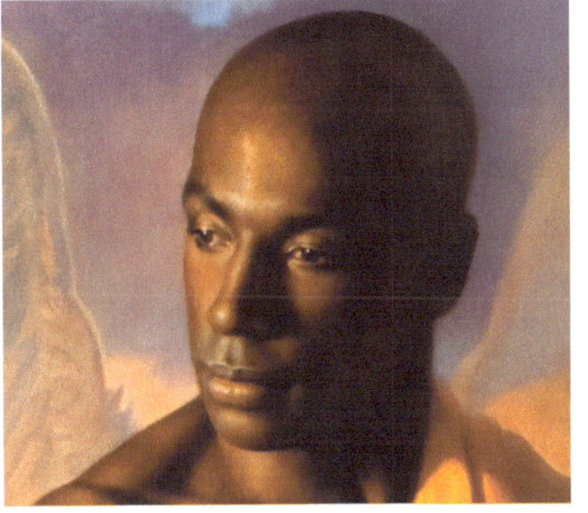

Right, five oil stages for the Angel's head.

Angel Wings

Angel wings can be some of the more difficult elements of the spiritual imagery I work on. I have tried to shoot wing reference in the past but nothing ever really works once I am into the painting stages. I know I want believable wings that look like they could actually work, but making something diaphanous and solid at the same time, inventing color and form, and then making it fit an Angel figure, is pushing the limit of what I am capable of rendering in a believable way. Still, I would not paint them unless they were enjoyable and meaningful to me, and they certainly give my work a sense of wonder and spirit and help the figures set a realm of possibilities.

I use wings as symbolism, in part, to help bring the idea of an Angelic spirit to the canvas. The wings enhance the figures and give them something of a timeless and weightless quality that somehow seems right for my work and thoughts.

Below, an extreme close up of a wing section from my painting 'Comes the Dawn' on page 55. You can see how multiple layers, thick and thin, warm and cool, all add to the effect in the final coloring that becomes a unified tone when reduced (inset) or the viewer steps back from the oil painting. By painting large, the work not only reduces down well, but the original forces the viewer back at least a few feet to see the full image in its entirety. If I could, I would paint most of my work at much larger, near mural scale, but that simply isn't feasible today.

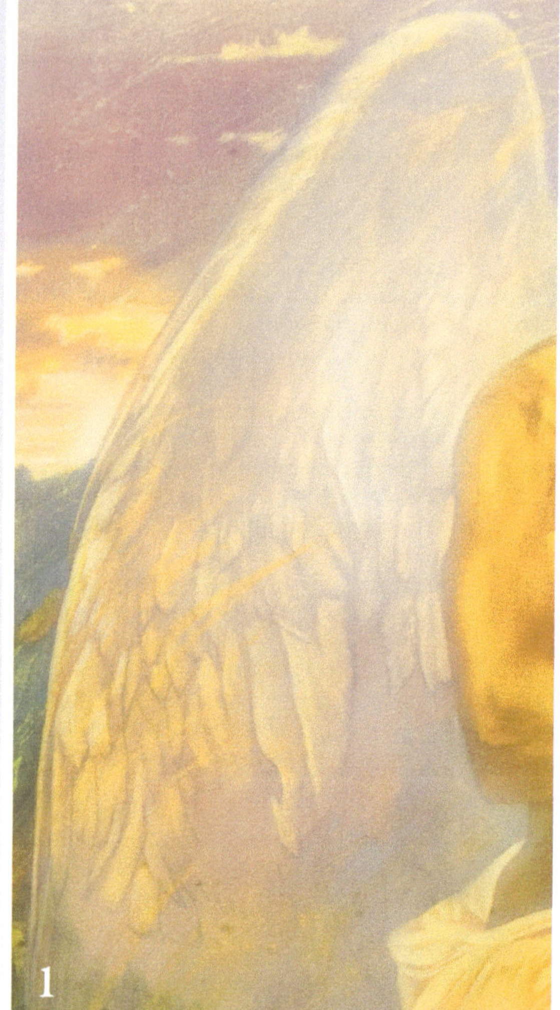

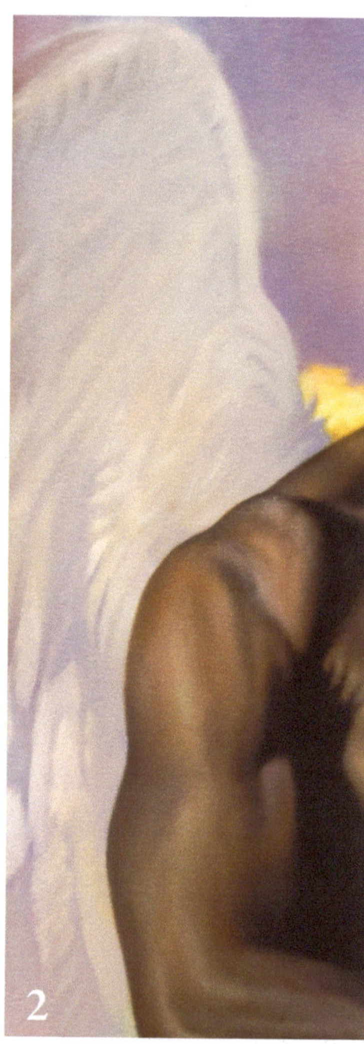

1- Gouache block in.
2- First opaque oil color over gouache, lights first.
3- Middle stage of wings. At this point, I was looking for a color solution that would be in harmony with the background.

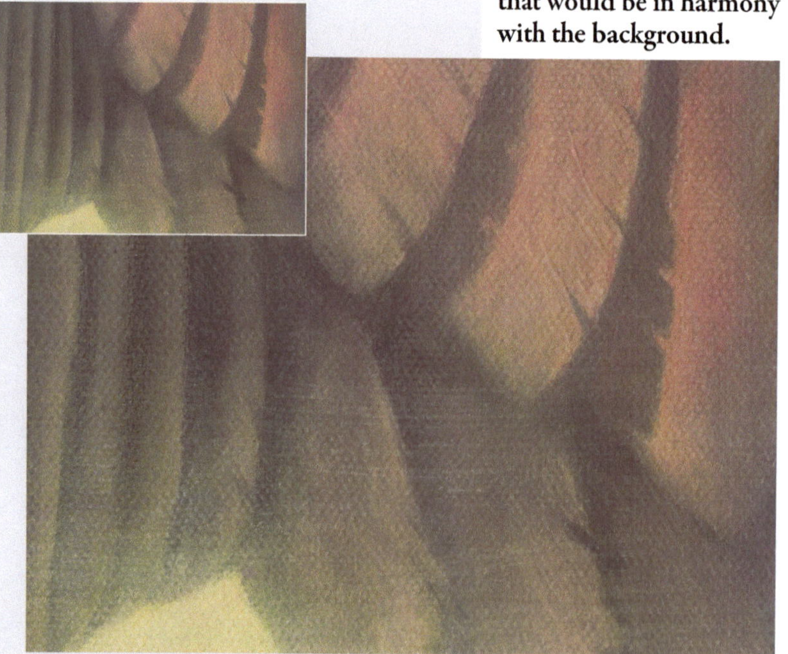

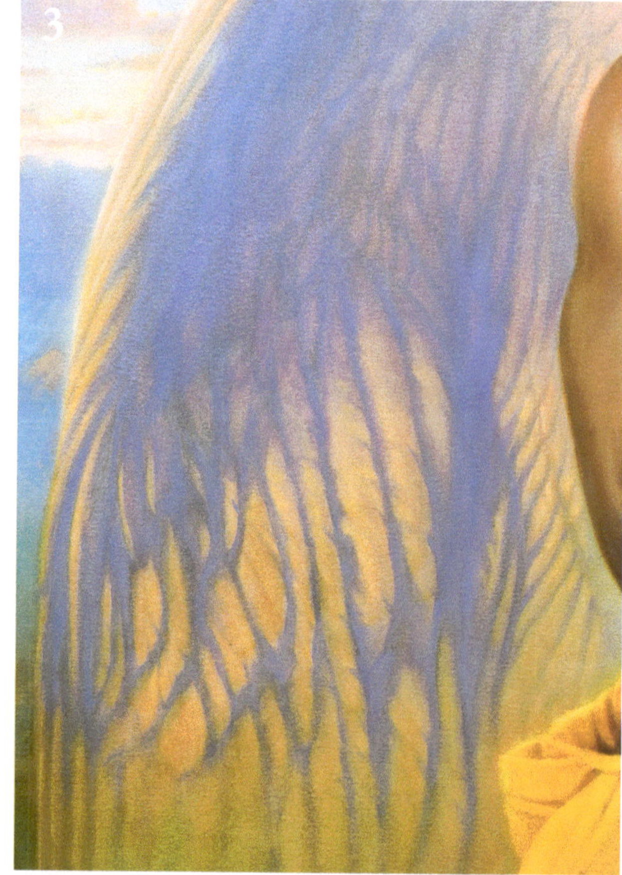

To round out the edge of the wing, I first softened the area with a haze by scumbling on a warm pink semi- opaque tone, giving the subtle pastel effect of an airbrushed look. Once dry, I added another glaze of hazy color and worked that over both the wing and background. I experiment quite a bit to test the effects I want, often working out several ideas until it begins to look close to what I imagined.

Where the soft background mountains meet the edge of the wing, I pushed the area back by misting the mountain into the sky, taking the sky color, the pastel pink tone, and dragged that into the blue of the mountain ridge line. Once that area visually dropped back, it told me how much I could soften the wing's curved edge, and how much should be left sharp.

Soft cool shadows only work if you use warm sunlight effects in equal measure. Everything we see is relative, so adding shadows without the dimensional light would look off to our sense of logical realism.

Alternately, painting hard shadows in soft light, like overcast or shade, doesn't make visual sense. Our mind tells us we need to see what light is causing such shadows to be cast.

To achieve a translucent effect, I first painted the background in opaquely, added a foggy glaze, and finished with a semi-opaque middle tone to enhance the area. This pushed the background back and brought the wings forward.

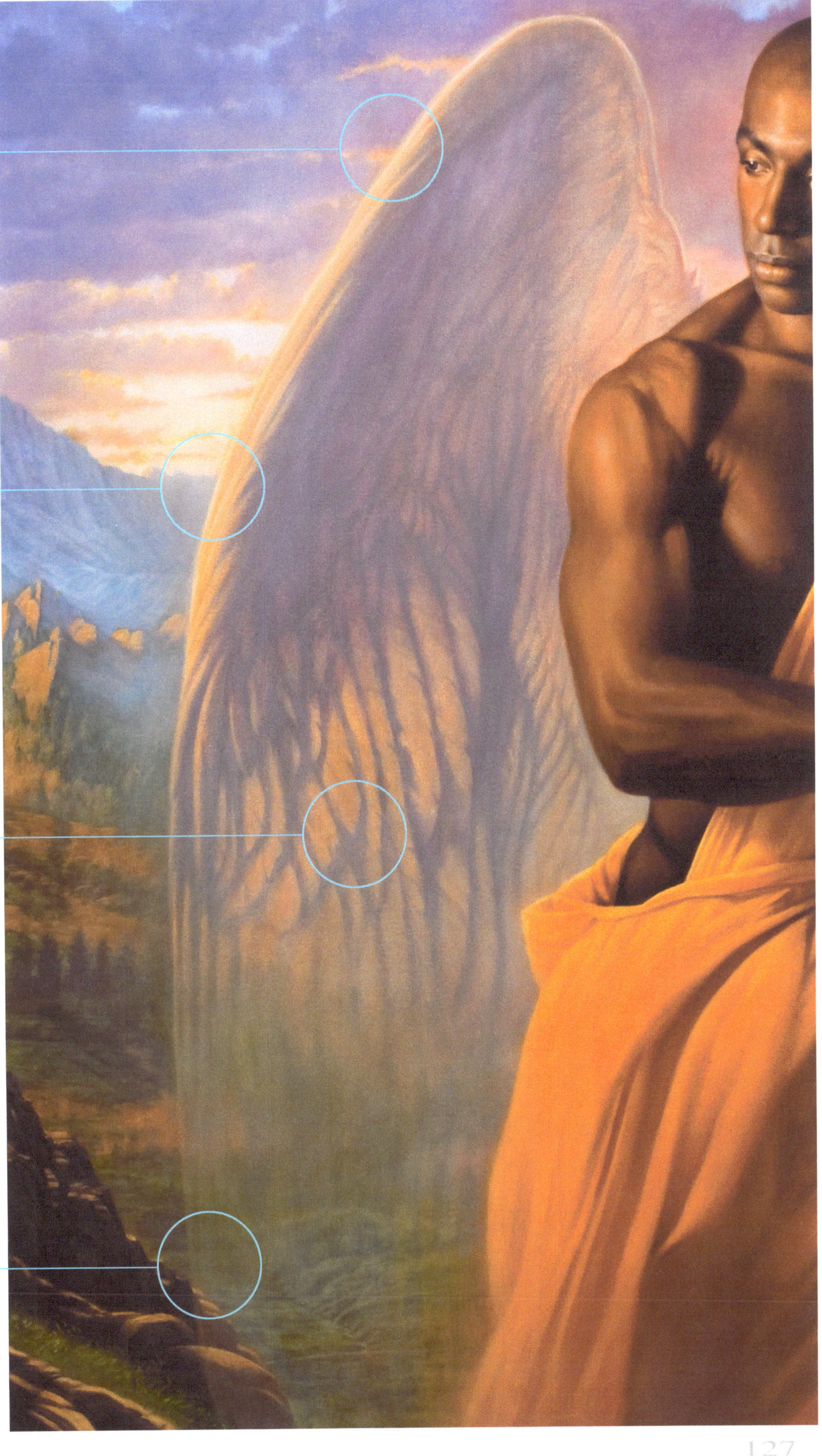

Time Passes

42 x 50" Oil over impasto texture (p. 63)

For this medium sized painting I added a few layers of textured gesso over the pre-primed canvas by dragging a wide stiff brush through the gesso mixed with a small amount of modeling paste. This gave the oil strokes more pull against the surface, allowing me a bit more freedom to do some interesting brushwork without losing any realism. It was effective in the building's stonework as well as the stand for the sundial. For faces, I don't want the skin to have a textured look beneath the paint, so I sanded that area down enough to smooth it out some.

The surface is both glossy and textured so I had to polarize the copy shots to minimize glare. I did this for the final high res shot, but left some of the glare in these demo shots so you can easily see how the texture is creating some nice effects, even in the subtle area of the fog.

I love doing Angel paintings where I combine themes that have spiritual content and emotion without slipping into the realm of pure fantasy. Keeping my figures life-like helps the imagery seem believable. While I enjoy fantasy themes for commercial clients, the work in this book is narrative fine art.

Around 1880-1920, a number of gifted realistic painters pushed for more creative themes. In Europe. painters like Waterhouse, Abbey, Solomon, and others were not only technically brilliant, but they chose to paint narrative imagery rather than traditional still lifes, figure studies, or landscapes that are still common today. Even Diego Velázquez spent much of his time doing traditional themes, but his brilliant work, in my opinion, was his more inventive pieces where his real technical mastery showed through.

I've realized, from those who have written to me, that the more creative work is what people enjoy the most, not just technique. It's what you paint- not how you paint it.

Below, for large paintings I usually start with larger piles of paint, premixed with extra walnut oil and a drop or two of oil of cloves for the earth colors.

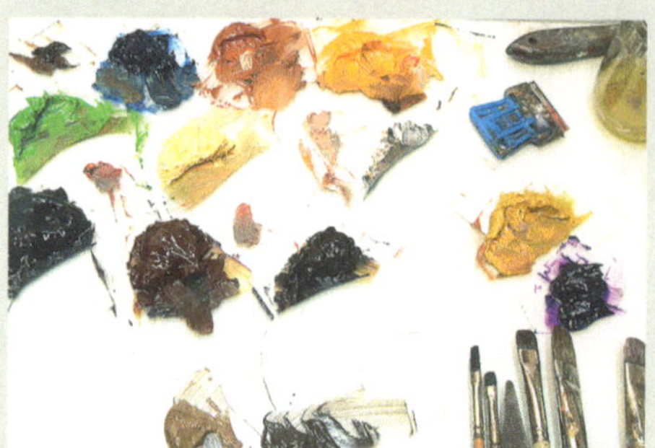

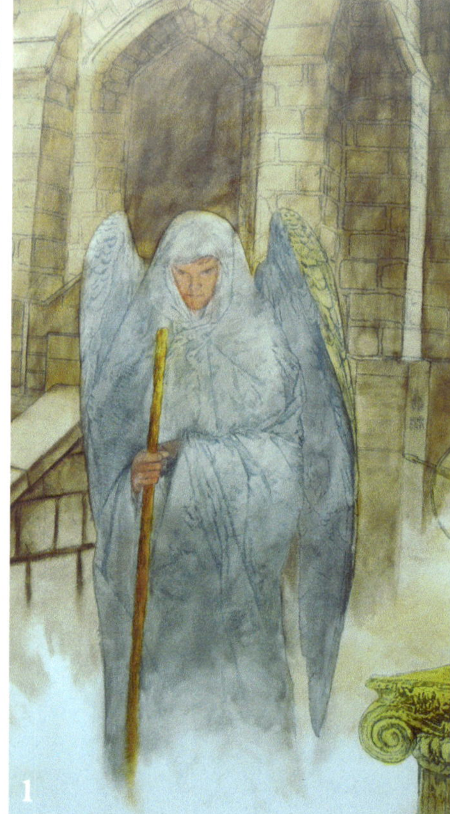

I started this piece like a watercolor, washing in the base colors using ample mineral spirits to thin down the oils and to get rid of the gesso white. The heavy texture adds to the watercolor effect.

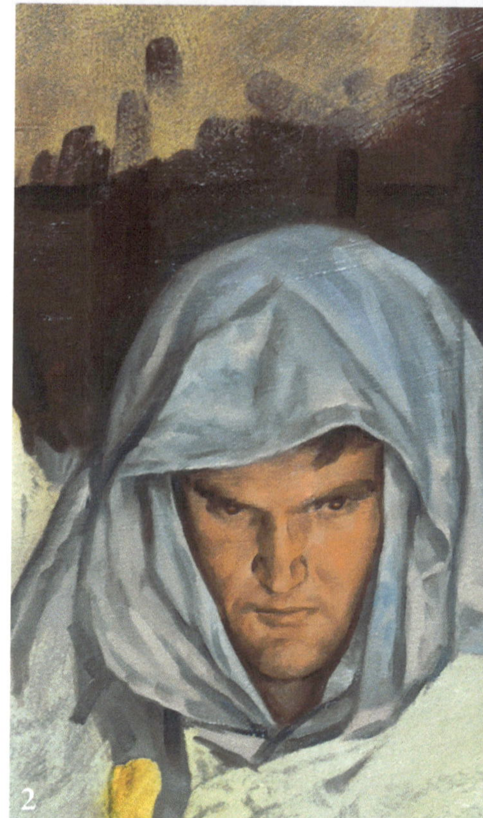

2, I knock out a quick head and leave it. I don't like overworking faces and try to do them within an hour or so. I can always glaze it darker when it's dry, if need be.

3, The stonework is laid in using large flat bristles, dragged across the heavy gesso surface by pulling the stroke nearly flat against the texture, enhancing it.

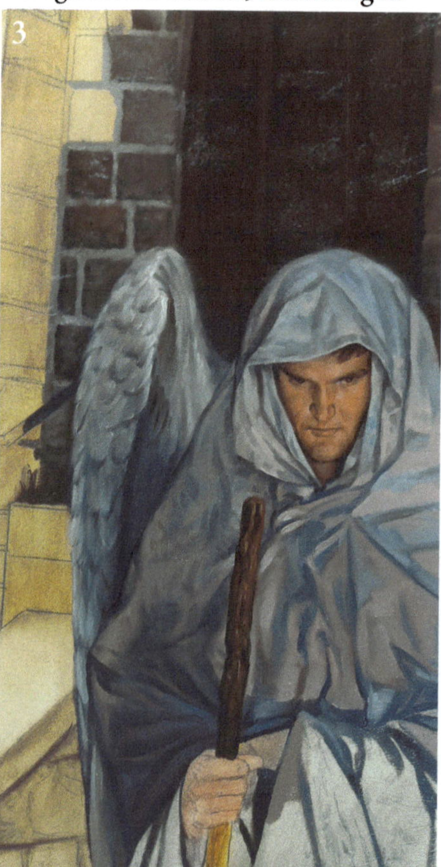

4, Usually, I do the foreground after the background so I can overpaint it, but with fog, the ideal is to work as much wet-into-wet as possible.

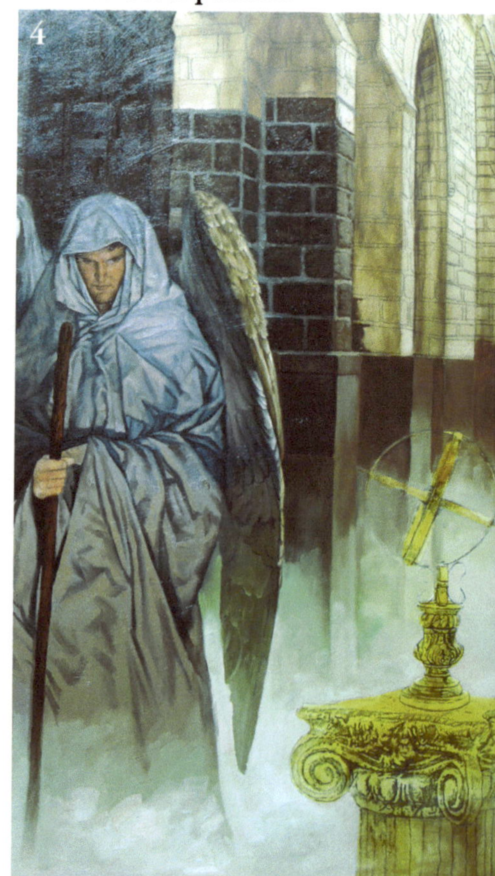

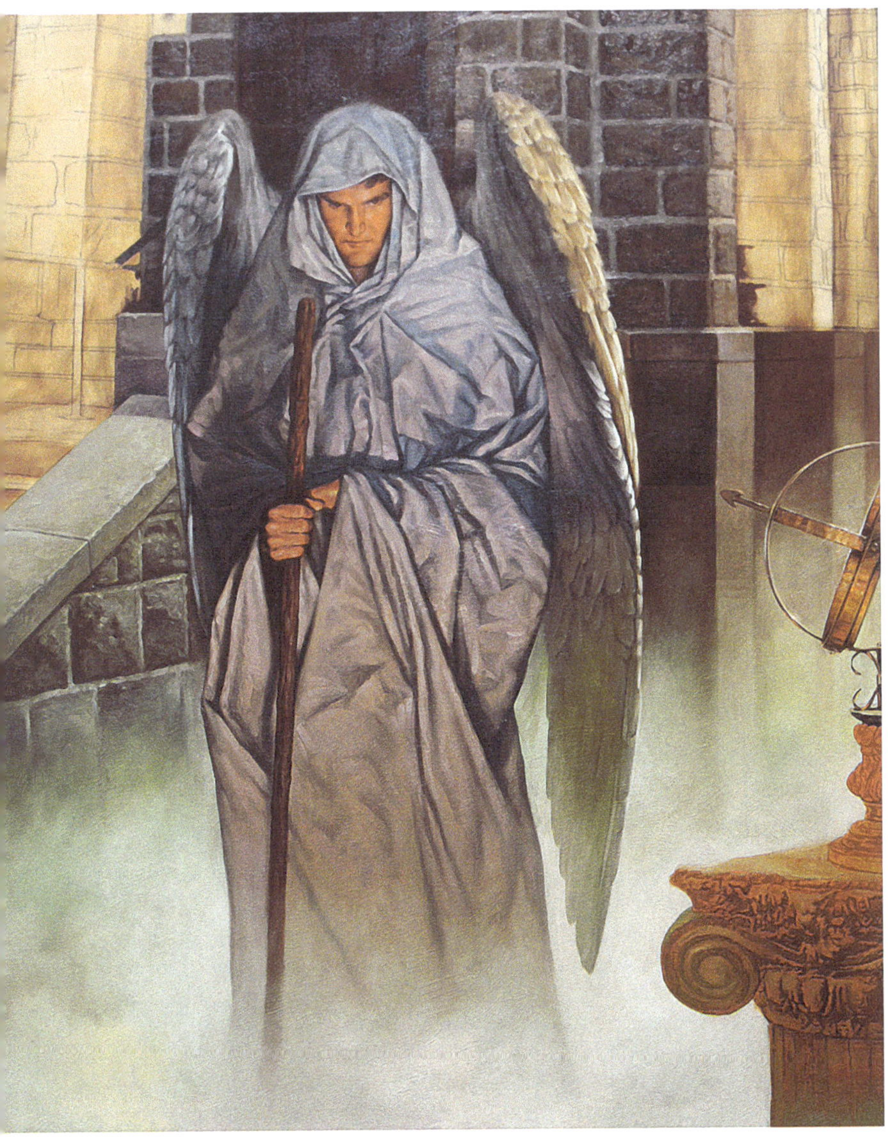

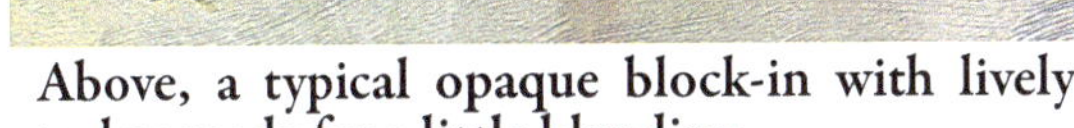

Above, a typical opaque block-in with lively strokes ready for a little blending.

Left, the quick blocked in strokes of the initial fog area were done with a 2 inch soft bristle flat directly into the base greenish-gray beneath. I did a color comp for this painting before applying any color. The comp color was still not what I wanted so I did a quick digital shot of it and brought the image into a color editing program on my computer so that I could adjust the color until it was closer to what I was seeing in my head. I printed this comp out so that I could use it as a loose guide to refer to as I blocked in the oil paint.

Most of the foreground is rendered out and ready for glazing, if needed. I continued working on the building until I had enough of it blocked in that I could melt some of the fog into the bricks and the Angel wings' edges into the fog and brickwork. It's by the melting together of these edges that the realism is achieved. Adding a final layer of semi-opaque greenish-gray around the wings' edges and fog area gave the image movement and illumination. For such layers, I usually loosely paint them in with a bristle round and then soften edges by scratching the wet layer into the dry layer beneath.

In this closeup of the final head, you can see some of the paint strokes where they pulled off my brush easily for two reasons-the heavy underlying texture, and the pull from the initial wash as it began to dry and leave a tacky feel that grabbed each stroke. This is when I have the most control, refining edges and laying on opaque paint. I work fast and direct, taking advantage of the hour or so working time before the paint becomes too stiff to work into freely.

Once the surface is dry, usually in a day or two, I can go back into these areas and selectively fine-tune details, add highlights and shadows, and enhance color. But the majority of my soft edges and focus effects come from the initial lay-in of the first opaque coloring over the wash.

Heavily textured underpaintings only suit some images. I've seen work that is technically weak but has very heavy impasto, and well executed work that seems too smooth. It always looks artificial when an artist tries to cover up weak work by using thick texture, when what is usually needed is more accurate drawing. It's each artist's choice, but I feel the work will dictate the effect needed and that only comes with experience and experimentation.

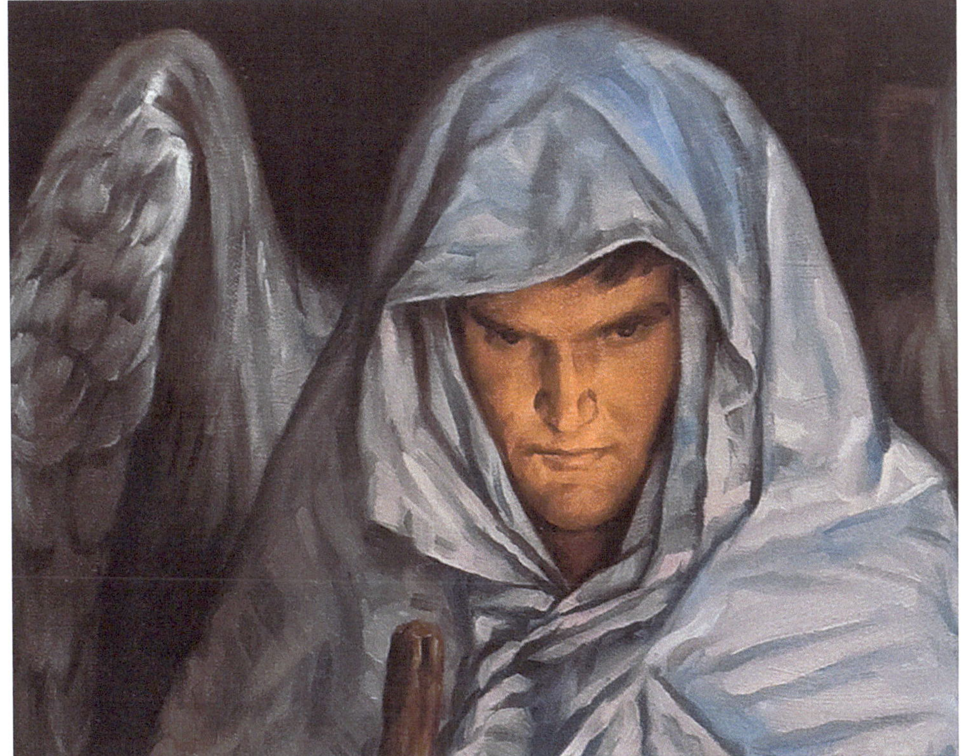

By the Sword

32 x 48" Oil on panel (p.36-39)

While I prefer the pull of canvas, painting on a smooth panel has its advantages. The best way I have found to prepare any wood surface is- 1, choose a flat 1/4" thick sheet of untempered masonite or pressed wood. Use the light ocher, not the dark brown, which contains oil. Hardwood panels are more expensive and heavier but may work as well, so long as they don't bow. Gluing 2-4 slats of 1-2" wood strips will help keep the panel rigid.

2, Scratch up the smooth side with light sandpaper, then lightly wash it with rubbing alcohol. 3, Use a wide house painter's brush to apply 3-4 coats of gesso in alternating directions. Allow each coat to dry for at least a few hours. You can sand between each coat for a super smooth surface or you can add some modeling paste for a textured base. I like rolling on the last coat with a half-worn house painter's roller, going back into the moist gesso to give it a light pebbly surface. Clear Gesso, made by Winsor-Newton, can be applied like gesso as the last coat if you want a sandy tooth that grabs the paint well. The small panels on pages 82-83 used Clear Gesso on masonite.

Panels are the most archival support for any paint. No matter how tightly you stretch canvas, it will still flex and buckle slightly over time, enough to weaken the surface and eventually cause cracking. I don't worry about it either way. With modern conservation techniques improving every year, I know most oil paintings done today will survive for much longer due to new plastic coatings that hold the oil to any firm substrate. Still, I strive for an archival approach.

A smooth gessoed surface will leave a cleaner stroke, which is great for linear effects and sharp edges, depending on the brushes you use. The paint sits on the surface rather than sinking in, so each stroke is more laid on looking. But because it's a smooth surface, it tends to smear, making it harder to blend, whereas canvas excels because of its natural drag against the brush strokes. Small brushes work better, if you have the patience and a light touch.

Drawing on gessoed panels is cleaner than canvas if you want an accurate thin line that is erasable. Erasing on canvas will leave smudges and an uneven line.

Many museums have fine examples of panel painting, from the earliest oils over egg tempera, to remarkably subtle realistic portraits that are photographically smooth because there is no canvas texture to work against.

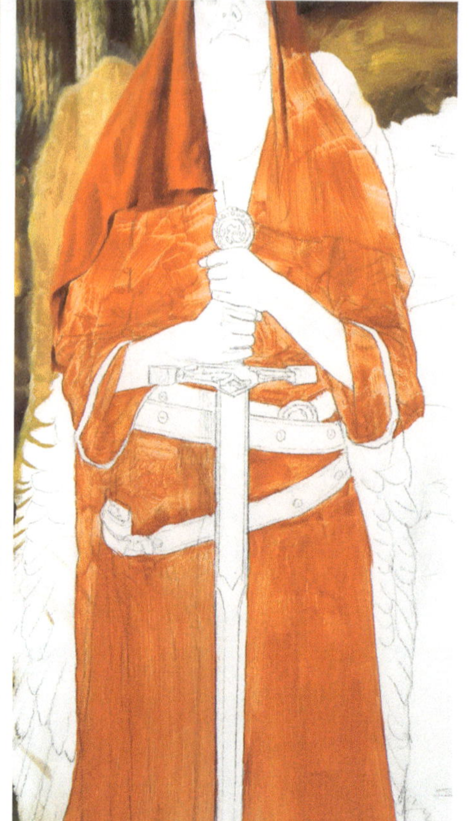

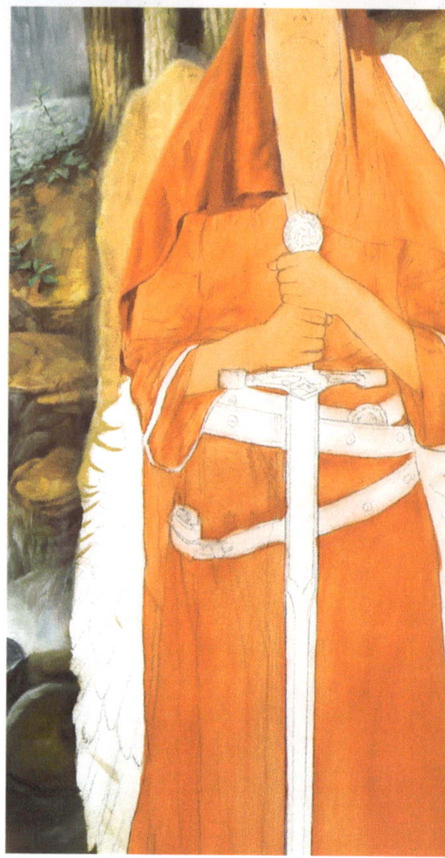

Above, these first stages of the figure show the semi-opaque wash for skin tone and the red cloth. I let this dry overnight and then worked more opaquely into the blocky thicker paint. I know I can get a very realistic effect by being patient and working in smaller sections as I move across the piece. Sables tend to work well on panels, but I prefer smaller bristle rounds and flats to tweak areas and scratch at edges. If the paint is too slick on the smooth surface, I add a bit of stand oil.

Below, for most landscapes I use direct opaque strokes and simply refine and noodle out the realism. Note how the opaque paint sits more on the surface.

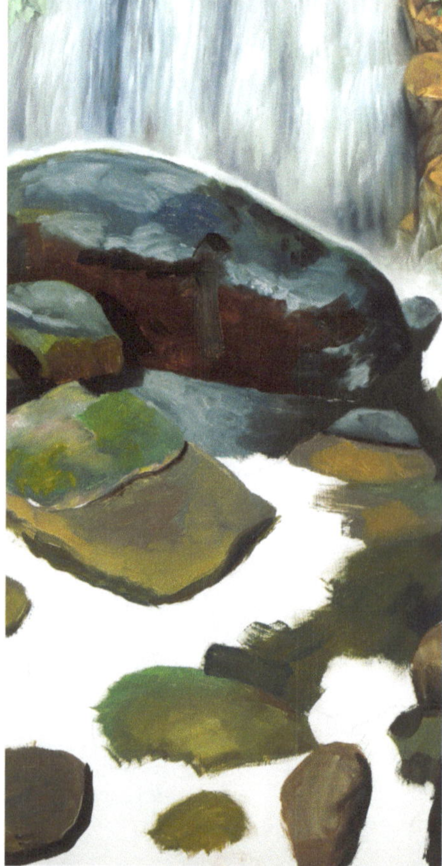

1

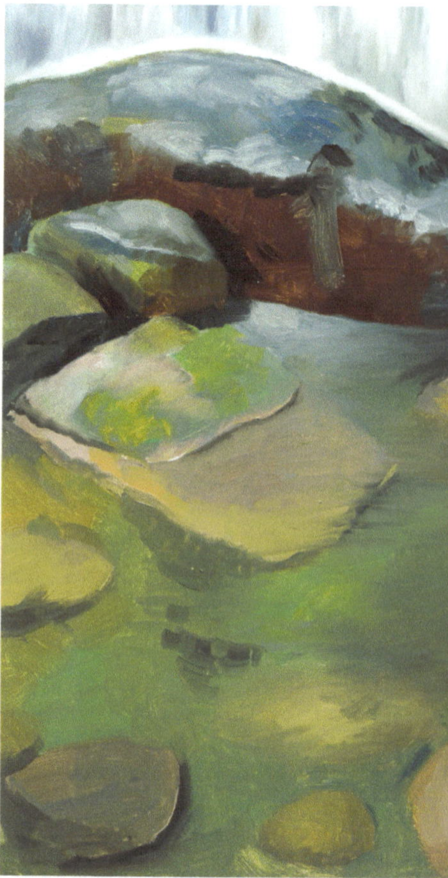

2

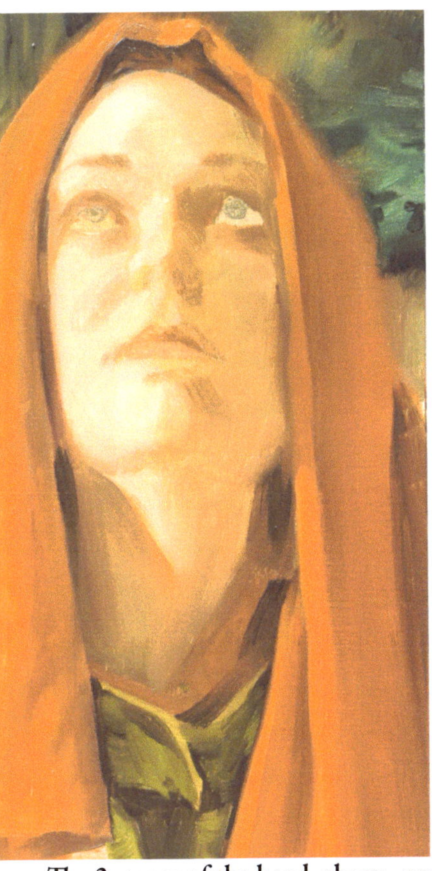

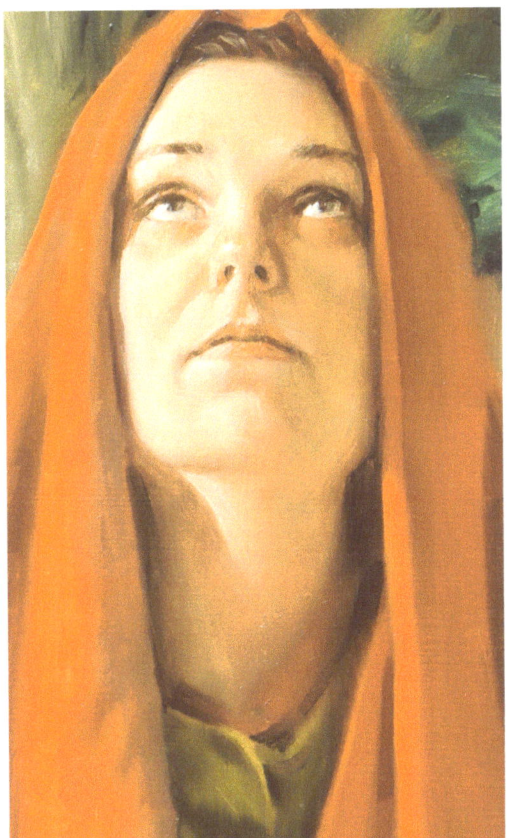

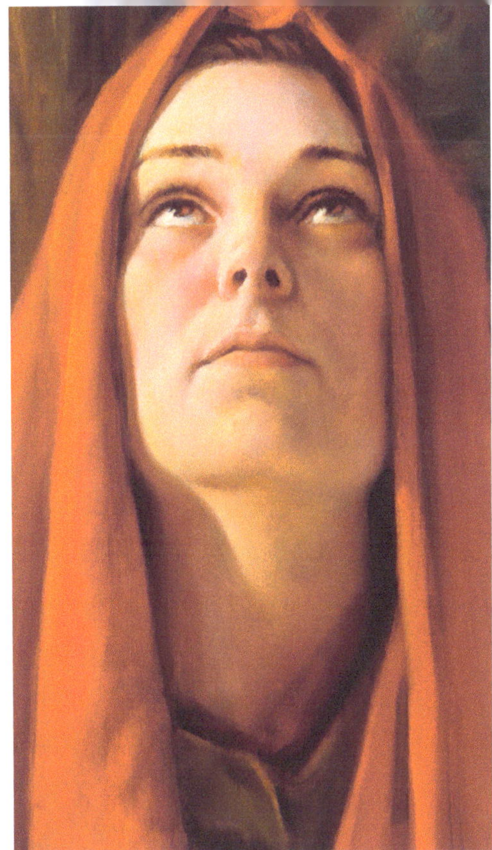

The 3 stages of the head, above- accurate direct block-in, smoothing out the rougher edges, then refining with smaller brushes by scratching and blending the wet paint. The final face has both cool and warm layers of at least 3-4 subtle coats.

Below, the smoother rocks and water set up the next strokes to stand out sharply against the softer edges. In the image to the far right, I have darkened the piece by adding a warm layer over the green. It's an interesting effect because it unified the water a bit more while adding an earthly depth to the realism. I always look for such effects beyond any photo reference I may have.

On the following spread, compare the finished close-ups to these prefinal stages. There is a lot of last minute tweaking and refining, not my favorite part of painting, but often necessary to get the painting to work. It can be exciting to see an edge or color shift suddenly with the right brushwork and then the whole piece seems to come together.

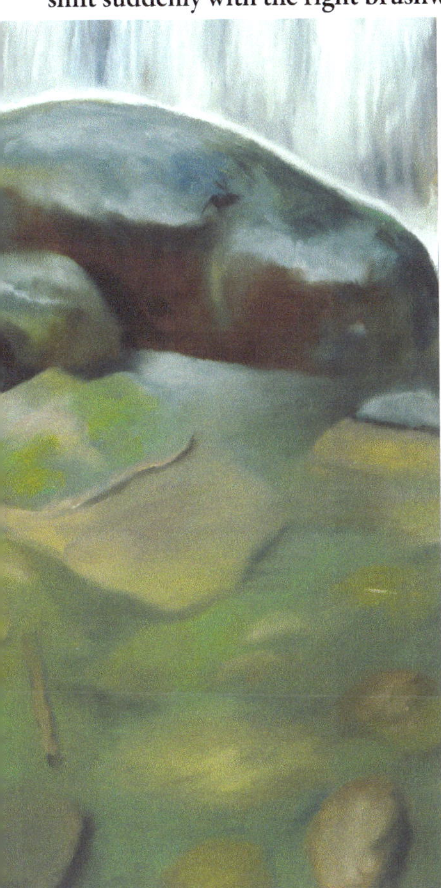

3

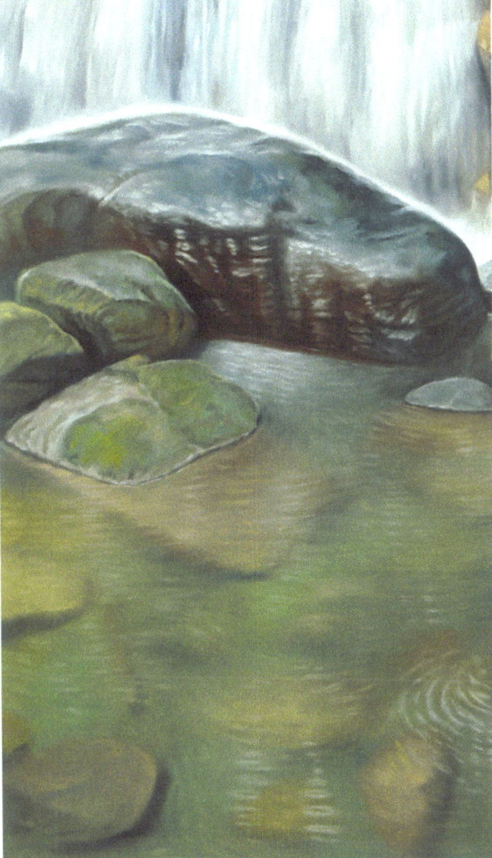

4

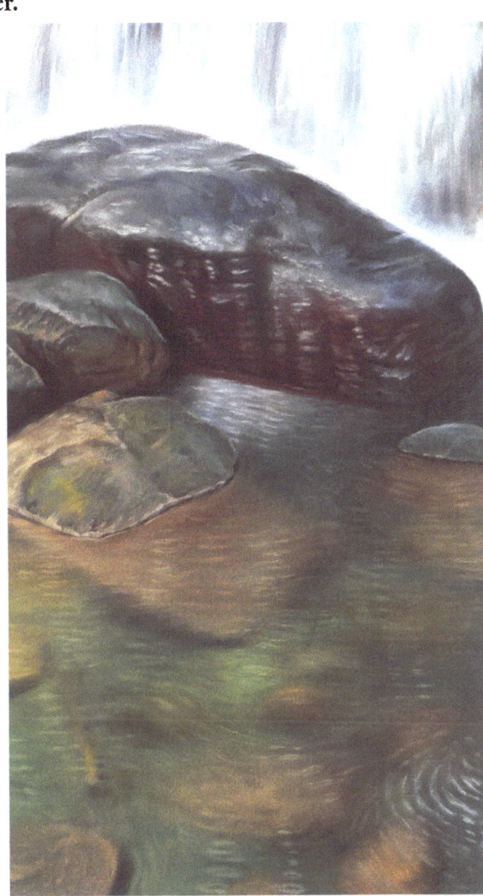

5

Below, an extreme closeup of the final face, not for details, but to show the finished panel surface as compared to canvas or textured gesso. Close-ups like this can show interesting brushwork beyond what you can see while painting, revealing the buildup of paint layers. The combination of strokes to create the solid form of the face shows evidence of this process. This is especially obvious in areas like the forehead where a variety of angled brushwork stands off the surface of the gessoed panel more than if I had worked on canvas.

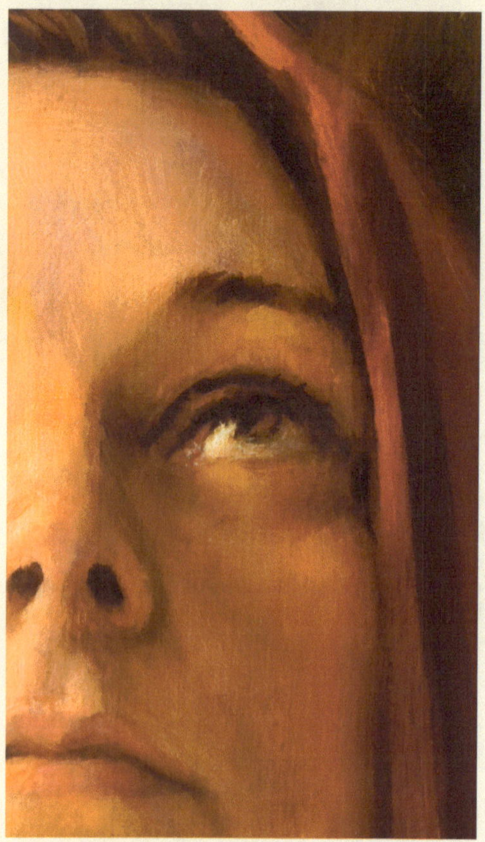

Below, panels are a great surface for expressive brushwork since the paint doesn't sink into the gesso or canvas weave. I used bristle flats here, sculpting the opaque paint with quick flat strokes.

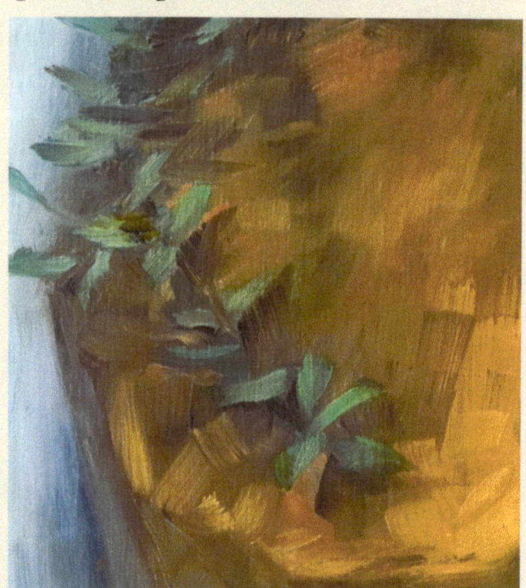

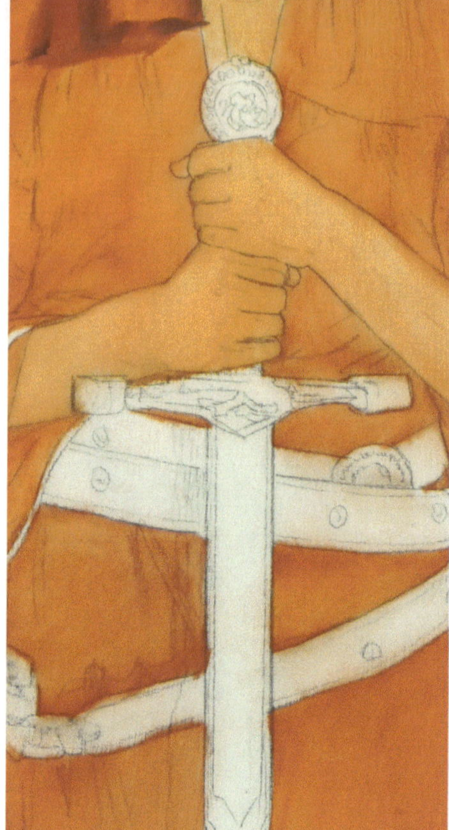

Above, the wash over my fixed pencil is translucent because of the mix of oil color with mineral spirits and a little Liquin medium to make it flow. I let this dry overnight, wanting just a base middle tone to work over the next day.

Below, for the background, I begin by blurring the initial mass of leaves.

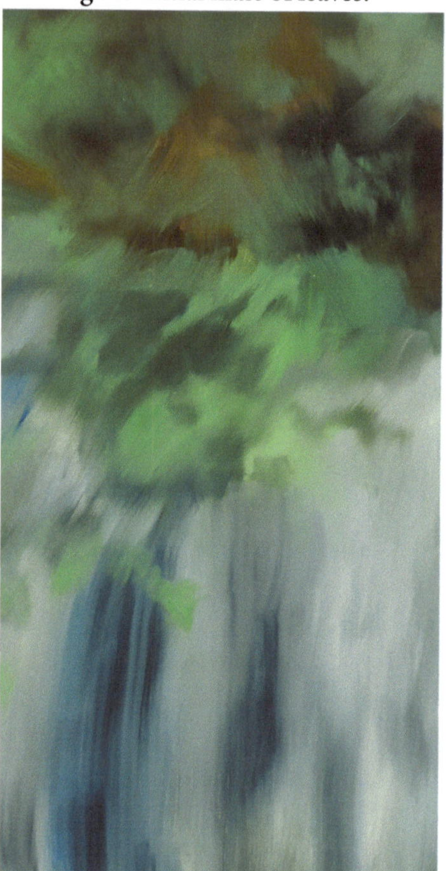

1

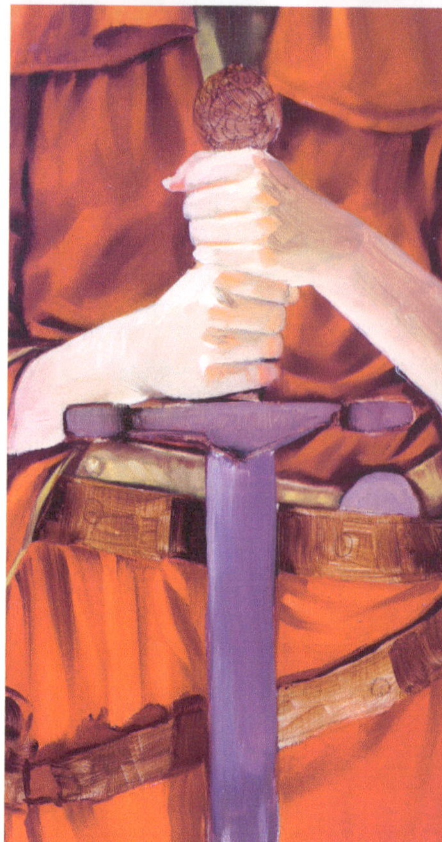

I block in more solid color. Had I not done the initial wash, the color would not have gone on as cleanly and I would be fighting the bright white of the gessoed panel.

Below, I begin to look for areas to drop in sharp blocky strokes, here and there.

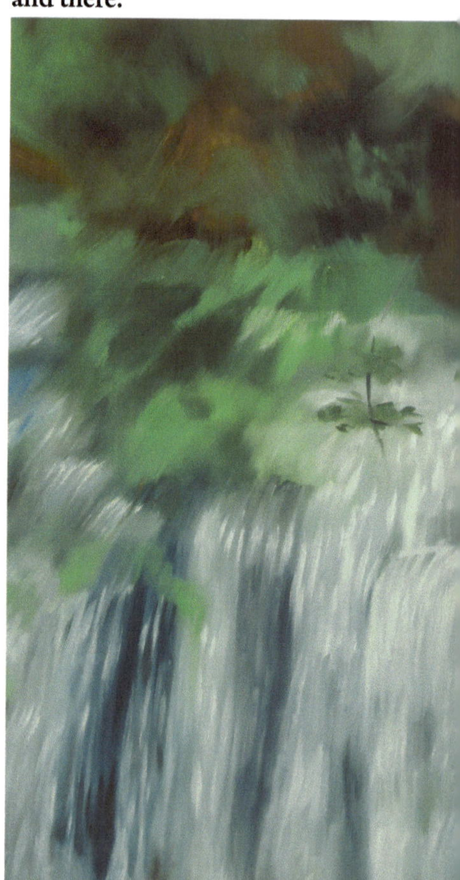

2

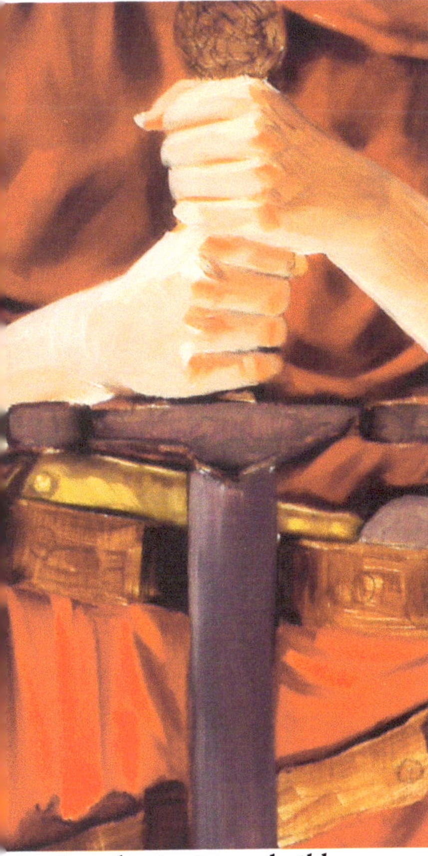

I am beginning to build up some dimension to the forms by adding darker, more solid coloring.

Below, the leaves come through the blurred mass. I made this area up, using what I know about shadow and light to lay opaque highlights over darks areas.

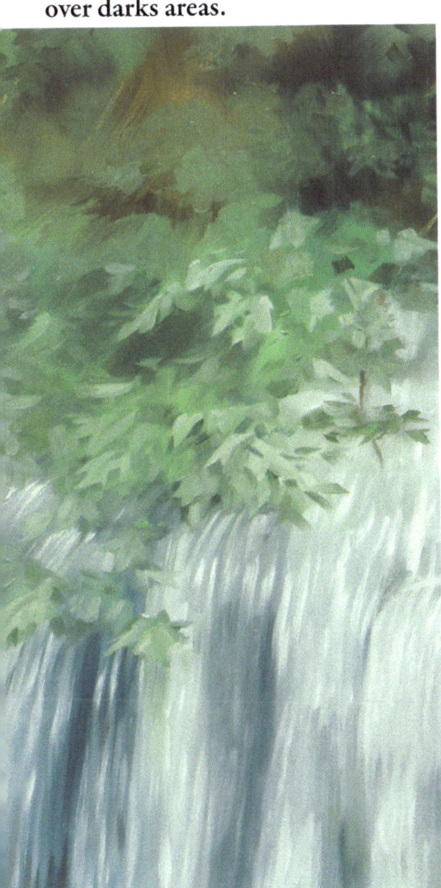

3

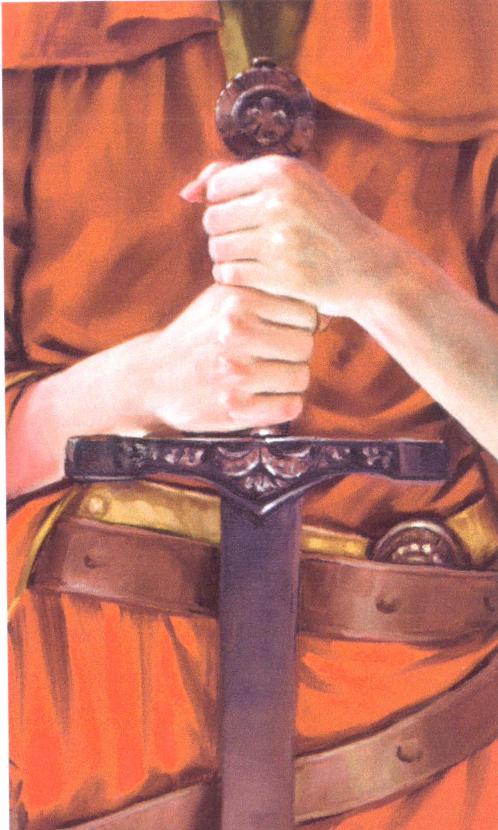

Refining stage 3, I try to work fast while the paint is wet. I begin using smaller filberts to model the edges and round out the forms. I use sable flats and rounds to finesse the details, like the sword's emblem.

Below, after about an hour of playing with shapes, the leaves feel more solid, so I drop in deeper shadows.

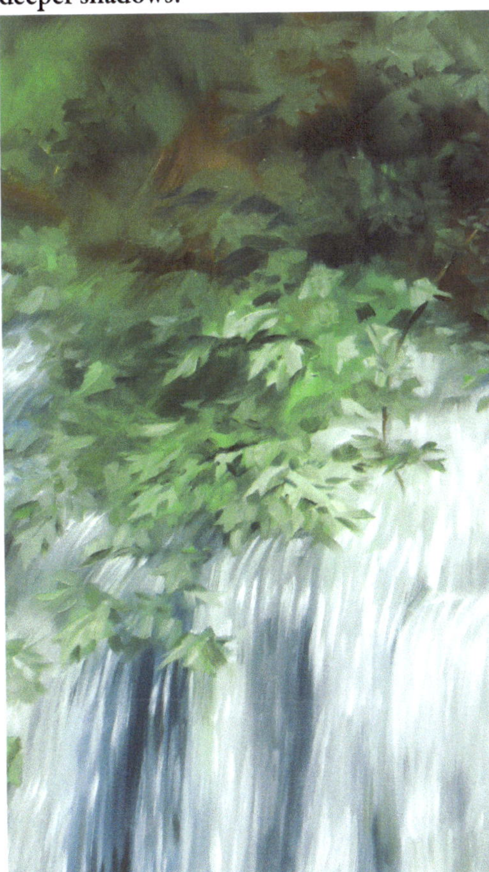

4

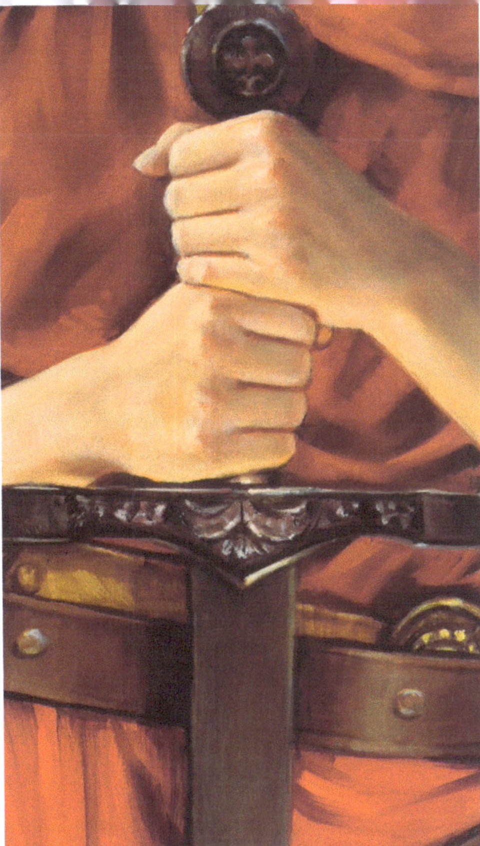

Both shots show the gradual edge refinements that go into pushing the realism toward a more believable result. I used big filberts for the initial strokes, then used flats to drop in edges and bring elements forward, controlling the focus and coaxing the viewer toward the figure of the Angel.

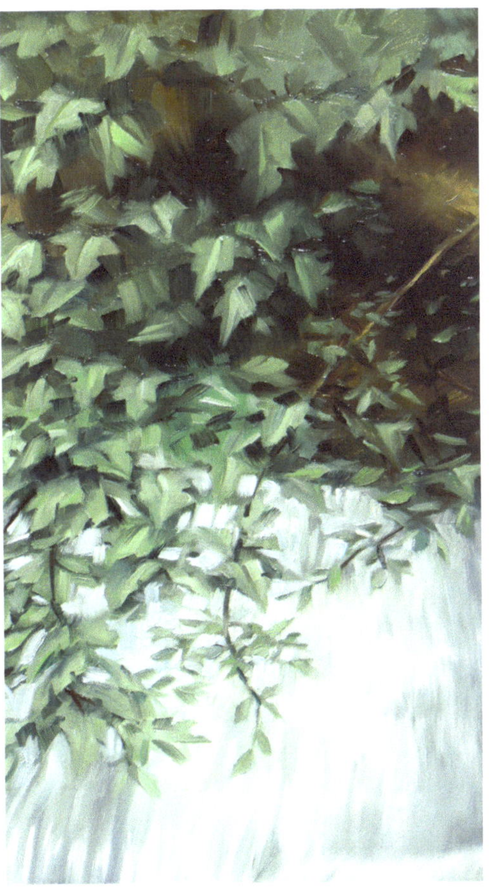

5

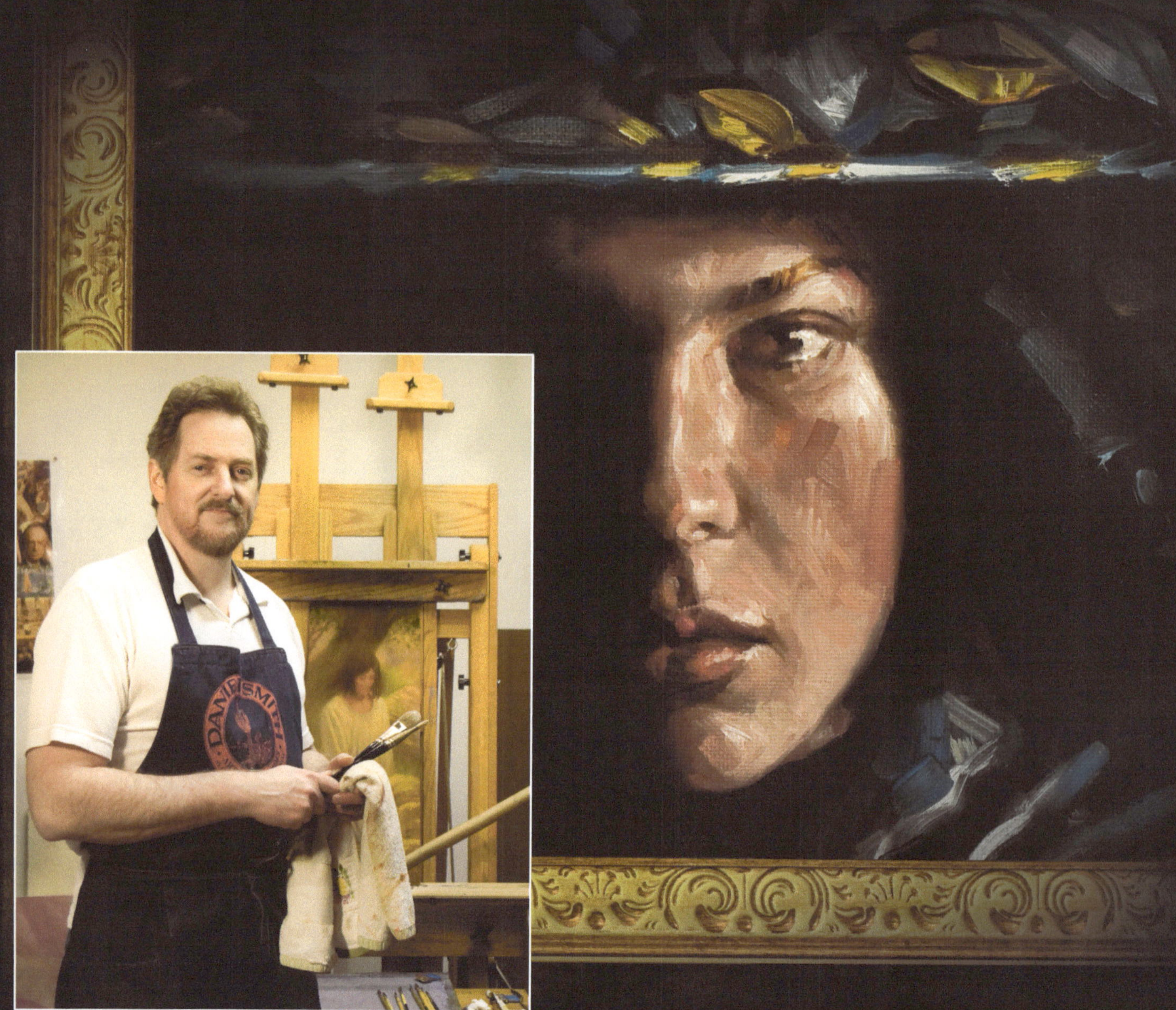

Philip Howe has been painting and illustrating for more than 30 years. His work is in many private and corporate collections worldwide. He has created over 4,000 illustrations for such clients as Microsoft, IBM, Intel, Dow, Nintendo, and has painted hundreds of magazine and book covers for most major publishers. He is also the author of the popular trilogy, The Rune Master.

Philip lives in the Pacific Northwest with his wife, Teresa, and their 2 crazy dogs.

You can contact the artist directly at
philip.howe@verizon.net
and visit his website at
http://www.philiphowe.com

www.ingramcontent.com/pod-product-compliance
Lightning Source LLC
LaVergne TN
LVHW070125110826
845147LV00002B/188